Praise for *Presence*

For those seeking to navigate this moment spiritually and culturally, I honestly can't think of many better guides than Jon Thompson. These are extraordinary days of both incredible kingdom opportunity and significant spiritual and cultural challenges. We desperately need wisdom and discernment, which make Jon's unique ability to fuse biblical revelation with prophetic insight an extraordinary gift to the church. His new book *Presence* will no doubt inspire, challenge, and stretch you, whilst simultaneously stirring a deep longing for God's kingdom to break in with greater measure.

—**Pete Hughes,** founding pastor of Kings Cross Church (KXC) in London, author of *All Things New*

Too many Christians know about God but don't walk with him. They've traded communion with the living God for busyness, noise, or shallow routine. In *Presence,* Jon Thompson invites the church back to what matters most, a daily, Spirit-filled, Scripture-rooted life with Jesus that changes how we witness! If you're tired of going through the motions and ready to encounter God again, read this book and see not only what can change for you but see the invitation for friends, family, strangers and enemies to encounter the Jesus you know.

—**Jonathan Pokluda,** lead pastor of Harris Creek Baptist Church, bestselling author, host of the *Becoming Something* podcast

There are not many thinkers in our time that can do and be what Jon does both in his life and also in this book. Deep, academic thinking, fused together with practical and spiritual application for us in the real world. I have to be honest, I have sent this book to more people this year than any other book—pastors, lay people, preachers, thinkers, all for the same reason: We need this book right now to navigate our posture as Christians in these complex yet exciting times. I actually have a text group on my phone filled with people who are reading it, and it is alive and well with people excited about Jon's ideas and approach. The first time I read it was with a pen, to highlight, mark it up, take notes, and learn how to think about our times. When I finished, I couldn't wait to read it again, this time for the heart of it, to see how I could pastor, lead, and live in the way Jon espouses here—to be a presence in a special way for our world, changed by the one who came to and was a presence for us.

—**Mark Clark,** senior pastor, Bayside Church, author of *The Problem of God, The Problem of Jesus,* and *The Problem of Life*

To put the whole of Thompson's book in three words (which are his words), God is working. In every life (even those we aren't so fond of) and in every culture and context, God is present and at work. Our part is to join what he is already doing, and that means seeking his presence and aligning our attitude and method with his heart. Such wisdom for twenty-first century evangelists! Everyone seeking the advance of God's kingdom should ingest this book and then get to work loving the place and people we've been sent to love.

—**Carolyn Moore,** bishop, Global Methodist Church

Few writers manage to hold conviction and compassion together without one collapsing into the other. Jon Thompson does, and *Presence* is the result. In a moment when too many Christian books either retreat into fortress mentality or quietly accommodate the spirit of the age, Thompson maps a third way: faithful, intellectually confident, beauty-attentive, Spirit-empowered witness that builds bridges rather than burning them. His Jonah framework—*do they deserve forgiveness, do they deserve the message, do they deserve my presence?*—is exactly the self-examination the contemporary church needs before opening its mouth. As someone working at the intersection of orthodox theology and pastoral welcome, I commend *Presence* to anyone tired of the fanaticism that, as Thompson rightly notes, almost always conceals a secret doubt.

—**Dr. David Bennett,** bestselling author of *A War of Loves*, research fellow in theology and ethics at the University of Oxford

At a time when many Christians feel pulled toward fearful withdrawal or reactive outrage, *Presence* offers a far better way. With theological depth, cultural insight, and a Spirit-attuned posture, Jon Thompson offers a hopeful and compelling vision for bearing witness to Jesus with humility, courage, and love. This book is a timely and much-needed guide for anyone longing to embody Christ faithfully in these turbulent times of change.

—**Ken Shigematsu,** pastor, Tenth Church, Vancouver, BC, and author of *God in My Everything*

With all the buzz, posts, and momentum around the world about revival, encounter, and outpourings, the church needs a translator and guide for this moment. Jon Thompson is a brilliant, biblical, and experienced friend . . . and I'm listening and learning from him.

—**Zach Meerkreebs,** pastor, speaker, author of *Lower: Igniting Spiritual Awakening Through Radical Humility*

I hugely appreciate all Jon writes in *Presence*. He offers an insightful diagnosis of the issues of our age and connects our lives to our calling and mission through deep biblical teaching and theology, drawing on his own passion and expertise as a pastor. Jon reads and studies widely and writes as a teacher, bringing clarity to his message through helpful stories, analogies, and metaphors. Thank you, Jon!

—**Archie Coates,** vicar of Holy Trinity Brompton

The book is brilliant, theologically astute, thoughtful, and prophetic! Throughout the ages the church has always needed wise and insightful leaders who teach and inspire its members to be faithful to the Great Commission in a confused and contradictory world. In this particularly complex and challenging cultural moment we are currently living through, Jon Thompson has proven once again through his latest book *Presence* to be such a gift to the body of Christ. In *Presence* Jon characteristically demonstrates his rigorous handling of Scripture, engaging wholeheartedly with the text in ways that exhort followers of Jesus to understand the times they are living in. Then he instructs them how to embrace the Jesus way and inspires them to seize the unprecedented opportunity for gospel expansion that currently lies in front of us.

—**Alain Emerson,** lead pastor of Emmanuel Church, director of the 24-7 Prayer Communities Network, author of *The Cruciform Leader* and *Luminous Dark,* and coauthor of *The God Story*

How can Christians witness well in this particular cultural moment and in ways relevant to all times or places? If you're looking for a book that truly answers that question, look no further. This is it! Whether he is analyzing the present post-Christian context, describing the various bridges that provide witness opportunities, expounding the uniqueness and richness of the Christian gospel, or underscoring the compassion and love which must motivate our witness, Jon Thompson has written a book filled with profound and perceptive insights. His engaging style, his deep dives into Scripture, his historical reflections, and his interaction with a wide range of contemporary literature all serve to ground and enrich the discussion. Read *Presence* and be enlightened, challenged, and inspired to be a faithful witness. I can't recommend this book highly enough.

—**Stephen Seamands,** emeritus professor of Christian doctrine, Asbury Theological Seminary, Wilmore, Kentucky

This book surprised me. I can't remember when I've last found myself smiling, as I've been kindly and effectively interrogated as a reader, challenged to slow down with Scripture, and asked to pray through the hard questions—all in a book written by a man with cultural insight, a biblically shaped imagination, and a heart for fellow laborers in the vineyard. I delighted in the surprise and am grateful for the encouraging challenge of *Presence*! If you are finding your ministry as a Christian leader both confusing and exhilarating, then Jon Thompson's latest book will be a bracing and future-focused guide. Naming the reality of our cultural moment, between retreat and revival, Thompson sets out lanterns—with an engaging mixture of theological, biblical, and cultural analysis—that the church can use to help guide the West back home to Jesus.

—**Jenny Andison,** former area bishop for the Diocese of Toronto, senior pastor, St. Paul's Bloor Street and St. George's Grange Park in Toronto

I found it very difficult to put this book down. Jon thoughtfully addresses some of the deep aches in the modern pastor's heart: How do we show up as faithful witnesses in a world where cultural tides are constantly shifting and familiar strategies are becoming redundant? He reminds us of the truth of the gospel, the power of the Spirit, and the steadfast love of the Father—all of which are essential for us to be rooted in if we are to be effective witnesses in this age. I am constantly surrounded by believers who either retreat or respond with militance due to the cultural complexities of our day and the ways they seem to challenge our faith. However, Jon's book imparts a humble courage, calling us to be loving and contextual yet unwavering in an uncompromised presence. My heart has been reinvigorated by the words penned in this book, and I know it will be an immense blessing to many.

—**Rev. Wole Agbaje,** priest, IMPRINT Church London

A wild, powerful, prophetic gift to the church. Writing with a pastor's heart and a prophet's fire, Jon beautifully frames the spiritual geography of this moment, helping map the tension of revival and revitalization. If you're keen to grow in your spiritual walk and break new ground, this book will be an invaluable friend.

—**Al Gordon,** author of *Spark*, leader of SAINT, and founder of RENAISSANCE

Reading *Presence* felt like I was observing Jon set a table for discussion with brothers and sisters who both agree and disagree with his theological and ecclesiological tradition. At this table, the goal is not to create uniformity but to showcase the strength of a united witness about the Lord Jesus in today's Western world. We, as followers of Jesus, serve as conduits of God's love, power, and presence in every sphere of interaction we find ourselves. Jon reminds us that our witness depends not only on us being conduits but also on our continual encounters with God's love, power, and presence.

—**Hakeem Bradley,** founder of Sacred Patterns

In *Presence,* Jon Thompson gives a thoughtful exhortation to the church on how to approach our cultural moment. Forged from decades of leading in one of the most diverse, multicultural cities in the world, he outlines a helpful theology of how we can live as exiles in our culture without falling into either withdrawal and retreat or compromise and syncretism. Jon gently, pastorally pushes against some of our ideologies that may be limiting the Western church from becoming the full expression of who Christ intended for us to be in the world. I hope you'll pick up a copy.

—**Luke LeFevre,** director of ministry engagement and Gen Z Gather25, author of *Holy unto the Lord*

In *Presence,* Jon Thompson gives the church a road map for renewal in an age of disconnection and disbelief. He clearly articulates that the hope of the world is not found in political power, cultural dominance, or nostalgic revivalism but in Christ. He calls the people of God to live as the tangible presence of Christ, empowered by his Spirit, grounded in his truth, and overflowing with his love. Presence, he reminds us, "is not just something we feel—it's Someone we carry."

—**Dwayne Cline,** executive director of TGC Canada

This book is both prophetic and brilliant. I adore it. This isn't the book you would write if you wanted to sell a million copies. This is the book you would write if God said, "Write this book." I mean that genuinely. *Presence* by Jon Thompson is brave and needed. This is seen clearly from the premise to the content. Whether or not the church wants this book, they need it.

—**Landon MacDonald,** pastor of Mission Church in Gilbert, Arizona

PRESENCE

PRESENCE

Resilient Witness in Times of
Retreat and Revival

Jon Thompson

ZONDERVAN REFLECTIVE
SEEDBED

ZONDERVAN REFLECTIVE

Published by Zondervan, 3950 Sparks Drive SE, Suite 101, Grand Rapids, MI 49546, USA. Zondervan is a registered trademark of The Zondervan Corporation, L.L.C., a wholly owned subsidiary of HarperCollins Christian Publishing, Inc.

Requests for information should be addressed to customercare@harpercollins.com.

Zondervan titles may be purchased in bulk for educational, business, fundraising, or sales promotional use. For information, please email SpecialMarkets@Zondervan.com.

ISBN 978-0-310-18306-8 (softcover)
ISBN 978-0-310-18308-2 (audio)
ISBN 978-0-310-18307-5 (ebook)

Published in association with the literary agency of Wolgemuth & Associates, Inc.

HarperCollins Publishers, Macken House, 39/40 Mayor Street Upper, Dublin 1, D01 C9W8, Ireland (https://www.harpercollins.com)

Cover design: Rob Jelsema
Interior design: Denise Froehlich

Printed in the United Kingdom

---

26 27 28 29 30 /CPI/ 10 9 8 7 6 5 4 3

Contents

PART 4: RESIDE

PART 5: REVIVAL

Coddiwomple: To travel purposefully toward an as-yet-unknown destination.

—OLD ENGLISH SLANG

The modern world is full of the old Christian virtues gone mad. The virtues have gone mad because they have been isolated from each other and are wandering alone.

—G. K. CHESTERTON

Our civilization was based on reason, writing, slowness, length, and the capacity for abstraction. The new digital civilization is based on emotion, image, speed, extract and culture of testimony ("me I"). No universal truth, no political consensus is attainable in such a media ecosystem. Each one replaces his self, his tribe.

—EUGÉNIE BASTIÉ

But in your hearts revere Christ as Lord. Always be prepared to give an answer to everyone who asks you to give the reason for the hope that you have. But do this with gentleness and respect.

—I PETER 3:15

Introduction

As I start to write this, my fourth book, I have just returned from a trip to Disney World with my family. I half-jokingly posted on Instagram that there are two kingdoms: one that will last and the other that will not last. One gives joy, and the other, momentary happiness. I belong proudly to both kingdoms.

I am a self-proclaimed Disneyholic. It's rooted in core childhood memories from when my parents were missionaries in Ecuador. Every time we came home, we would stop over for three days and visit Epcot and Magic Kingdom. If you can believe it, Disney World used to have a pastor and missionary discount. Sadly, as this whole book will show, that world is long gone. And yet Peter Pan's Flight, "it's a small world," Journey into Imagination with Figment at Epcot, that smell in Pirates of the Caribbean, and, of course, Mickey Mouse were all embedded in me.

So I have now passed this on to my family. Or perhaps some of you would say I've infected them. But no matter, because this was a special moment for us as a family. Thanks to some friends, we were able to book two weeks at a timeshare that was located right beside the parks. We bought our Park Hopper passes and got ready for an epic vacation. We couldn't wait to visit Star Wars: Galaxy's Edge, which was new for us. And there were so many other new rides also, like Remy's Ratatouille Adventure and Guardians of the Galaxy: Cosmic Rewind, not to mention the snacks, the Mickey ears—the list goes on and on. But there was a catch. Our trip would take place the last week of July and the first week of August. When we told people we were going to Florida at that time of year, most of them responded with, "Are you crazy? Do you know how hot it is going to be? You'll have to deal with humidity along with the crowds, plus possible hurricanes—this is nothing but disaster!" But while we heard them and knew they were likely right, we were still convinced that it would be fine. As we reminded them (and ourselves), the lines would be much shorter, so it would be worth it!

Well, we went and it was amazing. And it was so, *so* hot. Every day was between 97 and 102 degrees Fahrenheit. I'm sure you can picture it: the sweat, the smell, the lack of hydration, the meltdowns, the family fights. Every time it rained, we would put on the cheap plastic ponchos, which kept us dry but then acted like greenhouses making us sweat even more. It was exactly like Jim Gaffigan, one of my favourite comedians, says about going to Disney—nothing but pure insanity.[1]

And yet the food, the amazing rides, the pin trading, the exploring in a less rushed time—it was magical, immersive, and imagination-inspiring. Our kids actually ended up saying it was the best family vacation we have ever had.

In the middle of that Disney moment, I thought about this book. As I reflected on all the good, the great, the bad, and the ugly, I suddenly realized it wasn't just our family's experience but was happening to all the families around us as well. It was amazing, awful, hot, beautiful, joyful, and stressful all at the same time. We were all thinking: *Why am I here? Is it worth all this money? Get me out of here!* And at the same time: *I can't wait to come back again.*

Some of you are probably thinking, Jon, what does this have to do with evangelism, the global Church, repaganization, pluralism, renewal, and everything else we are facing? Well, I think the image of my family on vacation describes what it feels like for orthodox, historical, evangelical, Bible-centred, creed-confessing Christians to live in this new world. Now, I know my readers are members of different parts of the global Christian church, and though our unity is in Jesus, by the Spirit, our cultural realities are vastly different. And yet as I have lived in or traveled to over forty countries, and as I hang out with Christians from various different denominational and cultural experiences, I see a lot of commonalities, and I think that what I am about to outline is more or less shared by all of us.

Much of the time, we as Christians feel stirred, agitated, jittery, and out of place, and yet at the same time, we do enjoy life; we see good and beauty and God's ongoing work. Our experience is like my family's summer vacation in Disney—enchanting and requiring endurance, exhilarating and exhausting, beautiful and boring.

As I reflect, listen, pray, and lead, I think there are a few key reasons why on the best of days we feel conflicted about living "now" just as every generation before us has felt in some way. Yet as I am writing this in a quickly vanishing Christian West, as daylight seems to be fading, many of us either seem to be getting panicky, apathetic, and angry, or we are just slowly joining the shadows until no one can tell the difference between us and those around us. But when things start to feel darker, or actually get darker, when the dial moves, when the colour moves from grey to ink black, then the mood changes from *"I love this place"* to *"Get me out of here."* And then suddenly there is light, a burst of colour in the same place where the shadows are growing. We find retreat and revival in the same spaces, as we try to faithfully walk in the same holy routines the church has practiced for the last two thousand years.

So before we talk about how to witness well in this pluralistic, repaganizing, and revival moment in the West and across the world, let's all sit and take a moment to reflect on the tension of feeling at home and yet not at home. Why do we as Christians feel like my family did at Disney with all the good, bad, and boring all at once? Why do we feel and say things like, *"I love this place"* and *"Get me out of here,"* depending on the hour, the weather, or the ride we happen to be on? Or in real life, it can depend on politics, possible persecution, school and state programs, or family problems.

And if we could not be distracted or defensive for a few moments, let's explore how this affects how we see the world and our friends, family, faith, politics, and neighbours. The more open we can be, the more we can really get on to fulfilling Jesus's last words: Go into all the world, to all people. So let's explore together, and see if you see and feel the tension. And if you are willing, would you now stop and would you hear God's Word and pray the following prayer from Scotty Smith that God would speak to you even if you don't fully agree with all that comes next.

> If one gives an answer before he hears,
> it is his folly and shame. (Proverbs 18:13 ESV)
>
> Speak, LORD, for your servant is listening. (1 Samuel 3:9)

Dear Lord Jesus, I need these Scriptures today about listening, a lot. For more than once, people who love me have indicated their frustration with my listening skills—or worse, my commitment to take what they say seriously. You've given me two ears and one mouth, and the anatomical ratio is no mere accident. Help me become a much more engaged, attentive listener. Help me hear what people are meaning to say, not what interpretation I place on their words. Help me to listen with my heart, not just with my ears. Jesus, no one does this better than you. No one is more quick to listen. I never have to snap my fingers to get your attention. I never have to reel you back into focus. I never catch you looking away, as though you're bored with me. I never have to repeat myself several times to make sure you heard what I actually said.

You never interrupt me. You never spin what I'm saying. You never talk over me when I'm trying to tell you something. You never finish my sentences for me, though you could. There's no one who listens as attentively, respectfully, and compassionately as you.

Jesus, I don't think I need healing for deafness, but more grace for listening—first and foremost to you. You're always speaking to me through the Scriptures by the Holy Spirit, and you only speak words of life. What a foolish man I am not to hang onto every syllable you utter.[2]

PART 1

RESTLESSNESS

The inability to rest or relax as a result of anxiety or boredom

Do not have Jesus Christ on your lips and the world in your hearts.

—IGNATIUS OF ANTIOCH

Christians should live in the world, but not be filled with it. A ship lives in the water; but if the water gets into the ship, she goes to the bottom. So Christians may live in the world; but if the world gets into them, they sink.

—D. L. MOODY

The Christian inherits the pilgrim principle, which whispers to him that he has no abiding city and warns him that to be faithful to Christ will put him out of step with his society; for that society never existed, in East or West, ancient time or modern, which could absorb the word of Christ painlessly into its system.

—ANDREW WALLS

[Paul] proclaimed the kingdom of God and taught about the Lord Jesus Christ—with all boldness and without hindrance!

—ACTS 28:31

CHAPTER 1

This World Is Not My Home . . . Or Is It?

As we read the Bible, talk to other Christians, and read Christian history, there is a golden thread of tension that weaves itself through every single Christian community—Catholic, Orthodox, Coptic, Protestant, evangelical, charismatic, from the Mennonites to the Pentecostals, and from Baptists to Anglicans. We all struggle with living in the world but not being of the world (John 17). Not only that, but we're not even sure what it means much of the time. We really want to be faithful, but what does it look like on the ground, day in and day out? Of course, this might look vastly different depending on what culture or cultures you connect to or come from, right? In the middle of doing many kingdom activities in many different places, we are also called to be a holy presence and witness. But how?

I think much of the time, we feel caught between two extremes, two visions, two pictures—be holy and be separate and enjoy God's world and show others his very good beauty. Both seemingly rooted in the Scriptures and commanded by God—which leave many of us with contradictory feelings of joy and anxiety. So many verses call us out to be separate, to be holy. We are described as the "little flock" (Luke 12:32), commanded to not conform to this world (Romans 12:1), and called to be separate (2 Corinthians 6:17). And does not Paul say explicitly in 1 Corinthians 6:9–11:

> Or do you not know that wrongdoers will not inherit the kingdom of God? Do not be deceived: Neither the sexually immoral nor idolaters nor adulterers nor men who have sex with men nor thieves nor the greedy nor drunkards nor slanderers nor swindlers will inherit the kingdom of God. And that is what some of you were. But you were washed, you were sanctified, you were justified in the name of the Lord Jesus Christ and by the Spirit of our God.

Sounds pretty stark and straightforward. We used to be them, and we are no longer them. We were there, but we are over here now. We might struggle with the same wants, but our centre of gravity is now different.

So the question naturally comes to the surface: How do we create a parallel society whose roots are in the *not yet* and at the same time finds beauty and enjoys life *now*? Is that even what God wants of us? See, that is the rub. Things are evil and bad, right? Sin abounds, the demonic are real, world systems in many forms enslave billions, and all non-Christians are blind to the gospel (2 Corinthians 4:4), dead in their sins, under God the Father's wrath, and hostile to God (Ephesians 2:1–4). And yet the Bible says that there is, at the same time, joy, beauty, and life to be enjoyed. More than this, the church is said to be the declaration of defeat to all the enemies above (Ephesians 3:10) and the first fruits of what is coming (Romans 8:23, 29). How are we supposed to do both? I thought light and darkness don't mix?

As I look at my own life and the church I lead, and as I listen and read, I think the church in every culture and generation has felt a lot like the character Goldilocks, trying to find that perfect place: not too hot, not too cold, just right. But our attempts have often resulted in us getting burned or frozen. In many cases, pastors have preached and are preaching that getting burned or frozen is good and helpful, even though it hurts us and hurts others.

Can I encourage you to slow down and listen to what was said under the inspiration of the Holy Spirit by Solomon, the wisest man? He penned this so long ago:

> This is what I have observed to be good: that it is appropriate for a person to eat, to drink and to find satisfaction in their toilsome

> labor under the sun during the few days of life God has given them—for this is their lot. Moreover, when God gives someone wealth and possessions, and the ability to enjoy them, to accept their lot and be happy in their toil—this is a gift of God. They seldom reflect on the days of their life, because God keeps them occupied with gladness of heart. (Ecclesiastes 5:18–20)

Ecclesiastes, which is Scripture as authoritative as Paul's letters, seems to say that we are to love life and enjoy it to the full. This sounds very different from "run from all the darkness and shadow" and "most things are tainted, evil, and dangerous," doesn't it? As we read the whole Bible, we see that the fall affected everything, that is all was marred by sin, but not everything became totally evil, right? There is so much good still found in the world. We see it in art, beauty, nature, athletics, and food; we see love and acts of sacrifice in non-Christians and Christians alike. So how far is too far, we wonder?

Now, you might be asking, *Jon, why are we talking about this? Rabbit trail much?* Well, let me just begin to connect the dots. How we have this conversation (or our lack of it) shapes how so many churches and Christians talk with people and think about life, culture, and hope. It also becomes the place where churches and Christians attack each other, accusing one another of being fundamentalist, compromised to the spirit of the age, or somewhere in between. And yes, the truth is that in both extremes we find real heresy, but much of the fighting is actually around misunderstanding and people being a weaker brother or sister (Romans 14), not heretics. The difference matters not only for our unity but for our deeply needed presence, witness, and proclamation of the good news.

I became a Christian in a very conservative Baptist church. My early upbringing was filled with the message that the world is dangerous and we must be separate from it. I have this vivid childhood memory of going out to eat at Swiss Chalet, the Canadian version of Christian chicken. At that time in the early 1970s, if someone had stood up at Swiss Chalet and prayed at Sunday lunch, everyone in the restaurant would have bowed their heads. I could tell you what church was arriving depending on the time: We Baptists were always on time, the Salvation Army would be in the middle, and the Pentecostals always late. On this specific occasion, I was about four years old, and I saw an older man with tattoos all over his arms ordering a beer. On Sunday, in God's chicken restaurant! I was deeply concerned and told my dad this could not be right. What bothered me more was that he had been at church that morning. What scandal! There is no way this man was a Christian, I thought in my small four-year-old mind. The roots of deep, outward separation as the role, goal, need, and call of real Christians had already been rooted in me at four or five years old. But was that the real heart of the early church? Had my starting point set me up to distance myself from the world, to not be present for Christ in this moment that God's providence had placed me in?

When I was beginning to write this book, Tim Keller had just died. I watched many observations, slights, attacks, and tributes come across my screen from various political and theological backgrounds, but one in particular caught my eye. It was an article in *First Things* magazine written by Kevin DeYoung, who in many ways leans much more Reformed and conservative than I do. He was kind, thoughtful, and honest about his many disagreements and agreements with Keller, even though both were Presbyterians. What struck me was how he talked about there being three impulses in evangelical circles that drive everything and how, depending on how you prioritize the three, it changes how you think, live, view the world, and witness. The three impulses are right thinking (doctrine), right living (pietism), and improving society (cultural). Where you place the greatest emphasis affects how your presence and witness are worked out.[1]

DeYoung went on to say that Tim Keller was always fighting the "dangers of legalism, whereas I am more attuned to the perils of liberalism."[2] But it was this next paragraph that caught my attention the most. Kevin wrote, "Keller has acknowledged before that he is a culturalist first, then a pietist, then a doctrinalist. I would say that my order is just the opposite."[3] Did you catch it? Do you see how the order changes everything? Both are Bible teachers and pastors of great influence, but Keller obviously had the gift of evangelism, which changed his order. I remember tweeting a few years ago, "So many genuine theological disagreements between Christians are rooted in how much or how little the 'not yet' is guaranteed in 'the now.'" I would also now add this, "So many disagreements between Christians are about what order we should place the above three impulses in."

If we're going to witness well in this moment, or in any moment, we need all three. Otherwise, we will all, like Humpty-Dumpty, have a great fall, and never be able to be put together again. It is like a three-legged stool—remove one leg and, at best, it will wobble, but most likely it's going to break. So if you or your church or movement does not have all three, you cannot witness well. But the *order* you put them in shows your cards to other Christians and to those we are trying to reach.

I've seen this play out in my own ministry as well. I still remember the time a whole group of young adults in the church I was leading began listening to John MacArthur. All of a sudden there was lots of talk about how I was a Calvinist, yes, but not enough of one. I was complementarian but also compromised because we had women preachers. We believed in the use of all the spiritual gifts, and that was obviously wrong. We openly talked about spiritual warfare. You can imagine where it all went.

In one meeting, a friend of mine from this increasingly dissatisfied group said, "Jon, we must focus on the church; we have to get all of our own thinking and lives right and then we can start to reach out." My response was simply that if that is the starting point, we will *never* move beyond ourselves. Actually, if that was God's view, then Paul never should have left his own people and gone to the Roman world. But here it is again—the tension between those three impulses worked out in a local church, on the ground in real time. And that painful conversation took place in a less turbulent time than today.

This tension is being replayed over and over again as faithful Christians attempt to witness well in a rapidly changing moment. Just recently, I was in Los Angeles speaking to two church planting groups. After one amazing day with those communities, I was having dinner in Venice Beach with John Mark Comer. We had talked for years but had never met in person. The meal was excellent, the conversation robust, honest, and engaging. We talked; we debated; we prayed for each other. He told me I needed to repent of my Calvinism; I told him clear calling was a comfort I would never give up. We don't agree on so very much and yet we are family.

The next morning, back with the same group from the day before, I was in conversation with one church planter from Houston, a strong leader who had never wanted a megachurch, but under God's direction his church had grown into one. He had heard from others that I was with John Mark Comer the night before and said to me, "I really love so much of what he has written, but I'm afraid he will lead the younger generation away from what we need right now." "What do we need right now?" I responded. "More strong leadership," he said, "more direct engagement to culture, and more commitment in local churches to make an impact and to make a massive difference in culture." I smiled and responded, "I think you've missed the point. You are in Houston still fighting an older, different fight—the undoing of cultural Christianity. You're trying to lead people to truly encounter Jesus instead of just being 'Christian' because everyone else (sort of) is. John Mark is working in places where cultural Christianity is almost completely a thing of the past." I could tell this wasn't new information for this pastor from Houston, but the full weight and the reality of it had not yet fully landed where he serves.

So what is going to happen next in the United States? Will it feel more like Los Angeles, Houston, or both at the same time? As there is a growing cultural reaction to the Left, more conservative laws might be passed, and more people will want to protect or join cultural Christianity in some form once again. More places might stay like Houston while others become more like Los Angeles. As I am writing this book things seem to be swinging right more than left. And in all of this, let's be careful not to label the possible resurgence of cultural Christianity in certain areas as revival because it's not the same thing, right?

What many in the West and beyond do not yet understand is this: Evangelicalism, by nature, has always been more a renewal movement than a missions movement. Don't get me wrong, the global missions push has been massive (just look at the last three hundred years), but that is why there is such tension right now, at least in the West. The ground-breaking missions historian Andrew Walls brought this family debate home. Please slow down and read his words carefully because it really does matter. He wrote this,

> Evangelical religion was a product of Christendom, a civil society that nominally accepted Christian symbols and Christian norms but fell drastically short of those norms in reality. Evangelicalism was thus about "real Christianity" over against the formal and the nominal profession of it—about the inward religion of the heart turned toward God. Evangelicalism was of its nature protest religion, protest against a society that claimed to be Christian but denied that claim in practice. *Classical evangelicalism requires nominal Christianity in order to define itself and assumes the presence of a Christian, even if defectively Christian, civic society.* It was from these roots that the most influential strand of the Protestant overseas missionary movement sprang.[4]

Do you see it? So much of what we think we are as evangelicals is in response to something that is now gone or diminished. And so this must be the moment we move the majority of our focus from always fighting for revival and reformation only to mission and evangelism. Now, don't misunderstand me. Where there is church life and genuine Christian community—no matter how small or big—there will always be a critical need for reformation, renewal, and revival (more on this later). But overall, the time has come for evangelism and mission in ways we have not seen for generations.

Back to that conversation in sunny Los Angeles: I responded to my new friend that John Mark's cultural environment is, for the United States, a few years in the future (although for Canada, Australia, the UK, or Europe, this has been the reality for a long time) where the number of real and cultural Christians is steadily decreasing. Do you see what this small conversation reveals? It seems one leader is calling for a new form of a St. Patrick's monastic moment, gathering in so one can be sent out again; the other sees the need for bold, ongoing, in your face engagement into a majority Christian culture. One large, one small; one around tables, the other in formal known gatherings.

Here's the point: We need both! I tell this story to point out that there is so much behind all of this—mission, theological disagreement, culture, spiritual gifts, calling, unique assignments, personal experience, and different mixed environments. We need both at once because the gospel must reach different communities, physically and digitally, at the same time. Those two pastors are dealing with two different missional moments, two different tribes of people. They are in the same country during the same time, but it's almost like they're in different universes. If you hear people say this is *the* way or *the* answer for this moment, be careful.

Of course, living in Toronto, Canada, I relate much more to Los Angeles than Houston. But no matter where we live, the answer is not "an answer" but multiple seemingly contradictory answers that at their core are the same but whose expressions are vastly different in emphasis and shape. Better said, there is one ultimate answer but different expressions that will reach different people. Now I know, as the world is changing so many will think we need to go back to expressions of church that never change so we do not feel so lost. That is why so many are joining ancient high-liturgical movements like Eastern Orthodoxy or Roman Catholicism, because they appear more rigorous, stable, old, and tested. Yes, there is strength in these movements, but they are not *the* answer. More on this later.

Now, I know many who have read my other books have said to me, "I love much of your thinking, but I don't live in Canada. I live in a place where Christianity is still around. What you are addressing is not my world yet, and maybe it will never be." Great, but let me remind you, you and I live much of our time online. Every time you go online, you are immediately in a multicultural, pluralistic, multifaith, spiritual, secular, post-Christian, pre-Christian, and repaganized world. You can be living in the Bible Belt of the United States or in Kenya, but you need this full conversation just like the rest of us do.

Some of you might be getting nervous or defensive because you sense I might be already going too far, and you feel I am leading people to compromise. Well, ask yourself the question, could God be working from the inside and outside at the same time, even if it feels like contradiction? One biblical story where we see this oxymoron lived out is 1 Kings 18. God tells Elijah to confront King Ahab in the time when the queen, Jezebel, has been systematically killing God's prophets and dismembering the Jewish faith. As he goes, Elijah meets Obadiah, Ahab's palace administrator. Obadiah was working inside the system, but he was for God, not Ahab. He had hidden hundreds of prophets and given them food, water, and protection. Ultimately, he sets up the confrontation between God and Baal, Elijah and Ahab. So the question we should be asking is this: Which one was more faithful—Elijah or Obadiah? Which one was doing God's will and work in a dark time? The answer is yes. Both were. And that is my point. We live in a moment where we need both those working from the inside and those working from the outside even when they seem to be opposite sides. In the middle of this seeming contradiction is the work of God to bring new life. The gospel must incarnate; the gospel must be able to answer questions in many directions, to many different people in the same moment!

Hopefully you are beginning to see that we need an ongoing, pivoting gospel expression. We need monasteries *and* megachurches. Still, the tension is real, and we need to take the time to do this well. Why? Our faithfulness to God and our witness to the world and people he loves is at stake. If we are going to make a difference in the world, we cannot be totally separate from it. Right? Do you actually believe this?

We have to help our church and our leaders understand how to live in this tension well because the impulse to monastery away, to be completely separate, will not allow the last words of Jesus to take place. Of course, sometimes Christians are forced into isolation and exclusion, but in most cases it should not be our choice. And yes, some people are those called vocationally by God to be separated from the world, like St. Anthony of Egypt[5] or Julian of Norwich,[6] but this is not the whole community's calling.

Here are five images we need to reflect on. You cannot be Noah without being in the middle of the flood. You cannot be Elijah unless you are confronting Baal and, at the same time, living among God's people with folded hands waiting to see which way the wind will blow. You cannot be Ezekiel without being in the graveyard. You cannot be

Timothy unless you live with both wolves and sheep, and you cannot be the good Samaritan unless you are walking across the road to touch unclean people. Easily said but not easily done.

There is one other biblical image, given to us by Jesus in the Sermon on the Mount, which is the manifesto of our movement, that clearly demonstrates what living well in this tension looks like. If spiritual gifts are the only guaranteed place of power to see the kingdom grow, and if spiritual disciplines are the only guaranteed place of listening and transformation as we walk with the King of the kingdom, then the Sermon on the Mount is what the kingdom will look like worked out in everyday life. The sermon summarizes the ethics and lifestyle of those who are truly already in the kingdom of heaven. Dallas Willard described it as the grand "God based inversion,"[7] and N. T. Wright pointed out that, "Jesus here takes us through the sound barrier, where things begin to work backwards!"[8] It is what must form the foundation of our presence in this moment or any moment.

The image is found in a very famous verse that we have all read devotionally and that many of us have taught on: "You are the salt of the earth" (Matthew 5:13). Actually, this reads more accurately as "you *and you alone* are the salt of the earth."[9] Think about how crazy this is! There were no churches at that time, no billions of followers, no study Bibles, no seminaries, no Christian Bible colleges, and no small groups, only a few, mostly poor and uneducated, half-followers of Jesus together in the backwater of the backwater of the Roman empire. You alone are the salt of the earth? You? Among thousands of claims, thoughts, worldviews, and millions of people, you alone are the salt of the whole earth! This is either delusion, lie, manipulation, and emotionalism, or this is heaven-given, unnatural confidence because the One speaking knows what is coming—something that cannot be stopped, because the kingdom he is bringing and has brought is greater, bigger, stronger, and will last into eternity.

Why salt? In that culture, the main use of salt was to preserve food. No ice making machines and not one refrigerator or freezer existed on the whole earth, so the only way to deal with decay and decomposition was to rub food with salt or soak it in a solution of salt.[10]

Once again, Jesus is offending us and peeling back the veneer of civility and so-called order. Jesus says the world is always moving towards decomposition and rotting; it always moves towards pride and self-exaltation, and every generation is born already spiritually dead.[11] One wrote that Jesus is really saying, "Humanity without me is a dead body that is rotting and falling apart, . . . and you, my followers, are the salt that must be rubbed into the flesh to halt the decomposition!"[12] Do you think humanity is in that bad of shape? Really? Jesus says it is.

The world is a place where morals are always changing, but Jesus says that we who are part of the kingdom will slow down that rot as we bring him into all the places we work and live. We bring holiness, mercy, meekness, honesty, integrity, and truth. We stand for the most vulnerable; we love; we are the salt of the earth! As any historian will tell you, when Christians have been faithful, society has been affected in dramatic ways: legally, socially, and spiritually, in families, neighbourhoods, art, and culture. It all changes.

Oh, but there's more! Salt is a condiment, a spice. Just like salt is used to bring food alive, so Christians bring culture into right perspective. Art, culture, legal thinking, and philosophy can be saved and flavourful again.[13] We could call all of this beauty, which as we are going to see soon is a needed antidote to keep us as Christians from only seeing darkness and hating those we are supposed to love. Some of you think you put the *fun* in *fundamentalist*, but you don't. But salt brings freedom, fun, and beauty, which we desperately need.

Salt also creates thirst. A person only becomes poor in spirit when they thirst. With all that understanding in the minds of his original audience Jesus keeps going: "But if the salt loses its saltiness, how can it be made salty again? It is no longer good for anything, except to be thrown out and trampled underfoot" (Matthew 5:13).

Salt cannot stop being salt. It is a very stable compound, but when it is mixed with dirt or other things, it loses its power and becomes useless. Then you can't use it on food as a spice or preservative. When salt gets compromised, Jesus says it gets thrown out into the street, the ancient garbage dump.[14] If salt is mixed with other things and therefore thrown out, do you know what it ends up doing? It kills and sterilizes the soil and plants. It does the opposite of its purpose![15]

The image of salt found in this small section of Jesus's manifesto says something like: Yes, things are really bad—actually worse than most want to admit—and yet you have to be there in the middle of the decay or you cannot help. So we never fully feel at peace. The old Sunday school phrase "The Bible tells me so" does not fully help us draw close or move away because it seems the Bible tells us both to run away from the world and to settle down and enjoy home at the same time.

Which one is more important: (1) change the world and restore culture through evangelism, (2) be separate from it and speak the truth, or (3) just love God more? Each church does have an order they place these in, and so do you. And trust me when I say this: It directly affects our witness, especially in this new moment we're in that we have never really fully faced before.

Three marks of a moral revolution:

1. What was universally condemned is now celebrated.

2. What was universally celebrated is now condemned.

3. Those who refuse to celebrate are condemned.

—JON TYSON, ON THEO HOBSON

Christianity is often imagined as water. "But let justice run down like waters, and righteousness like an ever-flowing stream": the words of Amos 5:24, repurposed by Martin Luther King Jr. "He who believes in Me," promises Christ, "out of his heart will flow rivers of living water." Water baptizes, gives life, quenches thirst, purifies filth, expunges flames, transforms things for the better. If Christianity is water, then it is an unstoppable force: It will run down and seep up, no matter the impediment. But what if Christianity is not water? What if, instead, we understand the Christian era as a clearing in a forest? The forest is paganism: dark, wild, vigorous, and menacing, but also magical in its way. For two thousand years, Christians pushed the forest back, with burning and hacking, but also with pruning and cultivating, creating a garden in the clearing with a view upward to heaven. But watch as roots outstretch themselves and new shoots spring up from the ground. The patch of sky recedes. "Paganism has not needed to be reinvented," writes Steven Smith: It never went away. "In a certain sense, the Western world has arguably always remained more pagan than Christian. In some ways Christianity has been more of a veneer than a substantial reality." With no one left to tend the garden, the forest is reclaiming its ground.

—LOUISE PERRY

CHAPTER 2

The Decline of Christendom in the West

For us born in the West or who have immigrated to the West, there is a verse in Judges that gives a good summary of what is actually happening around us:

> The people served the Lord throughout the lifetime of Joshua and of the elders who outlived him and who had seen all the great things the Lord had done for Israel. . . . After that whole generation had been gathered to their ancestors, another generation grew up who knew neither the Lord nor what he had done for Israel. (Judges 2:7, 10)

I live in this amazing little town about an hour and twenty minutes outside of downtown Toronto. This little town is really special. It is, in North American terms, old (for global readers, you can just laugh). It is the closest thing we have to living in Victorian London. There are over three hundred homes built between 1790 and 1900. The downtown is the most preserved Victorian-style street in Ontario. There are massive Victorian mansions, beautiful older cottages, and row houses. Countless tourists come every year to do the garden tours and house tours. I live in a regency cottage built in 1875;

I wrote much of this book on its wraparound porch. There is a late-eighteenth-century Opera House currently being restored, a theatre that hosts plays and jazz concerts, and five churches with steeples surrounded by trees all along Lake Ontario. A river runs right through the town centre. Thousands come every spring and fall to fish for the trout and tens of thousands of salmon swim through as the seasons change. Many television and movie companies film in our town and in our homes. Its residents include former heads of University libraries, prima ballerinas, interior designers, and artists, and outside of town, many are farmers. It is this weird combination of urban and rural sharing a historic small town from a bygone era.

As you enter this amazing little place, right off the highway you see a large, old graveyard filled with headstones dating back nearly two hundred years. Beside the graveyard is a church, but it's newer, the original long gone. If you live in North America, you'll know this style of church: small (seating one hundred and fifty on a good day), built out of brown brick, a white steeple, and has what I jokingly call Baptist stained glass. You might know it, that orangey-brown glass from the 1970s that matched all the appliances like goldenrod and avocado.

Even though the building is newer, it's no longer a church, but a corporate office. Either they or the city cuts the grass in the graveyard. I was driving by one day in June—nothing unusual, it was a normal day—but as I passed by the former church, what I saw in those ten seconds became for me a picture of our moment, at least in the West: a graveyard no longer tended by the church. A church building that still has a bright white steeple, but the top has been removed and the cross is gone. The flag that was flying that day was the pride flag as June is pride month here. This is the picture of our moment, certainly here in Canada, but I would include much of the West to varying degrees, as well as other parts of the world. But then I drive forty minutes to my local church, which is attended by thousands of people from sixty nations. Such contradiction—from Christendom, to modernism, to postmodernism; from post-Christian to pre-Christian to repaganism once again. And yet in some places, like where I live, they all exist at the same time.

Many of you might relate to this similar perspective from Scotland, and even if you don't, it's good to hear from others about what life looks like for them.

> Let me take you to my own country. I can show you the William Carey Memorial Church in Leicester in the part of the country from which he came. It is now a Hindu temple—not because of some triumphalist Hindu expansionism but because no one needed it as a church anymore. Come to my own city of Aberdeen in the north of Scotland, and I will take you on a walk of the city centre. We will begin with the original building that housed Christ's College, where even in my own time, students were trained for the ministry of the Church of Scotland. You will still see on the front of it the memorial plaques to famous theologians who once taught there, but you will also see the contemporary sign that gives its contemporary name, Babylon, for the ultimate nighttime experience. Let us go up the street to one of the city's most imposing churches, Langstane Kirk, where a succession of famous Scottish preachers held large congregations spellbound. It is now a luxury bar and night spot called Soul and has been granted a license as a casino. Another church is now a nightclub called Ministry; its original title was the Ministry of Sin. I can take you to church after church that is now a store, an apartment block, a drinking hall, a nightclub, all because no one needed them as churches anymore. The country that once sent out more missionaries than any other has become a desert, desperately in need of the gospel—not a revival, it is too late for that, but primarily evangelism, cross-culture evangelism, for our culture is now a non-Christian one. Our God, if we have one, is Mammon, and the altars of Mammon are more gruesome than those of Molech.[1]

I fully can relate to all of what my brother sees and has experienced, although I would never say that revival will never be available at all. God is sovereign, and when there are any Christians left, then this is possible and seems to be happening in many places, especially among the younger generations, even in Scotland. But I don't think revival is the basket we can put all our eggs in. As I wrote years ago in my book *Deliverance*,

> We live in a post-Christian, de-Christian, postsocial, postmodern (yet modern), multicultural, radically globalized, fully mobile, highly personal world. One of the great paradoxes of life today is an ever-increasing level of connectedness, paralleled by increasing levels of fracturing. Social media offers the hope of bringing us all together but is often the instrument for tearing us apart. The long-held assumption that an increased awareness of diversity would easily lead to understanding and unity now seems to be morphing culture into something reminiscent of the ominous situation described at the end of the book of Judges: "*In those days Israel had no king; everyone did as they saw fit*" (Judges 21:25).
>
> I happen to live just outside of Toronto, Canada—one of the most global cities on earth. The fourth largest city in North America, it's rated as one of the top five most multicultural cities in the world, with over 150–300 languages spoken every day. It's an amazing place to live. Our city can be seen as a microcosm of the world, and we are trying to grow the church right in the middle of it.
>
> Here in Canada, as in much of the West, Christians find themselves more and more at the edge of society, not the centre. Along with marginalization, we now experience increased hostility and intolerance toward expressions of a Christian worldview. And more, with all the nations of the world here, Toronto is deeply religious, deeply spiritual, and deeply secular all at once.[2]

Whether you live in a city like mine or you just go online, this is our world. At one moment you are talking to a Muslim who wants to convert you, telling you the Bible is corrupt and your faith is weak. The next conversation is with a New Ager who thinks all roads are the same. The next is a Mormon claiming we worship the same Jesus. Then it's an Atheist declaring that God does not exist and to believe he does is intellectual weakness. And then you have a transgender activist saying your faith is the reason the world is so messed up, and you are responsible for the death of so many young people. On top of that, there is the person who just does not care, a person who calls themself a Christian but has a faith that is inherited and not rooted, a Hindu neighbour who really does want to understand why you believe what you believe, and so on and so on.

For some of us within the church community, we feel like we woke up, looked around, and said, literally, *"What on earth is happening?"* Many others of us are not shocked but have been waiting and working as the tides started to really turn. Others who have fled to or immigrated to the West from other parts of the world where the church is suffering and flourishing are saying, *"Do they not know what they had?"* They keep telling us: We have lived in the alternatives, and it's not as promising as you think. So many of us feel orphaned or culturally transplanted to unexpected places. Some of these places seem to be okay with our faith, other places are apathetic to Christianity, but many, many more are becoming not just uncomfortable with our faith but belligerent and hostile. And then there are the many churches and pastors that have given into the spirit of the age and the old shadow of heresy causes disunity and theological confusion. More and more often we feel small, unheard; we don't know who to trust or who to look to. The deeper truth is we suddenly don't have power like we once did, and it's jarring.

As you drive into Toronto from the east, you pass a Delta hotel just off the highway. The hotel used to seem huge. I remember eating at the sushi restaurant at the top of the hotel and being able to see the amazing downtown skyline of Toronto. But as Toronto grew, condos started being built around the hotel. The Delta has maybe fourteen or fifteen floors, but now the condos surrounding it have fifty, seventy, or one hundred floors. It is now dwarfed. Its former grandeur, its centrality, and its wow factor are now gone. I doubt that most people notice it anymore as they drive by. That is what it feels like these days as a Christian, at least in the urban centres.

I remember coming across this quote in my early years while doing my graduate work, but it summarizes everything I have been leading through for years:

> The church in North America for the most part has developed expectations of success and cultural status, either directly through

> participation in our culture or through standing in the shadow of those who led the way. We need to adjust this self-concept of the church to one that is able to accept a minority status and face cultural indifference. We will need to shake off the remaining vestiges of a Christendom perspective that expects the world to take the church seriously, refocusing our attention to how we should now seek out the world.[3]

Yup! And let me just throw out a grenade here: I think how we lose and keep choosing to lose might be so important to the long term. Yet as I look around, many spend most of their time trying to get the power *back*.

This year, I was reading a small, relatively unknown book by J. I. Packer called *Finishing Our Course with Joy*. It is a really helpful book on how to prepare to die well as a Christian, a topic rarely talked about but deeply needed. Although he was speaking to individual Christians and himself (as he was writing the book, he was preparing to die), this little section of wisdom for those more aged jumped off the page to me:

> Live in the present moment. Get into the way of practicing God's presence—more specifically, Christ's presence, according to his promise to be with us always (Matt. 28:20)—and cultivate the divine companionship. This, too, is an important and, I suspect, widely neglected spiritual discipline nowadays, and its importance also would seem to grow as we near life's end. Daydreaming and indulgence of nostalgia are unhappy habits, making for unrealism and discontent. Like all bad habits, they tighten their grip on us until we set ourselves against them and, with God's help, break them. Elderly retirees are prone to find that a disciplined breaking of them is an increasingly necessary task in life's last lap, in which steady looking ahead in each present moment becomes a bigger and bigger factor in inner spiritual health.[4]

Across the Western world, what we know and must accept is that Christendom is dying and in most places is already dead. By the way, do you know what Christendom is? Here is a great, simple definition:

> The European peoples accepted the Christian faith as entire communities and essentially in terms of law and custom. It is the nature of law and custom that no one is permitted to opt out. So Europe became Christian territory in which all were to be regarded as Christians, all baptized into the faith, with territorial churches, each family living in a parish with a church that would teach the faith and laws shaped by Christian teaching.[5]

So that Christian territory spread around the West and to everywhere the West influenced. Now there are still elements of this in America, England, and other Western places where there are large pockets of Christians. There are new versions of Christendom forming in Africa, Latin America, Asia, and the United States, and if you are from these places, pay close attention so you do not sin like we have before. But for us that are in the post- or pre-Christian places, I think Packer's reflection on death is so needed as we are facing the death of so much that was good and was not so good. Daydreaming and indulgence of nostalgia fills church membership meetings and the social media feeds of so many Christians, and it is not helping us with witnessing.

Which brings us to another question: What is going to happen next? Winter or summer, retreat or revival? No one can be sure, and I know things will of course work out differently in different places around the world. For example, when I hang out with my UK or Australian friends, they always say the modern/postmodern, post-/pre-Christian pagan moment is similar, but Canada seems to have jumped ahead to an extreme. Many of my continental European friends are like, "Welcome! We have been here longer than you can imagine." And my American friends, depending on where they live in their nation, say either, "Thank God someone is addressing what's going on here," or "It's not here yet, but we all feel it coming." More than a few don't want to know what is coming. Yet for others it is not coming at all, and there's a resurgence in the church. More of my global friends are facing very different issues, but there is always crossover for all of us.

But what I will say is that there is a growing sense of something more than apathy in many corners. This is best outlined in an interview with Canada's former Prime Minister, reported by the CBC years ago. Speaking before the Montreal Pride parade, Justin Trudeau said Canadians should stop talking about tolerance: "We need to talk about acceptance, we need to talk about openness, we need to talk about friendship, we need to talk about love, not just tolerance."[6]

Diana Eck from Harvard said, "Pluralism is not relativism. It does not mean we agree. It does not require us to leave our identities behind."[7] But these lines are being blurred, and that is the shadow so many are seeing. Many of us in Canada are deeply concerned when it comes to conscience around gender, sexuality, euthanasia, abortion, and exclusive faith claims. All of this is eroding so quickly that we wonder if parts of the Christian worldview will become a crime. Many are fighting back politically in Jesus's name, but is that what Jesus wants?

We have been here many times before throughout history—when our ancestors had to say, "No, Jesus is Lord." As Tim Keller once posted on X, "Roman Empire: 'You Christians are too exclusive. You threaten the social order because you won't honour all deities.' Modern West: 'You Christians are too exclusive. You threaten the social order because you won't honour all identities.'"[8] One of the lost moments in history where this became very real was during the French Revolution around priests and celibacy.

> French revolutionaries had raised doubts about celibacy along with so much else, and many intellectuals scorned it as "unnatural." Salacious popular literature mocked priests as sexually avaricious. Delegates to the National Assembly passed laws permitting priests to marry, and several thousand priests did. As the revolution descended into the Terror, celibacy became described as a "social crime," since married priests were presumed more likely to become good republican citizens. One Robespierre protégé denounced men vowed to celibacy "who wish to isolate themselves

> further from their fellow man and to violate natural and social law." Revolutionaries funded clerical weddings.[9]

This tradition of mockery in France still happens to this day. In the opening ceremonies of the 2024 Summer Olympics, there was what seemed to be overt mockery of the Last Supper with drag queens reenacting the famed moment. Others said that instead it was an homage to the Greek god Dionysus or inspired by the famous painting *The Feast of the Gods,* a seventeenth-century painting from Dutch artist Jan van Bijlert that depicts the pagan Greek gods of Olympus crowded around a long table with the sun god Apollo at the centre of the table, recognizable by a halo of light around his head. Those in charge claimed it was intended to celebrate community and tolerance and claimed it was not the Last Supper, but later some of the actors admitted online that it was, at least in part.[10] The point is mockery and paganism, and growing faith is the mix found in the West today. Just a few minutes from where this act of mockery took place, Notre Dame, now fully restored, is a physical symbol of what is happening in many other places, a coming back to faith. Once again retreat and renewal reside in the same place.

Simply put, in the French Revolution's political climate, the mentality was we will change your views through force because we have deemed them out of step with our own cultural ideals, wants, and worldviews. Tolerance versus acceptance is vastly different. Traditional tolerance, which much of the West is built on (sort of), says, "I tolerate you because we all have agreed upon ways of staying together, but I do not need to affirm or agree with you." As Christians our tolerance must be (though rarely is) made holy. Our tolerance cannot be standoffish. We are called to love people in a 1 Corinthians 13 way. We are called to have people over to our homes even when we do not accept much of their worldview or activities. But now the call in culture has become something much more than tolerance. It has become a mutated insistence of acceptance, which is an all or nothing demand.

As Rod Dreher said in *Live Not by Lies,* "Elites and elite institutions are abandoning old-fashioned liberalism, based in defending the rights of the individual, and replacing it with a progressive creed that regards justice in terms of groups. It encourages people to identify with groups ethnic, sexual, and otherwise and to think of Good and Evil as a matter of power dynamics among the groups."[11] There is a creeping, almost light totalitarianism happening, and I don't think we as Christians know how to talk about it. We sort of see it in the shadows, but we don't know what to call that thing.

Rod explores a book that has been mostly forgotten about. In 1951, a scholar named Hannah Arendt wrote this book called *The Origins of Totalitarianism*. She examined Germany, Italy, and the Soviet Union as case studies. After years of reflection, she described five signs that a society is ready for this experience. The first was loneliness as an experience of the majority of people in society.[12]

If this is true, then the West has never been so ripe for something extremely good or bad! Loneliness has been called an epidemic by multiple countries and health officials in our time. Social media has grown loneliness to historical highs. Arendt writes, "What prepares men for totalitarian domination in the non-totalitarian world is the fact that loneliness, once a borderline experience usually suffered in certain marginal social conditions like old age, had become an everyday experience of the ever-growing masses of our century."[13]

The second and third signs are the loss of trust in institutions and hierarchies and the desire to destroy and transgress.[14] Just look at your feed; look at our politics. Are we not an exhausted age—gluttons for information with very little wisdom? From racial unrest to political discord to vying for power, our trust in leaders and institutions is low, and society is filled with lust and love for sinful expression. Even more, society has been destroying systems and institutions without a plan for what would replace them.

The last two signs are just as eye opening: the willingness to believe useful lies and valuing loyalty more than expertise.[15] Are we not ripe for this? Dreher summarizes it this way:

> To grasp the threat of totalitarianism, it's important to understand the difference between it and simple authoritarianism. Authoritarianism is what you have when the state monopolizes

> political control. That is mere dictatorship—bad, certainly, but totalitarianism is much worse . . . a totalitarian society is one in which an ideology seeks to displace all prior traditions and institutions, with the goal of bringing all aspects of society under control of that ideology. A totalitarian state is one that aspires to nothing less than defending and controlling reality. Truth is whatever the rulers decide it is.[16]

As I write this book, both the political Left and the political Right are flirting with much of the above. As Christians we must be wary of this, but I fear we are getting sucked in by both extremes. At the same time, more and more non-Christians are becoming very uncomfortable with it all. There are signs of renewal, mass conversion, and revival-like experiences breaking out all over the world. From the urban core of London to university campuses in the United States, there are signs of real moves of God. Leading public thinkers are pushing back—just read Tom Holland (the historian, not Spider-Man) or Jordan Peterson or go on YouTube and listen to the recent conversion of Ayaan Hirsi Ali. In France, 12,000 people were baptized on Easter Sunday 2024 and 17,800 in 2025.[17]

The Asbury outpouring continues to ripple around the globe. Study after study now points to Gen Z being more conservative and wanting more than what has been. In real time as I am writing this, many of us are more openly wondering if a fourth awakening might be happening in Gen Z. Young men of all stripes are flocking back to churches. With the election of Pope Leo XIV, the young and old are deeply considering Catholicism once again. This is the embodied oxymoron of our time: We are living between retreat and renewal at once. The dividing lines are as much generational as spiritual. Whether you are in a majority or minority setting, this conversation matters so much.

A few months ago in London, the dating app Bumble had a billboard on the tube that read "Thou shalt not give up on dating and becoming a nun," implying that self-denial is awful and evil, and many shouted "Amen!" Yet at the same time, I see others, like my own children (both Gen Z and Gen Alpha) starting to agree with

C. S. Lewis's weighty statement, "One road leads home and a thousand roads lead to the wilderness."[18] Even the famous fundamentalist atheist Richard Dawkins has come out as a cultural Christian, deeply longing for what he has taken for granted.[19] He has now realized that the water he swims in (Christianity) is what lets him have the society he wants even though he still thinks the whole thing is a fairytale and scientifically impossible. He wants the social good without the fairytale.

So how do we respond to such death and life at once? What image could help us understand this oxymoron? Forest fires. When a forest fire rages and brings massive destruction, it tends to burn out all the underbrush that was choking out new life. For some the forest fire has not yet started, for others it is raging and is blistering hot, and for still others it has raged and raged and is now petering out. The new life after the fire is just starting to grow as the promises given have not yet been fulfilled, and more cultural Christians are becoming real Christians. But as this chapter ends, maybe your prayer—the simple yet dangerous prayer—should be "God, let it all burn if it leads to real life and to your kingdom really coming once again. And God, if the fire is done, please let the new growth be real as not what we used to have."

Are you willing to be so bold in your prayers? Or will you keep hedging because of comfort?

Don't turn the page until you decide.

The Incarnation is the ultimate reason why the service of God cannot be divorced from the service of man.

—DIETRICH BONHOEFFER

Our business is to present the Christian faith clothed in modern terms, not to propagate modern thought clothed in Christian terms. Confusion here is fatal.

—J. I. PACKER

The missionary spirit is the spirit of Jesus, the spirit of the incarnation and the cross.

—HUDSON TAYLOR

There is nothing so secular that it cannot be sacred, and that is one of the deepest messages of the incarnation.

—MADELEINE L'ENGLE

To the weak I became weak, to win the weak. I have become all things to all people so that by all possible means I might save some. I do all this for the sake of the gospel, that I may share in its blessings.

—1 CORINTHIANS 9:22–23

CHAPTER 3

The Incarnation as Our Model

One of the most consequential things to take place in history was that God took on flesh. It literally changed everything. You could say that the heart of the Christian faith is that God came for us when we could not get to him. For this journey that we are on together, the gospel of John is going to be the most helpful for understanding how the incarnation is the key to witnessing well in the midst of everything we've just looked at.

As Charles Swindoll observed, "Matthew wrote, 'This Jesus is the Messiah, is King; worship Him.' Mark wrote, 'Jesus is the Servant who serves all of us; let's follow Him.' Luke wrote, 'This is the only man among men without sin; emulate Him.' John says, 'This is God in human flesh; believe in Him.'"[1] That is why John uses the word *believe* ninety-eight times in his letter! Hear his heart, see his passion, feel his devotion, and sense the urgency he has for us, for you, and for the world both in his day and ours. Why did he write all this firsthand experience down? "But these are written that you may believe that Jesus is the Christ, the Son of God, and that by believing you may have life in his name" (John 20:31).

John calls us to say, "Yes, Jesus is Messiah; yes, Jesus is the only Son of God; yes, by trusting in Jesus I will have eternal life by his love, his work—by him alone!" But that's the end; we need to start at the beginning. In the very first verse of this gospel, John starts us in a very different place. He pushes to see if we really believe. He starts before Christmas.

Before the wise men with their gold, frankincense, and myrrh; before the star and before the songs of Simeon, Mary, and Zechariah; before Jesus was presented in the temple; before there was no room in the inn; before the birth of Jesus; before the shepherds and the choir of angels; before Gabriel spoke to Joseph; and before Mary; we are left with the question, where was Jesus just before? Did he exist beforehand, or was he created in that moment? Who was Jesus before Mary, before the manger, and before, well, everything? The answer to that question is central to everything we believe. So what does John tell us? "In the beginning was the Word, and the Word was with God, and the Word was God" (John 1:1).

These words throw you and me back to the moment time began, when life came to be. The very first verse in the Bible says, "In the beginning God created the heavens and the earth" (Genesis 1:1). Before space, time, and matter was God—in eternity past, before the clock started ticking—and in that eternal place, God began the largest artistic project that would ever be. Out of nothing, God created everything. At that moment, there at the beginning of history and at the root of the universe, was the Word, who, as we are about to see, is Jesus. And the word *was* in Greek means continually, so this really reads, "In the beginning was continuing the Word, and the Word was continuing with God, and the Word was continually God."[2] Or as another wrote, "Jesus always was wasing!"[3]

Swindoll wrote this about the Word:

> The Greek term is logos, a profoundly significant concept among philosophers for at least three centuries before Christ. It referred to an uncreated divine mind that gives meaning and order to the universe. John essentially co-opted the concept, saying in effect, "The concept pagan philosophers have theorized actually exists; He is God, and Jesus Christ is He." John continues to describe "the Word" by saying He was with God. . . . "The Word" and God the Father were existing close together, sharing place, intimacy, and purpose. In fact, the intimacy and familiarity was such that "the

Word was God." The Word and God share the same essence; therefore, all that is true of God is true of the Word.[4]

Before the manger, Jesus was with God and was God. John brings this home by summarizing in verse 2 that "He (Jesus) was with God in the beginning." Only God is eternal, and because the Word is eternal, Jesus must be God. Jesus is coequal, coeternal, and coexistent with the Father in eternity past. Then John moves from preexistence to the beginning, to the story of creation—from the not created to the created. Only God does not have a beginning; all of creation has a beginning. "Through Jesus all things were made; without him nothing was made that has been made" (John 1:3). The first act where God revealed himself was creation. The Father created, but he did it through Jesus. Jesus is the agent of creation. There are about one hundred billion stars in an average galaxy and about one hundred million galaxies in known space. That means there are ten *octillion* stars. Yes, that is a real number! That is a 10 with *27* zeroes behind it—10,000,000,000,000,000,000,000,000,000.[5] Jesus did all of that, and more!

Like with all great sequels, we see the full picture now. God the Father, through Jesus, created all things; God's creative capacity is expressed through the Word. Jesus was responsible for the creation of the World. The universe is not eternal; God is. The universe is not random; it is the act of an artistic and loving Creator. This is God's world! He created us and everything not because he was lonely but to bring glory to himself and to share his love.

At this point, you may be thinking, "Great, yes, we all believe this, Jon, but what does it have to do with presence, witness, and reaching our generation?" Stay with me, because it is the next grand moment in John 1 that brings us closer to our conversation today: "The Word became flesh and made his dwelling among us. We have seen his glory, the glory of the one and only Son, who came from the Father, full of grace and truth" (John 1:14).

The Word became flesh. The Word did not just appear to be human; he really became flesh! In the original language it reads like Jesus set up a tent: He "tabernacled" among us. Hundreds of years earlier, when

Moses was leading the Israelites in the desert, God would meet with them in a holy tent called a tabernacle. But now Jesus is the dwelling place, the glory, the permanent, ongoing place of encounter. That is why one of Jesus's names is Immanuel, God with us. Many Christians over the centuries have tried to help us understand this:

> In the 4th Century, Athanasius explained that the Incarnation was like a great king who journeyed to one of the villages of his kingdom to deliberately live as one among the ordinary people. Such action would bring that village honour above all others and would give profound dignity to all the residents. With the king physically present, it would be unlikely that enemies would harass or violate the citizenry. As late as the last century, still searching for a way to understand the Incarnation, Kierkegaard again used the analogy of a king. This time the king desired to marry a girl from among the common folk of his kingdom. In order to romance her he had to lay aside his royal robes and he, himself, went into the village to request her hand from the family, as would any commoner. He could not overwhelm the humble girl with an entourage nor could he send a messenger to speak for him. Kierkegaard had such a high view of the meaning of the Incarnation that he was reluctant even to speak of it in ways that are analogous to human experience. Yet, he concluded "love is exultant when it unites equals, but it is triumphant when it makes that which is unequal equal in love."[6]

This is essential to our faith: If you don't believe that Jesus is both fully God and fully human, you are not a Christian. But more than that, the incarnation also has massive implications for presence, witness, and evangelism. The message of Jesus and the person of Jesus never change, no matter the culture, but the incarnation shows us that each culture must accept him and invite him in within their own experience. "Incarnation is translation."[7]

Okay, let's really do some homework together. God wants to talk to, be in relationship with, and walk with human beings. God communicates. He lets us know who he actually is. God is the one who takes the initiative. God walked with Adam and Eve in the coolness of the day, and God went and found them when they had sinned. Over and over again, God keeps showing up through his presence (the physical glory of God in the wilderness, tabernacle, and temple), through his prophets, and ultimately, when he fully "moved into the neighbourhood" at Christmas. God wants to be understood, and the incarnation is God's best way to know him.[8]

Think about it: Jesus was a Jewish male who had a particular skin colour and who lived in a particular time and place. This act sets into motion the genius of God's mission, which is that every culture can connect with God through Jesus and by his Spirit alone within their own cultural expression and context. Now I will say this again and again: The message and the person of Jesus do not change and cannot change. When it does, we move into that old word "heresy." I love what Vincent of Lérins from the 5th century wrote, "'*dicas nove, non dicas nova*'; speak in a new way but don't say new things."[9]

Another way to understand it is to think about a seed. There's a protective coat or shell, and then inside that is the seed that brings life. The shell allows the seed to be protected and planted and allows the seed to become the plant it was created to be. The Christian message is like the inside of the seed that never changes, but there is an outside that can change, and must change, so the gospel can be planted in many different soils.[10] Or think about music. There are so many different expressions or styles: classical, pop, country, rap, reggae (Jamaica), flamenco (Spain), K-pop (South Korea), Afrobeat (Nigeria), tango (Argentina), bhangra (India), gamelan (Indonesia), fado (Portugal), rai (Algeria), Celtic (Ireland/Scotland), Tuvan throat singing (Tuva, Russia), highlife (Ghana), and the list goes on. We will all like some and loath others. They all can be redeemed, and what they communicate matters. This is the power of the incarnation. We must guard, confess, and have confidence in the gospel, in Jesus, and in God's Word, but we can expect and celebrate the vastly different styles of church and expressions even when they feel in conflict, because none of us own Jesus.

How does Matthew 28, the "go to all nations, all ethnic groups," look and feel? The incarnation modeled it for us: "Jesus came into the world to be at home with all people in every place. Therefore, they can welcome Him, knowing that He belongs with them and they with Him. Without this fundamental Word, there is no way to speak of appropriate Christianity. Through the Incarnation, God personally and intimately entered into the world of His own creation."[11] Another scholar said it like this, "Contextualization attempts to communicate the Gospel in word and deed and to establish the church in ways that make sense to people within their local cultural context, presenting Christianity in such a way that it meets people's deepest needs and penetrates their worldview, thus allowing them to follow Christ and remain within their own culture."[12]

This is why the family feels so much internal tension. We are all trying to reach out in multiple directions and to multiple people, whether online or in one neighbourhood, city, or country, but we also want everything and everyone to look the same, smell the same, act the same. We want to know whose team everyone is on so we can quickly look at their jersey and go, "Yup, they are with us (or against us)." But the incarnation does not make this so easy. The church must have vastly different looks, feels, and expressions all at once for us to be able to reach all the vastly different people in our world.

So much of the fighting we see between Christians is more about the husk than the seed. But when the husk becomes our majority focus, we all lose—our presence is weakened and our witness reduced. By the way, what we are exploring here is what makes our faith so different from other faiths and what helped it spread quickly before. It is our secret sauce. If we fully embrace this again, we can spread quickly in the West and around the world. This is why looking back matters!

One letter sent from Rome over 1,400 years ago brings home why incarnation and context matter and should make church look and feel drastically different across communities. Around AD 596, Pope Gregory the Great sent Augustine of Canterbury as a missionary to England and shared this advice with him as he went:

> Your brotherhood is familiar with the usage of the Roman Church since you have very pleasant memories of being raised and nurtured in that usage. But it seems to me that you should carefully select for the English Church, which is still new to the faith and developing

> as a distinct community, whatever can best please Almighty God, whether you discover it in the Roman Church, or among the Gauls, or anywhere else. For customs are not to be revered for their place of origin; rather those places are to be respected for the good customs they produce. From each individual church, therefore, choose whatever is holy, whatever is awe-inspiring, whatever is right; then arrange what you have collected as if in a little bouquet according to the English disposition and thus establish them as custom.[13]

Even more importantly, this highlights the great difference between Islam and Christianity. Make no mistake, these are the two faiths fighting for global influence in this moment. But listen to this:

> At the heart of Jewish faith, as at the heart of Islamic faith, is the Prophetic Word God speaks to humanity. At the heart of Christian faith is the Incarnate Word. God became human. The divine Word was expressed under the conditions of a particular human society; the divine Word was, as it were, translated. And since the divine Word is for all humanity, he is translated again in terms of every culture where he finds acceptance among its people. The unchanging nature of the Prophetic Word of the Qur'an, fixed in heaven for ever in Arabic, produces a single Islamic civilization recognizable, despite all the local variations, from Indonesia to Morocco. There can be no single Christian civilization; the Christian Scriptures are not, like the Qur'an, the Word of God only when delivered in the original languages. In Christian understanding The Word of God can be spoken in any language under heaven. The divine Son did not become humanity in general, but a specific man in a specific place and culture; he is, as it were, made flesh again in other places and cultures as he is received there by faith. Similarly with the Christian Scriptures; there is (for purposes of communication, at least) no such thing as language in general.[14]

And yet we are tempted again and again to make our own theologically informed, cultural style of church the only way, the right way, or the best way. For example, our Eastern Orthodox brothers and sisters insist that they are the only true faith passed down. Not just the core confessional beliefs but the style and liturgical expression of church is mandatory in their eyes. They use the language of being "maximalist" in their view of church orders, the role of sacraments, and authority passed down, with it being a precondition for church unity and the criteria for identifying where the true church is.[15] The problem is that often this has led to them being stunted in evangelism and struggling deeply with cultural boundedness, personal prejudice, and ethnic wants over evangelism. I remain a convinced Protestant. And this is just one of many examples, for there is more than enough critique to go around for the whole dysfunctional family called the church. The communities that I lead in and connect to have many other issues that must be called out, including pragmatism over theological reflection and different expressions of the Orthodox church's problem above, just wearing trendier clothing.

C. S. Lewis gave this brilliant advice to new Christians when he addressed church styles and denominations, making the point that you cannot just live in limbo (just you and Jesus) but must join one of the many expressions of God's community.

> The hall is a place to wait in, a place from which to try the various doors, not a place to live in. For that purpose the worst of the rooms (whichever that may be) is, I think, preferable. It is true that some people may find they have to wait in the hall for a considerable time, while others feel certain almost at once which door they must knock at. I do not know why there is this difference, but I am sure God keeps no one waiting unless He sees that it is good for him to wait. When you do get into your room you will find that the long wait has done you some kind of good which you would not have had otherwise. But you must regard it as waiting, not as camping. You must keep on praying for light; and, of course, even in the hall, you must begin trying to obey the rules which are common to the whole house. And above all you must be asking which door is the true one; not which pleases you best by its paint and panelling. In plain language, the question should never be: "Do I like that kind of service?" but "Are these doctrines true: is holiness here? Does my conscience

> move me towards this? Is my reluctance to knock at this door due to my pride, or my mere taste, or my personal dislike of this particular door-keeper?" When you have reached your own room, be kind to those who have chosen different doors and to those who are still in the hall. If they are wrong they need your prayers all the more; and if they are your enemies, then you are under orders to pray for them. That is one of the rules common to the whole house.[16]

What has been true in all times, but especially now, is that we need the church in all its forms—from free to liturgical, cathedrals to house churches, megachurches to the thousands of neighbourhood churches, ethnic specific to multicultural, and everything in between. This was always God's goal, and we must embrace, understand, and defend this diversity of expressions to reach out again in our very new, pluralistic, and repaganizing moment. Incarnation demands adaptation, and we adapt not for fun or because of some pragmatic need but to reach as many as possible! That is not to say there aren't major theological reasons for why we hold what we hold and practice what we practice, but what matters is the core, and if the core does not change, we are still swimming in the grand river of what God is doing.

But the incarnation is not the only lens we need in this moment. Once the plant is in the garden, weeds need to be replaced and removed from the garden. As the gospel becomes part of the culture, it must confront anything in the culture that is not of the kingdom of God. It must be welcoming, understanding, and personal but also prophetic, contrasting, and countercultural (though not anticultural). We must confess even when it hurts. We must be faithful and relevant at the same time. The community must, after being saved and formed by the timeless and transcultural Word of God, find what is good and right in each culture and critique, unmask, and challenge what worldliness looks like in that context.[17] This is where we are called to contrast, to be in but not fully in the world, to be a parallel community while still looking and feeling like those around us. Tertullian, the great church father, famously said, "What does Athens [human culture, context] have to do with Jerusalem [the gospel]?"[18] He pushed for more contrast than closeness.

Considering the American church experience, Stanley Hauerwas once wrote,

> Christianity's task, on the contrary, is to provide another story and an alternate community, based not on the abstract virtues of justice and freedom, but on the Christian beatitudes and the practices of Christian tradition. In contrast to an American culture of individualism and consumerism, Christians are called into a "community of character."[19]

We need to be in and not in; we need massive diversity with a never-changing centre. We need to realize that we will all reach different people. This was what I was hinting at back in 2018 when I wrote this:

> My current assignment is a megachurch in the suburbs of Toronto in the twenty-first century. So of course it can feel like Walmart or Starbucks to a degree. I don't expect that our style of church will be around in a hundred years, and that's the point. We should not theologically enshrine our temporal church culture but admit that our current iteration is only a model that can and must change. When we understand the difference between timeless and timely, we will see the convergence that can be found across all times and missional efforts.[20]

I love reading biographies, and I love hearing stories of how people come to faith or are exploring faith in Jesus. One that particularly stood out to me in recent years was about the historian Molly Worthen. She is an associate professor of history at the University of North Carolina at Chapel Hill. She has written for *The New Yorker, Slate, The American Prospect, Foreign Policy, The New York Times, Christianity Today,* and many more. She is an expert on religion and politics and teaches courses on North American religious life and intellectual culture, global Christianity, and the history of ideas.

Though she is a world class expert on early and American expressions of Christianity, Worthen personally did not believe in Jesus at all. As I listened to an interview where she shared about her history and journey to encountering Jesus, it was *where* she met Jesus that gave me pause: a Southern Baptist megachurch. *Wow. Really?* I love the church I lead, and I love the many similar larger expressions of church, but sometimes I long for an older, deeper, more reflective, quieter church to slow down and decompress. This is not saying I don't want the lively charismatic worship experience or to keep taking new ground, but when you have something, you can crave the other. And when I heard she had come to faith, I assumed she must have met Jesus in a Catholic community or an Anglican prayer service—something older, deeply rich in tradition and contemplation. She is a professor and historian, after all. Those communities have all the natural bridges to help her. But that is not her story. And I shouldn't be surprised because we see this happening all the time in the style of church I currently lead. Here is how Worthen described the experience in an interview:

> So I found myself sort of inexplicably drawn to worship, at like—I mean, it's Summit, the mothership in North Raleigh, because there's many campuses, the mothership is like the platonic ideal of a suburban, Southern Baptist megachurch. And it's frickin' awesome. I think for me, well, there's a few things going on here. One is I realize that for a person like me, who's a historian, there's a way in which the liturgical experience of high Anglo-Catholic worship gives the mind so many things to do that aren't Jesus. So my previous experience of church—I mean this sounds ridiculous to say, but I do think this is accurate—my previous experience of church was just not, I wasn't thinking about Jesus, like I was thinking about Thomas Cranmer. And what a genius he was and the Book of Common Prayer and the poetry in the stained glass windows and all of that, and there's a way in which megachurch worship, that the very simple kind of theologically to the point hymnody, the intense forty-minute sermon, deep dive, it helped me focus on what I needed to be focusing on.
>
> Also, the sort of giant anonymizing context of the megachurch was exactly what I needed. It was that there was this perfect combination of anonymity. I could go, it's dark, it's so loud, you can't

even hear yourself singing, no one knows who you are. Except I was becoming friends with the pastor. So when I could work up the nerve, which was not every time, I could go down in front afterwards and like check in with him. So it was this combination of friendship and anonymity on my terms. And the crucial intervention that J. D. made for me intellectually, that made it possible for me to even have this process, was to help me see that I had in my previous efforts—half-baked as they were—to investigate Christianity, I allowed myself to be overwhelmed by things that weren't the central thing. So if you're looking at converting to Christianity from the outside as a fully formed adult, you're not doing in the context of a family, it's a lot to take at once, right? So there's all the Jesus stuff, but there's lots of crazy stuff in the Bible. There's all the end times, prophecies, heaven and hell, the sexual ethic that is so at odds with everything our current culture says. It's so much at once. It is overwhelming, and you might begin to make baby steps on one point, but then you're like, "Oh, man, but all that other stuff was so bananas. I can't do this. I'm paralyzed."

What J. D. helped me see was that it stands or falls on the resurrection. And I could agree to struggle with all the other questions, like they're important, for sure. They're not the main thing. I could agree to struggle with them. It's all about Romans 10:9, right? It's all about confessing with your mouth that Jesus is Lord and believing in your heart that he rose from the dead. And I couldn't do that, because I'm a historian. And it turns out, and here again I feel so—I guess every conversion is a series of epiphanies, once you've had the epiphany, you're like, how could I've ever been so dumb, right? I mean, here I am, a historian of Christianity, certainly not a first-century specialist, but, yeah, a historian of Christianity, and I had always conceived myself as unusually open to the claims of Christianity—sincerely open. But I only realized in this process last summer that I really had not been, and that I had never—there were always resources for seriously investigating the claims of this religion, which is unique, and that it makes this singular historical claim and that that is everything, and there are the tools available to really engage with it, and make up your mind about it—and I had never done that. And I felt kind of ashamed myself. And so you know, over those months, I was praying for some warm and fuzzy, mystical intervention.

And it didn't happen. I just got to the point in August, where I thought, "Well, gosh, if I am a consistent pragmatist, I have to admit that I have gotten over that line of the resurrection being the best explanation for the historical evidence we have. And if that's true, I have to change my working hypothesis of the universe." And so there was this weekend where I switched how I was praying in private, from praying basically, simply for God to show himself to me to just seeing what it was like to say, "Jesus, you are my Lord and Savior." And then I met with J. D. the following week. And I remember that weekend, I said to my husband, I'm feeling pretty stressed out. I think I might be a Christian. And he said, "Well, why are you stressed out like that? That's not I mean, you don't have to go on wearing a sign. What's the big deal?" And I said, "You just don't understand. I mean, you're dealing with these Baptist, mission-minded types, like you can't—it is a big deal." So yeah, so I ended up making it official by doing the prayer in front of a Christian notary in the form of J. D. Greear in his office in August, and I got myself properly baptized.[21]

We need to see incarnation as the way we move forward—together, but in different expressions reaching different people and different communities. We must be slow to attack other expressions and slow to write off what others are doing. Don't presume which husk will reach which person! This lack of understanding is why we don't feel peace inside the church as the outside is raging. We need to change our expectations. Now again, this does not mean we leave room for compromise or heresy. Let me quote Vincent of Lérins once more, "Speak in a new way but don't say new things." If you think I am opening up Pandora's Box and not calling for a robust, historic understanding of our faith, I recommend reading chapters 10–14 in my book *Perseverance* where I lay out the need for theological perseverance in our post-truth moment. But what I *am* begging for is for us to slow down and root our kingdom attempts in incarnation first and confrontation second. Let me say that again: incarnation first, confrontation second.

We all must move from hubris to humility. It's time to acknowledge that it's easier to talk about and attempt renewal and reformation than witnessing. Can you do the more challenging work of incarnation? Are you willing to suffer when we must stand and confront? If we don't, trouble will only grow. It was St. Moses the Black (Ethiopian) who reportedly preached so long ago: "You fast, but Satan does not eat. You labor fervently, but Satan never sleeps. The only dimension with which you can outperform Satan is by acquiring humility, for Satan has no humility."[22]

Could you stop right now and pray for your humility and for your church or movement's humility and unity? Don't have the words? Well, our Anglican friends pray this time and again, and I think we should join them in this prayer for the church:

> *O God the Father of our Lord Jesus Christ, our only Saviour, the Prince of Peace: Give us grace to take to heart the grave dangers we are in through our many divisions. Deliver your Church from all enmity and prejudice, and everything that hinders us from godly union. As there is one Body and one Spirit, one hope of our calling, one Lord, one Faith, one Baptism, one God and Father of us all, so make us all to be of one heart and of one mind, united in one holy bond of truth and peace, of faith and love, that with one voice we may give you praise; through Jesus Christ our Lord, who lives and reigns with you and the Holy Spirit, one God in everlasting glory. Amen.*[23]

Reality cannot be ignored except at a price; and the longer the ignorance is persisted in, the higher and more terrible becomes the price that must be paid.

—ALDOUS HUXLEY

Every age has its own outlook. It is specially good at seeing certain truths and specially liable to make certain mistakes. Nothing strikes me more when I read the controversies of past ages than the fact that both sides were usually assuming without question a good deal which we should now absolutely deny. They thought they were as completely opposed as two sides could be, but in fact they were all the time secretly united—united with each other and against earlier and later ages by a mass of common assumptions. . . . None of us can fully escape this blindness, but we shall certainly increase it, and weaken our guard against it, if we read only modern books. Where they are true they will give us truths which we half knew already. Where they are false they will aggravate the error with which we are already dangerously ill. The only palliative is to keep the clean sea breeze of the centuries blowing through our minds, and this can be done only by reading old books. Not, of course, that there is anything magic about the past. People were no cleverer then than they are now; they made as many mistakes as we. But not the same mistakes. They will not flatter us in the errors we are already committing; and their own errors, being now open and palpable, will not endanger us.

—C. S. LEWIS

CHAPTER 4

Learning from the Past

It is one thing to watch a movie—nonfiction or fiction—like *Saving Private Ryan, Braveheart, The Lord of the Rings*, or *The Hunger Games*. It would be a totally other experience to live out those films we watch for entertainment from the safety of home.

This came home for me through an uncomfortable encounter with my grandfather, a World War II veteran. He was a member of the Canadian Forces that liberated Holland and Belgium and entered into Germany. As he went through this terrible experience, he, like many others, collected military items along the way. As a kid, I discovered all these many pins, daggers, medals, and hats tucked away in the back of closets and attics, and they sparked in me a real desire to learn about history and to collect historical items. For years I collected militaria from all sides of the conflict.

One day, our family was visiting my grandparents, and the original version of the movie *All Quiet on the Western Front* was on. I began watching it, but I was covering my eyes or walking out of the room at some points. And this original version was tame compared to the newer movie, which is one of the most honest and brutal expressions of war.

When my grandfather saw me covering my eyes, he, in an angry tone motivated by frustration, said, "You spend all this time reading books about and collecting military items from a war I lived through, but you can't even handle watching this movie." He had lived through the war. I just enjoyed thinking and watching stuff about the war. One was sanitized and safe; the other dangerous, breaking, and costly.

This is how many of us in the Western church have been able to live, with safety and nostalgia, but the luxury of what we have had is quickly disappearing or is already gone. Slowly but surely, we are joining the rest of the global church and the many that have gone before us. So why is this so hard?

Let's start inside. I have addressed this in my other writings, so forgive the repetition, but it matters so much. For years I have been begging Christians to fully and properly understand one of the great calls of the Reformation: *sola Scriptura* (the Bible alone). I keep asking everyone, but especially Christian leaders, to start reading church history and listening to today's global voices in order to prepare and sustain us. Yet in many conversations, the first is misunderstood and the second is willfully neglected, producing in many Christian circles a church versus church, anticulture mess that leads to fear mongering, overreaction, suspicion, unneeded division, and lack of being in the world at all.

Here is a simple summary of part of the problem: "Many modern theologians and Christian laypeople find themselves rootless and drifting in a barren, secular, and ecclesiastical (church) landscape, largely because they have forgotten their Christian past."[1] This explains why we feel angry, trapped, rootless, foundering, or excited because of new moves of God.

Let's start with this idea that "I just need my Bible." The most common assumption about *sola Scriptura* is that it means we need only the Bible and nothing else. But that isn't what it means. Let me share what I wrote on this in my book *Deliverance*:

> When Luther and others proclaimed "sola Scriptura," they were not saying there's no other source of authority or direction; they were saying the Bible was the Supreme Court, the ultimate authority before which other sources must remain submitted. But they did recognize the role of reason, experience, and tradition in reading,

understanding, and applying Scripture. Our forefathers and foremothers in the faith discovered over and over that Scripture can only be rightly understood and applied if we keep these three other "voices" in the discussion.

When we open our Bibles, we don't turn off our minds. We expect God's Word to stretch, heal, shape, and renew our minds even as we are using our minds to interact with what God has said. We don't close our eyes to our own experiences or the accumulated experiences of other believers (tradition) as we seek to rightly understand and obey God's Word. We as Evangelicals may treat tradition like a four letter word, but this overlooks the obvious facts that we have our own (not that old) traditions and that cutting ourselves off from the unbroken flow of God's work in His church over the centuries doesn't really give us the right to say, "We're not like those people any more" (we are their spiritual offspring); it also leaves us clueless about many important decisions and practices that believers have made since the close of the New Testament that do impact our lives every day.

Many of the doctrines we are most passionate about: the nature of Christ, the Trinity, and others stated in the creeds were hammered out from Scripture in the centuries following the days of the original church. They got some things wrong, but they also got a lot of things right that we can't afford to ignore. Most of the theological errors and heresies we deal with today are simply updated versions of mistakes made in centuries past. Our spiritual ancestors answered those challenges with biblical wisdom; why not at least consider their solutions instead of assuming that we know more and better today? Reason, tradition, and experience anchored and guided by Scripture still provide us with answers for whatever we face in these days.

So every time my church and I are confronted with experiential problems of a clearly spiritual nature or theological questions, we respond by asking, first, "What does Scripture say?" and then intentionally ask: "How have other believers dealt with this problem? What does history (both ours and ancient) tell us? What are the logical and reasonable aspects of this issue?" We have come

> to realize that the default answer among many believers, "Just read your Bible and everything will be okay" is neither a practical nor even a biblical response to real challenges.
>
> Although He was often confronted by both honest and devious questions throughout His ministry, Jesus never responded by saying, "Just go back and read the Bible." He even told the Sadducees they were diligently misreading the Bible! He brought reason, experience, and tradition to bear to silence opposition. But again, He also used Scripture to reasonably point out when tradition had gone off the rails. He understood that some things are beyond reason, "With man this is impossible, but not with God; all things are possible with God" (Mark 10:27). And in His experience of extreme hunger and temptation by Satan, He did not let His self-awareness or physical need overrule the truth of Scripture: "Jesus answered, 'It is written: "Man shall not live on bread alone, but on every word that comes from the mouth of God"'" (Matthew 4:4). This remains our model for obeying Scripture with reason, experience, and tradition in the conversation.[2]

Simply put, *sola Scriptura* is about authority; it is not a hermeneutic.[3] Why does this matter, especially for our presence and witness? First, it reminds us that we have been here before, so maybe we don't need to lose our minds and be so uptight. The Christians who lived in the Roman empire and in our first five hundred years also had to try working pastorally, theologically, and culturally through sexuality, gender, violence, pluralism, evangelism, retreat, revival, persecution, interaction with the government, and so on. All that we are facing with post-Christendom has tons of similarities with pre-Christianity. I put it this way in my book *Convergence*:

> If we categorically deny a vote to two millennia of accumulated Christian experience and pretend we have developed something new and unfettered by the past, we delude ourselves and fail to learn from either their mistakes or their excellence. G. K. Chesterton wisely described tradition as allowing our ancestors to have a vote. The application of this point is the call to know church history.

> There is very little we face today that hasn't confronted the church in the past. The fact that Christ's church has prevailed ought to be a clue to us that they figured some things out. Let's practice greater humility about the generations that have gone before us. . . .
>
> Not all church history speaks with equal clarity or helpful application either. I appreciate parts of Luther and Calvin for their immeasurable help with doctrine, but they also lived in Europe when everyone was considered a Christian (just the wrong type). That's why I read the church fathers more and more; they lived faithfully in a highly sexualized, pervasively violent, aggressively pluralistic environment. Today I live in Rome and Corinth, not Wittenberg and Geneva.[4]

We don't handle our Bible well, and we don't look back to those who have lived through similar situations. This is our "inside the church" struggle, which contributes to our current floundering, overreaching, and living in fear. We do this to our ongoing peril, which keeps us from not being able to handle this cultural moment or others.

But those are not the only reasons it is hard on the ground these days. There are other major cultural—outside the church—reasons we also need to explore. Many of you reading this might be doctors, lawyers, plumbers, stay-at-home parents, entrepreneurs, firefighters, or factory workers; the list is almost endless. Some of you are university educated, some by apprenticeship, and others of us have no formal education at all. But what is interesting is that so many of your professors, social-media feeds, and conversations over a Starbucks or beer are saturated with massive ideas that you might not catch, feel, or sense on the surface. Though I am not an expert, I would say we cannot dismiss the power of modernism and postmodernism at the same time. Though they are dire opposites, as we will see, they do come together in at least one way that affects your walk with Jesus and the church's witness. Within both of these sweeping and grand movements of thought are a deep suspicion against the old and ancient, which our faith is rooted in. Our mother is ancient and our father is old. We are truly born of both.

When the Enlightenment (modernism) came, it was all about

reason as the most important aspect of life. Reason was how humans could truly understand the universe and improve their own condition. The goals of rational humanity were knowledge, freedom, and happiness. Much good comes from these things, including the growth of science, medicine, and many of the freedoms we take for granted. One scholar pointed out the positive and negatives this way:

> Positively, many Enlightenment thinkers, horrified and repulsed by years of religious warfare, championed religious toleration, freedom of conscience, the expansion of political liberty, democratic principles and philosophy, legal reform and humane punishment. Peter Gay rightly reminds us that Enlightenment leaders were in the forefront of expanding freedom on a number of important fronts: "freedom from arbitrary power, freedom of speech, freedom of trade, freedom to realize one's talents, freedom of aesthetic response . . ."[5]

I think all of us reading along would say amen! Yes to that, we need that; all of those rights are such a gift, and it feels like we are losing them. Yes, yes, yes, but along with the rise of reason and science, the supernatural was dismissed, and the existence, involvement, and authority of God (if he exists at all) were removed. Just keep reading:

> With astonishing speed, the early Enlightenment thinkers were soon to cast aside the necessity of a Christian framework for interpreting reality. Atheism became a widely accepted philosophical option for the first time in Western history. Ludwig Feuerbach interpreted God as the projection of humanity's deepest hopes and concerns. Karl Marx portrayed religious belief as a narcotic designed to sedate the average person from rebelling against the injustices of the moneyed upper classes. Freud linked religious belief to deep inner neuroses in the human psyche, a reflection of an infantile search for security and unwillingness to mature. And Nietzsche, a philosopher whose system wore too heavily on his own psyche, clearly perceived that in a godless world all values become relative and truth merely a linguistic and cultural convention.[6]

Modernism was gift and poison all at once. Both the freedoms we love and cherish in the West and an almost full dismissal of our faith were found in the same box. It is like drinking salt water: You crave water, but as you drink, it just makes you more thirsty. The Enlightenment had all sorts of side effects. Even now as I am writing this, humanism, naturalism, individualism, and anti-authoritarianism—all remnants of modernism—do not have the power they once had but are still alive and well in certain segments of the population and academia. And they are definitely alive online.

Recently, I was having dinner with former students of mine, a couple. Years ago, Esther had brought her now husband to our youth group. At the time, her future husband was a sixteen-year-old Marxist atheist with Anglican family roots. I still vividly remember the moment of his conversion. I was preaching at one of our youth nights and saw a young guy with his hands raised. That did not happen much back then, so I remember thinking that a Pentecostal was visiting! But when I asked her what church he came from, she said that he didn't go to church, that he was an atheist, and that he had just encountered Jesus. A few weeks later, this very smart young man pulled me aside and asked, "Jon, what is a missionary? I really cannot get that word out of my head." I shared what it was, and together we prayed that if this was from God, it would happen in time. Well, all these years later, he is now a professor of philosophy at Cambridge University in England, and his wife is an editor for the Royal Society of Chemistry. I can barely keep up when talking to either of them. They would say they are missionaries to the intellectual elite of society. As we chatted, I learned that he is the only Christian in the whole Philosophy department, and all of his fellow professors are deeply modernist and still forming generation after generation of students in this worldview.

As I talk to my friends in Chinese churches across Toronto, they tell me about how they have many communities within one church, including many first- and second-generation people from Mainland China. They regularly struggle with the atheistic shadow that has made them antisupernatural in practice and functional atheists in everyday life. In their evangelism, they find that many from these backgrounds are steeped in Eastern and Western versions of atheistic modernism, which must be tackled for the gospel to grow in their large community across Toronto and beyond.

Along with modernism, the waters we swim in are also very much postmodern, with its questioning and/or outright denial of objective knowledge and inherent goodness. Postmodernism is all about all-inclusive systems and the affirmation of knowledge from all channels (rational, communal, and intuitive) leading to the rejection of the exclusive claims of truth (dogmatic and experiential) of the Christian faith.[7]

The mother of postmodernism is pluralism, which has now become the pragmatic experience of many of us. Os Guinness once defined this cultural belief in semimystical overtones: "We have reached the stage in pluralization where choice is not just a state of affairs, it is a state of mind. Choice has become a value in itself, even a priority. To be modern is to be addicted to choice and change. Change becomes the very essence of life."[8] Simply put, pluralism is founded on the belief that any ideological or religious claim that demands superiority and exclusivism is wrong, full stop.[9]

So we live in this crazy mix of modern and postmodern all at once. With these prominent worldviews side by side in our global village now in full effect, Christendom in the West has come to an end. The church no longer stands as the single moral, political, and religious voice. Years ago George Hunsberger pointed out that this has affected the church more than we might know, saying,

> The church, as a faith community, is relegated by the culture's frame of understanding to the private world of personal values, belief and opinions. By and large, the church has willingly (if not unknowingly) accommodated itself to that relegation and become a privatized, voluntary association for perpetuating its set of faith options. But for a church that believes that the gospel it embraces was God-given and intended as news for the whole world, for its public as well as its private life, there is a deep dilemma. We run the gauntlet between a failed Christendom and a false privatization.[10]

Do you understand that? That is really massive! Both ends we talked about are wrong, but almost all of us find ourselves flirting with either extreme.

And the grandchildren of all of these massive ideas have deeply affected the church. Just look at social media: Christians are posting so many things on TikTok, X (Twitter), or Instagram that are full of ideas that are actually against their Christian faith, but they don't even know they're doing it. This "X (Twitter) philosophy" only sees what seems to be okay on the surface but does not look deeper to see if the origins are poison. Last summer, I was reading the autobiography of Luke Timothy Johnson, a well-known Catholic New Testament professor, and was struck by how his experience in the field of New Testament studies so closely resembles what I see on my social feeds every day. I hear from people in my church parroting this mix of contradictions that feels helpful. Thinking about all the above he wrote this:

> The void left by the removal of canon [i.e., *Bible*] and creed was quickly filled by a variety of new ideological postures as new voices entered the scholarly arena: feminist, liberationist, postcolonial, and the like. Perhaps most problematic was the emergence of various forms of deconstructive criticism, which tended to reduce all texts to instruments of power needing to be purged of their oppressive force through "criticism." The animus toward ancient texts (defined as patriarchal, sexist, and imperialist) that was implicit in new ideological criticisms has become both more varied and more overt. Historical scholarship is at times viewed as a kind of therapeutic process designed to heal readers of the damages done them by ancient literature above all as wielded by oppressive forces within contemporary society.[11]

You might read that and wonder what any of it means. Simply put, many if not most of the old ideas—especially Christian ideas—have come to be viewed as dangerous by many today who say these ancient ideas are full of things that are evil and must be completely removed, rooted out, and burned to the ground so we can be healed from our generational trauma.

I know that for many of you, this all might feel really thick, boring, or irrelevant to everyday life, but you need to know that one of the reasons we feel the way we do right now as Christians, and especially Christian leaders, is because the outside culture, which is made up of different groups who view each other as the enemy, are both united around the belief that ancient texts and ideas are dangerous, that they should be viewed with suspicion, and that all old authority should be thrown out. They all have different reasons: Some say God is not needed (reason, progress, science), others say all paths are good and to say one is better is dangerous and evil, and others say that all ancient things are tools of oppression (patriarchal, sexist, and imperialist) and must be purged or just thrown out. And here we are, stuck between all three groups, holding our Bibles and over five thousand years of Judeo-Christian thinking, wondering why it seems like everyone is against us. This is why. And this is also why right now many in Gen Z are flocking back to the ancient. They have found the last three hundred plus years wanting, and they are mining history for the deeper things. But their exploration is not pure. They like most others still love that one last great-grandchild of this mess: the unashamed exultation of self. As Johannes Hartl brilliantly said, "Modernity has not abolished God; it has simply deified the self."[12] I am God, my loves are God, my views are God, my pleasures are God, my view of life is God, my cravings are God. And you can't say no to God! Where have I heard all this before? Oh right, from Satan to Eve and Adam. Did he not say to them, "You can be God, must be God, and cannot trust God"? Nothing is new under the sun.

So our educators are taught some mix of all the above (knowingly or not), and they pass it on to our children every single day. It is everywhere on blogs, podcasts, social media posts, and filling TikTok videos by the billions. Most people don't even know the source of these grand ideas or that they don't even fit together. The ideas seem like a weird buffet serving all sorts of foods that don't go together, but our culture says, "Who cares? It tastes good, and I like it!"

Let me state this again. The crazy thing is that we as Christians say our faith is rooted in what is old and ancient, that it is found in a historic book made up of sixty-six ancient letters and documents. And this old book is supposedly the ultimate source to form our faith, life, and practice. Not only that, but these ancient writings are inspired from God, right? We believe that ultimate authority is found in God and his Word, not science, reason, self, culture, feelings, or biology, a belief that leaves us trapped between all the people.

So from that university professor, to your friend, to the online troll, you are being told day in and day out that you are wrong, you are dangerous, and you really should leave all of that irrelevant, oppressive stuff behind. No wonder we're tired. But trust me, they are even more tired. And this exhaustion is one reason many are wondering if something ancient is the very thing we need once again. Many bridges are forming before our eyes to reach our neighbours. Let's not miss them.

The real Jesus of Easter is still controversial:

- *His cross too simple in a time of secularism and sophistication*
- *His love too expansive in a time of self-righteousness*
- *His ethics too restrictive in an era of individual self-expression*
- *His forgiveness of enemies too soft in a culture of grievance*
- *His righteous justice too harsh in a time of moral relativism*
- *His grace too scandalous in a cancel culture*

—DAN DARLING

If the fear of God is the beginning of wisdom, then to lose sight of God is the beginning of delusion.

—JOHANNES HARTL

The substance of the ancient doctrine of the deposit of faith is one thing, and the way in which it is presented is another.

—POPE JOHN XXIII

CHAPTER 5

Living in Retreat and Revival All at Once

So with all of the above converging into a real cultural moment, we might feel the tendency to only see evil, to keep turning on each other even when good is happening, to always react, to run and see no possible real redemption in the now. And many people just give in and slowly give their faith away.

I've talked a lot with my therapist friends about the basic human reaction that occurs when we are confronted with a problem, the famed flight, fight, or freeze. That is what so many Christians and churches are doing right now. Some of us are feeling the pull to retreat or have already started the flight process. "We need more Christian schools," they say, "more groups, house churches, and resistance through family." The call is old, monastic, and what Rod Dreher vividly outlined in his book *The Benedict Option*,[1] which is much more isolationistic than others. The Scottish Marxist turned Catholic philosopher Alasdair MacIntyre called this solidarity in the wilderness, "New forms of community within which moral life could be sustained, so that both morality and civility might survive the coming ages of barbarism and darkness."[2]

There is a growing call by many from different churches and kingdom movements to build strong communities of faith based on traditional Christian values and confession. In their eyes, the only way to intentionally withstand the corrosive rot of the secular and un-Christian spiritual culture we now live in is by living on the margins. Other Christians, however, are fighting back through various forms of Christian nationalism[3] (such as in Hungary, Poland, and parts of the United States) or by using the power of politics and protest. Trump coming to power again in the United States is evidence of this. Enough is enough, they say. It is time to counter evil with good laws and Christian populism. This is God's world, and Jesus owns everything, including politics, so it is time to use the levers of power for common good under the influence of God's Word. We must vote, protest, and use legal power to get back to what we had and enshrine more laws that guard our religious freedom and keep Christian values, whether the culture wants them or not. In parts of Europe, this is rooted all the way back in the grand clash between Islam and Christianity, one which has never been resolved and, with immigration, is coming to a head once again.

There is a need for some of this, which we'll get to later, but the unsettling truth for many of us is that *how we lose* will ultimately be more important than winning. It's not about how we get power back or bring back Christendom 2.0 but about how we become meek and look like fools. Just look at Jesus: His chosen loss was rooted in a robust trust in the sovereignty of God, and it is the clarity of that understanding where the real winning does come and will be final. One scholar put it like this:

> I actually think that one of the good things that is happening today is the loss of our status and power in the wider society. This growing loss is making us free. We as Christ's disciples ain't got nothing to lose anymore. That's a great advantage because as a people with nothing to lose, we might as well go ahead and live the way Jesus wants us to. We don't have to be in control or be tempted to use the means of control. We can once again, like the first Christians, be known as that people that don't [BS] the world.[4]

Nothing is new under the sun, right? The culture that Jesus lived in and spoke into had all of this too. Think about all the political and religious Jewish groups that supported, questioned, attacked, and killed Jesus. Are they not just like what we see on our Christian social-media feeds? Are they not filling many of our pulpits today?

> There were the Zealots, who felt their task was to achieve Israel's political independence through armed struggle. In contrast, the Pharisees saw their task as "making actual the ideal of the Holy People of God through strict observance of the Law," believing that this would prompt God to send the Messiah. The Essenes withdrew from all others and looked for the abrupt cataclysmic appearance of the Son of Man in clouds and glory to receive his eternal Kingdom (Daniel 7:13–14). Because of the widespread popularity of this apocalyptic yearning, Jesus frequently rebuked those preoccupied with a kingdom about which people will say; "Here it is," or "There it is" (Luke 17:21). Finally, there were the rationalistic Sadducees, who saw Israel's only hope through playing the political game with Rome. They had long since lost interest in any hope of divine deliverance.[5]

We have our share of Zealots, Pharisees, Essenes, and Sadducees within the church today, all doing their best to keep faith alive, honour God, and see the world become a better place. But just like back then, many of them keep missing Jesus, the God they are trying to represent. We, like all who have gone before us, are tempted by the ghosts of these four groups.

So what to do? I mean, many of those who we thought were speaking for God have turned out to be untrustworthy, making things even more confusing. So many leaders and Christian movements have been exposed for grave sins, which only feeds into our apathy, anger, or timidity. In our honest moments, I think a lot of Christians are wondering why God seems so quiet or silent. I feel the need to mention that when the apparent silence of God is mixed with pain, shame, lost expectations, and anger, it can seem too much for us to handle. When fear is stronger than faith, and when self-sufficiency and survival seem stronger than salvation, the story always takes a sinful turn. The painful story of Sarai and Abram with Hagar shows us the results. The church today keeps doing this, and I think there are too many Ishmaels and too few Isaacs.

Outside of those who are in flight or fight mode, I think most Christians are somewhere in the middle—deeply aware of the growing changes around us and hoping the storm will pass. The truth is, many are freezing like a deer in the headlights, not sure what to do. There is so much change, so much history, so much hostility, and so many voices; it is just too overwhelming, like trying to swim in a tsunami. But in a tsunami, most people don't swim or survive; they drown. So beyond flight, fight, and freeze, is there another possibility? Yes, I think there is, even if it is only for a brief time. The above summarizes where we are now. But if you are reading this years from now or generations long after I am dead, you will be in a different world. Though you will be living in vastly different times the principles—the seed—will remain the same and must stay the same.

In this cultural moment, I think there are ways forward. I have no intention to rely on cheap words or glib answers, but I do believe it is possible for the church to witness well in this growing or transitional moment. There's a word from the world of plants that I heard a few months ago, and as soon as I heard it, I knew it was the word we need right now. The word is *verdure,* meaning "the greenness of growing vegetation" and "a condition of health and vigour."[6] I have even heard it used to describe freshness or greenness in a dry or desert-like condition. It is a great word, a great image, and it could be us.

So how do we witness in this moment? We all know we need to respond, but the greatest of questions is how? How do we say with Paul, "For I am not ashamed of the gospel, because it is the power of God that brings salvation to everyone who believes: first to the Jew, then to the Gentile" (Romans 1:16)? I am going to try to walk through this by using five Rs: restlessness, revelation, renaissance, reside, and revival. We have already explored restlessness. I think just naming them can begin to show us that this is no cookie-cutter moment. As we walk with the Holy Spirit in this conversation, it might be disruptive, but not in the places you might expect.

Think of this book as a road map. Or better yet, this might feel like a book some of us who are older might remember, a "choose your own adventure" book, where you have to make decisions as you read that lead to different endings. Though most of us reading this book share similar cultural experiences, what we each need to do will end up being different depending on the city, town, ethnic community, or social situation you are in.

The goal of this book is not to create some six-step program or some new strategy or political rallying cry. Much of this starts with us and our church and what we think God is saying. Be wise and discerning as you read, but remain open, because God so loves the world and we should too, right? No, really, do you love the world? I think this Japanese proverb by an unknown author is very helpful and a needed redirection: "If you feel like you're losing everything, remember, trees lose their leaves every year, yet they still stand tall and wait for better days to come."[7] I think leaves are starting to bud.

As we now begin to explore how to respond, let's stop and pray an old prayer that St. Thomas Aquinas used to pray before studying and trying to be better formed by God. This prayer helps us prepare to receive God's word, to hear his Spirit, and to prepare to keep stepping out no matter what has changed.

> *Creator of all things, true Source of light and wisdom, lofty origin of all being, graciously let a ray of Your brilliance penetrate into the darkness of my understanding and take from me the double darkness in which I have been born, an obscurity of both sin and ignorance. Give me a sharp sense of understanding, a retentive memory, and the ability to grasp things correctly and fundamentally. Grant me the talent of being exact in my explanations, and the ability to express myself with thoroughness and charm. Point out the beginning, direct the progress, and help in completion; through Christ our Lord. Amen.*[8]

PART 2

REVELATION

the supernatural disclosure
to humans of something
relating to human existence
or the world

Do you believe the Bible is basically about you or basically about him? Is David and Goliath basically about you and how you can be like David? Or is the story basically about Jesus, the one who really took on the only giants that can really kill us and whose victory is imputed to us? Who's it really about? That's the fundamental question. And when that happens, then you start to read the Bible anew.

—TIM KELLER

All other great religious teachers subordinate themselves to their message. They pointed away from themselves to their teachings. For instance, Buddha said, "look not to me, look to my dharma (doctrine, teaching)." But Christ said, "Come to me" (Matt 11:28). Buddha said, "be lamps unto yourselves." But Christ said, "I am the light of the world" (Jn 9:5). Moses and Muhammad claimed only to be prophets of God, Jesus claimed to be God (Jn 8:58). Any other religion could survive the loss of its founder. If Muhammad or Buddha or Confucius were proved to be mythical and not historical figures, the religions that stem from them might still survive. But Christianity could never survive without Christ. For other religious founders only claimed to teach the truth; Christ claimed to be the Truth (Jn 14:6).

—PETER KREEFT

Jesus answered, I am the way and the truth and the life. No one comes to the Father except through me.

—JOHN 14:6

CHAPTER 6

Who Is Jesus?

So with that "small" overview of where we are, with our mission from Jesus still clear, and with the assurance that every tribe and tongue will be around the throne (Revelation 7:9), we are compelled to keep bringing the kingdom of God into this time and place, no matter how complex or complicated things are. So we are going to look at how to do that well, but first we need to ask what we are actually giving to others. Who is Jesus and what is the gospel? In a post-truth world, many will co-opt or highjack ideas and divorce the words from their meanings. Things can sound the same or feel the same but not at all be the same. And in this conversation, the stakes are eternal, so we must be clear.

Where do we begin? I think the person to help us is Peter. Why? Because Peter is found at the centre of the two most important moments of not only Christian history but human history. The first is a conversation, the other a sermon. When these two moments are brought together, they provide a crystal-clear understanding of who Jesus is and what he means for everyone.

I was preaching in the east side of London in Hackney at an amazing church called Saint. It was a beautiful Sunday morning. The whole week before had been an experience of a lifetime as God had moved in a revival-like way with an intensity that I've never seen before. That morning I had been invited to preach. Months before I had prayed and was led by the Holy Spirit to speak out of Peter's confession of Jesus. I started my sermon like this:

> It's a great honour to be with you here today as a Canadian. I'm a little bit jealous because I love England, and I love London even more. Actually, this is my favourite city on earth. You've done many good things for the world, but I think one of the greatest things you've done is the invention of the *Antiques Roadshow*. I love it. I know it makes me sound old, but I love it. The reason I love it is the repeated story that is told time and time again.
>
> For example, I was watching the show (the UK version) a few days ago. A woman walks in with a large ceramic bowl, and the appraiser says, "Oh my goodness, I can't believe you brought this in!" And the woman responds with something like this: "My cat sleeps in this bowl," or "It's usually underneath my bed," and the appraiser's face is saying, "Stop doing that." But instead of rebuking the woman, the appraiser simply asked where she got the bowl. "Well, my father was in Japan after the war, and he bought it from a dealer." The appraiser responds, "Well just so you know this is not Japanese ceramic. It's actually Chinese ceramic. The Japanese collected them in this certain time period . . . blah, blah, blah." Again she repeats, "Well, my cat sleeps in the bowl." And he's like, "Well, don't do that anymore because it's worth £10,000!" The shock, the crowd, and then the *Antiques Roadshow* music ushers us to the next boom or bust moment.

When I preached out of this passage in my context, I added an example from the American version when a man was in for a surprise when he brought in a painting of his great-grandfather, Lea Febiger. The piece was done by a friend of Febiger's, the artist Frederic Remington. This striking picture included a letter from the painter to the subject. Appraiser Colleene Fesko told the owner his piece would likely sell for between six hundred thousand and eight hundred thousand dollars at auction.[1] Wow! Don't we all want this moment?

The point is, we all want the ceramic bowl or the family picture underneath our bed. We want to find the thing that looks plain and normal but is actually much more than it appears and has the ability to change our lives. This is what Jesus is for the human experience: plain, not beautiful, not from power or privilege, and yet he is the most valuable find ever. We see this in the way Jesus chooses to transition his entire ministry in the most unlikely of places, and it is here where we begin to answer the question: Who is Jesus?

So where is this unlikely place? In Matthew 16:13, it reads like this: "When Jesus came to the region of Caesarea Philippi." The vast majority of people who lived in Caesarea Philippi were Greek, Syrian, or Roman. This place served as a border between Jew and non-Jew, clean and unclean, those who were in and those who were out, with God and against God.[2] And Jesus chooses to cross this border with grand intention. He will be understood and found in the most unlikely of places. Pay close attention, for here Jesus is already showing us how to do this well in our own time.

Caesarea Philippi was a dark place, one that had been dedicated to the Roman god Pan. Here is how one historian describes it, giving us real insight into this place,

> The steep cliff overlooking the city was home to caves and a natural spring.... The deepest crevices of the depths of the caves were believed to be the gates to the underworld, the gates of hell. The spring that came from there was believed to be the mode of transportation from hell to earth. However, as every year is different, the people felt the need to entice the gods out at the beginning of every spring season to make sure their harvests would be fruitful. They did this by committing sinful sexual acts (such as sexual relations with goats, as Pan was half-goat) at the shrines located at the entrances to the caves.[3]

This was also a place named after Caesar, and people here honoured Caesar as a god, as the prince of peace, as lord. As you go back in history, the more interesting, clarifying, and darker it gets. In the Old Testament, this region, and this very site, was one of the central places where the Canaanites worshipped Baal.[4] And it is here, where generations of false worship both human and demonic has taken place, that Jesus chooses to do something massive. Here is where he chooses to fully reveal himself and begin his journey towards the cross. Do you see it? Jesus comes to a bunch of orthodox Jews living in a region of non-Jews, surrounded by darkness. This was a sign that his coming was for the whole world and again becomes a convicting picture for us in this moment. We cannot leave; we cannot fortress away. Jesus walks into darkness, not away from it, and so must we. Okay, back to the moment.

Matthew 16:13 says, "When Jesus came to the region of Caesarea Philippi, he asked his disciples, 'Who do people say the Son of Man is?'" That name, the Son of Man, is significant so let's slow down and really understand this. This is not some generic name. Every single Jew knew this was a huge deal. We will only fully understand the grandness of this title, Son of Man, by looking both forwards and backwards. At the end of the Bible we read,

> On the Lord's Day I was in the Spirit, and I heard behind me a loud voice like a trumpet. . . .
>
> I turned around to see the voice that was speaking to me. And when I turned I saw seven golden lampstands, and among the lampstands was someone like a son of man, dressed in a robe reaching down to his feet and with a golden sash around his chest. (Revelation 1:10–13)

This is connected all the way back to Daniel 7:9–14,

> As I looked,
>
> thrones were set in place,
>   and the Ancient of Days took his seat.
> His clothing was as white as snow;
>   the hair of his head was white like wool.
> His throne was flaming with fire,
>   and its wheels were all ablaze.
> A river of fire was flowing,
>   coming out from before him.

> Thousands upon thousands attended him;
> ten thousand times ten thousand stood before him.
> The court was seated,
> and the books were opened. . . .
>
> In my vision at night I looked, and there before me was one like a son of man, coming with the clouds of heaven. He approached the Ancient of Days and was led into his presence. He was given authority, glory and sovereign power; all nations and peoples of every language worshiped him. His dominion is an everlasting dominion that will not pass away, and his kingdom is one that will never be destroyed.

What Daniel saw long ago will be fully understood later. The Ancient of Days is God, and the Son of Man is Jesus. But when you read Revelation 1, you see that the Father and the Son are equal, so the descriptions of the Ancient of Days used by Daniel are used for Jesus in Revelation. Every Jew hearing Revelation 1 would understand that this is a powerful statement. In Jesus, we see the Ancient of Days fully through the Son of Man, because they are equal and because they share essence and worship. But Peter and others are not fully there yet. This is the page turning moment between the bookends of Daniel and Revelation. In this passage, we get a clear picture of who Jesus is. Back to the passage you have read, preached out of, and listened to so many times:

> When Jesus came to the region of Caesarea Philippi, he asked his disciples, "Who do people say the Son of Man is?"
>
> They replied, "Some say John the Baptist; others say Elijah; and still others, Jeremiah or one of the prophets." (Matthew 16:13–14)

Some at that time said Jesus was Elijah, the famous miracle worker of the Old Testament. Others thought he was the great preacher and prophet who had just been killed, John the Baptist. Calling him Jeremiah is very interesting because he was the prophet called by God to tell the Jewish leadership that they would be judged by God and that the temple would be destroyed. Jeremiah was ultimately attacked and resisted by God's own leaders. Jesus is about to imitate this very journey again.[5]

But nevertheless, of course the average Jewish person would think that Jesus is like or is one of these prophets! Jesus had fed thousands with five loaves and two fishes; he had healed the blind, the sick, and the bleeding; he had cast out demons and preached powerfully. It would make sense to think he might be this person or that prophet. Yet none of them guessed the true nature of Jesus.

Really, nothing has changed. Our family, friends, neighbours, and enemies all have many views about Jesus. All sorts of people talk and reflect on Jesus—some are nonreligious or just sort of spiritual, others belong to different formal religions, and many are those who have taken the name Christian but in reality are not. The world today says Jesus was a great man, a prophet, a miracle worker, one form of God, an inspired humanitarian, a revolutionary, a person of historical significance, or a gifted religious leader. Others say he was just a myth, or that he was a liar, a false prophet, or a man who did nothing but was later elevated by zealots and religious crazies.

But in the face of all these opinions, held both then and now, Jesus asks the real question, "'But what about you?' he asked. 'Who do you say I am?'" (Matthew 16:15).

Jesus comes to us—in every generation—and asks the question that transfers theology from an armchair discussion or some online blog debate to an uncomfortable, very personal, dialogue between us and God. The response of the disciples comes from the leader of the group, Peter: "Simon Peter answered, 'You are the Messiah, the Son of the living God'" (Matthew 16:16).

Peter moves from the wrong understanding and imposed views of others to a full confession: You are not just a prophet or spiritual teacher, not just a political revolutionary, not one incarnation of God or one path to God of many. You are not crazy or a liar; you are not Satan the deceiver. You are the Messiah, the long awaited one, and the Son of the living God. You are the only one who has seen God face to face because you and the Father are one. You can speak with authority that stems from yourself because your identity and all you do is grounded in who you are—God in flesh, Immanuel, God with us!

The Son of the living God! I love this confession, for there in Caesarea Philippi, in that very place of false worship, Peter declares that Jesus is not some demon or dead god like Baal or Pan but the Son of the *living* God! And Jesus replies, "'Blessed are you, Simon son of Jonah, for this was not revealed to you by flesh and blood, but by my Father in heaven'" (Matthew 16:17).

Peter is blessed, because while everyone else was guessing, God himself chose to show him who Jesus really is. Peter didn't understand because he was more open or intellectually aware, and it wasn't because he saw Jesus heal, cast out demons, or give the Sermon on the Mount. Only God can open our hearts to his gospel; only God can show us who Jesus is. We cannot see past our own sin, our deadness, and our spiritual bondage unless he cuts through all of it (see Ephesians 2:1–4).

Then Jesus turns around and says to Peter, you have declared really huge things that are true about me, now let me do the same to you. "'And I tell you that you are Peter, and on this rock I will build my church, and the gates of Hades will not overcome it'" (Matthew 16:18).

Jesus changes his name from Simon to Peter. *Simon* means "the Lord heard." *Peter* is a Greek name that means "rock." So Jesus is going to build his church on the rock, but what does that mean? Well, people answer that question in at least three ways:

1. Jesus will build his church on Peter, the first leader. So you would read this as "You, Peter, are rock and on you I will build my church."
2. Jesus is saying, "Hey, Peter, I will build my church on this rock" and points to himself, not Peter. "You are a rock, but I am the more important Rock." Even in Peter's later writing we see this image being used by Peter about Jesus. "As you come to Jesus, the living Stone—rejected by men but chosen by God and precious to him" (1 Peter 2:4).
3. The third option is that Jesus is saying it is the confession of

> Peter that is the rock he will build his church on. So it's like Jesus is saying, "Peter, your confession is about me, and I will not build my church on you personally but on the confession God allowed you to understand and say."[6]

Seeing the wordplay, I think the most natural reading of this is that Peter has the foundational role to play. He is the rock. Now the Roman Catholic Church took this to an extreme and built the papacy out of it, which I don't agree with, but there is no doubt that Peter is the first among equals. As I will point out below, one reason why I must arrive where I do is because two chapters later Jesus gives the same authority to all of his disciples, not just Peter. Whether you agree with me or not, let's just keep reading together:

> And I tell you that you are Peter, and on this rock I will build my church, and the gates of Hades will not overcome it. (Matthew 16:18)

This is the first time the word *church* is used in Matthew. In Greek, it was a common word used for an assembly of people. In Jewish writings, however, this was a term for the people of God, and Jesus says here that *his* people are the true people of God! And in Greek, the emphasis is on the word *my*—this is *my* church, Jesus says. This is wild if you sit with it. Jesus claims, "I am the place where Jews *and* non-Jews become the people of God. I will do this. I have authority to do this. I am the fulfillment of all of the Old Testament."[7] This is what Paul later wrote about in Ephesians: "You are no longer foreigners and strangers, but fellow citizens with God's people and also members of his household, built on the foundation of the apostles and prophets, with Christ Jesus himself as the chief cornerstone" (Ephesians 2:19–20).

And then we come to that amazing, much-needed promise that has helped the church persevere in every generation and must be the central promise we cling to now in this global, cultural midwifing moment. Jesus declares, "I will build my church, and the gates of Hades will not overcome it" (Matthew 16:18).

Can I get an amen? Jesus is there, looking at the caves where Pan was worshipped, the literal gates of hell, and says they don't win! The gates of Hades (or hell) is not just metaphor for the demonic; they are the gates of death, which are not able to be opened and when you pass through them there is no way out. Death had the final say.[8] But who owns death? Well, Hebrews is really clear: "[Jesus] too shared in their humanity so that by his death he might break the power of him who holds the power of death—that is, the devil—and free those who all their lives were held in slavery by their fear of death" (Hebrews 2:14–15). Jesus is saying something like, "Death will no longer have the final say, nor will the demonic. The gates of hell will not overcome *my* church." And then he looks at Peter and says, "I will give you the keys of the kingdom of heaven; whatever you bind on earth will be bound in heaven, and whatever you loose on earth will be loosed in heaven" (Matthew 16:19).

Again this steps us closer to how to witness well. Binding and loosing is critical to this. But what does that even mean? Because of history and theology, we tend to get into the Catholic, Orthodox, or Protestant view. This passage is why Catholics say all the successors of Peter have unique authority. I would humbly say the problem is that two chapters later Jesus says the same thing to all of his disciples (see Matthew 18:18).

Peter is the first among equals, but binding and loosing is not about kingdom governance—it's about evangelism. This is about who gets saved, who enters the kingdom of God, and who does not. Peter is the first to know, by revelation, that Jesus is the one who allows us to come home. All this becomes clearer when we understand binding and loosing, which was a common idea connected to Jewish rabbis. The language of binding and loosing is a rabbinic way of indicating what is a yes and what is a no, what is allowed and not allowed, who is in and who is out. It is not about who oversees the church.[9]

This gets to the very heart of witness. By what terms, what conditions, does God allow entrance into his kingdom? Peter is the first to point to Jesus as the one, the only one, that allows entrance into the kingdom. Binding and loosing are not about authority over the church (or demons either) but about access. That is why when Peter preaches the very first Christian sermon in Acts 2, he tells his fellow Jews that they must come home through Jesus. When Peter ends up at the house of Cornelius, a Roman officer, an occupier and oppressor of Peter's people, he says the same thing: Jesus is the only way home. Binding and loosing is about the forgiveness of sin and the barrier-shattering declaration that you can come home.

But then the next thing happens in the story, something we deeply need to not only hear but embrace, as shadows grow and fear seems so strong. This next part is needed for our presence in this moment because what Jesus confronts then is what needs to be confronted now so we don't lose witness. After this history splitting confession, Jesus "ordered his disciples not to tell anyone that he was the Messiah" (Matthew 16:20).

Why would he do this? Well, to answer this, we have to look at what the Jewish hope was for the Messiah. The answer should feel familiar. Much of the Jewish community were still lured back to wrong thinking and wrong desires. They wanted a territorial kingdom, a national kingdom, a political kingdom, and if they heard that Jesus was the Messiah, they would naturally expect him to deal with the Romans and destroy all the enemies of the Jews. He would make Israel great again! He, as the new David, would immediately establish Israel as the centre of the world by religious and military might. The promised warrior king had come! Well, yes to worshipping and warrior, but not in the ways they wanted. No, Jesus's kingdom starts with suffering not power.

> From that time on Jesus began to explain to his disciples that he must go to Jerusalem and suffer many things at the hands of the elders, the chief priests and the teachers of the law, and that he must be killed and on the third day be raised to life.
>
> Peter took him aside and began to rebuke him. "Never, Lord!" he said. "This shall never happen to you!" (Matthew 16:21–22)

Peter looks into the face of the Messiah, the Son of God, and rebukes him. What? Have you really sat with this? Peter in effect is saying to Jesus, "You will not be taken out by religious leaders; you will not be taken out by Rome. This is not God's will for you; this is not your job! Stop talking like that; it is embarrassing. Do your job." Did you catch it? Peter is telling Jesus that he doesn't need to suffer because he's the Messiah. "You are in charge; take control by any means necessary! It's really bad out there, so you need to get your crap together." Sound familiar?

In that moment, what Jesus can see that Peter and others cannot see is what is wandering over from those caves. Satan, Baal, Pan is in the room. Right after Peter makes his amazing confession: He is being influenced by Satan. Satan always tries to kill things before they can be born. This, by the way, is Peter's first betrayal of Jesus. Peter is already giving in to the devil even though Jesus had just said the devil would not be able to destroy his church.

Does Peter's language feel familiar to you at all? It should. At the beginning of Jesus's ministry, he was tempted by the devil. Satan, who is Baal, who is Pan, and who is deeply connected to Caesar's world, had already said to Jesus in the third temptation, "You don't need to suffer."[10] "Again, the devil took him to a very high mountain and showed him all the kingdoms of the world and their splendor" (Matthew 4:8). Remember, the devil did and does own all the kingdoms of the world and could offer them to Jesus. Even after Jesus's ascension, 1 John 5:19 says, "the whole world is under the control of the evil one."

Everything—all the colour, all food, all sexual pleasure, all the treasure, all the military, all of physical reality—Satan owned it all. And his goal was to get Jesus to be king the wrong way. This was an attack on his identity by tempting him to bypass his call. God had already promised Jesus the whole world way back in the Psalms.[11] "I will proclaim the Lord's decree: He said to me, 'You are my son; today I have become your father. Ask me, and I will make the nations your inheritance, the ends of the earth your possession" (Psalm 2:7–8).

Satan's goal was to give the earth, the nations, and all authority in heaven and on earth to Jesus, the Son of Man, without the mission of the cross and without the establishment of the church.[12] You can be king, powerful, in control, self-made. You don't need to suffer to follow God or his commands; there is an easier and more fulfilling way to get what you deserve.[13] "'All this I will give you,' he said, 'if you will bow down and worship me.' Jesus said to him, 'Away from me, Satan! For it is written: "Worship the Lord your God, and serve him only"'" (Matthew 4:9–10).

But now Satan is back with the same temptation: You don't need to suffer or build the church. All that was offered in Matthew 4 is now offered again through Peter. This is what John Macmurray once wrote in his book *Persons in Relation*: "The maxim of illusory religion runs: 'Fear not; trust in God and he will see that none of the things you fear will happen to you'; That of real religion, on the contrary, is 'Fear not; the things that you are afraid of are quite likely to happen to you, but they are nothing to be afraid of.'"[14]

How did Jesus respond to Peter? With a statement that was shocking to Peter and to us: "Get behind me, Satan! You are a stumbling block to me; you do not have in mind the concerns of God, but merely human concerns" (Matthew 16:23). Peter, the gates of death and the gates of the demonic will not overcome my church, but you are already compromised and don't even know it. And Satan, I say again to your offer, no. No to your temptation through Peter's mind and mouth; no to your influence, no. I will suffer, I will die, the church will be born, you will not overcome, and in the end you will be destroyed!

This passage is foundational for us in knowing how to witness well in our current pluralistic, repaganizing, and possible renewal moment. I think we all need to hear a few truths here. As I am writing this, I think Jesus himself might say this to some of you personally. First, if Jesus could use Peter, he can use you. (That will preach all day long!) Second, in this moment we must pray out of this promise of Jesus; we must preach out of it and regularly remind each other again and again that death does not have the final say; the demonic do not have the final say. The church will not be overcome, for Jesus's victory is final and total. He has won and he will win! This is one of the ways we persevere in this midwifing cultural moment! Jesus has been, will be, and always is Lord. Yes and amen, but . . .

For this book, two major ideas emerge that need to be clear and tested in our thinking. One is relevant in every generation, and the other ebbs and flows based on what temptations are being offered to the church in that season. The first is obvious, "Who do people say the Son of Man is?"

This is the greatest of all questions. This is the most important question in all of history. Jesus, by his deeds, self-declaration, and teaching, claims to be the Son of God—God in flesh. He must be confessed as such and nothing else. If our presence will ripple into eternity and have effect now, we must declare Him as heaven revealed to Peter and Jesus affirmed. As C. S. Lewis wrote:

> A man who was merely a man and said the sort of things Jesus said would not be a great moral teacher. He would either be a lunatic—on a level with the man who says he is a poached egg—or else he would be the Devil of Hell. You must make your choice. Either this man was, and is, the Son of God: or else a madman or something worse. You can shut Him up for a fool, you can spit at Him and kill Him as a demon; or you can fall at His feet and call Him Lord and God. But let us not come with any patronizing nonsense about His being a great human teacher. He has not left that open to us. He did not intend to.[15]

There was an old Sunday school chorus I used to sing that said, "Jesus is the answer for the world today." Yes, that is what we have said for two thousand years. In a world divided by race, gender, education, the mistakes you made, the people you know, in a world of violence, political extremism, family breakdown, and religious fanatics, a world coming closer and yet never being as far apart, full of abused, disconnected, lonely, questioning people, a world with eight-plus billion people and growing, is there any person or movement that can meet the needs and answer the questions found in your children, family, and coworkers? Is there anyone who can give you honest peace, a new start, forgiveness for all the stuff you have done in secret, and freedom to forgive all who have hurt and let you down? Yes. Jesus, God in flesh, came and lived a life we could not live, died a death we deserved, and when he was raised from the dead, every sin, every demon, and every experience of death was overcome. When you meet him, he takes you—good and bad, even very good and terribly bad—and he chooses you, gives you access to him, makes you holy, makes you belong to him, gives you a new family, and calls you out of darkness into light. You are made a citizen of a new spiritual nation, not one based on ethnic nationality or geographical boundaries but on a personal relationship with God through Jesus Christ. This is the Jesus we must point everyone to!

The second insight, however, might be more difficult to swallow. Peter's rebuke of Jesus is based on his own wants and desires for Israel over God the Father's desire for all nations. This political religious mix is happening in real time today as we are feeling increasingly oppressed and marginalized and as fear grows. As globalism is being tested and challenged by nationalism (both in good and bad ways), and as Christians that belong to many different countries, tribes, and ethnicities, we should be aware of the danger of nationalism over and above the kingdom of God.

Ask yourself: Do you love the whole world? Do you love people, *all* people? Do you love your ethnic group or your country more than or at the expense of the gospel and the kingdom that will last? Again, why give your life to Jesus if you don't? Why try to fulfill his last words if you don't? It was French Jesuit Henri de Lubac who was always trying to help Christians see the difference between what he called "honourable patriotism" and "destructive nationalism." He was deeply worried that the church could be manipulated spiritually, emotionally, or politically to the point where it might become "an instrument of device to national passions."[16] When we love our country, tribe, or community more than the gospel, we become that contaminated salt we talked about earlier. During the rise of the Nazi regime in Germany, certain Christian leaders felt and saw where the kingdom was replaced by nation in the most extreme of ways. This from a Catholic vantage point,

> From his nuncio's office in Munich, Cardinal Eugenio Pacelli watched the growth of the Nazi Party with foreboding, especially since the movement at its origins counted many Catholic members eager to demonstrate their patriotic bonafides. Hitler's own anti-Catholic rhetoric soon soured many of these Catholics, notably his

attacks in *Mein Kampf* on ultramontanism and the futility of an international church attempting to represent the "feelings of the German people." Still, Pacelli privately speculated that nationalism might be the "most dangerous heresy of our time."[17]

It's that line, "nationalism might be the most dangerous heresy of our time." "Yes, yes," we all say, "but I am not giving in to some Nazi regime." Fine, but slow down and sit with this because we will not witness at all, let alone witness well, unless we let the Bible actually form us. You know we all share the same ancestors, right? And at the end of the day, humans are all the same, right? You believe this to be fully and deeply correct? Arthur Glasser said it like this,

> The dangers inherent in nationalism militate against the Bible's view of the common ancestry of all human beings. . . . Christians must be supportive of the hungering of formerly subjugated peoples for self-expression and self-determination. However, this can degenerate into a new obsession with human power. Militant nationalism can easily become a tangle of myths and actualities, truths and errors, and begin to assert itself aggressively, even to the point of precipitating aggressive war. This form of national exclusiveness and cultural arrogance appears on the surface to meet certain fundamental needs of people: their desire for purpose in life, for individual significance, and for personal security—all gained through losing themselves in a cause greater than themselves. But within any nation or racial enclave it soon becomes a demonic force through discrimination against minority peoples within its borders and persecution of citizens whose loyalties extend beyond their political boundaries. This form of exaggerated nationalism eventually results in the oppression of anyone who challenges its presuppositions. Militant nationalism is especially challenged by those whose sense of loyalty and obligation extend beyond racial and political fidelity. Those who embrace all members of the human family must call it into question. These issues constantly raise tensions between the church and the state.[18]

I know that's a mouthful, but it sure shows how dangerous nationalism is to our witness. For example, my country of Canada will not last in the new heavens and new earth. Your country won't either. Nations are God's ideas for a time, but not forever. I am not a globalist in the secular form, but I do try to place nations in their right place. I love Canada and believe it is an amazing country. Of course, I would say it is the best country in the world, but it is not more important than God's kingdom. And if the people we lead or influence cannot see the difference, then we have become compromised.

Beyond nations, our ethnic experience will not be wiped out in the new creation. It is clear from Revelation 7 and the resurrection that we keep our gender, skin colour, and ethnic overtones, but they will be experienced in their rightful place. I have many times ended up talking to many of my pastor friends with growing or larger platforms, and I keep reminding them that because of social media and their church's global platform, they must always ask: What am I preaching? Will it help or hurt the global church, not just my church? Am I aware when my desire for America, or Canada, or your own nation could quietly override how I need to disciple not only my own people but also the global crowd that now listens? Am I clear when I express my hope or opinion versus what God wants? Does my tone or emphasis change between this is God's Word and this is what I hope for? If everything comes across similarly, how do people pick up the difference? Again, when any Christian group begins to chant, "Make (fill in the blank) great again" (not just a shot at my American friends; this is everywhere and in all our hearts), be very careful. You might be rebuking Jesus to his face even though you confess him correctly.

Paul also had to deal with this head on. Just read this summary:

> "Christianity," writes Eugen Rosenstock-Huessy, "came into a world of divided loyalties." Each race, tribe, class, nation, and empire lived to itself. Peoples had different gods, different customs, different political structures. Each pagan history "begins somewhere within time," with the founding of Rome or the Olympic games, and each history is therefore the history of a single people. Pagans had no single history because paganism did not conceive of

> the human race as the kind of thing that might have a single history. Paganism meant "disunity, dividedness of mankind." Christianity did not "simply erase these loyalties," which would have been nihilism. Jesus came not to abolish but to fulfill, and "by its gift of a real future, Christianity implanted in the very midst of men's loyalties a power which, reaching back from the end of time, drew them step by step into unity." This is what salvation means, "the advance of the singular against the plural." Salvation enters a world of "many gods, many lands, many peoples," many histories, and it proclaims instead a set of singularities: "one God, one world, one humankind." Rosenstock-Huessy is right; "One God = one humanity" is axiomatic for Paul. The reunion of humanity in Christ is the gospel, the revelation of the one God against his many rivals. The unity of the church is an "evangelical" unity, a unity proclaimed in the good news of Jesus, a unity that must be realized among those who believe it.[19]

Preach! Can I get an amen? Is your white hanky out yet? You should have just said, "Yes, yes, yes!" Do you want to witness well? Don't give your whole life and energy—in person or online—to things that will fade. I will talk later on about how we are called to be involved in our societies, but at this point in the book, this is a soul check moment. Don't think you are the Peter in the first half of the story only. Many of us find we cannot be present well or witness well because we are rebuking Jesus to his face through our blogs, family meal comments, online thoughts, and mixed preaching. If you have the courage, ask Jesus right now as you end this chapter, ask the living Jesus by his Spirit to reveal to you which Peter you are—the confessing one, the demonized one, the one rebuking Jesus, or a mix of all three. And when he shows you, ask by his Spirit to change you so you can reach out to your family, friends, and your own "Caesarea Philippi" all at the same time. A new, unnatural unity has always been the heartbeat of the One you sang to last Sunday.

Many people today assume that Christianity is a religion, a moral system, a philosophy. In other words, they assume that Christianity is about advice. But it wasn't and it isn't. Christianity is, simply, good news. It is the news that something has happened as a result of which the world is a different place. . . . One can debate the merits of a religion, moral system, or philosophy, but a news event is discussed in a different way. Either the event happened or it didn't; if it did happen, either it means what people say it means or it doesn't.

—N. T. WRIGHT

I need Christ, not something that resembles Him.

—C. S. LEWIS

Testimony is telling people what Jesus has done for me in my personal experience, but evangelism is telling people what Jesus has done for the world in history.

—ROY CLEMENTS

God weeps with us so that we may someday laugh with him.

—JÜRGEN MOLTMANN

Let us eat, drink and be merry, for yesterday we were dead.

—RUSSELL MOORE

CHAPTER 7

What Is the Gospel?

Another one of my favourite global cities is New York City. The people, the food culture, the coffee, the intensity, the museums, the history, all of it. I know it's a bit touristy, but one spot I always go is Rockefeller Center. If you have not been, this is where the famous ice rink is, where the Christmas tree is lit, where you can visit NBC Studios, where *Saturday Night Live*, *The Kelly Clarkson Show*, *The Tonight Show Starring Jimmy Fallon*, and *Late Night with Seth Meyers* are filmed. And it's where you can go up to the famed Top of the Rock Observation Deck to take in amazing views of New York City.

At one entrance of Rockefeller Center is the famous Atlas statue, made of bronze and bearing the weight of the world. There he stands, day in and day out, straining in his own power to hold everything on his shoulders. He is monotone, only a dark bronzed colour. Right across the street, you'll see the heart of the Catholic community, St. Patrick's Cathedral. As you walk in to this beautiful church, you are washed in light and colour from the 3,700 stained-glass panels lining the cathedral, including a twenty-six-foot-wide Rose Window above the entrance. The cathedral's replica of Michelangelo's *Pietà* is three times larger than the original sculpture in St. Peter's Basilica. And as you lift your eyes above the high altar, beyond the throngs of tourists, as you look through the colour and wafting incense, you will see a very different image than the one across the street. There, in the middle of it all, is the cross of Christ. This to me has always been one of the most striking ways to see what the gospel is and isn't. Self-sufficiency versus salvation, burden versus freedom, darkness versus light. The strongest humanist, the most devout religious person, the "spiritual but not religious," and the kind agnostic are all the same (though they all tend to view the others as the problem with the world). All four are Atlas—their salvation, purpose, and advancement have "self" at the centre. But across the street is the image of a Saviour, one who steps in to deal with a situation that cannot be resolved by us. As Richard John Neuhaus wrote about this very place while reflecting on Good Friday:

> In the Good Friday liturgy, the priests and deacons lie prostrate, collapsed, before the cross. St. Patrick's Cathedral in New York is directly across from Rockefeller Center, and at the entrance to Rockefeller Center is the great sculpture of Atlas holding up the world. On Good Friday, the doors of the cathedral are cpened, and you can see the great cross from the street. Turn in one direction and there is the mythical Atlas holding up the world, turn in the other, and there is the One broken by the world. Which image speaks the truth? Is the world upheld by our godlike strength or by the crucified love of God? Upon that decision everything, simply everything, turns.[1]

And this very image, one missed by most on Fifth Avenue in New York, brings us back again to this most critical of questions: What in the world is the gospel? Before we embrace something, defend it, live out of it, and offer it to others, we have to know what it is. You could call that kernel the pure gospel. Others might call it the naked gospel. When you strip all the cultural trappings and incarnational expressions. When you strip away the other important issues, who is the person of Jesus, and what did he offer that we are now called to offer to every person no matter their gender, sexuality orientation, religion, worldview, ethnicity, or place?

For a number of years now, the Church of England has been engaged in a long, drawn-out process called "Living in Love and

Faith" that aims to build unity through diversity in a family that is deeply divided. The process has exposed deep rifts in the English church about sex, marriage, relationships, the nature and authority of the Bible, and the gospel. I was following with keen interest as the debate over same-sex blessings went back and forth in their synods. One interview I saw included the Church of England Evangelical Council president, an Anglican priest, and a lay person. The lay person, Helen Lamb, pointed out simply that the debate was exposing what the gospel is and what it is not, and how something can look and sound right but actually stop being the gospel.

> The gospel is good news for all of us because we are all sinners and we need redeeming. But Jesus came to seek and save the lost. He came for those that are sick and need a doctor, not the healthy. And both of those mean we are all changed as we encounter him. And that is a different gospel than one that says God loves us and love is love and whatever makes us feel loved is what God wants to affirm in us. And we have two different gospel messages. And it was very clear, and there was honesty from people arguing both directions, that this is at the heart of our disagreement. Do we believe that gospel is God affirming us as we are, or do we believe that the gospel is a call to repentance and transformation into the likeness of Christ which is for all of us no matter our particular experience?[2]

We will never be able to witness well in our global, pluralistic world unless we know who Jesus really is and what that means good or bad for the human family. Again let us see what the original seed is. For me, one of the best places, if not the best place, to start is the very first Christian sermon given through Peter, who under the power of the Holy Spirit outlines this new gift of God so well. This first act of witnessing takes place during Passover. After the upper room moment with the wind and tongues of fire, Peter's call and clarification answers the question: What is the gospel?

He begins: "Fellow Jews and all of you who live in Jerusalem, let me explain this to you; listen carefully to what I say. These people are not drunk, as you suppose. It's only nine in the morning!" (Acts

2:14–15). In that culture, the first meal didn't take place until ten in the morning, so Peter says, somewhat sarcastically, this is not drunkenness, and you know it![3] We are all Jews or Jewish converts here, right? Hello! How are you missing this? What is happening right now in front of your face is what for generations we as a people have prayed and hoped for. Did God not promise Isaiah, Ezekiel, and Joel that there would be an outpouring of his Spirit and the making of a new community?[4] Our God promised this, and you are missing it! Let me remind you of what it says in our Scriptures; Joel 2 is happening in front of your eyes.

> In the last days, God says,
>   I will pour out my Spirit on all people.
> Your sons and daughters will prophesy,
>   your young men will see visions,
>   your old men will dream dreams.
> Even on my servants, both men and women,
>   I will pour out my Spirit in those days,
>   and they will prophesy . . .
> And everyone who calls
>   on the name of the Lord will be saved. (Acts 2:17–21)

Do you see it? The last days have been around since this moment. The *last days* refers to the last epoch, the last run of history. We as Christians do not believe in the myth of unending progressive history; we believe it has a beginning and an end. Since Jesus has come and gone, and since the giving of his Holy Spirit, we have been living in the end times for two thousand years.[5]

The sign of the last days is that God places His Holy Spirit in people permanently. The image from Joel is powerful. In desertlike conditions during a short raining season, there are torrential downpours on land that for most of the year is parched, barren, and filled with death. But in a moment, when the rain comes, the desert becomes full of life. So the same with us: We are broken, barren, parched, and spiritually dead, and the rain—the Holy Spirit—brings life!

Why is this such a big deal? As many of you might know, in the Old

Testament the Holy Spirit was given only for a season. He was given selectively and occasionally to prophets, prophetesses, or kings. But now, as promised in Joel, Ezekiel, and so many other places, the Holy Spirit will be given to anyone who meets Jesus. Age, gender, social status, education, or economic levels are swept aside, and now God permanently gives his Spirit to anyone![6]

Peter's Jewish audience would get all the references, but they had to ask what it had to do with salvation and a new move of God. Peter answers with one name: Jesus. "Fellow Israelites, listen to this: Jesus of Nazareth was a man accredited by God to you by miracles, wonders and signs, which God did among you through him, as you yourselves know" (Acts 2:22). Peter reminds them: Jesus of Nazareth was a man, a real living man; they had all heard about him, and many of them saw him. Yes, Jesus was a man, but he was a man divinely accredited by miracles. Jesus healed and delivered with authority like no one had never seen. He healed the blind, the deaf, those unable to speak, those who were bleeding, those gripped with death, demonic, and mental illness. He brought people back from the dead, and when he touched people, incurable illnesses, like leprosy, were just gone!

The point is you shouldn't just dismiss this. All the signs and miracles of Jesus were evidence that God is among us and the kingdom is here. The powers of the coming age are at work in the now, sent up like flares. They are tastes or appetizers to what the main meal will be like.

But Peter is not done. He keeps pointing to Jesus, now taking his listeners behind the curtain, revealing everything. "This man was handed over to you by God's deliberate plan and foreknowledge; and you, with the help of wicked men, put him to death by nailing him to the cross" (Acts 2:23). Jesus's coming and death were always the plan. Oh, yes, the Romans and some of our Jewish religious leaders (and some of you!) got him killed, Peter preached. They said Jesus was guilty of treason against Caesar and guilty of blasphemy because he claimed to be equal to God and able to forgive sins. The Romans and religious leaders thought they were in charge, but they got outplayed.[7] Jesus's death was God's plan all along. Later Paul would repeat the same idea in his letter to the Romans: "God presented Christ as a sacrifice of atonement, through the shedding of his blood—to be received by faith" (Romans 3:25).

Let what Peter and Paul said sink in—God gave over Jesus. Before the beginning of time, God decided to give himself for our sakes. Salvation is free for us, but it cost heaven everything. *Everything.* God gave Jesus up, gave him over, to deal with our sin. All the terrible events of Good Friday—the murder of Jesus—were the plan of God to bring deliverance to the world. Is this some weird form of cosmic child abuse? No, this is God himself so loving the world that he sent himself. As John Piper wrote, "If God were not just, there would be no demand for his Son to suffer and die. And if God were not loving there would be no willingness for his Son to suffer and die. But God is both just and loving. Therefore his love is willing to meet the demands of his justice."[8]

But Peter has more to say: "You, with the help of wicked men, put him to death by nailing him to the cross" (Acts 2:23). The group Peter was speaking to included many that were actually involved in calling for and participating in the killing of the Messiah they were waiting for, but the Bible teaches that we—all of us—are guilty of putting Jesus on that cross. The very first Christian sermon calls out all people; our condition is not downplayed at all.

Oh, how I love this next verse: "But God raised [Jesus] from the dead, freeing him from the agony of death, because it was impossible for death to keep its hold on him" (Acts 2:24). All the statements, all the sentences passed by human leaders, all the decisions of human courts, and the carrying out of that sentence by the Roman occupation are now rejected, reversed, rescinded! This is physical resurrection, not resuscitation or the walking dead! Resurrection is an all-or-nothing deal, all in, total sum gain!

Catch this, we as Christians unashamedly root ourselves in history itself, not myth. We don't run from history because we believe the resurrection was a historical event. Our movement is based on the idea that Jesus was really here, was really killed, was really dead, and then really physically rose from the dead. See that word *agony* in verse 24. In the original language it means "birth pains." So this verse says that the death occurred during labor but could not hold back the delivery of Jesus![9]

At this point the Jewish audience would be confused. They had been taught that the Messiah would never suffer. They had been taught he would restore the religious political kingdom and win. He was supposed to cleanse the temple, destroy the Romans, and restore the glory of David and the kingdom of Israel. To hear that the Messiah suffered is, as one scholar put it, like hearing you can fry ice.[10] But Peter asks: Why did we as Jews ever start thinking that the Messiah would not suffer? After all, David, our greatest king, the man after God's own heart and the one to whom God gave the promise that his line would change the world, predicted the Messiah's suffering. Peter was saying something like: Have we all not heard, read, and memorized Psalm 16?

> I saw the Lord always before me.
> Because he is at my right hand,
> I will not be shaken.
> Therefore my heart is glad and my tongue rejoices;
> my body also will rest in hope,
> because you will not abandon me to the realm of the dead,
> you will not let your holy one see decay.
> You have made known to me the paths of life;
> you will fill me with joy in your presence.
> (Acts 2:25–28)

But David is dead, right? His tomb is just down the road; we could go visit it. He has been abandoned to the realm of the dead; he has experienced full decay.[11] Obviously, David had to have been speaking about someone else.

> Fellow Israelites, I can tell you confidently that the patriarch David died and was buried, and his tomb is here to this day. But he was a prophet and knew that God had promised him on oath that he would place one of his descendants on his throne. Seeing what was to come, he spoke of the resurrection of the Messiah, that he was not abandoned to the realm of the dead, nor did his body see decay. (Acts 2:29–31)

It's Jesus. Jesus fits the pattern; he fulfills the prophecy. Jesus was dead but not abandoned to the dead. His body did not see decay. He is the one David was talking about all along, and he is alive! "God has raised this Jesus to life, and we are all witnesses of it" (Acts 2:32).

We do not shrink from the resurrection being the place of validation. Jesus was dead, and God brought him back from the dead. Right there, on day one, Peter says, this is real: "We are witnesses." This is not invented or borrowed myth. The resurrection actually happened. Before you as a modern person say, "Well, Jon, you know, two thousand years ago people did not have iPhones, the internet, or all our advances, so they were a little stupid and gullible," just stop. This chronological snobbery is unfounded!

As Tim Keller wrote in *The Reason for God,*

> In his landmark book *Jesus and the Eyewitnesses,* Richard Bauckham marshals much historical evidence to demonstrate that at the time the gospels were written there were still numerous well-known living eyewitnesses to Jesus' teaching and life events. They had committed them to memory and they remained active in the public life of the churches throughout their lifetimes, serving as ongoing sources and guarantors of the truth of those accounts. Bauckham uses evidence within the gospels themselves to show that the gospel writers named their eyewitness sources within the text to assure readers of their accounts' authenticity.[12]

This is why Peter is so bold and countercultural.

Peter keeps preaching, "Exalted to the right hand of God, [Jesus] has received from the Father the promised Holy Spirit and has poured out what you now see and hear" (Acts 2:33). Oh, the scandal! Jesus, the carpenter's son from Nazareth, is at the right hand of God? In the Bible, the right hand is the place of all authority, all power. When a king extended his right hand, it meant life or death, blessing or war. It was the place of and sign of ultimate decision. And here, Peter, this Galilean fisherman, is saying that Jesus, who had been executed fifty-three days earlier, was at the Father's right hand with supremacy over the whole universe. And don't miss this: Jesus has been given the Holy Spirit. Jesus is pouring out the Holy Spirit! The implication comes home, for only God can give and pour out his Spirit. So Jesus must also be divine?[13]

Filled with bold confidence, Peter says, "Therefore let all Israel be assured of this: God has made this Jesus, whom you crucified, both Lord and Messiah" (Acts 2:36). And there it is, the first, holy, universal confession of our movement. *Jesus Christ is Lord!*

Remember the quote from Joel 2 that Peter had used a few verses earlier, "Everyone who calls on the name of the Lord will be saved" (Acts 2:21). Think about the power of this statement knowing many in the crowd's complicity. David Gooding brings this home: "They had murdered God's Son; he was offering them his Spirit. They had crucified the second person of the Trinity; he was offering them the third. They had thrown God's son out of the vineyard in the hope of inheriting the vineyard themselves; now he was inviting them to receive God's Spirit not just into their vineyard but into their hearts."[14]

Peter's words hang in the air. What would happen next? Would there be mob violence if Peter and the others were killed like Jesus? Would the crowd just walk away and say they are buzzed, high, or crazy? Or would there be acceptance? Would there be holy fire for these people as there had been on those speaking? "When the people heard this, they were cut to the heart and said to Peter and the other apostles, 'Brothers, what shall we do?'" (Acts 2:37). Cut to the heart! When you get cut, man, do you feel it! Notice they are not just feeling anxiety or a vague awareness that something is wrong. They are now looking in the mirror and seeing clearly their complicity and guilt. They know they have done something very wrong, and they are afraid. As orthodox Jews, they are feeling something like this: "Is there anything we can do about this? Or are we doomed to suffer God's certain wrath on the day of the Lord?"[15]

This brings up the need, the deep need, for the fear of God to be brought back into not just our preaching but our witnessing. I love the way Grace Hamman talks about this:

> So why use the baggage-laden word *fear* instead of *awe* or *respect*? The difference between awe or respect and fear is the difference between seeing the skeletons of dinosaurs at the Denver Museum

> of Nature and Science and witnessing a dinosaur in the flesh. A skeleton I would gape at, impressed that something so gigantic was once alive. Then I'd go about the rest of my day. But if I saw a live Tyrannosaurus rex, I would feel small down to my toes in the presence of its enormous power. Seeing the T. rex would determine my next action, my next thought. Perhaps I would tremble or hide or give thanks. I would keep a healthy distance from said dinosaur to avoid imitating *Jurassic Park*. This fear gives birth to humility, to the healthy recognition of my humanity and natural limitations.
>
> It is healthy and reasonable for humans to be afraid of anything bigger or more powerful than we are. We *should* be cautious around large animals, venomous spiders, oceans, and dark places while surfing, skiing, or rock climbing. Small children must learn to be careful when jumping off furniture or walking by the edge of a pool. It would be bad for their formation if they did not learn this level of caution. Reasonable fear gives us the gift of remembering our limitations and practicing good judgment while enjoying a proximity to beauty, power, and the thrill of taking risks.
>
> We fear Christ as we fear the ocean: for the staggering beauty and uncontrollable power.[16]

When we realize how far we are from God, that we can do nothing to match his holy law and holiness, and when we see our sin, our contribution to the murder of God's Son, our sickness, and our separation, we, like the Jewish people in this story, cry out, *"Is there anything or anyone that can help?"*

How do we get out of this mess of our own making? "Peter replied, 'Repent and be baptized, every one of you, in the name of Jesus Christ for the forgiveness of your sins. And you will receive the gift of the Holy Spirit'" (Acts 2:38). There are three steps: repentance, faith, and baptism. They may not always be in that order, but all three are always there.[17]

Repentance: an attitude of turning back to God, involving remorse over the past. It is admitting that I have sinned, I am guilty, and I need help.

Faith: understanding and surrender. It is not enough to know that Jesus existed; we must personally ask him to cover us. Faith is not a blind leap but informed trust in the work and name of Jesus Christ.

Baptism: the image of inclusion, the outward symbol of already done inward work, and the confession of death and resurrection of Jesus and in Jesus, being clean, new life.

Then you will receive the best gift. You will be baptized in the Holy Spirit. As Paul would later write, "It's in Christ that you, once you heard the truth and believed it (this Message of your salvation), found yourselves home free—signed, sealed, and delivered by the Holy Spirit" (Ephesians 1:13–14 MSG).

Peter just keeps going. "'The promise is for you and your children and for all who are far off—for all whom the Lord our God will call.' With many other words he warned them; and he pleaded with them, 'Save yourselves from this corrupt generation'" (Acts 2:39–40). Corrupt generation! Really? Let's not forget when this first Christian sermon was given. It was Pentecost, celebrated fifty days after Passover. Pentecost is one of the three pilgrimage festivals, where Jews would travel to the temple in Jerusalem from all over the known world to give offerings to God. Hundreds of thousands of orthodox Jews and those who had converted to Judaism (giving up so much to follow the true living God) gathered to meet God in Jerusalem. So there, during a significant religious gathering, full of really good people who were giving up time and money to worship the true God, Peter tells them they were all still corrupt. Having the law, reading the law, being circumcised, or being ethnically part of those called the children of Abraham does not save. As one author wrote, "The Jew's assumption of superiority over non-Jews was not a matter of ego or personal boasting. Out of all the nations of the earth, God had chosen Israel as his people. Surely, the Jews reasoned, as God's chosen people they are immune from judgment—his 'tolerance' and his 'kindness' will always cause him to overlook our sin."[18] This is what Paul would later write in Romans 2. Being religious, even sincerely religious, does not save you. It's not what you do, but what another does for you!

In one day the church was born, and within hours they added three thousand people from all over the world: "Those who accepted his message were baptized, and about three thousand were added to their number that day" (Acts 2:41). And just so nobody misunderstands, after they repented and said yes to Jesus, after they became Christians by faith, they got baptized to declare it to everyone. Baptism does not save; it evidences the yes. These people were not trusting in a new moral system, a moral code, or more religious actions, but in a living, loving person—Jesus the Son of God, the Son of Man, the Messiah, the Lord who came to seek and save the lost.

And there it is, the heartbeat of the Christian faith, spelled out on day one. Jesus sums up the Old Testament. Jesus fulfills the Jewish faith. Jesus was a real man whose life was marked by miracles. Jesus from Nazareth was crucified. Jesus physically rose from the dead, just as God planned from the beginning. Jesus is king and is reigning right now. All human beings are corrupt and all sin. Even the most religious people are guilty. All of us need a Saviour. Jesus is not just a man but is God in flesh. If you accept Jesus, you will be forgiven of your sins, and you will get the greatest gift—the Holy Spirit. You can join God's movement no matter your history or background. God is holy. God is love. God is not silent; God reached out! And everyone who calls on the name of the Lord will be saved.

For us today, beyond the crystal-clear summary of the good news as seen in Peter's message, there are two other insights we need to recover to witness well in this very difficult moment. The first is the undoing of sincerity, and the second is the push beyond comfort.

The gravity of the situation is more dire than we think. Late medieval churches saw a trend in religious art called "Doom paintings." They tended to be the largest piece of art in the church building. As the priest would preach and distribute the Eucharist, those in attendance would look up to see Jesus as judge and wonder if mercy or judgment would move them to him. I love this summary, and I will help connect the dots in a moment:

> The second coming of Christ was painted according to the same formula from about 1100 to 1500. In every Doom, Jesus sits in

> authority, towering over the multitude gathered beneath him. On an arch at the parish church of St. Thomas in Salisbury, England, painted around 1470, Jesus sits upon a rainbow, with his feet on a smaller rainbow. The rainbows remind us that he fulfills all his promises. A red cloak is draped around his shoulders and knees, with his chest bare and hands extended to clearly show the wounds of his passion. On his right is Mother Mary, to his left John the Evangelist. Angels hover around him, some holding the instruments of the crucifixion. Below Christ sits the twelve disciples. Further below, the action of doomsday crackles. On the left, naked bodies emerge from the ground, helped out by angels. They are the dead, rising from their burial sites to join Jesus in heaven. On the right also, the dead come forth. Yet devils are herding them into the mouth of hell. Despite their nudity, many figures on both sides curiously wear hats. Crowns, floppy farmer hats, miters, and papal tiaras perch incongruously atop naked bodies rejoicing with the angels or wailing in the fire of hell. The hats reveal that damnation is equal opportunity: king, pope, and peasant alike must account for their choices. This picture of damnation as equal opportunity is a word of comfort along with fear.[19]

What was painted in those medieval pictures is what we see preached in the first Christian sermon. Great and small, powerful and powerless, known and unknown, great writers, generals, poets, actors, thinkers, politicians, religious leaders, kings, queens, and the billions of normal people of history—all will stand before God and face Jesus from Nazareth.

This is what Peter demonstrates, that is, the undoing of sincerity as the grounding of salvation. No matter their status, all will be held accountable. Wealth, power, position, race, colour, nationality, heritage, philosophy, education, religion, looks, fighting for justice, serving the poor, and *fill-in-the-blank* count for nothing when it comes to salvation. "But I am sincere," you might say. "I am a church member, I am from a Christian family, I am spiritual, I give up so much for others, I give to the United Way, I serve at a homeless shelter, I sponsor kids through World Vision." Yet none of it will move

God! Jew, non-Jew, right believing, wrong believing—the measuring rod will be the same for all of us!

This passage mentions fifteen geographical areas with their own languages. When you consider where they all come from, it is even more amazing. We often don't catch this because we don't know the ancient world, but the list moves from east to west and north to south. It starts with Parthians and ends with Rome, the farthest eastern and western borders of the Roman Empire. This moves you from desert to islands and everything in-between.[20] God answered their cry and gave them the ability to speak all at once in many languages they did not know, and this began the process of bringing the world back to God through Jesus. Notice, it was not Greek, the trade language of the day, or Hebrew, the faith language of the Jews, but heart languages. God speaks to me in my language, in my culture, to me personally. Yes, God loves you as you and wants to speak to you in the way you understand and feel. Back to incarnation we go!

This moment is the undoing of Babel at its very root. The whole human family, years after Noah's flood, have heard the whispers of that ancient snake, those poisonous seeds that say, "Don't trust God, God is afraid of you, God is keeping so much from you, you must do something!" And so humanity in that space and that time declared this, "Then they said, 'Come, let us build ourselves a city, with a tower that reaches to the heavens, so that we may make a name for ourselves; otherwise we will be scattered over the face of the whole earth'" (Genesis 11:4).

God had said, be fruitful, multiply, and spread over the whole earth. We said, no! This was the first great human project; it is the unity of unbelief expressed through a city—by our own actions we can reach to the heavens, live among the gods, and access the divine.[21]

If human beings are blocked from Eden, then we will force ourselves into heaven.[22] Three things are born here: secular humanism (we don't need God; we will save ourselves and control history), religion (we will save ourselves by our own spiritual actions), and spirituality (we will enlighten ourselves). Some people love one of these and think that the others are the enemy of human happiness and flourishing. But from God's view, all three are the same. That again is the scandal of Christianity, that the most ardent scientific atheist, the most devout Hindu or Muslim, and the yoga-going, United Way–giving New Ager are all lost in self-saving activity.

The problem was a heart issue. Taking out the tower would do nothing in real terms. Since this was a heart issue, the common connection was language, which had to be broken. This is how God keeps his word to Noah to not destroy the world again, by breaking our linguistic unity.[23] But now, on a side street in Jerusalem, God creates a new unity out of human diversity through God-given languages. In Jesus, through the Holy Spirit, a new humanity will be created and the old dividing walls will be abolished, day one.[24] As one brilliantly wrote years ago,

> If God had perceived that our greatest need was economic, he would have sent an economist. If he had perceived that our greatest need was entertainment, he would have sent us a comedian or an artist. If God had perceived that our greatest need was political stability, he would have sent us a politician. If he had perceived that our greatest need was health, he would have sent us a doctor. But he perceived that our greatest need involved our sin, our alienation from him, our profound rebellion, our death; and he sent us a Saviour.[25]

This gospel message is for everyone. It's really bad out there, and it's really bad inside us. But there is good news for everyone, and his name is Jesus. Or as my son's kid devotional once said, "God made it, we broke it, Jesus fixes it."[26] If we preach anything other than that, we are not preaching the gospel, and we will not make eternal impact.

Everyone is looking for rest, which is just another way of saying we're looking for an identity, a story that gives us the kind of gifted swagger of being known, named, and offered a map home.

—JAMES K. A. SMITH

What we are experiencing is not the eradication of God from the Western mind, but rather the enthroning of self as the greatest authority.

—MARK SAYERS

The 80s: serving yourself
The 90s: finding yourself
The 00s: accepting yourself
The 10s: expressing yourself
The 20s: marketing yourself

—SAM ALLBERRY

I am loved. Therefore, I am.

—N. T. WRIGHT

CHAPTER 8

What Is Our Identity?

When we moved a few years ago, our new home came with used appliances. During the walkthrough and even after we moved in, they all seemed to be fine and in good working order. Then a strange thing began to happen. We started noticing small tears appearing in some of our clothing. For the life of me, I could not understand what was going on. Time and time again, we would find a new tear, but could not find the source. Then one day I was cleaning out the lint drawer in the dryer, and I saw it. The plastic lint catcher was broken at the top, stopping it from inserting fully. Every time our clothing went through a drying cycle, it would catch on that small piece of jagged plastic, and bit by bit the tears would form, destroying much of our clothing. The damage was small at first, almost unseen, but then it became repetitive and, in the end, destructive.

This is what happens to us spiritually because of pain, sin, the world, the demonic, our current moment, and so on. Suddenly, after going through another tumble in life's dryer, we wake up, look around, and find that the gospel has gotten lost or muddied, and the gravity that holds us in place moves just a little, bringing catastrophe. If the Earth moved by even one degree, all seasons would end, there would be extreme day-night cycles, and it would eventually lead to the end of all human life. The same is true for us: If we move even slightly from our gravitational centre, the results for us and those around us are catastrophic.

Here is my point: We cannot witness well in any moment, let alone this one, if we are not clear about Jesus, clear about the message itself, and if we don't see, know, and feel the gospel in our own lives. If we become unsure of our belovedness, for example, we are done and become some form of the living dead. The living dead cannot make any difference. As we witness to others, we must keep witnessing to ourselves so we don't compromise or give up.

We must know who we really are and who we really know. You need to know who *you* are before you can help others know who they might become! "Yes, yes, Jon," you might say, "this is so obvious." But is it? There is something more here, something deeper. While many of us might not think about it this way, living out our God-given identity is nothing less than an act of rebellion. You might say that's dramatic, but have you actually pondered what *rebellion* means? Rebellion, by definition, is the action or process of resisting authority, control, or convention.[1] Yes, this is the word we need. To have a clear understanding of identity and then live out that understanding is rebellion, because the world, the flesh, and the devil are all trying to form you, mold you, and disciple you. As one pastor posted, "If we are not being intentionally formed by Jesus himself, then we are being unintentionally formed by someone or something else."[2] So true! The 24–7, nonstop access to everything is vying to change you, silence you, distract you, and shape you to look, feel, act, and think in the ways of the spirit of the age. Ongoing rebellion is deeply needed.

In the blistering heat on that Disney trip I mentioned earlier, my eye caught two different T-shirts on two different days. Among the thousands of Mickey ears and Figment, Donald Duck, and Goofy swag, these two stood out as different from the others. Both were rooted in defiance, both rooted in self-determination, both, I am sure, a reflection of the political mood of the day within the United States. The first one had the words "Don't be a sheep, be a lion!" written across it. The other had large letters emblazoned on the back that said, "becoming ungovernable." Both are deeply embedded in the American psyche, but both are actually more deeply embedded in the human condition. Be strong; the weak die. I will determine my life, my hopes, my happiness, my life. This is rebellion in the wrong direction. Both contain the seeds of the fake news spoken by the snake in the garden and are the opposite of Jesus's demonstration that meekness is where power is.

All those rivers and oceans of thought we talked about in the first section of the book are constantly trying to form your identity, even after your conversion. They are trying to claw back your identity because it is now formed by another. People like Sigmund Freud say you are not free, and your subconscious determines you. Neo-Darwinists say your biology, your DNA, and the process of evolution determine you. The full expression of the sexual revolution says your feelings, cravings, and passions form you, not self-denial or covenants.

So many voices tell us where and how to find the floor of our identity! You are determined by nature, biology, psychology, skin colour, ethnicity, upbringing, socioeconomic pressures, and group affiliation. And yet many others say actually, your identity is not determined at all. It is fluid and needs to be discovered or built by you. Just be a good person and follow your heart; your happiness is all that matters. Be true to yourself, put yourself first, look inside yourself, listen to yourself. Your rights and your ability for freedom of expression are what's most important to build identity out of. Work harder, play harder, be entertained, and feel good about who you are. All this freedom has caused not only harm and confusion but outright exhaustion. The ongoing pressure to discover yourself, to keep on finding, expressing, defending, adjusting, and defining, is exhausting. On one side is the call to the never-ending, relentless discovery process, and on the other, the unchanging trap of determinism. Again this is why Gen Z is saying enough, we cannot survive like this anymore.

Now I am not saying that history, biology, gender, and place do not form part of our identity. Of course they do. But for Christians, our core identity is given from an outside person who enters into our very essence. The image is not just of changing the rooms of our lives. This is not like redecorating a house and moving from a coastal or mid-century style to modern or traditional. Jesus comes in and translates, interprets, and transforms the whole house! Our deepest identity comes from outside in, not inside out. I have no idea where I heard this but it is so insightful: If your identity is achieved, not received, it will always be threatened and changed, and you will always be led to look down on others to prop up your fragile, self-constructed world.

In an Instagram post, while reflecting on how sexuality is viewed in this extended cultural moment, Jon Tyson pointed out that for the secular world everything revolves around identity, rights, ideology, pleasure, consent, and sociology. On the opposite end of the spectrum, religion is deeply connected to shame, which leads to legalism, moralism, literalism, fear, secrecy, and hypocrisy. But real faith, religion that stems from living contact, is sacred and leads to formation, fulfilment, theology, grace, transformation, and belonging.[3] *Belonging*—that's the word, the place where the called-upon holy revolt and rebellion begins.

For Christians, our identity is given through relational encounter with Jesus. Peter preached out of his confessional relationship with Jesus. At the end of the day, our epistemology (the study of *knowing*) and ontology (the study of *being*) are relational. Our core understanding of self is connected to encountering the true, living God, the one we are made in the image of. This is the ground floor of Christian identity: "So, whether we live or die, we belong to the Lord" (Romans 14:8).

I love what former Archbishop of Canterbury Rowan Williams wrote in *Resurrection: Interpreting the Easter Gospel*: "The gospel will not ever tell us we are innocent, but it will tell us that we are loved; and in asking us to receive and consent to that love, it asks us to identify with, and make our own, love's comprehensive vision of all we are and have been."[4] And this, make no mistake, is nothing less than rebellion. It is rebellion against our own hearts, rebellion against the demonic and all they want us to become or accuse us of being, and a marked rebellion against the multiple expressions of the world. So let me preach it again: Christian identity is rooted in another.

But then we must have a growing, clearer picture of God before you know what he thinks and how he perceives you. God cannot be a projection of ourselves.

The danger, as many have pointed out through the centuries, is that when we as Christians don't have the right picture of God, we end up shaping him into something he is not, which of course ends up being an idol that deforms our identity. In the book *The Trivialization of God, the Dangerous Illusion of a Manageable Deity*, Donald McCullough rightly argues that many of us reduce God to our comfort, our success, or our political bent. He wrote,

> The problem arises when we forget the vast difference between our *view* of God and the *reality* of God, when we equate the picture in the lens with the whole of divine truth. Any god I use to support my latest cause, or who fits comfortably within my understanding or experience, will be a god no larger than I and thus not able to save me from my sin or inspire my worship or empower my service. Any god who fits the contours of *me* will never really transcend me, never really be God. Any god who doesn't kick the bars out of the prison of my perceptions will be nothing but a trivial god.[5]

Ah yes, this is it. When God is clear and we encounter God personally in an ongoing way, our identity becomes not only clear but secure, established, and knowable; it is a gift.

I used this quote by David Benner in my book on pastoral perseverance, but I must go back to it here once again:

> Knowing ourselves must therefore begin by knowing the self that is known by God. The possibility of knowing yourself is grounded in the fact that yourself is already known to God. . . . Similarly, the possibility of knowing God is grounded in the fact that God already knows you. J. I. Packer correctly captures the priority in all of this knowing. The matter supremely, therefore, is not, in the last analysis, the fact that I know God, for the larger fact which underlies it is the fact that he knows me. . . . Genuine self-knowledge begins by looking at God and noticing how God is looking at us. Grounding or knowing of our self and God's knowing of us anchors us in reality. It also anchors us in God.[6]

Sometimes I think about our Christian identity like our solar system. All that makes us "us" is like the planets revolving around the sun. The gravitational force of the sun keeps the solar system together and gives heat for life (at least on earth). If the earth was just slightly off, we would all freeze to death, or burn to death, or just float away into the void of space. So it is the same with us: The true God is always the centre, and he is the one that brings order and symmetry to life, nothing else and nobody else. But if we do not know where our identity comes from, and who gives it to us, we will be tossed by so many winds that we will most likely float off into space. Then we will have no ability to witness, to show others that there is something more beautiful, restful, and forming than all the other voices. You and the church as a whole must rebel and resist identity theft!

Speaking of witnessing, you cannot truly give what you do not have, and you cannot invite others to know the one you don't actually know. If you have flown on an airplane, you have heard this warning given a hundred times over: In case of emergency, put your own mask on first, then others. If you don't have a steady flow of oxygen, you not only cannot help others but might die yourself. This chapter is like that warning. I know many of you reading this might be leaders, pastors, and long-term Christians, so you might not "learn" anything new in this chapter. But don't treat this moment like most of us do when "watching" that pre-flight safety presentation. This next section is the ground floor. If this is not stable, everything else crashes down. Think now about the complicated moment we are leading in as you hear the gospel again and again to see if you really do know, believe, and live out the good news of God.

Peter said, "Therefore, my brothers and sisters, make every effort to confirm your calling and election" (2 Peter 1:10). The invitation here is not some extreme, fear-inducing call that leads to continual crisis, but an invitation to rest and peace! As Neil Anderson wrote, "The most important belief we possess is a true knowledge of who God is. The second most important belief is who we are as children of God, because we cannot consistently behave in a way that is inconsistent with how we perceive ourselves."[7]

When I preach sermons, I tend not to use alliterations, but I will give in here. The three major planets forming the solar system of our identity are three c's: called, children, and Christian. Let's talk about each one in turn.

One of the most grounding, most assuring parts of our identity is that we are *called*. It's like in John 3 when Jesus uses the powerful image of conception, telling Nicodemus, "You must be born again" (v. 7). We don't choose to exist. Someone else chooses, and then we exist. Likewise, we are called into faith in Jesus Christ by the election of God the Father by the power, revelation, and faith-giving Holy Spirit. Most of us have heard this (at least in part), and we may take different views on calling (election, predestination, etc.). But could we just hear it afresh, no matter priest, pastor, bishop, and fellow Christians?

Paul wrote,

> Praise be to the God and Father of our Lord Jesus Christ, who has blessed us in the heavenly realms with every spiritual blessing in Christ. For he chose us in him before the creation of the world to be holy and blameless in his sight. In love he predestined us for adoption to sonship through Jesus Christ, in accordance with his pleasure and will. (Ephesians 1:3–5)

I would say that Ephesians is the strongest letter in the whole Bible to build a theology of Christian identity from. There's almost enough in just the first five verses. Here is the foundation of our unity in the church and the core of human identity: saint, grace given, peace with God, included in Christ, blessed and seated in the heavenly realms with every spiritual blessing in Christ. You are chosen, called, foreknown, and adopted children of God, sons and daughters. You are forgiven, redeemed, sealed with the Holy Spirit, and God's possession! Many of us bristle at the idea of someone owning us, but I want to be God's possession. Just as I see my kids deep down wanting my approval, presence, and love, so too we want that from God. The truth of calling is not a curse but a comfort; being predestined is a promise, not a problem; being elected is enough to get you through all the storms of life you face. This is a core part of our identity as Christians.

The second core part is, I would say, the most important aspect of your life—the most significant, most overarching theme, influencing factor—and that is that you are a *child of God*. Both John and Paul talk about this, and before you skip this section and say, "Jon, I don't need a small preach today," hold on because I think we might. Why? There seems to be quite a bit of confusion about what it means to be a child of God. From sermons to social media feeds, I keep hearing Christians say that all people are children of God, and that is just not true.

Paul said it like this: "For those who are led by the Spirit of God are the children of God" (Romans 8:14). Okay, it's important to be very clear: Every human being is made in God's image. We all have the same Creator. But that does not mean every human is a child of God. You only become a child of God when you receive the Holy Spirit, and you only receive the Holy Spirit when you accept Jesus. Paul is only repeating what John wrote: "Yet to all who did receive him, to those who believed in his name, he gave the right to become children of God—children born not of natural descent, nor of human decision or a husband's will, but born of God" (John 1:12–13). Those who receive and believe in Jesus become children of God—*only* those who believe, who trust, who rely upon, who have confidence in Jesus. Don't skip the part where John says that it is God who gives the right, ability, and capacity to meet him, know him, and walk with him in relationship.

The most religious person on earth who does not know and embrace the person, work, and saving power of Jesus is not a child of God. But when you do accept him, well, everything changes! Just go back to Romans 8 and keep reading: "For those who are led by the Spirit of God are the children of God. The Spirit you received does not make you slaves, so that you live in fear again; rather, the Spirit you received brought about your adoption to sonship. And by him we cry, '*Abba,* Father'" (Romans 8:14–15). Paul says we have been adopted to "sonship." We can miss the power of Paul's word choice without understanding history, but every first-century Roman hearing this would understand its power. Sonship, at that time, was a legal term, which is why you cannot translate it as "son or daughter" here. Augustus Octavian was the adopted son of Julius Caesar, so all that was Caesar's became Octavian's. As one historian put it, "In the Roman world of the first century AD an adopted son was a son deliberately chosen by his adoptive father to perpetuate his name and inherit his estate; he was in no way inferior in status to a son born in the ordinary course of nature, and might well enjoy the father's affection more fully and reproduce the father's character more worthily."[8]

That is the opposite of rejection. And the power of rejection is one reason why so many Christians do not make it to the end well, let alone at all.

> The feeling of being rejected is all too common in our world. Husbands reject wives and wives husbands as the divorce rate soars. Parents reject children and children parents. High school students reject other students because they do not fit with the "in group." Every reader can fill in the blank with his or her own experience of rejection. The sad fact is that it is increasingly difficult to find a secure and permanent relationship. As a result, people feel uneasy and uncertain. I know wives married twenty-five years to loving husbands who find it hard to trust their husbands because of the broken marriages they see all around them. Of course, no human relationship can ever provide ultimate security. The best-intentioned spouse can die at any time. But what our fellow humans can never supply, God does. In the midst of our disillusionment and doubt, he offers the most secure relationship imaginable: adoption into his own eternal family.[9]

So we are called, *and* we are adopted. We become children, and this brings us to the pinnacle of our most personal and shared faith. We get to call God Almighty—the Creator, the Great I Am, the God of Abraham, Isaac, and Jacob, the Eternal One—Abba, dear father, Dad. The Jews would address God as Father in worship, but not like this! As one historian wrote, "Jesus alone used it, and this was no doubt considered scandalous by his enemies. . . . Jesus through the Spirit, has given us his own special name for God, and it has become our natural cry to a loving Dad."[10]

As if that was not enough, "The Spirit himself testifies with our spirit that we are God's children. Now if we are children, then we are heirs—heirs of God and co-heirs with Christ" (Romans 8:16–17). The Holy Spirit leads us time and time again to one place, one declaration, one grounding—to that life-changing, life-giving, all-consuming point. The Creator of heaven and earth looks upon you, in your good, bad, sin, family history, and says, with an almost indescribable smile, "You are my precious child." Then we get to run back to him and say, "Thank you, Dad!" And other than his worship, he will share everything with us. As one said, Romans 8 is the inner sanctuary within the cathedral of Christian faith.[11] Why? Because it speaks of what Jesus has made us by his Spirit.

We are called and we are God's child, and lastly, we are *Christian.* That title, Christian, is first used in the New Testament in Acts 11:26: "The disciples were called Christians first at Antioch." Christian was originally an insult that meant "little Christ" or "little Jesus." But the name stuck, and it moved much deeper than insults or some surface description of us. It became our core identity as followers of Jesus. Within years, the name that was an insult became our chosen marker. Peter, near the end of his life, uses it: "However, if you suffer as a Christian, do not be ashamed, but praise God that you bear that name" (1 Peter 4:16).

Christian. I am a Christian. If you are a follower of Jesus, this title is not attached to your identity; it is no add-on. This is not like clothing you wear; that is not really you. This is central to everything you are, how you live, how you act, how you think. It doesn't remove your gender, ethnic background, history, economic status, or education level, but it is the grounding of your identity, and if you are a follower of the Way, it affects all of the above. As one wrote, "The basic calling of a Christian is to identify with 'the name' wholly and simply, in a way, that one's confession of Christ becomes the most essential fact of one's life."[12]

One way I express this identity publicly is by crossing myself when I pray. Because I live in such a pluralistic, multicultural city, many other people pray to many things and gods, and I want to publicly declare Jesus is Lord. I want to publicly declare the power of the cross and the person and God I am walking with and praying to.

Called, child, and Christian—this is who you are, who *we* are! Because this is true, there are other experiences connected to identity that embody all we have already talked about. Peter lists them over two simple verses: "Peter, an apostle of Jesus Christ, To God's elect, exiles scattered throughout the provinces of Pontus, Galatia, Cappadocia, Asia and Bithynia," and "Dear friends, I urge you, as foreigners and exiles in the world, to abstain from sinful desires, which wage war against your soul" (1 Peter 1:1; 2:11). Exile, alien, and stranger are smaller planets in this solar system of our identity. These truths should form us deeply, and as they do, they will help us navigate such diverse times. We are really spiritual refugees and ambassadors at the same time.

For the Jewish community, exile (after Babylon) had loomed so large that it shaped their identity and thinking, even to this day. N. T. Wright says that this unresolved exile became the controlling narrative, the grand story, or the metanarrative for Jewish living in the Second Temple period. He argues in most of his books that unresolved exile fundamentally shaped the thinking of both Jesus and Paul.[13] I suspect that exile is one but not the only driving factor, but no matter. Clearly, living in exile left a deep, unhealed wound among the Jewish community, even post-Babylon, because they struggled with their continuing lack of freedom. Why are we home, but still in exile at the same time?

> What then does "exile" mean, in this continuing sense? Answer: the time of the curse spoken of in Deuteronomy and Leviticus, a curse that lasts as long as Israel is "the tail and not the head" still subject to the rule, and often the abusive treatment, of foreign nations with their blasphemous and wicked idolatry and immorality. As long (in other words) as the condition of Israel is much like that in Egypt, they will be waiting for the new exodus. As long as Persia, Egypt, Greece, Syria, or Rome are in charge, the exile is not really over.[14]

For Christians, the ongoing exile is resolved through the person and work of Jesus Christ, who constitutes the climax of the salvation-historical story of Israel.[15] But we still feel it as we live in the here and now, just as our spiritual ancestors did. Though we now see the ultimate answer in Jesus, exile is in our identity as it was in theirs. And why does this matter? Because the tension, the cognitive dissonance, reminds us we are home, sort of. If we don't feel the tension anymore, we are in danger. I love how the actual life of Augustine brings this part of our Christian identity home for us:

> Augustine was an African who ventured to Europe looking to make a name for himself—to "arrive" in both senses of the word, thereby securing his identity. . . . He found there only a new sense of alienation. A provincial in the centers of cultural influence (first Rome, then Milan), he realized the limits of his welcome into the upper echelons of power. As his biographer Peter Brown reminds us, "Even the fully Latinized African of the fourth century remained somewhat alien.". . . .
>
> But when he returns to Africa, he finds himself suspect there now too. His meteoric rise through Roman channels of power is a sign to some African compatriots . . . that he's gone over to the other side. He is tainted with "foreignness" even at home now . . . "Augustine's restlessness," González observes, "was not due only to his distance from God, as he tells us in his *Confessions,* but also to the inner struggles of a person in whom two cultures, two legacies, two world visions clashed and mingled." . . . Even Augustine's home was hybrid.[16]

Yes, and so the same for all of us—hybrid homes. And yet, if we stop knowing exile, we stop living out of our identity as alien and stranger, and that will prevent others from coming to faith in the first place because there will be no difference between you and those you are supposedly different from.

Which brings me back to where we began: rebellion. Jesus, in the parable of the sower, is very clear about why people ultimately do not become part of the kingdom. But have you ever read this parable and reminded yourself that the very things preventing people from entering the kingdom of heaven do not cease to exist when we are called and when we become children and Christians? These forces and opportunities do not remove us from God's love, but they do become the place where identity is marred and tarnished and where it puts the solar system out of sync. Just read the passage below with fresh eyes:

> Some people are like seed along the path, where the word is sown. As soon as they hear it, Satan comes and takes away the word that was sown in them. Others, like seed sown on rocky places, hear the word and at once receive it with joy. But since they have no root, they last only a short time. When trouble or persecution comes because of the word, they quickly fall away. Still others, like seed sown among thorns, hear the word; but the worries of this life, the deceitfulness of wealth and the desires for other things come in and choke the word, making it unfruitful. (Mark 4:15–19)

Personal shallowness kills the reality of faith. Trouble, like suffering, sickness, job, family, life, affects us. Persecution, when following Jesus actually costs you something, affects us deeply. Are not all of us marred by the worries of this life and the cares of this world? Take the time to write a list of these struggles—worry, illusions, wrong perceptions, job, possessions, self-image. The list is probably longer than we want to admit. Another writer put it this way:

> Personal trauma, the fear of rejection, or the influences of the pursuit of a life of comfort often play a dominating role in our lives. If most people were honestly asked to consider how much of their time and energy are spent coping with these issues, most of us would agree they consume the majority of our energies. Yet too often we accept their impact on us as an unavoidable given. It is easy to see why Jesus names the things he does that get in the way of our bearing fruit. Nonetheless, a life dominated by these concerns is not headed for spiritual fruitfulness. A little booklet entitled "The Tyranny of the Urgent" was popular when I was in college. It argued that often our lives are driven by that which throws itself into our lives and demands our attention and fixing.[17]

Of course, in the West, wealth chokes out God's work. Wealth offers but cannot deliver what the human heart cries out for: intimacy, connection, unconditional love. Money, house, cars, trips, furniture, food—none of these things are evil. In fact they are all gifts. But they can grow and grow and choke out Jesus and his kingdom. One author wrote this about church in the West:

> Why are we dying seems very simple. It is hard to be a disciple and be rich. Surely we may think, it cannot be that simple, but Jesus certainly seems to think that it is that simple. The lure of wealth and the cares of the world produced by wealth quite simply darken and choke our imaginations. As a result, the church falls prey to the deepest enemy of the gospel—sentimentality. The gospel becomes a formula for "giving our lives meaning" without judgment.[18]

Jesus boldly says that competing pressures like tribulation, persecution, worldly cares, wealth, sensual offers, and the king of the other kingdom, the Evil One himself, kill the work of God. And I would say that even postsalvation, these very things attack and corrode our identity and then slow or stop us from the ability to see God's heart and join God's mission. Theologically, we would call this sanctification, the struggle to become like Jesus, but we must also see this ongoing internal struggle in the light of our holy presence as witness. And it's not just sin or guilt that we all wrestle with, but also shame. Do you know, according to psychiatrist Curt Thompson, it takes less than three seconds to feel shame? Yet it takes thirty to ninety seconds to receive a compliment.[19]

When we face shame as Christians, our hearts and the demonic usually tell us to suppress what we feel, desire, struggle with, or what we are. The world, much of the time, will call us to embrace and become these things, build our identity on these things, and, most importantly, celebrate them. But those of us who walk with Jesus should never respond with suppression or denial but with transparent surrender as ultimate rebellion. When we know we are loved by the Father through the Son by the Spirit, we need not hide anything. Suppression leads to apathy, guilt, hypocrisy, or a shipwrecked faith. Transparent surrender allows authenticity and costly worship at the same time, which truly is normal Christian discipleship.

One of my favourite shows on Netflix is *The Crown*. I'm sure many of you know about it or have seen it, but if you don't know, it follows the life of the English royal family in three generational phases all around the late Queen Elizabeth. The acting is incredible, the sets magnificent, and the story line full of pain, drama, victory, and global events. It was amazing to watch. There were two moments over those six seasons that jumped out to me. Both are connected to Queen Elizabeth's grandmother Mary of Teck, whose full name was Victoria Mary Augusta Louise Olga Pauline Claudine Agnes. She was the Queen Consort of the United Kingdom and the British Dominions.

The first moment is a letter Mary wrote to Elizabeth after her father died and the other a conversation between the Queens on when (and how) to speak and when not to speak. She sits in one of her royal rooms and writes this,

> Dearest Lilibet, I know how you loved your papa, my son. And I know you will be as devastated as I am by this loss. But you must put those sentiments to one side now, for duty calls. The grief for your father's death will be felt far and wide. Your people will need your strength and leadership. I have seen three great monarchies brought down through their failure to separate personal indulgences from duty. You must not allow yourself to make similar mistakes. And while you mourn your father, you must also mourn someone else. Elizabeth Mountbatten. For she has now been replaced by another person, Elizabeth Regina. The two Elizabeths will frequently be in conflict with one another. The fact is, the crown must win. Must always win.[20]

The second notable moment occurs when the two of them are sitting together in Queen Mary's bedroom as she was dying. The conversation goes back and forth, and then Queen Mary says to Queen Elizabeth:

> Monarchy is God's sacred mission to grace and dignify the earth. To give ordinary people an ideal to strive towards, an example of nobility and duty to raise them in their wretched lives. Monarchy is a calling from God. That is why you are crowned in an abbey, not a government building. Why you are anointed, not appointed. It's

> an archbishop that puts the crown on your head, not a minister or public servant. Which means that you are answerable to God in your duty, not the public.[21]

Now this is not a comment on the monarchy or the British Empire, but what I loved in those two personal and dramatic moments in the show was the way they encapsulate what we are called to do related to identity. In the end, we are fully accountable to God,[22] but more, the struggle between the old us and the new us is real. And the new us, the us "in Christ," must always win. For though our identity is given by God and cannot ultimately be removed, it is the goal of the demonic, the many contradictory world systems, and even our own sin to distort, mute, and dampen that identity—to get us to hate ourselves or this world too much, or to love ourselves and this world too much. We live out of what we are and what we love. Ongoing and given identity is key to faithful witnessing in this moment, for if this is lost, then all is lost.

So before you keep going, you should stop and pray about identity. In fact, it would be great to pray out of one of the oft-neglected "I am not" statements of Jesus from John 8 where you find not only all the above but also the seeds for new life. You can pray:

> *Jesus, just as you said, now I can say: I am not alone. I stand with the Father who sent me (v. 16), I am not of this world (v. 23), and I am not seeking glory for myself (v. 50). Help me to believe this, to live out of this, to know this. Help these truths to shape me and not just shape me but the church around the world. Amen*

PART 3

RENAISSANCE

a revival of or renewed
interest in something

Beauty is a relic of Eden—a remnant of what is good. It comes from a deeper realm. It trickles into our lives as water from a crack in a dam, and what lies on the other side of that dam fills us with wonder and fear. Glory lies on the other side. And we were made for glory.

—RUSS RAMSEY

Sometimes, witnessing to Christ will mean drawing out of a culture the full meaning of its noblest intentions, a fullness that is revealed in Christ. At other times, witnessing to Christ means challenging that culture, especially when the truth about the human person is under assault.

—JOHN PAUL II

The entire cosmos is one vast burning bush, permeated by the fire of the divine power and glory.

—KALLISTOS WARE

It is not a Darwinian advantage to be merciful to the poor, love your enemies, and also to create beauty.

—MAKO FUJIMURA

CHAPTER 9

Seeing Beauty with New Eyes

There is a word we need in the western Church right now—an idea, a time period, an experience. It is the word *renaissance*. It's a word that brings up many images, museums, and thoughts, but what does it really mean? Renaissance refers to a revival of or renewed interest in something. And what do we as orthodox, creed-confessing, Bible-holding Christians need? We need a renaissance; we need a renewed interest in beauty. Yes, the world is complicated, unjust, and so much light seems to be vanishing. Yes, the world, the flesh, and the devil—as we have seen above—are large and overbearing. Yes, they are real and their influence is massive, but still, beauty is everywhere. If you don't look for those fingerprints of God, you will be awash in the darkness, and you won't want to witness and bring more beauty because you will be tempted to give up and say all is lost. Without seeing the beauty, we either lose hope or just want to burn it all down and start over like some Christianized Thanos from the Marvel universe. In the next chapter I will walk through how beauty is key for witnessing in this cold, calloused, and increasingly bitter moment, but for now we need to talk about how seeing God's beauty will help *us* to not grow cold and bitter inside before we move to share that beauty with others! I love what Russ Ramsey said in his book *Rembrandt Is in the Wind*, reflecting on our deep, core need for beauty as Christians:

> We have a theological responsibility to deliberately and regularly engage with beauty for three reasons. First, God is inherently beautiful. The book of Exodus tells us that Moses' desire to see God was a hunger to look upon beauty. King David expressed the same longing in Psalm 27:
>
> > One thing have I asked of the Lord,
> > that will I seek after:
> > that I may dwell in the house of the Lord
> > all the days of my life,
> > to gaze upon the beauty of the Lord
> > and to inquire in his temple.
>
> Moses and David didn't just want to see beauty. They wanted to see God. They knew there was no greater beauty to see. Second, God's creation is inherently beautiful. There is beauty all around us, and it points to the glory of God. When God rested from creating, he said the world he made was "very good." This goodness is not according to the world's standards, but to God's word. And in God's kindness, the fall did not erase the beauty of creation. It's there to behold, if we'll only look. And when we see it, it will teach us about the Author of beauty. Third, God's people shall be adorned in beauty for all eternity. Those who are in Christ will one day be "prepared as a bride adorned for her husband." Psalm 149 describes this beauty as the glory of being "adorned with salvation." These verses are meant to draw us a response of praise. We should engage with beauty deliberately and regularly because these are the clothes we will walk around in for all of eternity.[1]

Thomas Aquinas, while struggling to work out revelation, evangelism, apologetics, and the fall, came to the conclusion that revelation is like a two-story house. You can enter the house (come to know that God exists) through nature, philosophy, reason, beauty, moral experience, and so on, but to go to the second story of the house, you need divine intervention. This is special God-given faith (specific revelation), not just reason.[2] We'll get into more on that in the next chapter, but for now, why does this matter for your faith, your hope, and your soul in this very different and difficult moment?

Well, as Christians, we know God personally through Christ, by the Holy Spirit. We know him up close. For us God is not far away, hidden, obscured, or lost. We have been given special revelation. Even though we know the beginning and the end, we should not and cannot diminish or ignore what God has given all around us. Actually, we need to spend more time on the first level of the house, so we don't lose hope for our now and be tempted to live only for the "not yet." The apostle Paul fights for this, walking us back downstairs with his most famous grouping of thoughts about anxiety, joy, suffering, and beauty. We will get there in a moment, but first, let's zoom out.

Hope. It is a small word and a big word. It has become a churchy word, but it is a needed word. Hope is at the epicentre of the Christian faith. Christian hope creates the environment and the foundation for another rare item—joy. And the reason hope and joy are both powerful, authentic, inspiring, threatening, and life changing is because of where they are the strongest—when God redeems, reuses, and clarifies our suffering. Suffering is where the brightest Christian hope and Christian joy shines.

Christian hope and joy are supernatural, are connected to Jesus, and are gifts. Say that again? Christian hope and joy are unearned gifts. That's right. Jesus said there would be many troubles in this world, yet we are called to have hope and joy—unexplainable, contagious, outrageous, infectious, unnatural hope and joy. The only way this can happen is when we walk with, under, and alongside of Jesus. What did Jesus promise us if we know him and obey him? "These things I have spoken to you, that my joy may be in you, and that your joy may be full" (John 15:11 ESV).

We are not called to live under the weight of our circumstances, nor are we called to live above them; we are called to walk *in* them, empowered by the Spirit of Jesus day by day. We cannot avoid fear, worry, stress, or darkness. But we are called to walk with Jesus through them.

This is why Paul not only wrote conceptually about hope and joy but actually experienced them both. I think we need to be reminded sometimes that Paul was just a person like you and me, who struggled, wondered, and experienced life. And his life was actually much more difficult than many of our lives! Listen to what he went through after becoming a Christian and beginning to talk about Jesus to others:

> I've worked much harder, been jailed more often, beaten up more times than I can count, and at death's door time after time. I've been flogged five times with the Jews' thirty-nine lashes, beaten by Roman rods three times, pummeled with rocks once. I've been shipwrecked three times, and immersed in the open sea for a night and a day. In hard traveling year in and year out, I've had to ford rivers, fend off robbers, struggle with friends, struggle with foes. I've been at risk in the city, at risk in the country, endangered by desert sun and sea storm, and betrayed by those I thought were my brothers. I've known drudgery and hard labor, many a long and lonely night without sleep, many a missed meal, blasted by the cold, naked to the weather.
>
> And that's not the half of it, when you throw in the daily pressures and anxieties of all the churches. When someone gets to the end of his rope, I feel the desperation in my bones. When someone is duped into sin, an angry fire burns in my gut. (2 Corinthians 11:23–29 MSG)

Okay, that is a serious list. Paul should be burnt out, angry, jaded, tired, done, hating those he was supposed to love, neurotic, and nothing more than a power-driven shell of a church leader. He should have moved to some sort of agonistic worldview, crying out, "It's too much to handle! Where are you, God? If this is what I got called into, I am out!"

(At this point you might be saying, *Jon, beauty. I thought this chapter is on beauty.* Yes, it is, just give me a moment. Back to Paul.)

Despite all of his hardships, Paul is not a destroyed leader or a despondent Christian. Somehow he is living in the environment of Christian hope and is marked by deep joy. And he chooses to express this joy in great detail in the most unexpected place, writing a letter to the Philippians while he's under house arrest in Rome, two years before he was murdered for his faith.

Paul helped found the Philippian church around AD 50. It was probably the first church established on European soil. You can read that story in Acts 16.[3] But it has been ten years since then. Paul is in jail, the Philippian church has grown, and under the guidance of the Holy Spirit, he writes this letter thanking them for their gifts and urging them to keep going. It is a letter of friendship and encouragement, not of persuasion or dealing with false teaching, which is why so many love it. It is one of his most personal letters, if not the most personal, written to a church.

The book of Philippians is only 104 verses long and is filled with grand themes about the centrality of Jesus, the power of the gospel, the call for community, and faithfulness in suffering. But underneath them all is the grand theme of joy. It acts like the foundation, the infrastructure, the bedrock; it's like an underground river that seeps in and through the whole letter. Joy bubbles up time and time again. And one of the clearest places he unpacks joy and peace is in one of the most quoted group of verses. These verses have been written on Bibles, on mirrors, journals, printed on stickers, scribbled on sticky notes, and posted on social feeds many times. But—and this is huge—most of us never slow down enough to hear, let alone understand, what is being promised (and its connection to beauty).

Okay, to the famous verses we go: "Rejoice in the Lord always. I will say it again: Rejoice! Let your gentleness be evident to all. The Lord is near. Do not be anxious about anything, but in every situation, by prayer and petition, with thanksgiving, present your requests to God" (Philippians 4:4–6). Do not be anxious about anything. What a shocking command! But what is anxiety anyway? Anxiety can be expressed in many ways. I still have not been able to recall where I heard or read the ideas below but they are so helpful.

Worry: something that may or may not occur
Stress: strain over a situation we cannot control
Fear: uneasiness over possible danger, evil or pain
Darkness/Fear experience: the actual touching of danger, evil, or pain

Since this passage in Philippians is often preached quite badly, let's not forget its original context: The section about anxiety refers to persecution—getting beat up or losing a job, experiencing death, imprisonment, or intimidation, losing friends or family because of your public faith in Jesus. Both Matthew and Luke used the word *anxiety* when relaying how Jesus taught the Twelve to not worry when they would face local religious councils, kings, or governors. Paul is not talking about normal fear, nor is he talking about anxiety rooted in mental illness. As one author wrote, "Since their present suffering is at the hands of those who proclaim Caesar as Lord, they are reminded that the true 'Lord' is near!"[4]

Since the Lord is near, thank God that you get to suffer as Jesus did and don't forget to come to me in prayer, God says. So in the face of real anxiety and mistreatment, pray with petitions and thanksgiving! And what is petition again? Petition is asking God into situations, asking God for things, asking God's will into all we face. I love what Spurgeon wrote, "Whether we like it or not, asking is the rule of the kingdom."[5]

But it's not only about asking. Our prayers must be filled and grounded in thanksgiving. We must recall God's mercy, love, and works done in the past, present, and future. We must express joy to the Lord, thanking God for his faithfulness, protection, and benefits and, most importantly, for the crystal clear and certain future of the resurrection and Jesus making all things right. Another author wrote,

> Lack of gratitude is the first step to idolatry (Rom 1:21). Thanksgiving is an explicit acknowledgment of creatureliness and dependence, a recognition that everything comes as gift, the verbalization before God of his goodness and generosity. If prayer as petition indicates their utter dependence on and trust in God, petition "accompanied by thanksgiving" puts both their prayer and their lives into proper theological perspective.[6]

The believer should pray, Paul says, about every circumstance and should couple those requests with thanksgiving. In that, the peace that passes understanding will come: "The peace of God, which transcends all understanding, will guard your hearts and your minds in Christ Jesus" (Philippians 4:7).

Paul is not talking about the peace we experience between us and God through the work of Jesus—that is right standing. But from that foundation, we receive this peace: God will make all things right. As you read Philippians 1–2, Paul says that in transitional times, in difficult times, in dangerous times, we must work out our troubles with each other because of Jesus's work in us. He instructs us to be gentle to those who attack us because of Jesus's work in us. But then he goes somewhere most of us do not. Paul invites us (or really, commands us) not to be consumed by fear and worry because of Jesus's work in us. And then he is like, "Just stop. Look up and around and see that God, his work, and his beauty will be found even in the midst of persecution and suffering. All around you there are not just echoes of Eden, but signs of what is to come." And so we come to these often quoted yet rarely well-interpreted group of verses: "Finally, brothers and sisters, whatever is true, whatever is noble, whatever is right, whatever is pure, whatever is lovely, whatever is admirable—if anything is excellent or praiseworthy—think about such things" (Philippians 4:8). Okay, let's just walk through these one by one.

Whatever is true: In Paul, this is narrowly understood. It is fully expressed and defined by God—his gospel and his laws that reflect his truth. It is specific revelation. That is truth.[7]

Whatever is noble: What is sacred, what is holy, what is majestic—these are things that are still connected to God himself.[8]

Whatever is right and pure: That is what is correct, what is moral, what is specifically God-given: his life-giving laws. Since we now have the whole Bible, Paul would instruct his readers to think on, be formed by, swim in all of Scripture, from Genesis to Revelation. That is right and pure.[9]

And this is where most preaching and most Bible studies end. Most say, what else do we need? We have God, his Word, his law, his grace, his revelation. That's enough. But Paul says that it's not enough, especially not during violent times. Paul goes further. He pushes us to see the world through God's eyes. Just keep reading.

Whatever is lovely and admirable, excellent and praiseworthy: Paul tells us to think on and look at what is lovely and admirable. This is what theologians call common grace, God's fingerprints all around us. Yes, we live in a fallen world. Yes, it is totally depraved, but it is not *utterly* depraved. Much in creation, in humans (including those who don't have a personal relationship with Jesus), and in culture is not evil. Some of it is even excellent and praiseworthy. Paul is teaching the church that, as things get darker and more difficult, we must not see evil and retreat, but we must not run into the many forms of an anti-intellectual, anticulture, antineighbour mind-set.[10]

Here's my favorite summary of Paul's list:

> Perhaps Paul knows that since the people are being persecuted by the society around them, they will be tempted to reject everything outside the church as indelibly tainted with evil. If so, then this list, with its admonition to look for the virtue in the wider world, reminds the Philippians that, although society sometimes seems hostile and evil, it is still part of God's world and contains much good that the believer can affirm.[11]

Let me put it this way: We must look for and find beauty in God's world. Beauty is key to preventing Christians from becoming angry fundamentalists. It does not dismiss the reality of darkness and total depravity. It does stop us from acting as if everything and everyone is utterly depraved. We must choose to look for beauty. It was Rich Mullins, the author and singer, who put it best: "There's so much beauty around us for just two eyes to see. But everywhere I go, I'm looking."[12]

So I would like you to stop and ask yourself: When was the last time you looked for beauty in other people—or in art, nature, or some movie or show that is not Christian? When did you last slow down and look at a painting or a bird and see the expression of God's beauty? When was the last time you enjoyed a meal or laughed with friends and realized that much of creation is still good? You might not be deeply moved by nature or art like some, but beauty is found in many places. It would be good for some of you to stop and make a list of the many beautiful things besides God and his Word. Thankfulness is crucial, and beauty is a powerful way of prompting thankfulness. Darrell Johnson once told me that when things got really dark for him, he began this daily spiritual discipline of stopping to name or list twenty things he was grateful for every day. We could all benefit from that.

To intentionally find beauty as Christians is a command of God in Philippians 2. This is not just some nicety or add-on. This command is as strong as "read your Bible regularly" or "worship God properly." If more Christians would seek beauty and spend less time online attacking others or "doomscrolling," we would see a massive attitude shift that would at least partially produce the stamina we need to keep going in this transitional moment full of darkness and possible mass renewal. Again, there is no "fun" in the worldview of cultural or religious fundamentalists. That is why we need to keep finding beauty as Christians. Beauty lets us see God, see hope; it fills our soul. God's world is full of beauty. Admitting this does not dismiss the reality of darkness and total depravity. Yet sin and darkness do not prevent us from seeing and loving whatever is true, whatever is noble, whatever is right, whatever is pure. Finding God-given beauty does stop us from acting like everything is utterly depraved. Christianity requires a chosen default setting that is not cynicism. Find beauty and rest a bit. If we don't, our presence will be anxious, our presence will be deformed, our presence will not be beauty producing or beauty giving.

He has made everything beautiful in its time. He has also set eternity in the human heart; yet no one can fathom what God has done from beginning to end.

—ECCLESIASTES 3:11

God did this so that they would seek him and perhaps reach out for him and find him, though he is not far from any one of us.

—ACTS 17:27

This Creator God has not created a hunger for God within humankind only to leave it unsatisfied.

—JAMES DUNN

CHAPTER 10

Seeing Bridges That Already Exist

I think many of us have experienced occasions where science came to life as a teacher showed us some experiment. The teacher took some boring principle and brought it to life right before our very eyes. In my generation it was building the famous papier-mâché volcano. The moment when your volcano really worked was so cool. You carefully added the baking soda to a cup in the middle of the volcano that you'd worked on for so long. Then, of course, you added red food dye and, finally, the vinegar. Then, fizzing and bubbling, the fake lava erupts and pours out across the helpless Lego city below!

Another (admittedly less amazing) science moment for me was when we started to learn about the law of attraction demonstrated with magnets. One simple rule to remember with magnets is that opposites attract. Each magnet has a north pole and a south pole. When you try to place two of the same poles together like north to north, they will repel each other. They cannot come together, as hard as you might try. But when you place the opposites near each other, they cannot *not* come together.

For us, the greatest point of connection is not what is common, shared, or agreed upon, but opposites, things of hostility, contradiction, and differences. The magnetic points we have with those who are not Christians (whether they are religious, spiritual, or secular in all their different forms) are found in the places where we would normally expect to encounter the greatest resistance. Keep this picture in mind as we continue, for it will be so helpful as we seek to reach out in this moment.

But first, we must continue our conversation about beauty. As we turn outward and look at the world around us, the stark and needed question we must face down is this: Is there anything left for those who do not know God? And the answer, of course, is yes! And this then becomes the hinge moment—moving from inside to the outside, from family conversations to missional outreach to the billions who are not yet within the family of God.

Let me pose the question like this: What is the role of beauty in witnessing? This is a question for every generation, but especially ours. What is the role of beauty in this never previously experienced moment in Christian history, in this "post-Christianity"? As society becomes unglued, cold, and violent, and as "winner's justice" replaces mercy, grace, and the Judeo-Christian view of informed justice, what do we do?

It is helpful for us to go back to one of the greatest church fathers from medieval times: Thomas Aquinas. While thinking about evangelism, Aquinas struggled deeply with what sources of truth to use in order to witness well. How would he speak to multiple audiences in multiple directions at the same time, the great call and struggle we are all now called into as we live in this global, digital, virtual, multicultural, secular, spiritual, religious, pluralistic, and secular age?

You can hear Aquinas's heart, concern, and struggle as you listen to his thoughts expressed in his commentary on Ephesians. In it, he rightly admits that faith is a gift from God and cannot be found or obtained by reason: "Free will is inadequate for the act of faith since the contents of faith are above reason. . . . That a man should believe, therefore, cannot occur from himself unless God gives it."[1] Of course, the blind cannot make themselves see; the dead cannot produce life; one cannot start their own conception.

But the question remains: Is there common ground that can be accessed in the journey, in the process of being found by Jesus? Well, the language is old, but listen again to Aquinas as he struggles with the challenge of giving the gospel to Jews, Muslims, false Christians, and many others who are tied to differing faiths and old pagan systems all at once:

> Thus against the Jews we are able to argue by means of the Old Testament, while against heretics we are able to argue by means of the New Testament. But Mohammedans (Muslims) and the pagans accept neither the one nor the other . . . we must, therefore, have the recourse to the natural reason, to which all men are forced to give their assent.[2]

Now there is much that could be unpacked here. Aquinas focused much on the role of philosophy and also had a more positive view of human nature after the fall than I and many others would.

When dealing with Aquinas and the limits of reason, it is important to understand the Catholic view of the image of God and how sin has affected this given image. In Genesis 1:26–27 it says,

> Then God said, "Let us make mankind in our image, in our likeness, so that they may rule over the fish in the sea and the birds in the sky, over the livestock and all the wild animals, and over all the creatures that move along the ground."
>
> So God created mankind in his own image,
> in the image of God he created them;
> male and female he created them.

Many in the Catholic world would look at the words *image* and *likeness* in this passage and see them as two dimensions of the image of God. This concept began to be developed by the church fathers and has been debated until the present. Irenaeus was the one who set a strong foundation for this medieval theological understanding. He argued that *image* referred to Adam's reason and free will and *likeness* was "some sort of supernatural endowment which Adam possessed through the action of the Spirit."[3] He did not consider these two to be original righteousness, but instead he saw them as a seed that contains the right material for Adam to grow into what God wanted him to. This view was later developed by the medieval scholastics. The difference between image and likeness and also the effects of the fall were understood through image and likeness. Image was defined as, "man's natural resemblance to God, the powers of reason and will."[4] Likeness was lost but the image was still intact. One theologian helps us understand:

> This perspective of course involves a conception of the nature of sin and the fall, but it also involves a definite idea of the nature of man. One's human nature is unitary and relatively immune to the damaging effects of the fall. Even non-Christians and marginal believers are as fully human as are sanctified believers. All men possess the ability to evaluate evidence, to recognize the truth, to choose on the basis of knowledge of the truth. This leaves open the possibility of a rational or natural theology. Even without special revelation all persons are able to find some true knowledge of God. It also leaves open the possibility of a natural ethic. Being free, man is capable of doing some good works apart from grace. On the seemingly innocent distinction that while the likeness of God was lost, the image was not leaving open the possibility of a natural theology and a natural ethic, the whole system of Catholic theology was built.[5]

Now many Protestants would, rightly so, react against such an idea. They have shown that likeness and image are the same (two words meaning the same thing) and that "all" of us have been marred by sin.[6] And yet even if everything is touched by sin, it does not mean beauty does not have a role. Nature, natural theology, and beauty are key starting points to joyful witnessing. Yes, of course, you will never know the nature of God (Trinity), the incarnation, or the need for and reality of the atonement without God's intervention.[7]

So in this repaganizing and pluralistic moment, what does beauty mean for witnessing? To answer this, we must stop and let Scripture speak to what is left after the fall. In the middle of the world's systems, the vastness of original sin, our ongoing sins, and demonic, is there anything good left? The answer is yes—so much yes. Remember, the difference between total depravity and utter depravity really matters.

Let's set the stage with what theologians call common grace or natural theology. God left his fingerprints all around us and his mercy to all of us is an everyday occurrence whether we see it or know where it truly comes from.

The Dutch Reformed side of the family got this right when in 1924 the Christian Reformed declarations said that God's grace is found in three areas. First, God gives good things, like rain and sunshine, to all. Second, he is actively restraining the human race from moving from all things touched by sin to *only* living out of sin. God, in mercy, is restraining us from going fully to where we would naturally trespass to. There was a time in our history that we as humans were utterly sinful. Just listen to God's view just before the Noah event. "The Lord saw how great the wickedness of the human race had become on the earth, and that every inclination of the thoughts of the human heart was only evil all the time" (Genesis 6:5). God has stopped this from happening again. Third, there is good in the world of leadership, what we might call civic righteousness.[8]

Even Calvin said the world and non-Christian thinking, "though fallen and perverted in its wholeness, is never less clothed and ornamented with God's excellent gifts."[9] Jesus, in the Sermon on the Mount says,

> He causes his sun to rise on the evil and the good, and sends rain on the righteous and the unrighteous. If you love those who love you, what reward will you get? Are not even the tax collectors doing that? And if you greet only your own people, what are you doing more than others? Do not even pagans do that? (Matthew 5:45–47)

God gives common grace to all; he shows love even by giving life to everyone. Jesus says that even the Jewish tax collectors—those known for corruption and theft, the ones who were collaborators working for an occupation government—knew God's grace. Jesus says again that pagans—people with no faith in the true God, no presence of the Holy Spirit, but who worshipped the demonic and human idols—experienced God's grace. There are fingerprints of God even among those collaborators and those in darkness.

Paul says it like this in Romans 1:19–20: "Since what may be known about God is plain to them, because God has made it plain to them. For since the creation of the world God's invisible qualities—his eternal power and divine nature—have been clearly seen, being understood from what has been made, so that people are without excuse."

Hey, everyone, it's plain. Nothing is hidden, Paul says. This is not a secret. You don't need to be a great intellectual to see him. He has shown himself. This act is definite, powerful, unequivocal. The knowledge of God has been made known to us.

We cannot know everything about God from creation, but we *can* know he is a creator, a God of order, an artist, and a moral God. From the fine tuning and order of the universe to the untaught moral code shared by all cultures, to our desire to worship someone or something, God's invisible qualities are clearly shown. Observation says yes, moral insight says yes, spiritual intuition says yes, beauty says yes. As Russ Ramsey wrote,

> We save our vacation days, plan our itineraries, and make our way across oceans, over mountains, through cities, and down the long stretches of highway that span the countryside to take our place in line to catch a glimpse of the deeper glory we know we were made for. Elaine Scarry said we make sure that we are "looking in the right direction when a comet makes its sweep through a certain patch of sky." We go to the Louvre in Paris, the Met in New York City, the Rijksmuseum in Amsterdam, and the Academy in Florence. We go to the Grand Canyon of the American West, the Giant's Causeway of Northern Ireland, the forests of East Asia, and the islands of the South Pacific. We go to a pizza place in Brooklyn, a pub in Oxford, a vineyard in the Sonoma Valley, and a café in Paris. Why? All to join the carnal to the divine. All to get closer to glory.[10]

The best passage for me that holds this reality in tension is found in the Psalms. Remember, we are trying to be honest about everything—the radical fallenness of humanity, the uniqueness of the gospel, and the call to be holy, along with the call to find common ground, the call to find beauty, the call to witness, and the call to have hope. The Psalms took a thousand years to write and compile, and as you read, pray, sing, and think about the Psalms, you will discover there are three major groupings (praise, lament, and thanksgiving) but more than ten types, or styles.[11] Think about Netflix with the different genres you can choose to watch depending on your mood. Or think about a golf bag that has different clubs for different parts of the course. The same is true here in the Psalms. We are given the languages of sadness, joy, terror, hope, boredom, worship, and vengeance—all in liturgical form to pray our lives back to God.[12]

One style is called creation Psalms. They focus on God as creator and remind us that God is the sustainer, the one who stabilizes the universe. They tell us that creation is good, that God speaks through creation. These Psalms call us to look at the artistry, complexity, beauty, order, and rhythm of creation as a source of seeing God, hearing from God, and worshipping God. The most famous of these is Psalm 19:1–4:

> The heavens declare the glory of God;
> the skies proclaim the work of his hands.
> Day after day they pour forth speech;
> night after night they reveal knowledge.
> They have no speech, they use no words;
> no sound is heard from them.
> Yet their voice goes out into all the earth,
> their words to the ends of the world.

Creation, all of it, from angels to atoms, from whales to trees, from sea to sky, from the billions of stars to the billions of bugs, from mountains to lakes, from humans to flowers, from rocks to mountain tops, from diamonds to dirt, all of creation, in all of its complexity and colour, proclaims the existence of God and nature of God. Day and night, seven days a week, twenty-four hours a day, this creation, this chaotic order, in all of its pageantry, beauty, sweetness, and terror, announces, informs, and points humans to their Creator!

This soundless speech is everywhere, and it is available to every human being on earth. Creation announces, creation informs, creation literally gushes forth the reality of God. It is actively speaking, actively giving knowledge, singing, speaking, and pointing out that there is a Creator who is different from, higher than, and the source of creation.[13] This is why the Apostles' Creed, the best summary of true Christianity, begins with God and creation.

But what is so interesting about Psalm 19 is that it starts with common grace (beauty) and then moves to specific grace. It moves from the second level of the house to the first floor, to use the image from the last chapter. It shows the progress that always takes place when God moves into a person's life, and actually, it shows the tensions and needed conversations that will fill the rest of this book.

See, Psalm 19 is not just praise or worship. It isn't just a list of facts. Psalm 19 is polemic. It says that the many religions of Jewish people's neighbours are wrong. They all worship creation—sun, moon, and the stars. But no, no, the Bible cries! There is only one God, and what the rest of you worship is no god at all. The things you worship are made by God. Your gods are false, and all fall under the one true, only uncreated God.[14]

The Bible is clear about this: When we lift up ourselves, when we put anything in front of God, when we end up worshipping not the Creator but the created, there is nothing but brokenness. The heart of sin, of trespass, of iniquity—the root of all brokenness is misdirected worship, what Paul wrote so clearly in Romans 1. Christian philosopher Soren Kierkegaard described sin as building our identities on anyone or anything other than God.[15]

Returning to Psalm 19, the song moves from all of creation to focusing on the sun. "In the heavens God has pitched a tent for the sun" (Psalm 19:4). We often miss the power and offence of this. The sun was worshipped as a deity by the Canaanites and many other cultures that surrounded the Hebrews. No, the Psalms say, the sun is not a god but has been created and set in the heavens by our God. Yahweh is God, not the sun or anything else.[16]

The psalm keeps going:

> It is like a bridegroom coming out of his chamber,
> like a champion rejoicing to run his course.
> It rises at one end of the heavens
> and makes its circuit to the other;
> nothing is deprived of its warmth. (Psalm 19:5–6)

The sun is like a groom on his wedding day, dressed up and beaming with excitement. He is like a champion, a warrior, a mighty man ready to fight and win the day, ready to compete and win the race. And nothing is hidden from the sun, for the circuit of the sun over twenty-four hours arcs over all of creation, over every human being. Nothing escapes its light and so also, nothing escapes the Creator's view.[17] And yet this is not enough. There is such a God, but can he be known? He is involved, but is he good or evil? Again we feel the limits; we experience the tension of being on the first floor and needing to find the stairs to the second floor. So many people live as if the house is only a bungalow and not a two-story house.

So now we move from creation and general revelation (beauty) to specific revelation. We move from knowing that *some god* is out there to knowing that *this God* speaks and can be known. Amazingly, in the first six verses of Psalm 19, the name for God in Hebrew is El, the most generic name for God. But in verse 7 his name changes to Yahweh, God's covenant name, the one used when God entered into relationship with his people. Here, the names for God show the relational progression from outside the house, to the first floor, and up to the second floor.

Again, I need to point out that knowledge, from a biblical worldview, is not merely intellectual but deeply personal and experiential. In different connotations, the same word is also used in the Bible to mean sex, to "know" your spouse. To know about someone or to know someone at the deepest level is the difference between thinking about something and knowing something. The one who knows God personally knows him as Yahweh. They are in relationship with him and his word is life. That is exactly where the Psalm goes next:

> The law of the LORD is perfect,
> refreshing the soul.
> The statutes of the LORD are trustworthy,
> making wise the simple.
> The precepts of the LORD are right,
> giving joy to the heart.
> The commands of the LORD are radiant,
> giving light to the eyes. . . .
> The decrees of the LORD are firm,
> and all of them are righteous. (Psalm 19:7–9)

I love what one Old Testament scholar wrote:

> The ancient gods of polytheism operated with just as twisted a moral standard as humans. They lied, cheated, stole, were sexually promiscuous, and generally outdid their human servants with their lack of consistent morality. They were distinguished from humans by only two major characteristics: They were powerful, and they lived forever. Therefore, whatever the gods demanded had to be obeyed because they had the power to make human existence miserable, and there was no hope of out-living them.[18]

But not so for our God, thank God! And if you keep on reading this Psalm, it goes on to speak about knowing the true, living God, walking in his ways, and seeing the world. It's about walking into and living on the second floor of the house through his written Word.

For witnessing in such a divided and polarized moment as this one, I want to start outside the house and spend time on the first floor. We tend as Christians to run upstairs, but if our presence is going to have real effect, we must discipline ourselves to stay below for a while. Why? Because those magnetic poles that attract others are everywhere if we choose to look. The front door of the house is wide open. As the gospel went into new areas for two thousand years, this idea of finding the natural connections, finding the magnetic connections (of which beauty is one of the most important expressions), has been critical in reaching out as witnesses.

Famous Christian thinker J. H. Bavinck points to five key places that act as natural magnetic connections, these existing bridges we get the privilege of walking across. In time, if they are utilized, then godly shame, guilt, repentance, faith, and trust might take place (2 Corinthians 7:10), but we must start with these five areas:

1. One's relationship to the world (creation, shared creation story, and death)
2. One's relationship to what is shared by all of us as normative (shared law of right and wrong, transcultural values)
3. The question of existence (can one encounter a personal God)
4. The need for salvation (the drive to the religious, good works, idols, to eliminate or overcome death)
5. The fundamental belief in a supreme power.[19]

There are two other ways to define the bridges and find these magnetic points. As we will see in a few chapters, Paul points out three major bridges in Athens, three massive ideas that every single human wonders about: What is the origin of life? What is the meaning of life? And what happens at the end of life?[20] Each one has magnetic pull.

I would add one last critical thought that I believe is necessary in our presence and in our witness in all moments, but especially this one. If the above are all questions, bridges, or magnetic points we all commonly share, then how do you begin to walk across them? The answer is love, power, and word, which are the same categories that the spiritual gifts are grouped into. Love gifts demonstrate the love of God, word gifts define who God is, what he wants, and power gifts evidence his reality in the moment.[21]

These three expressions allow the church to pivot to different people in seconds and provide bridges and magnetic connections in multiple ways. I wrote this in *Convergence*,

> The spiritual gifts in their three groupings are like three doors that must be opened and used at all times. Many will come to faith through being loved into the kingdom. Others will be taught or

> thought into the kingdom. Yet my on-the-ground experience and growing conviction is that the vast majority will come to faith through power, through an encounter with Jesus. Now all of these doors must lead to the real Jesus of Scripture, and there must be repentance of sin, faith in Christ's work and person for salvation, and the hope of physical resurrection. But if you don't have all these gifts working well in your church, doors to evangelism will be closed that don't need to be. Even as all these gifts work, some doors will have little or less attractive power to certain ages or stages or some ethnic or religious communities. This is why all the gifts must be understood and used. Whether it's a Muslim having a dream about Jesus; a university student listening to a Christian Oxford professor on the historical validity of the resurrection; a sick person being loved, cared for, and prayed over by that Christian nurse; that sermon by the preacher; or that deliverance that broke the power of darkness, the point is that in a pluralistic, multicultural, socioeconomically diverse world, we need all God's doors open to see the kingdom of God in its fullness on this side of the new heavens and new earth.[22]

Most Christians tend to only be comfortable in one or two of those categories, and the same is true for most churches. But we need them all to have kingdom presence and witness well in a repaganizing, pluralistic, and possible-renewal moment.

We are about to move into the book of Acts next to see various acts of witnesses in their raw form, and we must let the Scriptures speak for themselves. I hold the view that these encounters are not just recorded acts of history but case studies to show us not just "what" was done but "how" in our day. These are real moments of salt and light, what on-the-ground presence looks like as we work towards orthodox theology and orthopraxy. Without this secondary step, God is reduced to history and future, with very little attention given to the "in between," where we do all of our living.

Do you even want to see the magnetic points or have you just dismissed them? Are you working hard to find the God-given bridges, or would you prefer to pretend they are not there? Or worse, do you choose not to cross them? Maybe you want to burn some of them depending on where they might lead. If love, word, and power are all critical, where are you on this part of the conversation? Do you see all three areas at work in your church and in your ministry? Do you have a robust understanding of all the gifts and the need for them in each church community? Do you believe some do not still function? Or do you believe they do but are afraid of them? Are you looking for, welcoming, fighting for, and expecting God to do amazing work in all three ways? Are you open to being used in any way God chooses? If not, you or your church are already on the back foot and will not be able to truly reach the West and the world as it is.

When non-Christians are confronted with the message of Christ, most will at first have moral and cultural blocks to even considering it seriously. It is a costly message for it involves renouncing one's past life and embracing Christ as Lord. Thus, unless there is some compelling evidence that will move their hearts, people will not regard it as worthy of consideration.

God often uses actions of Christians—such as deeds of kindness, miracles, and blameless lives—to incline the hearts of people favorably toward the gospel. Once the heart is open, it is possible for the will to be oriented to accepting the gospel. People will be able to regard its teaching for what it is worth without their earlier prejudices and fears. They will realize it is something worth committing their lives to. . . . Though ultimately people put their trust in Christ based on the words they hear, deeds often act as a trigger to open them to considering the words.

—AJITH FERNANDO

Jesus Christ is Conqueror
By his resurrection he overcame death itself
By his resurrection he overcame all things
He overcame magic
He overcame amulets and charms
He overcame the darkness of demon possession
He overcame dread
When we are with him
We also conquer

—AFRICAN HYMN

CHAPTER 11

Power Within Our Presence

When I was in a youth group, a new teen started attending, and we became friends. He was South Asian in background, from India or Sri Lanka, and Hindu by faith. He began coming to youth group to check out Christianity. He came to youth services, watched us pray, asked tons of questions, and played all the games. So a normal youth group moment in the early '90s. Then one day he disappeared and never came back. A few years later, either near the end of high school or during my early university years, I happened to run into him again. I reintroduced myself, and we struck up a longer conversation. After a while, I asked him, "You just disappeared one day; what happened to you?" "Do you really want to know?" he replied. I assured him I did. In my head I was thinking that it might have been about culture. Back then we were basically an all-white youth group. Joining any group where you are the minority is always challenging on the best of days, and I guarantee that at that time our cultural EQ was not high. So I asked him straight up if we had made some cultural mistakes. Surprisingly, he responded, "No, no, nothing like that." "Then what happened?" I asked. "My mom got really sick," he said. "I asked Jesus to heal her, and he didn't. Then I went back to my Hindu gods and asked them to heal my mom, and she got better. So obviously the gods of my ancestors are either more real or have more power than your God, so I'm sticking with them."

Just sit with that for a moment. This is not an unusual experience; it happens all the time. And it brings home the need for spiritual power in our witnessing. As we begin to cross different bridges, we have to be ready to have messy conversations. And one of the key issues we will need to face is where in the world power comes from.[1] What role do power experiences play in evangelism? How do we evaluate if the power is real, and how do we know where it's coming from?

As I have shared in previous chapters, one of the things I love about my city is that the whole world is here. For those of us who have lived elsewhere or are from other parts of the world, we know the vast majority of people who become Christians do so first through experience and secondarily through rational ideals. We need both word and deed, power and gospel proclamation. But how and why and when? This is why these two small stories found in Acts 13–14 are so helpful on the ground. In this part of Acts we get to see not only the need for the power of the Holy Spirit to win large parts of the city but also how this can go wrong so quickly. At a church gathering, God told Barnabas and Saul to leave that amazing church in Antioch: "While they were worshiping the Lord and fasting, the Holy Spirit said, 'Set apart for me Barnabas and Saul for the work to which I have called them.' So after they had fasted and prayed, they placed their hands on them and sent them off" (Acts 13:2–3). They worshipped and listened (through the use of spiritual disciplines and spiritual gifts), and prompting led to planning. The leaders placed their hands on them, not giving them a new spiritual gift or more power, but as an expression of connection, a way to affirm they were being sent out.[2]

Then it continues: "The two of them, sent on their way by the Holy Spirit, went down to Seleucia and sailed from there to Cyprus" (Acts 13:4). Luke again shows us that it is the Holy Spirit who sends. The Holy Spirit is the one who moves Jesus's body to do Jesus's bidding which is the Father's command. And just like with Jesus, the Holy Spirit is sending them into a spiritual war zone. They end up in Cyprus, a land occupied over history by the Greeks, Egyptians, Phoenicians, Assyrians, Persians, Ptolemies, and later annexed by

Rome. During the time of Augustus, it was a separate province and under the leadership of a proconsul,[3] who was about to come to faith in Jesus.

The story continues: "When they arrived at Salamis, they proclaimed the word of God in the Jewish synagogues. John was with them as their helper" (Acts 13:5). They first go to the east coast of this island and go to the Jewish worship houses called synagogues. Paul follows this pattern almost everywhere. He starts with those who have the most in common, the most bridges already built. Remember, Christianity is not a separate religion from Judaism; it is the Jewish faith fulfilled through Jesus the Messiah, the Son of God. That is why Paul wrote in Romans 1:16, "I am not ashamed of the gospel, because it is the power of God that brings salvation to everyone who believes: first to the Jew, then to the Gentile."

But after preaching in the synagogues, the scene changes drastically: "They traveled through the whole island until they came to Paphos. There they met a Jewish sorcerer and false prophet named Bar-Jesus" (Acts 13:6). The men travel west ninety miles to the seat of the provincial government,[4] and it is here again that another known pattern emerges. Every time the good news is spoken and miracles are done in Jesus's name in a new territory, there is a turf war. That is, there is a demonic encounter meant to abort, thwart, or delay the work of God. The Bible teaches that Satan is the god of this world, and the kingdom of God—beginning with Jesus and continuing through his followers—keeps pushing the kingdom of darkness back. So we see in the book of Acts the demonic using both Christians and non-Christians to try to stop the kingdom of God. It happens in Acts 5 with Ananias, with Simon in Acts 8, here in chapter 13, and later again in chapters 16 and 19. Every time the gospel comes to a new place, a new family, a new people group, there is a clash.[5] These turf wars still happen today. Every time we witness to a new community, new neighbourhood, new ethnic group or family, we should expect a clash. There is always a battle before the battle.

This coming clash is very important, so lean in. Luke wants to make sure (and so must we) to distinguish between the power of the Holy Spirit and those of the demonic. Luke never doubts the ability or gifts of those empowered by evil. To him the issue is not the weirdness or the presence of spiritual gifts, but the *source* of the gifts. The demonic do acts of power similar to those who are empowered by the Holy Spirit. The demonic even do good things, like healing people to keep them deceived. They look the same but serve different purposes. The ability is not fake; it's evil.

The scary fact is the spirit of antichrist looks like, acts like, and does things like Jesus and his church do, but the source of those things is not Jesus Christ by the Spirit of Christ. Their goal is to deceive and destroy, not save and bring peace, and most importantly to give glory to God the Father. That is why you must not only know the Bible well but also have all the gifts in operation in a church community, like the gift of discernment to test what the real power is behind all of these moments.

The clash comes very quickly: "Bar-Jesus . . . was an attendant of the proconsul, Sergius Paulus. The proconsul, an intelligent man, sent for Barnabas and Saul because he wanted to hear the word of God. But Elymas the sorcerer (for that is what his name means) opposed them and tried to turn the proconsul from the faith" (Acts 13:6–8). Sergius Paulus was a very interesting guy. We know from historical sources that there is a great chance he was part of a political family that was highly esteemed within the first and second centuries and that he was known at the highest courts in Rome.[6] Then there is Bar-Jesus, a syncretistic Jew who mixed Jewish faith with the occult. *Elymas* is a Hebrew word meaning male occultic worker or sorcerer.[7] He is within the proconsul court because the belief was that he had the ability to break the bonds of fate and give power to his employer.[8] He could help with real world political power by using other worldly power such as telling the future. Sergius Paulus is hedging his bets with advisors from all areas, including the supernatural.

The kingdom of darkness, knowing the good news was coming, already had a key player in this place of power: Bar-Jesus. The goal here is to confuse and confront Jesus's people. By the way, *Bar-Jesus* means "Son of Salvation." Make no mistake, his name fills the room with confusion. So which Jesus is right? Which Jesus is Saviour, Jesus from Nazareth, the Son of God, or Bar-Jesus, the son of salvation? And all of them are Jewish, which would confuse Sergius for sure.

There is a human agenda, a demonic agenda, and a God-given agenda in the same room. Bar-Jesus does what he can to stop his boss from listening because if he embraces another spiritual source, leader, or worldview, then his job and role would be endangered. Yet at the same time, the spirit or spirits that gave Bar-Jesus these ungodly abilities would also be opposing the Holy Spirit found in Saul and Barnabas. It's a clash of kingdoms, a turf war—God and Satan, good and evil, true gifts and false gifts, one person plugged into the spirit of antichrist and the others filled with the Spirit of Christ himself.

Why fight here and why fight now? This is the first presentation of the Word of God to the Roman world formally given on Roman soil with access to the Roman political system. So the clash begins like this: "Then Saul, who was also called Paul, filled with the Holy Spirit, looked straight at Elymas and said, 'You are a child of the devil and an enemy of everything that is right! You are full of all kinds of deceit and trickery. Will you never stop perverting the right ways of the Lord?'" (Acts 13:9–10). Filled with the Holy Spirit and using the spiritual gift of discernment, Paul exposes this man for what he is and confronts what inspires him. He asks a piercing question: Will you not stop making crooked the straight paths of the Lord? Those words might feel very familiar, and they should. We hear these words at Christmas in Handel's "Messiah," which come from Isaiah 40:4 about John the Baptist and Jesus: "Ev'ry valley shall be exalted, and ev'ry mountain and hill made low; the crooked straight, and the rough places plain."

This is the great difference between good and evil, peace and chaos, level and unlevel, straight and crooked. Paul, using the spiritual gift of discernment along with common theological understanding, says that this guy is a Jew but a child of the devil. He says something like, "You are false and your power is false. You're not here by mistake. The devil has placed you here to stop, thwart, confuse, pervert, and overcome the good news of Jesus so it cannot take a foothold in the Roman world. But we are here by God's command. We have been here sent by the Holy Spirit."

Then Paul moves from discernment to the gift of miracles: "'Now the hand of the Lord is against you. You are going to be blind for a time, not even able to see the light of the sun.' Immediately mist and darkness came over him, and he groped about, seeking someone to lead him by the hand" (Acts 13:11). This battle is not between Paul and Bar-Jesus; the battle is between the Holy Spirit and the spirits in Bar-Jesus. And there is no doubt who wins! So God, through Paul, blinds Bar-Jesus for a time. God's acts of discipline always have silver linings of grace and provide space for someone to move towards salvation. Remember Babel. God could have destroyed everything, but he didn't. He only broke up their languages. Remember the Flood. He saved the human race through Noah, and the rainbow was given as a sign of coming salvation. Remember Jonah. He fled God and was thrown overboard, but God saved him by a fish. Remember Paul, the guy that just cursed Bar-Jesus. I guarantee you Paul was thinking about his own conversion story from a few years earlier, when he fought God and was blinded by Jesus for three days.

Now Paul is used by Jesus to blind another man supernaturally for a time. One huge reason that I believe the blinding is not permanent is that God is giving Bar-Jesus a warning while also giving him space to become like Paul, who turned and followed Jesus.

Then we come to the needed moment. Power encounters are never the real story. Eternal life always is: "When the proconsul saw what had happened, he believed, for he was amazed at the teaching about the Lord" (Acts 13:12). Here we see the power of "both-and" and the biblical rejection of the "either-or" view in evangelism. First, the proconsul saw what happened, the power encounter. This miraculous event was the door being opened, the trigger, the taste, the affirmation that Paul might be right. The power encounter directed the proconsul, but the act of preaching, the foundation of truth, is what he believes upon. God-given power is clarified by the gospel! Without that clarification, it's just power, and *both* sides have power that produces good temporary results. At this point many theologically conservative people's default position is, "You'd better not do the power stuff and stick with proclamation." No. The possible perversion or abuse of something true does not make it untrue. It simply must be clarified. If churches are going to reach a world that is deeply intellectual and experiential, secular and spiritual, then the case study in Acts should not be the exception but the norm.

As I was finishing this book, I was teaching a seminary class on spiritual conflict, which at its heart is about spiritual theology, the systematic evaluation of spiritual experiences from a biblical perspective. We walked through spiritual gifts, spiritual disciplines, and other experiences trying to work out what is from God, what is from the demonic, what is human, what is psychological, and what is simply too much Netflix or yesterday's pad thai. After the second full day, one student asked if she could stay after class. With tears in her eyes, she started telling me her story. She is a relatively new Christian, having left her Hindu faith only two years ago. Her conversion was dramatic, with dreams, the demonic, Jesus, and the Scriptures all playing a part. She is still the only Christian in her family, and as a young twenty-something, it has been difficult. But it was what she shared next that grieved me. She thanked me for affirming her conversion story, for giving her biblical categories and language for all she had been through and was going through. Then she told me about how she had joined a local Reformed church when she got saved. She was the first adult baptism in that church in ten years. The pastor was so excited, and so was she. But after she wrote out her testimony in full, with all that had happened, the pastor took it and cut out every single supernatural story and encounter. He did not have the categories to understand it and thought the congregation would have been fearful. As a result, this young woman was deeply hurt and confused, and the congregation was not stretched and pushed to step out. This story shows us that when theology is rooted in fear, it stops witnessing in its tracks. But we are not done yet. Back to the biblical account we go.

In Acts, we move from the chambers of Roman power to the religious everyday life of many people as Saul and Barnabas go next to the Roman colony called Lystra: "But they found out about it and fled to the Lycaonian cities of Lystra and Derbe and to the surrounding country, where they continued to preach the gospel" (Acts 14:6–7). There is no Jewish gathering in this city, so they begin to share the good news with people from all sorts of religious backgrounds. Now let me slow you down so we all catch this: Every person hearing their preaching was a religious pagan, which means they either followed the Greco-Roman gods, believed in fate, were part of secret religious cults, or held some other false worldview. The goal for Paul and Barnabas was to first show them that there is only one God and then to point out that God is only found through Jesus. This strategy was outlined by Paul in 1 Thessalonians 1:9–10: "They tell how you turned to God from idols to serve the living and true God, and to wait for his Son from heaven, whom he raised from the dead—Jesus, who rescues us from the coming wrath."

With pagans who have no Jewish understanding, this is a two-step moment: first, point them to the only true God (not demons or idols), and then preach Jesus who reveals God. So here in Lystra, the gospel is repeated. "These idols or worldviews you trust in have no power! You must encounter the true living God, and you meet him through Jesus, who was raised from the dead." Though not directly mentioned in these verses, we know that this is being preached.

Then suddenly the next event begins to unfold: "In Lystra there sat a man who was lame. He had been that way from birth and had never walked" (Acts 14:8). Don't read this too quickly: This was a real person. His whole life he had lived with a difficult disability. Some of you know what that is like, watching people take for granted things you would give everything to just experience. This man had never walked. Remember, there were no wheelchairs, no disability insurance, no building regulations for accessibility, nothing. So this man, in his never-ending brokenness, is listening to Paul preach, and as he listens, the Holy Spirit fills the space, the moment, the environment: "He listened to Paul as he was speaking. Paul looked directly at him, saw that he had faith to be healed and called out, 'Stand up on your feet!' At that, the man jumped up and began to walk" (Acts 14:9–10).

Now Jesus had done this very act, and so had Peter and John at the Jewish temple. But this is different. This is not in a Jewish context, not near the Jewish temple, not with a religious common understanding, and not many clearly agreed-upon bridges. As we've already talked about, it is not about the miracles, but the source. Where did the power come from, and will the miracle get people to the place where they can see that Jesus is the answer to every human craving and question? Well, Paul and Barnabas know, of course, that it's the Holy Spirit who points to Jesus and reveals the Father, the Creator of all. But the onlookers interpret God's work very differently. Lean in, because this happens in our world today all the time.

What Paul and Barnabas did not know is that in this very town there was a famous story put into a poem by a man named Ovid. Jupiter and Mercury, which are the Latin names of Zeus and Hermes, came to the next town over. As the myth goes, Jupiter and Mercury disguised themselves as humans and visited a thousand homes to see if anyone would welcome them and give hospitality. At home after home, they did not receive welcome until they got to the home of a very old couple, whose names were Baucis and Philemon. This couple, unlike all the others, welcomed them in. Then and only then did these two gods reveal their true nature and rewarded the couple. But as the legend went, the homes that rejected the gods were punished terribly.[9]

So in light of this commonly known story, watch the confusion unfold as these two Christians witness through the power of the Holy Spirit, using the gifts of the Spirit, and see how the act is reinterpreted through a pagan lens to the point where the gospel is about to be lost completely: "When the crowd saw what Paul had done, they shouted in the Lycaonian language, 'The gods have come down to us in human form!' Barnabas they called Zeus, and Paul they called Hermes because he was the chief speaker" (Acts 14:11–12).

In almost every culture on earth, the supernatural is normal and expected. In this place they worship Paul and Barnabas, because, according to their stories, this had happened before. But this time they dare not anger the gods; they dare not withhold hospitality to the gods like they had before. Once you know the local lore, their responses make much more sense. They call Barnabas Zeus because he is older, and Paul is called Hermes, the god of interpretation, the messenger of the gods, because of his preaching.[10] Now Paul and Barnabas don't speak the local language, so they don't know what is really happening.[11]

> The priest of Zeus, whose temple was just outside the city, brought bulls and wreaths to the city gates because he and the crowd wanted to offer sacrifices to them.
>
> But when the apostles Barnabas and Paul heard of this, they tore their clothes and rushed out into the crowd, shouting. (Acts 14:13–14)

I can imagine the moment in my mind, their faces turning sad, angry, confused, as they're filled with revulsion and yelling, "This is terrible! This must stop right now!" The crowd would have stopped in shock as they watched the so-called gods tearing their clothes and shouting at them. Notice Paul and Barnabas don't stay in front of the crowd but join them. They are physically demonstrating that they are just people, only people, nothing more! But now we know the local legend. I am sure the priest and crowd got scared that they had done something wrong and that the gods might kill them or curse them.

Then Paul addresses the crowd:

> Friends, why are you doing this? We too are only human, like you. We are bringing you good news, telling you to turn from these worthless things to the living God, who made the heavens and the earth and the sea and everything in them. In the past, he let all nations go their own way. Yet he has not left himself without testimony: he has shown kindness by giving you rain from heaven and crops in their seasons; he provides you with plenty of food and fills your hearts with joy. (Acts 14:15–17)

God is no longer allowing you to go your own way; the time of ignorance is over. Notice how Paul starts with the created order—general revelation, beauty, and food. The miracle was the first magnetic connection, the first bridge. Now beauty is the second bridge. Paul is preaching Romans 1:20: "For since the creation of the world God's invisible qualities—his eternal power and divine nature—have been clearly seen, being understood from what has been made, so that people are without excuse." And yet even with the clarification, the battle to root the source, to show the truth was difficult. The old ways of thinking were so ingrained: "Even with these words, they had difficulty keeping the crowd from sacrificing to them" (Acts 14:18).

And then the scene closes.

In both case studies, the gospel confronts personal sin, worldliness, and the demonic. The kingdom of darkness, realizing it will lose power over many people, does not attempt direct confrontation but the more subtle approach of syncretism. Syncretism is the mixing of truth and error. But more than lessons on turf wars, these two case studies remind and challenge us in two directions.

First, we must see the place and necessity of Holy Power in witnessing. Our world, cities, families, and online interactions are full of people from other faiths and pseudospiritual experiences, so acts of God will be received and expected. We are called to preach and pray for the miraculous, which open doors and provide access to the bridges that connect us with others. Angels, demons, miracles, deliverances, dreams, visions, healings—none of it should be dismissed. Rather, we should use it to walk people across the bridges to the great Deliverer, Healer, and Saviour. This also addresses some of the greatest needs found in many people and cultures where they live in fear of the demonic and see no escape.[12] The fear of the demonic, the gods, the burden of fate, the hopelessness of trying to make sure you appease all sorts of forces is massive, oppressive, and slavery-inducing, but we have the answer.

Of course, churches can be imbalanced. Many charismatic communities focus so much on the miraculous that they forget that signs only point to and affirm God's presence and his good news. The message still must be spoken and submitted to. Others reject all forms of the miraculous as dangerous, or simply not necessary. "Just preach. You need nothing else." Yet this stops the pattern we see in Jesus's life and the book of Acts, where four generations of people, not just the apostles, used power. In the works of Paul, Peter, and the author of Hebrews, ongoing power gifts are expected, clarified, and referred to. The miraculous should not be stopped out of fear, theology, unbelief, past pain, or possible abuse. Miracles do not replace preaching, but they are the handmaiden that prepares people from many backgrounds, both Western and non-Western, for the good news. And while we're here, if I might be able to just call something out? Please stop saying that miraculous "stuff" works over "there." Over where? What does that even mean? Let's be honest, when many people say that, it is rooted in pride and bias. This Western-centric statement has shadows of racial and colonial missteps. God's power works everywhere, with many people from many backgrounds. We need power in Germany, Australia, Canada, the United States, and Poland, just like we need it in Singapore, Sudan, or Vietnam. Missions in this global moment is to everywhere from everywhere. The only gravitational centre is God himself.

I know many amazing God-loving cessationists will say God still does the miraculous under his sovereignty, even though they hold that the power gifts have ceased, and in this we can say amen together. And we should always know the difference between those hardcore cessationists (like B. B. Warfield or John MacArthur) and the many that would have accepted this view but still experienced the unusual power of God on a regular but not continuous basis.[13] Either way, cessationism is rooted more in fear and reaction than in Scripture.

Cessationism feels very similar to the oral law of the Pharisees. They, as good Orthodox Jews, deeply wanted everyone to love the Lord God with all their heart, mind, soul, and strength. The oral law was built so no one would violate God's actual law. It was like setting up multiple fences that you would trip over so that you never crossed a red line that could have eternal consequence. The idea was rooted in a deep desire for holiness, but it was also rooted in fear. Cessationism follows the same pattern. It is deeply concerned that the average Christian will fall into false teaching and nonbiblical mysticism that violate the authority of Scripture. So cessationists set up multiple fences to keep us from even getting to that point. The problem is that this idea is not easily found in the biblical texts. It is imputed on the texts. It does not bear out exegetically, nor can it be at all defended historically.[14]

Don't misunderstand me; I'm not calling my brothers and sisters Pharisees or making the equivalence that cessationism is connected to salvation. My point is that cessationist theology grieves the Spirit, grieves evangelism, and violates the very book they love and appropriately defend. Admittedly, cessationism is easier because it just cuts everything out, but as Paul, Peter, Luke, James, the author of Hebrews, and Jesus demonstrate, our responsibility is not to dismiss experience but interpret it, case by case, and lead people into the fullness of the Spirit and away from spiritual darkness. Cessationists will, of course, accuse me and others of elevating experience or tradition over the Word of God. And yet time and time again as I've interacted with my cessationist friends, I hear them argue that the gifts have been so abused or that they have not seen this in their church, which is itself an argument from tradition and experience. They become what they are against, putting the final authority on their experience (or lack thereof, which is itself experience) and not on the Word of God. Not until the perfect comes (1 Corinthians 13:10) will we all become willingly joyful cessationists. Right now, we need the ongoing power of God expressed through his sovereign, unique acts and through *all* the spiritual gifts at all times.

So many times I have seen a word of knowledge cut through the most ardent atheist's pain and arguments. In my own church context, the story of our former HR director brings this home. She had grown up and attended church most of her life in the United Church of Canada, a liberal denomination that no longer holds to the gospel or even the basic creeds of our faith. Then her daughter had an encounter with the true Jesus and was radically converted. Her daughter invited her to church. Week after week, she went, cautiously. Week after week, she heard the gospel, heard the Scriptures explained, and so many light-bulb moments happened. Her social, moral-only church experiences turned into a personal, alive faith in Jesus. After preaching one morning, I was led by the Holy Spirit to speak to them. I knew the daughter but not her mother. As we talked and discussed some questions about the Christian faith, the Holy Spirit said, "Jon, ask the mom if her husband is a Mason." So I did. They were shocked and said, "Yes, he is." I shared how this was one of the main blocks to him seeing Jesus clearly. The agreements he had made by oath enforced great blindness. I assured them it did not matter if he believed any of it or not, an agreement is an agreement. They said, "But he is an atheist." I shared that they should begin to pray for all blindness to be removed and all agreements to be broken. Well, to my surprise, they went home and shared the story with him. He said something like, "Is your pastor a psychic? How did he know about this? Who told him?" They said, "Jesus told Jon." That was the moment the father began to wonder if there is more than just this materialist world. He started to come to church, attended Alpha, met Jesus, got baptized, and has served in our church ever since. The point is, it was the use of God-endowed power that was the door-opening act.

Countless times I have seen deliverances lead families to faith. I was just talking to urban missionaries in Toronto who are working with Tibetan Buddhist teenagers and seeing them come to Christ. Often it is the power of Jesus over the demonic that shows them that the fear that binds them is not stronger than the power and love of God. The act of power alongside preaching moves the needle and not some talk about the resurrection being historically valid. They are wrestling with questions of which power is more loving, more powerful, and more life giving. Another guy who comes to our church saw a demon while he was high. He was so terrified he called his Christian friend, who attended our community at the time. She laughed and said, "Oh they are real, but don't have power like ours; just tell it to leave in Jesus's name." He did, it left, and now he comes to church and reads theology at a PhD level. But his starting point was the power of Jesus experienced while he was high on weed.

How many Muslims have come to faith in Jesus through dreams? I was attending a conference in London a few months ago, and a Christian leader from a Muslim dominated former Russian satellite country told a story that is becoming so familiar. A young boy knocked on his door and asked if this is where the Jesus people meet. The pastor, very hesitant because of persecution and ongoing harassment by local authorities, asks the young boy (who the pastor thinks is a plant), "Who told you about this place?" The young boy says, "I had a dream. Jesus was in my dream. He told me this address and told me you people would tell me what to do next." Praise God, the boy meets Jesus and then leads others in his family to Jesus. Even a few weeks ago I was speaking to a former site pastor that has gone into the corporate world as a missionary. He and his boss are Christians and have a careful but open faith. One of their Hindu colleagues has talked about faith more than once. But more recently she has had a series of dreams where there was a large banquet, and she sees my friend and his boss, but she is never there. She simply asked my friend, "What is this banquet? Why are you there and I am not? I want to be there. Can you tell me how to get there?" Just amazing.

The goal is never to dismiss power or experiences but use them to help people come to Jesus. Years ago, when I was a youth pastor, all the churches in the area held a massive outreach for teens in our area. It was a powerful display of unity. Baptist, Evangelical Free, Anglican, and Pentecostals all worked together. And God moved in dramatic ways.

One night a young girl came up to me and told me she was a witch. I politely asked if she practiced black or white witchcraft? She said she was a Wiccan witch. I took the time to apologize for any Christians that had called her a Satanist. She was shocked that I had not yelled at her, called her a child of the devil, and that I knew the difference between styles of witchcraft. I told her, "I don't doubt your power. The beings in you that allow you to do what you do are real and powerful, and I know you think they allow you to do good. But the power in you is nothing compared to the power that resides in me. Would you like to see who is stronger?" From there I shared the power of Jesus, the true nature of the Holy Spirit, and her need to renounce one power for a greater power. She did not become a Christian that night, but the point was, I knew this was a moment to find the magnetic point, the bridge. The connection was that we were both possessed by non-human supernatural beings. We were both walking with a power that was not human. I did not dismiss, mock, yell, or make fun of her beliefs. Instead, I invited her to holy, life-giving, and true belief. Full of grace, full of truth, walking across the bridge, not burning it. Let me say this again, we must walk across bridges not burn them. The nature and use of power is key to win today.

Just as we saw in the Acts account, many will want to take the miracle without the miracle worker. They will want to use our Lord's power like it's magic. Years ago I received a call from a man who was deeply distressed. He said he was demon possessed and heard that I had the power to remove demons, so he called me. I asked some questions, and at the end of our conversation it was clear his life had real darkness. He started telling me about how he tried to get help from New Age healers and indigenous shamans. He had done so many rituals and gone to so many non-Christian spiritual retreats looking for relief. I simply shared that I was only a man, but the person I knew, Jesus Christ, the Jesus from Scripture, had the ability and power to set him free. Then I shared the full gospel with him and asked if he was willing to accept Jesus as Saviour, leader, and Lord. Would he repent of sins? Would he trust in Jesus's work alone by the Holy Spirit's power alone? His answer was a clear no. "I do not need Jesus's saving. I just need you to relieve me of this darkness." I told him the Scriptures were clear that I could cast out what was in him but then he would be empty and seven more wicked demonic beings would come back. His life would be worse. He demanded. He begged. I had great compassion for him, but he did not want the source of my power. He did not want a relationship with God through Jesus by the Holy Spirit. He wanted to be relieved from the demonic by Jesus's power but with no relationship. I told him I couldn't help him. I told him this was not like magic but was relational. He hung up the phone without getting the help he needed, but I would not proceed because he wanted power without the gospel.

But this brings me to the second point: We must always clarify power encounters with the gospel. Imagine with me right now that suddenly every person on earth is healed. Every single doctor and nurse is out of a job. We no longer need medical research. The world would certainly be a better place. But it would not be a saved place. Let me say that again: The world would be a better place but not a saved place. We must preach the gospel. Christian justice, mercy (as we will see below), and miracles open the door to the gospel and provide evidence for the gospel, but they are not the gospel. If you begin to think these things are the good news, you have fallen into syncretism and are preaching a false gospel. If you stop after miracles or power encounters, they will most likely be reinterpreted through the lens of other powers, the universe, or chance. Will the people be thankful? Yes. Will they still be lost? Also yes. What Paul wrote in

1 Thessalonians is critical: "[Turn] to God from idols to serve the living and true God, and . . . wait for his Son from heaven, whom he raised from the dead—Jesus, who rescues us from the coming wrath" (1 Thessalonians 1:9–10).

Religion cannot be a matter of coercion.

—LACTANTIUS

When force is applied, the will cannot be aroused. You can be compelled to enter a church against your will; to approach the altar against your will; to receive the sacrament against your will. But you cannot believe against your will. No one can believe except willingly.

—ST. AUGUSTINE

The link between holy living and effective evangelism could hardly be made more effectively. In particular, Christians stood out for chastity, their hatred of cruelty, their civil obedience, good citizenship. . . . They did not expose infants, they did not swear. They refused to have anything to do with idolatry and its by-products. Such lives made a great impact. Even the heathen opponents of Christianity admitted as much.

—MICHAEL GREEN

The willingness of Christianity to care for others was put on dramatic public display. . . . Pagans tried to avoid all contact with the afflicted, often casting the still living into the gutters. Christians, on the other hand, nursed the sick even though some believers died doing so. . . . Christian social services also were visible and valuable during the frequent natural and social disasters afflicting the Greco-Roman world. . . . "The impious Galileans support not only their poor," complained pagan emperor Julian, "but ours as well."

—RODNEY STARK

The test of Christianity is not loving Jesus, it's loving Judas.

—GEORGE WOODRUFF

CHAPTER 12

Make Christianity Weak Again

Now we turn to the next bridge, to a place where so many magnetic points grow stronger and break down barriers through the good news of Jesus. Here we see the power of God-given love, mercy, empathy, and radical forgiveness. And yet for this to have strength, we must face quickly the temptation to use political force or even violence to maintain any form of cultural Christian presence or power. Do you care more about the eternal destiny of people or about your own comfort or your desire to maintain some semi-Christian presence that is cultural but not personal? In this moment, the temptation is to try to hold on to something that is not rooted in personal conversion. The temptation is to feel safe, to feel culturally protected, but ultimately, this is not Christian. You could put it this way—here is the difference between crusade and mission. This is how world-renowned historian of missions Andrew Walls defines it. Read this slowly and absorb what he is saying. We desperately need to not only understand but feel this difference. He wrote:

> The crusading model and the missionary model are sharply differing methods of extending the Christian faith. They grew up in the same areas in the same period; they coexisted and went on side by side. But they are totally different in concept and in spirit. The

> crusader may invite, but in the end, he is prepared to compel. The missionary cannot compel, the missionary can only demonstrate, explain, entreat and leave the rest to God. . . . If the missionary cannot compel, then entrance is possible only with the consent of those to whom the missionary goes. It is necessary to find a place, a niche, within the society. The fundamental difference between the crusader and the missionary is that the missionary lives and works on someone else's terms. Though the colonial period brought all sorts of modifications, the generalization remains broadly true even today. The fundamental missionary experience is to live on terms set by somebody else.[1]

Are you by reflex crusader or missionary? Really ask yourself this question. There are no global Christian crusades movements taking place at this moment, but the dark shadow of compelling people to the ideas of our faith is everywhere, and it grows as fear grows. All across my social media feeds, as young men react to the Left, their memes are full of references to the crusades and Cromwell's puritan armies. The image is to recapture the strong, faithful, and violent days. Have we not yet learned from history? The love of a "Christian" country over the gospel goes against the very fabric of our faith. And so we turn to a section of Acts where we are given a master class in what it looks like not to cheapen our faith but to confront several shadows that haunt us.

We join Paul and Silas as they bring the good news to Philippi in Macedonia. Our journey begins on a Saturday morning: "On the Sabbath we went outside the city gate to the river, where we expected to find a place of prayer" (Acts 16:13). Question one: What is a place of prayer? When there were not enough Jewish men to start a synagogue (there had to be ten), the small Jewish community would then establish a place of prayer to the true God.[2] These gatherings would be made up of Jewish men and women as well as non-Jews who worshipped the true God, which again gives us the first clue of what we should be doing to witness well today. As already pointed out, Paul always started with those he had the most in common with and the most bridges with, which for him were Jewish communities.

So Paul and Silas went to the place of prayer, and as they do, it says they "sat down and began to speak to the women who had gathered there. One of those listening was a woman from the city of Thyatira named Lydia, a dealer in purple cloth. She was a worshiper of God" (Acts 16:13–14).

Lydia was not Jewish but rather a convert to the Jewish faith. She was a dealer in purple, which means she would have been a very wealthy woman. In our language it means she dealt in Gucci, Louis Vuitton, Versace, Dior, and Hermes. Listening to Paul and Silas, she encounters the fulfilment of the Jewish faith she had embraced, and "the Lord opened her heart to respond to Paul's message" (Acts 16:14).

Never ever forget this! Lydia was not more open or more intellectual than others; it always takes God to open our hearts to his gospel. We cannot get past our sin, our deadness, our spiritual bondage unless he cuts through it. And when he does, the results create a domino effect: "When she and the members of her household were baptized, she invited us to her home" (Acts 16:15).

Fast forward to another Saturday, and the church is gathering in the place of prayer and now also in Lydia's home. On their way to that same place of prayer, suddenly the next major turf war between the kingdom of God and the kingdom of darkness takes place. Why? Well, this is the first time that the gospel is being preached in Europe: "Once when we were going to the place of prayer, we were met by a female slave who had a spirit by which she predicted the future" (Acts 16:16). This woman is not fake; this is not some fortune teller just putting on a show. This poor woman is filled and owned by the demonic. What resides in her helps us understand the area. Her spirit has been translated *python* or a "spirit of divination." *Python* would make sense, for the prophetess of Delphi was nearby. She was supposedly inspired by the god Apollo who defeated the dragon python. So she used pythons in magical rituals just down the road. She was one of the most famous pagan prophetesses in the Greco-Roman world. This slave woman is connected to a source of dark power in the region,[3] and "she earned a great deal of money for her owners by fortune-telling" (Acts 16:16).

Now let's pause for a moment. This was a real person, and this is a real story. This poor girl was a slave in so many ways. Not only was she owned by men who used her, she was also a slave to an unholy, false spirit. This was no act; she was no fraud. She was possessed by a thing—a living evil, an ancient darkness that would take over her mouth and mind! Her so-called gift was nothing but a living hell, used and abused by both her human and satanic masters. There is no escape for this girl. She is owned by hell and men, and she would be used till she died.

But that is not the end of the story. As Paul and Silas walked by, that python-like spirit saw the Spirit of Jesus in them and cried out, trying to confuse and trying to confront. Just like with Jesus, heaven acts through those who follow and represent him now. "She followed Paul and the rest of us, shouting, 'These men are servants of the Most High God, who are telling you the way to be saved.' She kept this up for many days" (Acts 16:17–18).

Hold on, hold on. Are you confused? Why is the kingdom of darkness affirming that what Paul is saying is true?[4] The demon keeps saying, "Listen to these men; they know God!" And it is that statement and the chosen name of God that reveals the brilliance of evil. Watch this. To the Jewish mind, the cry of the demonized woman rings of truth. "Most High God" would be "holy God" or "*El Elyon*." But to the non-Jews, these shouts undermine the message that would bring the light of the gospel into this area. The divine name being used is generic, allowing each listener to fill in the identity of that god according to their own beliefs. She's telling the truth in a way that undercuts the truth—and this irritates the apostle.[5] As one Bible teacher summarizes, "There were many 'highest gods.' This title had been attached to Zeus, Isis, the mother-goddess of the kingdom of Lydia in Asia, and Baal. A pagan hearer would understand the term to refer to whatever deity he or she considered supreme."[6] Everyone hearing this would fill in the blanks and go, I already know that god, or that spirit. I already have the good news; I have heard all of this before. It is a way to undo and even neuter the gospel in real time as it is being proclaimed.

But Paul has had enough: "Finally Paul became so annoyed that he turned around and said to the spirit, 'In the name of Jesus Christ I command you to come out of her!' At that moment the spirit left her"

(Acts 16:18). In that moment, she was free. No more nightmares, no more ownership, no more perpetual darkness, no more haunting, no unholy thing speaking out of her mouth, taking over her mind. I wonder if she began to cry as the idea of freedom washed over her. Or I wonder if she got angry because she had just lost her power.

As usual, not everyone is happy that Jesus has shown up through his people: "When her owners realized that their hope of making money was gone, they seized Paul and Silas and dragged them into the marketplace to face the authorities" (Acts 16:19). No more money, and no more ability to manipulate and control. So these slavers, these evil men, use the justice system to get their revenge. Don't forget Paul and the others are Roman citizens and were not allowed to be punished without trial, but interestingly, Paul does not bring it up. You might want to underline that. At this time Philippi was a Roman colony run by magistrates. It was not against the law to speak about Jesus, but they would not tolerate threats to peace or order.[7]

Things go from bad to worse, and "the crowd joined in the attack against Paul and Silas, and the magistrates ordered them to be stripped and beaten with rods" (Acts 16:22). Okay, the rods. Magistrate's assistants carried around bundles of rods with an axe in the middle that symbolized their right to give out corporal punishment. Likely this beating was done with one of these rods.[8] Regardless, this was bad, humiliating, and left them with open wounds: "After they had been severely flogged, they were thrown into prison, and the jailer was commanded to guard them carefully. When he received these orders, he put them in the inner cell and fastened their feet in the stocks" (Acts 16:23–24). Paul and Silas are stripped naked in public, beaten, flogged, and thrown into a maximum-security prison. The inner cell was reserved for the worst criminals, murderers, rapists, and insurrectionists. Placing them among the most dangerous is meant to humiliate them further. But it does not stop there. This is a form of torture.[9]

Despite the injustice, despite the humiliation, despite the pain, despite the unjust assault for being Christian and setting people free, they are not overcome. Think on Paul and Silas's experience; they could easily have been bitter, angry, depressed, and asking where God is. "Why is this happening? I hate Romans!" They helped someone out of spiritual bondage, and this is the thanks they get.

But what do we find? "About midnight Paul and Silas were praying and singing hymns to God, and the other prisoners were listening to them" (Acts 16:25). Would you be singing "Amazing Grace" or "Saviour King"? I wouldn't be. But here they are, breaking out in song, singing to God. You see, singing is a form of prayer. Perhaps they understood something that many of us do not yet fully grasp: Singing about and to God is a discipline that brings hope in hopeless times. And worship is a guaranteed place of encounter. Remember that God inhabits the praises of his people, and Jesus said, "where two or three gather in my name, there am I with them" (Matt 18:20). One writer observed:

> Christians today who have not won the battle with bitterness over misfortunes they have faced, should look to the prescription hinted at by Paul by praying and singing. If we are hit by a painful or humiliating blow, we can plan revenge; give in to self-pity, or immerse ourselves in an attempt to get out of the problem. While this last option may be appropriate, we still could carry an unhealed wound, we may eventually act in unchristian ways. We must discipline ourselves to let the eternal truths of God impact the situation so that the sting of the pain is removed. With that perspective we can react positively to the crisis, and singing along with prayer helps give birth to that perspective.[10]

What a word for the church today! Pain, misfortune, humiliation, and injustice can lead naturally to bitterness, revenge, and self-pity. Does this not sound like so many blogs and Christian social media feeds in the West right now? Are these not the very reasons why many want a muscular version of Christian statehood and faith?

Prayer and worship through song bring us into the presence of God. Worship reminds us that we are not alone. Worship is beyond emotion. Worship brings us to the reason we exist: to know God and enjoy him forever! Worship moves us from sin.

In the middle of this injustice, with wrongdoing and worship in the same space, God intervenes in the most dramatic of ways:

> Suddenly there was such a violent earthquake that the foundations of the prison were shaken. At once all the prison doors flew open, and everyone's chains came loose. The jailer woke up, and when he saw the prison doors open, he drew his sword and was about to kill himself because he thought the prisoners had escaped. (Acts 16:26–27)

The jailer knows Roman law. There is a good chance he was a former Roman soldier or officer.[11] He knows that according to Roman law, like the Code of Justinian, if someone gets away, then you face the same penalty the escapee would have faced. So he knows he will be tortured or executed and decides it is better to take his own life.

But before he falls on his sword or cuts his throat, with no way out, in deep darkness, suddenly, just like the earthquake, mercy breaks out across that broken jail. Paul and Silas choose to stay! They stay in the injustice and show empathy, mercy, and forgiveness: "But Paul shouted, 'Don't harm yourself! We are all here!'" (Acts 16:28). To the jailer, who arranged for Paul and Silas to be tortured, Paul says, "Don't harm yourself." Most people would say, "Kill yourself! You deserve it!" Winner's justice is everywhere these days. Yet in this case, hospitality replaces hatred, and radical forgiveness replaces revenge. I am sure the jailer was thinking, "Why did you stay? I heard you were singing. I heard what you were preaching around town. Why would you love me like this? Why would you spare my life and my family's life?"

Bleeding, tired, and dirty, the two Christians respond, "Jesus."

> The jailer called for lights, rushed in and fell trembling before Paul and Silas. He then brought them out and asked, "Sirs, what must I do to be saved?"
>
> They replied, "Believe in the Lord Jesus, and you will be saved—you and your household." Then they spoke the word of the Lord to him and to all the others in his house. (Acts 16:29–32)

This is the mini version of what Paul writes in Romans 10:9, "If you declare with your mouth, 'Jesus is Lord,' and believe in your heart that God raised him from the dead, you will be saved."

Right here the gospel is given. What must you do to be saved? Confess that Jesus is Lord and king; Jesus is more than Caesar. Jesus shares the name, nature, holiness, authority, power, majesty, and eternity of God because he is God! Believe that God physically raised Jesus from the dead. This is the kernel, the baseline, the core gospel given again and again and again, no matter the audience, culture, place, or time.[12]

You might be thinking, *"Jon, when are we getting to more loving, kind, second chance stuff?"* Hold on, it's coming, but there are a few more things to really wrestle through. One of those very important moments is in the next verse: "At that hour of the night the jailer took them and washed their wounds; then immediately he and all his household were baptized" (Acts 16:33). This is the second time that an entire household, not just a person, comes to faith in Jesus. We saw it in Lydia's home and now this home. Personal faith can come through family decision. Welcome to the ongoing, pivoting gospel. How certain cultures choose is profoundly different. And since we now have access to the world online, and since many of our neighbours and friends are from community-first and individual-second cultures, this matters. Below is another older, historic example, but it is a total repeat of what we read in Acts. This is the actual story of how the appointed leader of Iceland converted to the Christian faith, and how that decision affected the whole nation, not just himself:

> At the Althing, the general assembly of the heads of families in Iceland (there is no king in Iceland; it is a democracy), a heated debate is in process. The issue is whether or not the community should become Christian. Powerful speeches for and against are being made, but there is no sign of agreement. It has been necessary, therefore, to go to arbitration and place the decision in the hands of Thorgeir, one of the most respected elders. He sits, hour after hour, in silence, a cloak over his head, as day passes into night and night into day again. At length he rises, throws aside the cloak, and announces his decision: "We will be Christians," keeping the festivals of Easter and Christmas. There will be a grace period of six months during which those who wish to use the shrines may

> continue to do so, after which they will be closed. The practice of putting female children out to die is to cease. There is grumbling and manifest disappointment on the part of those who favoured maintaining the old customs, but they accept the decision. . . . It is unlikely that Thorgeir, as he sat under the cloak, was agonizing over the doctrine of the Trinity. It is more likely that he was pondering questions of customary law, of spiritual resources for the community, and of the general well-being of the society. But why was his arbitration necessary? To modern minds, it seems obvious that the solution was for Christian families to follow Christian ways and for traditionalists to follow the old ways. No one in Iceland ever suggested that—it was a recipe for civil war. A single people must have a single code of conduct: "This is our custom."[13]

In time, we want to see if and where faith has really taken root, but we must become okay with and even expect household conversion once again in a post-Christian, pluralistic, and multicultural world.

This is demonstrated by Paul and his mentorship with Timothy. Both Timothy's mom and grandmother came to faith in Jesus Christ. Both of these Jewish women encountered Jesus, the Messiah, the Son of God, and shared this new fulfilment of their faith with Timothy. How do we know this? Because just before the greatest description of the nature of the Bible, we read these words: "From infancy you [Timothy] have known the Holy Scriptures, which are able to make you wise for salvation through faith in Christ Jesus. All Scripture is God-breathed and is useful for teaching, rebuking, correcting and training in righteousness" (2 Timothy 3:15–16).

By the time we get to Timothy, his family is already three generations into their faith being passed down, and Paul gives this important insight: "I am reminded of your sincere faith, which first lived in your grandmother Lois and in your mother Eunice and, I am persuaded, now lives in you also" (2 Timothy 1:5). Timothy's faith is sincere, and Paul says that this faith, which was on the inside of his mom and grandma, now also lives in him. Household faith, but personal encounter.

Let's get back to the jailer for a moment. Sometimes when we listen to this case study in a sermon, we miss the danger of this moment. We don't feel the risk. This jailer is hosting political prisoners at his home. And what's more, he cleans their wounds with water. This could get him and his family jailed, tortured, or killed. But the results are amazing. After the torturer washed his prisoners' wounds with water, Paul and Silas turn around and baptize him and his household with water to symbolize that the jailer's wounds before God are now clean. What gospel is this?

Don't take your gaze away from the food. The meal matters: "The jailer brought them into his house and set a meal before them; he was filled with joy because he had come to believe in God—he and his whole household" (Acts 16:34). They eat together! Jesus unifies us. Our unity is not ethnic, not monetary, not educational, not a common experience or history, not political. Our unity is in Jesus. Jesus brings us all to the table. Can you imagine sharing a joyful meal with your enemies? Hold on, let me ask you again: Can you imagine eating with your enemies with joy? This is God's heart for the West, for the whole world. You believe this, right? With your whole heart? We are getting closer to the role of love in crossing cultural bridges for the sake of the gospel—hospitality, not using political rights quickly.

Yet the greatest act of love in this increasingly cold moment is radical Christian forgiveness. Forgiving others—family, friends, coworkers, enemies—is the ultimate expression of love. This love is deeply jarring to many and deeply wanted by most people around us. Theologian Miroslav Volf beautifully confronts us all with this summary of forgiveness:

> Forgiveness flounders because I exclude the enemy from the community of humans even as I exclude myself from the community of sinners. But no one can be in the presence of the God of the crucified Messiah for long without overcoming this double exclusion. . . . When one knows that the torturer will not eternally triumph over the victim, one is free to rediscover that person's humanity and imitate God's love for him. And when one knows that God's love is greater than all sin, one is free to see oneself and so rediscover one's own sinfulness.[14]

Wow, wow, wow! This takes us to a deeper place that ripples into eternity. But the story is not yet complete.

If we keep reading, we come to an often skipped or missed point. Paul, after all the humiliation, after all the physical and emotional torture, after the injustice, finally brings up his political rights, but only after the gospel has taken root, not before. It's as if Paul embodies what William Shakespeare wrote in *The Merchant of Venice*: "Though justice be thy plea, consider this: that in the course of justice none of us should see salvation. We do pray for mercy, and that same prayer doth teach us all to render the deeds of mercy."[15]

> When it was daylight, the magistrates sent their officers to the jailer with the order: "Release those men." The jailer told Paul, "The magistrates have ordered that you and Silas be released. Now you can leave. Go in peace."
>
> But Paul said to the officers: "They beat us publicly without a trial, even though we are Roman citizens, and threw us into prison. And now do they want to get rid of us quietly? No! Let them come themselves and escort us out."
>
> The officers reported this to the magistrates, and when they heard that Paul and Silas were Roman citizens, they were alarmed. They came to appease them and escorted them from the prison, requesting them to leave the city. (Acts 16:35–39)

Paul says something like, "You broke the law, and you need to acknowledge it." The government officials, deeply concerned, play nice. So laws and rights are needed, important, and can be used by Christians. We will talk more about this later. But before you start wanting rights and political cover, let this part of God's Word confront you: Paul and Silas did not use their rights before, only after. Is this your natural Christian response and instinct? Is this your holy reflex? Am I willing to forfeit my rights so that others might come to faith in Jesus?

They rejoice in suffering. This not only makes them look more like Jesus but also results in a family of enemies becoming an eternal family. What are you willing to lose so that others might be granted eternal life? Does this mean we should let injustice go unchecked or allow abuse? No, but do we ever consider that Jesus wants to save our enemies? And what can we do about it? If these are not your deepest questions, you will never help win back the West or anywhere at all.

The story in Acts ends like this: "After Paul and Silas came out of the prison, they went to Lydia's house, where they met with the brothers and sisters and encouraged them. Then they left" (Acts 16:40). God uses different ways to reach people—preaching, the power of Jesus in miracles, earthquakes, and undeserved mercy. Conversations take place in different ways depending on the culture or situation. Think about the makeup of the church in Philippi: a formerly demonized slave, a non-Jewish successful entrepreneur with her family, and the head of the Roman jail and his family. And this is the church that Paul would write a letter about joy to a decade later: Philippians.

The focus of this chapter has been on why biblically expressed love, mercy, forgiveness, and hospitality are the best ways to walk across the cultural bridges left for us by God. So here are some critical reflections.

How we lose might be more important than how we win. Attacking others without knowing them personally is prevalent in our world today. Political attacks, put downs, unfair generalizations, and insulting memes fill our social media feeds. Our conversations are full of spiteful name callings, divisive satire, and facts without fact checking. And conspiracy theories abound. We know that we can grow movements (even churches!) quickly by tapping into preexisting feelings of resentment, anger, and apathy. During the COVID-19 pandemic and in many other moments, the fastest growing churches have been angry churches. But this is not our jam, this is not our source, this is not our calling. We can get seduced quickly into seeing anger as true spirituality, but it's misplaced. Passion, yes. Conviction, yes. But not anger. And so much of what we want to call "holy anger" really isn't holy at all when we're honest.

In the end, Paul and Silas did use their political rights, but they did not use them quickly. Why? The gospel mattered more. Paul would say to us today that his suffering allowed his enemies to be given eternal life. As he later wrote to this very church: "Whatever happens, conduct yourselves in a manner worthy of the gospel of Christ.... For it has been granted to you on behalf of Christ not only to believe in him, but also to suffer for him" (Philippians 1:27–29).

What power would you give up? What safety would you give up? What cultural comfort would you give up? What political agenda would you give up? This forces us to place our love of history, family, or country in their rightful place. It was Lesslie Newbigin who powerfully reminded us that "a church that sees the cross of Jesus as the central event of history can never identify any political order with the reign of God."[16]

What national right would you give up so that those you hate, those you struggle with, those who fight for everything you don't agree with could become your brother or sister in Jesus? Can you imagine, or stomach, the idea of that person or those people sitting at a table with you and then seeing them baptized? There is no winner's justice in that reality.

And this brings us to the power of hospitality as a door-opening event. As the West and much of the world is now calling loneliness an epidemic, despite all our access to each other, can the church, can we, can you, not see that hospitality is one of the greatest secret weapons to our being salt and light? But you can only be hospitable in relationship with people. Most cultures around the world lead with hospitality. We must open our homes, our tables, and our lives to others.

We must understand that hospitality, dealing with social concerns, fighting for justice, and offering racial forgiveness creates such strong moments that not only legitimize our presence but also act as grand moments to witness, no matter how dark, cold, or ideologically diverse things get. The Salvation Army has understood this since its inception. William Booth simply said, "Soap, soup and salvation."[17] Billy Graham once said, "The Salvation Army serves with the cup of cold water in one hand, and the Gospel in the other hand."[18] And as the great antislavery advocate William Wilberforce rightly said, "A private faith that does not act in the face of oppression is no faith at all."[19] Edgar Elliston summarized this reality for every church and each one of us as Christians.

> To evangelize with no intentional concern for the social or physical situation will result in a truncated evangelism and disobedience to the command of the Lord to love our neighbours. To do development without an intentional concern for discipling the nations will likely lead to a disobedience to the Lord's command in the Great Commission. And to disregard the context—social, physical, and spiritual—will lead to dysfunctions with both the evangelistic and cultural mandates.[20]

Read God's Word below. Ask the Holy Spirit to pierce you with verses you know so well, that you have preached, studied, posted on Instagram, or have on your mirror.

1. Let everyone see your good deeds (Matthew 5:16).
2. Love your enemies, and do good to them (Luke 6:31–35).
3. It is more blessed to give (Acts 20:35).
4. Overcome evil with good (Romans 12:20–21).
5. Do good to all people (Galatians 6:9–10).

We believe in a holistic kingdom—physical, emotional, and spiritual in Jesus's name! Whether it's the ongoing fight against human trafficking, helping the millions of children living in orphanages globally, stopping mandatory circumcision of girls, eliminating child marriages, working for affordable housing, helping immigrants adjust and feel welcome, fighting for religious freedom for all, protesting in the streets for the life of the unborn, resisting euthanasia, fighting against governmental overreach related to abuse of power, helping indigenous communities gain lost memory, working to get clean water, or cleaning up the planet, Christians must be at the centre of acts of kindness and justice. When done for the glory of God in Jesus's name, they are showing the kingdom of God is among us.

But as we do any of these activities, we must also preach the gospel. Hospitality is not the gospel; better laws are not the gospel; social justice is not the gospel. Imagine if all wars stopped or if all racism was removed from every human heart and every system. The world would be such a better, more enjoyable, and safer place, but it would still be a lost place. Christian justice, mercy, and miracles open the door to the gospel and provide evidence for the gospel, but they are not the gospel. If you begin to think this is the good news, you have fallen into syncretism (mixing truth and lies) and are preaching a false gospel.

And let us not forget history. Years ago I was at a conference when they talked about leadership and shadow missions. This is when an unconscious, destructive, or distracting goal derails an individual or organization from their true purpose.[21] In that talk, the speaker pointed to the many movements that started for the kingdom and then were lost when the gospel was made secondary. Here are three examples. In the late 1800s in Britain, a group of bank-owning Quakers joined together to serve God by supporting businesses that provided useful products and paid just wages. Today, the only vestige of its Quaker roots is the name of its morning management meeting, which is still called "prayer." The bank is Barclays of London. It followed its shadow mission, and the gospel is long gone.

Another organization, started in 1863 in Switzerland, was founded by a fervent evangelical and high-minded Calvinist. One founder said his idea of the organization was a direct inspiration from God. Another founder said he had been guided by the example of the good Samaritan to assist those wounded in war. Yet the organization has little overt Christian witness. The Red Cross followed its shadow mission, and the gospel is long gone.

Another familiar organization's original mission was to be a social movement for those in whom the love of Christ has produced a love of men. They were called to meet the young stranger as he enters the city and take him by the hand. At one time this Christian organization could boast that one in every six college students in the United States attended one of its Bible studies. This organization sent student missionaries around the world and invented two Olympic sports: basketball and volleyball. But few people would consider the YMCA (Young Men's Christian Association) an organization with an authentic Christian mission. It followed its shadow mission somewhere along the way and rebranded itself as the YMCA. The gospel is long gone.[22]

Some of you might have been feeling tense as you've been reading this section. Why? Because much of the time we as all-in, Bible-loving, Jesus-worshipping Christians cannot agree on what social justice is or which social causes are the correct ones. There is so much division and debate between Christians that, much of the time, this group of bridges seems to be burned down in the crossfire between Bible-believing Christians. One group weaponizes the fight calling it "woke," and the other weaponizes it as "racial or economic privilege." My church and your church can find no agreement. One group of Christians believe racism is still systemic in society; others believe that "systemic racism" is a progressive program to redistribute wealth and power to angry radicals and is a threat to liberty for all. They see it as a way to make others into scapegoats. There is a cultural battle in all our conversations, and we don't even tend to see it. The tension between individual and group, the essence of intercultural conflict, is at the core of so many of our cultural and theological red lines.[23]

But all is not lost. There is one place that we can all agree has the strongest magnetic pull and is the largest bridge to cross. And so I must end this chapter here. As already stated, the most glaring and brightest act of love is the forgiveness modelled by Paul and Silas. This cannot be debated politically.

The magnetic effect of forgiveness is costly but has been demonstrated for over two thousand years. In 2006, Charles Roberts walked into the middle of an Amish school house and killed five children. Immediately, the families gave forgiveness. I remember the shock and disbelief of reporters in the weeks that followed. The world held their breath at the forgiveness. But as the world moved on and the next tragic moment filled our feeds, this story of forgiveness just kept growing. More than ten years later the mother of the killer had been embraced by these families as friend.[24]

In the massive HBO hit *Ted Lasso,* you see the power of forgiveness. Though the show is far from Christian, it contains deep themes of love, mercy, forgiveness, and hope. You could feel the draw to the simple purity of Ted by the millions watching, longing for something that had seemed to be lost. Scenes like this one kept mercy and grace front and centre:

Rebecca: Ted, I lied to you. I hired you because I wanted this team to lose. I wanted you to fail. And I sabotaged you every chance I've had. Ted, I'm so sorry.

Ted Lasso: I forgive you.

Rebecca: You . . . What?! Why?!

Ted Lasso: Divorce is hard. You and me . . . we're okay. . . . It makes folks do crazy things.[25]

How we lose matters more than how we win, and the greatest expression of this is forgiveness. The church—you and I—must be like Jesus at the cross, saying, "Forgive them, Father." As God has done this for you through Jesus's work, so we must extend forgiveness to others. God's forgiveness comes first, and then he moves us to do the same. Forgiveness is not forgetting, and it is not lack of justice. Either the wrath for the injustice you forgive has been placed on Jesus, or the unsaved person will have to give an account on judgment day. Forgiveness is a choice, a crisis of the will, and a giving up of your rights to God to hurt them back. I have no clue where I heard this, but it is powerful and it is true: "Forgiveness is assuming personal responsibility for the emotional pain and consequence of another's sin."

How radical is your gospel? As I've heard others say, Paul entered heaven to the cheers of those he murdered. This is what we believe, right?

Forgiveness is not just for us to become like Jesus, or to be free and not controlling, but it can open the doors for witnessing. How serious are we about the gospel going out to those we are uncomfortable with, let alone our enemies? I invite you to slow down and pray this prayer:

> May God bless you with discomfort
> At easy answers, half-truths,
> And superficial relationships
> So that you may live
> Deep within your heart.
>
> May God bless you with anger
> At injustice, oppression,

And exploitation of people,
So that you may work for
justice, freedom, and peace.

May God bless you with tears
To shed for those who suffer pain,
Rejection, hunger, and war
So that you may reach out your hand
To comfort them and
To turn their pain into joy.

And may God bless you
With just enough foolishness
To believe that you can
Make a difference in the world,
So that you can do
What others claim cannot be done
To bring justice and kindness
to all our children and the poor.

—A FRANCISCAN BENEDICTION[26]

Men despise religion. They hate it and are afraid it may be true. The cure for this is first to show that religion is not contrary to reason, but worthy of reverence and respect. Next make it attractive, make good men wish it were true, and then show that it is.

—BLAISE PASCAL

It is Jesus in fact that you seek when you dream of happiness; he is waiting for you when nothing else you find satisfies you; he is the beauty to which you are so attracted; it is he who provokes you with that thirst for fullness that will not let you settle for compromise; it is he who urges you to shed the masks of a false life; it is he who reads in your hearts your most genuine choices, the choices that others try to stifle. It is Jesus who stirs in you the desire to do something great with your lives, the will to follow an ideal, the refusal to allow yourselves to be ground down by mediocrity, the courage to commit yourselves humbly and patiently to improving yourselves and society, making the world more human and more fraternal.

—JOHN PAUL II

CHAPTER 13

Answering the Right Questions

I first visited Paris in the summer of 2000 when my wife and I were on our honeymoon. We saw all the sites—the Palace of Versailles, the Opera house, Napoleon's tomb, Galeries Lafayette, Notre-Dame, Sacré-Coeur, the sculpture garden at Musée Rodin, and much more. My wife loves the impressionist painters, so her favourite museum ended up being the Musée d'Orsay, the old train station in Paris filled with impressionist art.

And of course, in the middle of all the tourism, is the grand and famous Louvre Museum. This jaw-dropping museum has a collection of 500,000 items, old and new, ancient and modern. On average, they display somewhere between 35,000 and 45,000 of those items at a time. They say it would likely take three full days just to see every single thing on display, and that still is not even close to all they own. But most people have one thing, one painting, in mind that they want to see when they go to the Louvre: the *Mona Lisa*. So we had to see it. Among four hundred exhibition halls, we finally found it. It was behind barriers and tons of glass. I was taken aback by how small it was.

Hundreds and hundreds of people crowd around trying to get a glimpse at this tiny painting. And for good reason. The *Mona Lisa* is an amazing piece of art. This and many other of Leonardo da Vinci's paintings are stunning. But I noticed something: Very few people turn around to see what's on the opposite wall across from the *Mona Lisa*. When I turned around, all those years ago, what I saw took my breath away. I stood, mesmerized, looking the opposite way when everyone else was vying for space to look in the opposite direction.

Across from the *Mona Lisa* is another famous painting by a guy named Paolo Veronese. He painted many amazing pieces, but this one is at a whole other level. Veronese's painting is called *The Wedding Feast at Cana* based on John 2:1–11. It's magnificent and monumental—six meters high and ten meters wide. It's all about Jesus turning water into wine, his first miracle. I think my experience between those two paintings is a brilliant representation of our world today. People crowding in and around a good, beautiful thing. The crowds are moved there, everyone is focused there, but hardly anyone turns around to see the miracle just behind them that is more monumental, more life-giving, actually *eternal* life-giving! Even *Mona Lisa* spends all her time looking at Jesus, but everyone else is looking at her. I wonder if she would want to cry out to the masses: "Turn around and look at the Creator of the one who created me!"

This is the third way we cross bridges and find the magnetic connections with those we are witness to. We need to turn people around to see the whole room. We do this not just through power and love but by intellect as well. We must engage with ideas to show that the Christian faith not only answers humanity's most deeply held questions (Why am I here? Is there a God? What happens after death?) but that our worldview is also the most beautiful and most helpful option, all while being intellectually rigorous.

So now we come to Acts 17, one of the most important passages in the Bible when it comes to knowing how Christians are called to engage intellectually with culture. This case study is truly a masterclass on how to access culture not only religiously but intellectually while remaining faithful, avoiding compromise, and still giving the gospel clearly.

First, let's remember that at this moment in the world there are no church buildings, no crosses as symbols of hope, no completed Bibles with the Old Testament and New Testament. At this moment there was no Christian concept of human rights gripping Western thinking. All of this comes much later because of Christianity, not before it. And it is from this place—with no power, no prominence, and no religious, political, or cultural acceptance—that the Christian faith engages fully with all of what the Greco-Roman world held so dear.

We have been exploring the stories in Acts 13–17. Three groups of people are exposed to the new gospel message in these chapters. The first are those with specific, agreed-upon theological knowledge—Jews and converts to Judaism. This is the group with the most bridges, the most overlapping worldview. The second group are those involved in non-Jewish religious practices, both formal and informal. We have seen the role of power and love in crossing these bridges over the last few chapters. But now we enter Athens, the home of Socrates, Plato, and Aristotle. Now the message of Jesus is coming for the third group: intellectuals with knowledge outside of God's specific working in holy history. Here, the intellectuals and philosophers of this age are presented and confronted with the gospel of the Christians.

By Paul's time, Athens had lost some of its grandeur but still stood as a symbol of great philosophical power. Yet the city was still unrivalled in its status when it came to thinking and architecture.[1] Athens featured a blend of spirituality, with the ongoing worship of many Greco-Roman gods, and enlightened philosophy. To use today's language, you had New Age, mixed with formal worship of the accepted gods, mixed with a passionate university philosophy department. And they did not agree with each other. Many in the university department didn't believe in the religious stuff anymore but still loved it for its culture and artistic beauty alone. "We have grown and abandoned all that childish thinking," they would say.[2] Not the easiest place to share the good news about Jesus, right? If you live in any major city on earth or just go online for a while, Athens should feel right at home.

As we come to Acts 17, Paul is in Athens waiting for Silas and Timothy to rejoin him. He is in one of the most beautiful cities in the world. We would tell Paul to take a vacation, enjoy the hummus, gyros, and olives, go to a museum, take a breath. Paul has given so much—and suffered so much. What a good time for a vacation. But as

Paul walked through the city, something massive began to stir within him—anger. Anger like he used to feel against Jesus's followers, but now this is a purified anger, a clarified anger, a holy anger. As we will see, it was not an anger rooted in religious pride but in sadness.

"While Paul was waiting for them in Athens, he was greatly distressed to see that the city was full of idols" (Acts 17:16). The city of Athens was home to both glorious temples like the Parthenon and thousands of smaller temples, all filled with idols and shrines. They were beautiful, the very centre of culture. Many still go today to see what is left, but this was at their height. Yet Paul's reaction was distress. The Greek word has real power, meaning "to be provoked or upset someone/something that causes severe emotional concern."[3] The word means to despise or revile and was used to describe God being against idolatry (Isaiah 65:3, Hosea 8:5).[4]

Paul can see beyond the human-created beauty. He knows that behind all this cultural glamour, expressed as a forest of idols, is human pride, the shadow of Babel, the presence of the demonic. Paul's heart is broken, deeply disturbed. And yet what he does next is so powerful and shows us how to engage our own world in deeply distressing moments: Paul shows restraint. He shows respect, and he works even harder to find common ground and cross the bridges so he can point many to Jesus. How different is his response to what we often see today! Many of us love to quote Paul, but we cherry-pick his theology, which hamstrings us and makes us ineffective.

Here again, Paul follows the classic pattern: "So he reasoned in the synagogue with the Jews and the God-fearing Greeks" (Acts 17:17). As we have already seen, Paul starts with those who have the most in common, with whom the most bridges are already built. Remember, Christianity is not a separate religion from Judaism; it is the Jewish faith fulfilled through Jesus the Messiah, the Son of God. But then he does not stay in the shelter of the familiar. Paul reaches out to two worlds at once. Both groups are so different, so opposite, so opposed, yet both are so very lost. Luke records that Paul also went "in the marketplace day by day with those who happened to be there" (Acts 17:17).

This marketplace is called the agora. This is not just some public park but the main public space of the city. In this one place, the economic, political, religious, social, and culinary parts of life all come together.[5] For Canadians, this is a mixed Bay Street, Ottawa, the local mall, Starbucks, Loblaws, farm markets, and great food. If you are American, picture Wall Street, Washington, and Whole Foods surrounded by a forest of idols for miles, and with really good coffee.[6] For those reading in other parts of the world, just add your own political place of debate, with a top university, your best grocery store, museum, and a ton of great restaurants.

Day after day, Paul is at the centre of culture, preaching and debating. In doing so, he slowly begins to encounter some of the greatest thinkers of that day: "A group of Epicurean and Stoic philosophers began to debate with him. Some of them asked, 'What is this babbler trying to say?' Others remarked, 'He seems to be advocating foreign gods.' They said this because Paul was preaching the good news about Jesus and the resurrection" (Acts 17:18).

Let's slow down and understand who these Epicurean and Stoic philosophers were. First, they rejected all the Greco-Roman gods that many others within the city still worshipped. They both believed in one god, sort of.[7]

Epicureans were all about living life to the fullest. For them the goal of life was pleasure, the absence of pain or disturbance. They were deists. They believed that god, whoever or whatever that is, was not really interested in life. God simply set up the world and walked away. At the end of the day, they believed life was all about chance.[8] To use our language, they were secular and agnostic, and I think the best summary of their view of life is by the ancient thinker Diogenes: "Nothing to fear in God; Nothing to feel in death; Good [pleasure]can be attained; Evil [pain] can be endured."[9] To the Epicureans, the idea of resurrection was not on the table.

The Stoics, on the other hand, did believe in a supreme god but were pantheists, meaning that god is everywhere and in everything. They taught the opposite of the Epicureans. "The world is divine, so deny yourself." They made life about self-sufficiency, courage, and duty. Self-denial was the key to life.[10] Resurrection was not on the table for them either. This group eventually came to believe in the immortality of the soul but nothing else.[11]

Both groups were a mix of light supernaturalism and scientific naturalism. And as they debated with Paul, we get such an interesting response! "'What is this babbler trying to say?' Others remarked, 'He seems to be advocating foreign gods.' They said this because Paul was preaching the good news about Jesus and the resurrection" (Acts 17:18). The word *babbler* comes from the image of a bird picking up and dropping a seed. A babbler is a person who picks up bits and pieces of information and then pretends to know what they are talking about. The word can mean "gossiper," "peddler of a second-rate religious opinion," or "show off." A good modern statement is "third-rate journalist."[12] Let's just say we have a real babbler epidemic, as most so-called experts pick up bits and pieces of information online, which seems to be resulting in the death of expertise. This comment towards Paul, however, was untrue and insulting—it reflects pride, vanity, and superiority. Why such a response? Because of what Paul was saying about the good news and the resurrection.

Their reaction to Paul still matters today. The internet is full of garbage on the resurrection and claims about what people really believed two thousand years ago. Many call Christianity a scam and lie. (See the QR code on the inside of the front cover for additional resources.) The accusation that it recycles older religious ideas is widely used but not historically true. This rejection of Paul's ideas reflects the true state of belief held by the average intellectually informed non-Jew of that time.

The only people who believed in physical resurrection were Jews, but even that was a resurrection that would occur at the end of time, involving everyone at once. That is why when Jesus rose from the dead, the disciples did not believe at first, because it violated what all Jews were taught was supposed to happen!

Pagans did not believe in resurrection at all. Greco-Roman thinking and myth is not at all full of physical resurrection ideas or beliefs. In one of the largest studies on pagan thinking about physical resurrection, N. T. Wright in his book *The Resurrection and the Son of God* concluded that "Christianity was born into a world where its central claim was known to be false. Many believed the dead were non-existent, outside of Judaism nobody believed in resurrection."[13]

Yes, many believed in an afterlife, in Hades, or in eternal bliss, but there was no coming back. Actually, they did not want to come back. In the golden age of Greco-Roman thinking, spanning over a thousand years, most people believed that the physical side of us was bad—a prison or temporary—and the good in us is the spirit. So death was liberation. Why, then, would anyone want a physical resurrection? Simply stated, the millions living in the Roman empire and beyond did not teach, believe, desire, or hope for physical resurrection of people.[14]

Well, things in Athens escalate. Paul is invited to Mars Hill, a large hill across from the Acropolis and the centre of philosophy and pagan religious thought: "Then they took him and brought him to a meeting of the Areopagus, where they said to him, 'May we know what this new teaching is that you are presenting? You are bringing some strange ideas to our ears, and we would like to know what they mean.' (All the Athenians and the foreigners who lived there spent their time doing nothing but talking about and listening to the latest ideas.)" (Acts 17:19–21). Paul is now taken to a venerable institution, the court of the Areopagus. Please don't misread this. Paul was brought not to stand trial in a forensic sense nor to be examined with a view to being licensed as a public lecturer but simply to have an opportunity of expounding his teaching for the experts of the day.[15] *Why this gathering?* Historians and scholars tell us, "These people on the one hand were famous for incorporating all sorts of new gods into their pantheon. On the other hand they believed they must stay vigilant lest 'new gods' undermine the morals of the state. So the issue here is understanding followed by evaluation: is this something good or not?"[16]

What was the response from all the religious leaders and philosophers of the day? Did they say, "Ah, yes, resurrection. We all know about that. Oh right, you are just using older myths from Egypt and Babylon and reinterpreting them." No, they either mocked or showed interest in it because it was *new*, completely foreign to them. This gets at one of the most prominent ideas floating out there in movies, podcasts, and books, that Jesus's resurrection is just another religious story that everyone sort of held and was just adapted by Christians. No, it was not.

Now we enter the masterclass we all need in our moment, as Paul demonstrates what it looks like to access three bridges that already exist: "Paul then stood up in the meeting of the Areopagus and said: 'People of Athens! I see that in every way you are very religious'" (Acts 17:22). The first bridge is crossed when he says, "You are very religious." He starts with their belief in God or many gods, the supernatural, dreams, miracles, angels, or something like an intelligent designer. This bridge begins the conversation. But quickly he moves to the next bridge, something they all knew, something found in culture, architecture, beauty, and religious history: "For as I walked around and looked carefully at your objects of worship, I even found an altar with this inscription: TO AN UNKNOWN GOD. So you are ignorant of the very thing you worship—and this is what I am going to proclaim to you" (Acts 17:23). Now bridge two is history and philosophy. Paul declares to these thinkers, "I know this unknown God." Okay, we need to stop and ask *why they built this altar.* The answer would have seemed obvious to them and still seems obvious to many around the world today. The people of Athens wanted to appease all the gods, so they had an unknown god altar to avoid missing a blessing or unintentionally angering a god they didn't know about. They were hedging their bets. This is a religious insurance policy motivated by fear and the unknown.[17]

But there is more going on here. Paul uses this altar's history as a bridge too. Notice, Paul has not quoted any Bible verses. He only used their history and their philosophy. So why is this altar here? We find the answer in the historical cultural context:

> Recorded as history by Diogenes Laertius, a Greek author of the third century A.D., in a classical work called *The Lives of Eminent Philosophers*. The basic elements in Diogenes' account are: Epimenides, a Cretan hero, responded to a request borne to him from Athens by a man called Nicias, asking him to advise the city of Athens in the matter of a plague. Arriving in Athens, Epimenides obtained a flock of black and white sheep and released them on Mars Hill, instructing men to follow the sheep and mark the places where any of them lay down.

> Epimenides' apparent purpose was to give any god concerned in the matter of the plague an opportunity to reveal his willingness to help by causing sheep that pleased him to lie down to rest as a sign that he would accept those sheep if they were offered in sacrifice. Since there would have been nothing unusual about sheep lying down apart from one of their usual grazing periods, presumably Epimenides conducted his experiment early in the morning, when sheep would be at their hungriest. A number of sheep rested, and the Athenians offered them in sacrifice upon unnamed altars built especially for the purpose. Thus the plague lifted from the city.[18]

Paul knows this history because he is about to quote this very person later. Paul is saying Epimenides, and now many of you, sort of know that God is out there, but I'm telling you that you can know his name. You can know for sure what God is like. I can move you from ignorance and mystery to revelation and relationship.

Paul responds to their idolatry while also agreeing with some of what his critics believed: "The God who made the world and everything in it is the Lord of heaven and earth and does not live in temples built by human hands" (Acts 17:24). He finds the truth in their philosophy. God is creator of all things, and he is the Lord of heaven and earth. This is, of course, a key name for the true living God as found in the Old Testament. He is the supreme Lord of creation and worthy of our allegiance. Paul looks across the landscape of Athens, filled with shrines and temples, and says, "None of this is him, nor will you find him in any of these so-called houses of encounter." Since the Stoics and Epicureans did believe in a god, they would be like, "Yup, we're with you so far."

Notice Paul is accessing everything they have in common—religion, history, and philosophy. But going one step further, Paul says with gentle boldness: These altars don't contain God! We cannot make him in our image; we cannot control him or keep him in these temples: "He is not served by human hands, as if he needed anything. Rather, he himself gives everyone life and breath and everything else. From one man he made all the nations, that they should inhabit the whole earth; and he marked out their appointed times in history and the boundaries of their lands" (Acts 17:25–26).

When we read this on a surface level, most of us would miss that Paul is still walking across their bridges. As one scholar wrote:

> He drew on the Epicurean idea that the gods, if they exist, need nothing from mankind (he is not served by human hands as if he needed anything) and the Stoic idea that the divine is the source of all life (because he himself gives all men life and breath and everything else). But all the time he is using their clothes to present his (biblical) message. Sometimes he has been rebuked for not quoting the Old Testament. But of course he does not do that here, as he would in a synagogue, because the Athenians did not know the scriptures nor recognize them as an authority. In apologetics you can exercise no leverage unless you use an authority your opponents recognize.[19]

God is sovereign; God makes humanity. He is the provider of all, the sustainer of life; he does not need our offerings. He started with one man (Adam) and has built humanity, planting the nations. We believe we are in control, or that fate moves the world, or that it is all random evolutionistic chance, but reality is God truly is sovereign.

The divine thumbprint is in the creation order: "God did this so that they would seek him and perhaps reach out for him and find him, though he is not far from any one of us" (Acts 17:27). We cannot know everything about God, but we can know he is a creator, a God of order, an artist, and a moral God. God's invisible qualities are clearly shown, from the fine tuning and order of the universe, to all cultures having a shared and untaught moral code, to our desire to worship someone or something. Observation says yes, moral insight says yes, order says yes, spiritual intuition says yes! The search for God is not fruitless. Notice how Paul uses the magnetic point of meaning and longing—namely, an intellectual and emotional ache we all share.

But Paul's not done. He crosses a third bridge by way of their own religious writings: "God did this so that they would seek him and perhaps reach out for him and find him, though he is not far from any one of us. 'For in him we live and move and have our being.' As some of your own poets have said, 'We are his offspring'" (Acts 17:27–28).

Paul demonstrates why we must use other people's blogs, art, writings, and religious thought. If there is any common ground, we must find it. The goal is to tear away as many barriers as possible so they can see fulfillment where it truly is or, I should say, where he is. To do so, Paul quotes two very well-known pagan philosophers: Epimenides of Crete ("in him we live and move and have our being") and Aratus ("we are his offspring").

Did you catch that? Epimenides of Crete was a catalyst that led to the altar to an unknown god. But what is more shocking is that the second phrase, by Aratus, was used in a hymn to Zeus: "Let us begin with Zeus. Never, O men, let us leave him unmentioned. All the ways are full of Zeus, and all the market-places of human beings. The sea is full of him; so are the harbors. In every way we have all to do with Zeus, for we are truly his offspring."[20]

Paul uses their own writings but is saying they missed the right "who." Zeus is not the true and living God; the God of the Jews is. I love what Michael Green, who spent most of his life being a pastor in Oxford, wrote:

> It would be easy at this point to suppose that Paul had given too much away to pagan thought. Far from it. He is very ready to challenge their deeply held prejudices. The Athenians prided themselves on being indigenous, and therefore superior to others. Paul maintains that all people spring from one source (Adam) and that it is God who allots to each nation their territory (vrs 26). That would have been painful. As we have seen, the Epicureans were materialists and the Stoics believed in cosmic reason rather than God. Paul asserts boldly to both groups that God exists, that he is personal and that we are made in his image. That is why the idolatry that both the Stoics and Epicureans practiced was wrong.[21]

Paul goes on the attack in all three directions: "Therefore since we are God's offspring, we should not think that the divine being is like gold or silver or stone—an image made by man's design and skill" (Acts 17:29). First, he says that all idolatry is unnecessary and wrong. Then he also rejects pantheism (the belief that we are all God or all part of God). We are the created, he is the Creator; we are made in his image. Paul then comes to the centre of his passion, his love, his only hope and tells the Epicureans that God *is* involved in this world, ultimately displayed through Jesus! God *can* be known and the universe is not run by chance or by random restructuring of atoms.

And again we return to what we have repeatedly seen, from Jerusalem to Paphos, to Lystra and Philippi, and now in Athens—repentance and resurrection: "In the past God overlooked such ignorance, but now he commands all people everywhere to repent. For he has set a day when he will judge the world with justice by the man he has appointed. He has given proof of this to everyone by raising him from the dead" (Acts 17:30–31). We are not God, nor are our inventions (idols) God. We must turn from false notions of God to see God through the person and message of Jesus alone. Jesus has physically risen from the dead and sits at the right hand of God; this is proof of his claims and his authority as advocate and judge. God has and continues to intervene. This worldview skirmish on Mars Hill has happened time and time again over the centuries.

The first man in space was Russian Yuri Gagarin. According to Soviet propaganda at the time, Gagarin went to space and did not see God, so atheism must be true. What was wrong with this concept is that they believed that going higher in our own reality means finding God. They not only had the wrong expectations but also the wrong understanding. C. S. Lewis heard about the Soviet propaganda and wrote this brilliant response:

> The Russians, I am told, report that they have not found God in outer space. . . . Looking for God—or Heaven—by exploring space is like reading or seeing all Shakespeare's plays in the hope that you will find Shakespeare as one of the characters or Stratford as one of the places. Shakespeare is in one sense present at every moment in every play. But he is never present in the same way as Falstaff or Lady Macbeth.[22]

Lewis's point is amazing. The only way Lady Macbeth or Hamlet, for example, would ever meet Shakespeare is that he would have to show himself—let them see him, interact with him. And the only way that could happen is if he had written himself into the play. Only then would they be able to not only know about him and see him but also recognize him. And that is what Christmas is all about! God wrote himself into our story.

The result of accessing all those bridges and finding all the magnetic points has been and will be . . . mixed. And yet what we see in Acts is the power of not only being confident in our message but being willing to engage other worldviews intellectually on their own ground, with their own ideas as a starting point for conversations, but always with the goal of pointing them to Jesus. We see the need to pivot, to look in multiple directions towards multiple contradictory audiences in the same cultural spaces. But in this global transitional moment, we must relearn the following: *Our answer is more satisfying and more beautiful than all other answers.*

For some the questions are: Is this real, is this true, is this verifiable, is this logical, can you prove it? And we can say yes. But others don't care if it is true. Truth is not the standard. They ask: Is this good, is it helpful, is it inspiring? And it is. We have the most truthful, satisfying, and life-giving answer. We have good news to share like Paul did:

> What good news Paul had for the Epicureans and Stoics living as they did under impersonal change or fate. Behind or within reality stands neither of these but a rather gracious, personal Creator, Ruler and Sustainer of all. For modern scientific humanity, living as it does within an impersonal universe that evolved quite by chance from the big bang to the last whimper of a dark and frigid night without star fire, Paul's message is also very good news. And for postmodern humanity this gracious, personal God breaks the bonds of pantheistic karma.[23]

Many of the other answers seem amazing until you live with them and see what remains after they affect one's life. We must show where so many of our friends, family members, and enemies will end up when they trust in or believe in other gods, ideas, and worldviews.

We must show them where the bridge ends and move them from rationality to revelation. Again Michael Green gives the best summary of Paul's moment:

> As we look back over this remarkable address, we can see that what Paul is really doing is offering them a fresh starting point. Paul was actually anticipating a situation of cultural collapse that had already begun but would fully emerge in Augustine's day. He insists on a new beginning, an entirely new approach. Reason, which made classical culture so great, can only get you so far. It can only operate on the data provided. Revelation offers a new starting point. Paul invited the Athenians to consider revelation. Classical thought had given the world so much, but was unable to overcome the divide between reason and will, between the spiritual world known by the mind and the physical world known by the senses. Blind fate would ultimately prevail. They were torn between two dominating forces, two goddesses as they saw it, Chance and Necessity; or, as we would put it, freedom and determinism. Truth was ultimately unknowable.[24]

When we read church history, we could say that Augustine's moment is now our moment. Read slowly and thoughtfully because he is hinting at the place we must go soon:

> Cynicism took over. This was a situation ripe for despair. The barbarians were at the gates. Augustine faced this situation by taking an entirely new starting point from the humanist assumptions of classical culture. He began with revelation. He proclaimed *The City of God*, and saw everything else in its light. Here was a new interpretation of the world, based on the living God. By it Augustine was able to conserve the best parts of classical culture, to which he was heir, and value them in the light of the gospel. And by it he was able to inculcate a new hope which dominated Europe for a thousand years. Our situation today is somewhat similar. The rationalistic worldview of the modern era has collapsed. It had imprisoned the human spirit and offered no rescue from the horrors of scientific materialism gone mad. We, like the Greeks, are torn between randomness

> and determinism. There is today no overarching framework for thought and action that carries conviction any more. We are strong on analysis but weak on meaning and purpose. Human origins are taught in every classroom but there is an uncanny silence about human destiny. Modern thought has been split between a quest for (unattainable) objectivity on the one hand and, on the other, a morass of subjective feeling. We need a new starting point.[25]

So many around us are longing for a fresh start and a new starting point. The person of Jesus is both. But we must not run from idolatry and non-Christian thought. Find the fingerprints of God and the common longing of the human heart.

I don't know if you noticed, but I didn't use the language of "bridge building." We are not building bridges. They already exist. We just need to find them and cross them. Do you see them, and do you want to cross them? I am not saying that if you struggle with something, you should place yourself in a context that would lead you to sin (Galatians 6:1). This is not a call for salt and light without considering temptation and sin. But the truth is, we tend to avoid too much and miss the bridges that lead to eternal life. And before you say, "That is so unbiblical and so compromising," I remind you that Paul just did this, right? You and I are not better than Paul. And more so, it was another missional thinker that reminded us what the church father Origen pointed out so long ago:

> Perhaps the proper conclusion is one that was pointed out to us by Origen long ago. Think, he says, of the gold cherubim that surrounded the tabernacle. Think of the gold vessels. Where did the gold come from to make the tabernacle in the wilderness? The answer, of course, was that the Israelites had spoiled the Egyptians. It is Egyptian gold that decorates the tabernacle; it is Egyptian gold from which the signs of God's presence are made. The tabernacle is hung with curtains of Egyptian cloth. It is the business of the people of God, Origen goes on, to take the things that are misused in the heathen world and to furnish from them things for the worship and glorification of God.[26]

Preach! This needs to be recovered big time in so many church communities. This is a truth that must cut through Christian tribalism. What "pagan gold" is around you that could become the place your neighbour, friend, or enemy encounters the true and living God and tabernacles with him?

Our arguments are not weak, as we will briefly explore in the next chapter. But are you trying to find the already existing bridges around you, or are you just shutting yourself off from all that you consider dark, worldly, threatening, and lost? As I pointed out before, why did *Ted Lasso* affect so many of us? Because in the middle of all the sexual stuff, swearing, and pagan thinking was an honest conversation about frailty, human longing, love, forgiveness, and the shallowness and hollowness of so much of what is believed on, fought for, and offered.

One of the best things you could do before the next chapter is to list all the intellectual bridges (shows, movies, blogs, songs, religious thinking, philosophy, art, nature, family struggles, personal experiences) that you could use to point people to Jesus. If your list is short, you are swimming in the shallow end at a time when the world needs deep-sea-diving Christians.

Religion likes to pretend its God is good and loving, but in reality, all religious devotion is fuelled by a secret dread that He is looking for an excuse to condemn those who do not please Him. While a holy God must punish sin in accordance with justice, He does not delight to destroy what He created and crafted with such care. God is the Author of life; sin is the cause of destruction. Whereas religion worships a sinister, sadistic god who delights in the suffering and destruction of people, Jesus reveals the true nature of God. He longs to see His creation saved from the just penalty of sin and to thrive forever in His presence. Therefore, the Son of God came to earth to save all humanity from judgment. What hope!

—CHARLES SWINDOLL

The lesson I learned from my years with the Muslim Brotherhood was the power of a unifying story, embedded in the foundational texts of Islam, to attract, engage and mobilize the Muslim masses. Unless we offer something as meaningful, I fear the erosion of our civilization will continue. And fortunately, there is no need to look for some new-age concoction of medication and mindfulness. Christianity has it all. That is why I no longer consider myself a Muslim apostate, but a lapsed atheist. Of course, I still have a great deal to learn about Christianity. I discover a little more at church each Sunday. But I have recognized, in my own long journey through a wilderness of fear and self-doubt, that there is a better way to manage the challenges of existence than either Islam or unbelief had to offer.

—AYAAN HIRSI ALI

CHAPTER 14

Finding Bridges to Religious People

As we have seen, God-given spiritual power, Christian love, and thoughtful Christian argument are all deeply important for reaching out in different directions to different people all at once. Our cultural moment is full of hope and opportunity. Seeing the gospel permeate the West and beyond for the first time or all over again is possible, not just plausible. This book is not a book on apologetics, nor can I speak into all the different Mars Hill moments we are being confronted with. But the next two chapters will summarize and reflect on how we cross the many bridges for those who are against or curious about our faith—the Stoics and Epicureans of our day. But before them, I want to start with those who have more magnetic points, more in common, more shared understanding of worldview and authority, that is, religious people.

Some of the hardest people to bring to Jesus—those who find Jesus the most unreasonable—are good people, those who are moral, kind, and nice people in all forms. Also spiritual or actively religious people find Jesus hard to meet when they begin to understand his call. Jesus says that being good, kind, or religious does not give you access to God. It is not life-giving; it will not pierce heaven.

There could be several more chapters on what to do and how to do it, but I want to at least take a few moments to summarize some critical thoughts on the *what*. The vast majority of people in the world are spiritual and religious, so bridges are everywhere. Muslims, as one example, talk about Jesus, Mary, and the role of Jews and Christians, and they are monotheist. You can go online and see grand debates between Christians and Muslims about the many issues, which might be helpful for you to do. You can listen or read the works like *Seeking Allah, Finding Jesus* by Nabeel Qureshi[1] to review the way we are called to respond. If you choose to read Qureshi's story, for example, you will see the need for responding intellectually to the questions and criticisms Muslims have, but very quickly you will also see the role of miracles and dreams in his conversion story.

In a major study done by the famed Muslim missiologist J. Dudley Woodberry, he and others summarized 750 interviews with former Muslims. They surveyed people from thirty countries and fifty ethnic groups. The researchers ranked the order of influences on why people left Islam for Christianity:

1. The lifestyle of Christians
2. The power of God in answered prayers and healing
3. Dissatisfaction with the type of Islam they had experienced
4. Spiritual truth in the Bible
5. Love expressed through the life and teachings of Jesus[2]

Do you see them—love, word, and power? But don't miss the rankings. Clearly, our basic, boring, everyday lives can influence others.

Are we willing to reach out to Muslim friends? My oldest daughter, Hannah, was once in a long-term conversation with a devout Muslim friend. Back and forth they went on questions like: Is the Bible corrupt? Is Jesus more than a prophet? What does her friend do with Mohammad's sexual life towards children? What do we do with Jesus's claims that go beyond prophet? The conversations were tough and challenging for both of them, but respectful. At the end, my daughter simply said to her friend, "When I look at the life, teaching, and character of both leaders, Jesus shines the brightest." These are the conversations we must be having with our religious friends in many directions at the same moment.

Many cry out that we have opened our doors too wide nationally to those who might want to replace or destroy the West and that there might be a coming existential threat to democracy. But many of those who have immigrated have done so wanting *more* democracy and *greater* freedom. And by the way, fifty percent of immigrants and refugees to the West are Christians—your brothers and sisters.[3]

As Christians, we must try to see from heaven's perspective. God, who controls history, has brought all people groups and all nations to us, so we must rejoice and get to work. It has never been easier to have presence with those different from us. Generations of Christians before us prayed for this, fought for this, died for this, but now that the moment is here, do we want God's answer to their prayers?

Of course, each conversation will be different, depending on who you are talking to—from a conversation with a Muslim friend, to showing the Jewish community that Jesus is the Messiah, to telling New Agers that the power they trust in is deceptive and not life-giving. Like a three-legged stool needs every leg to balance and work, so we also need power, love, and intellect.

As Christianity is diminishing in parts of the West, millions of people still claim to be Christians, and some are returning. And yet many of them (though I would say a shrinking percentage as there is not cultural cover or value left) are nominal Christians. They are Christian by ethnic history, family, or political bent or have Christian memory and experience. The Lausanne statement on nominal Christians provides the best summary:

1. One who attends regularly and worships devoutly, but who has no personal relationship with Jesus Christ.
2. One who attends regularly, but for cultural reasons only.
3. One who attends church only for major church festivals (Christmas, Easter, etc.) and ceremonies (weddings, baptisms, funerals).
4. One who hardly ever attends church but maintains a church relationship for reasons of security, emotional, family ties, or tradition.

5. One who has no relationship to any specific church and who never attends, but yet considers himself a believer in God in a traditional Christian sense.[4]

I remember having a conversation with one of my high school teachers when I was in grade 11. He was talking to me about my faith and why I needed to tone it down. I asked if he had Christian connections. To my shock he said, "Yes, I go to church all the time." As we talked, it became clear. He said he loved the music, the stained glass, the whole vibe of church. I said, "What about Jesus, the resurrection?" His response was agnostic at best. He loved the history and community but did not believe what Christianity was about. It's like looking at a beautiful painting but not wanting to meet and know the painter. He was a classic nominal Christian. And yet as we try to witness well, many people still are culturally Christian, and they are very important in this battle for the heart of the West and beyond.

The best-case study for how to witness to religious people is the late night interaction between Jesus and Nicodemus. Jesus uses their shared worldview, their agreed-upon authority (the Torah, the Prophets, the Writings) to point to himself. Just because there is common ground does not mean there will not be painful moments. Jesus's words are offensive and piercing, and it seems just a little too simple!

Could we read this case study together from John 3? "Now there was a Pharisee, a man named Nicodemus who was a member of the Jewish ruling council" (John 3:1). Three things set the stage: Nicodemus is a Pharisee, part of the ruling council, and is called Israel's teacher later in verse 10. Why does this matter? Well, this guy is amazing. He's a really good guy but does not understand his real need. And why would he? He was already better than most people.

So, first, he was a Pharisee. If you have been to church a lot, you know Pharisees get a bad rap. But don't miss this: The Pharisees were really good people, and in most places, they are viewed as better, more religious, more honest, and more helpful than almost everyone else. The average person in Israel looked up to the Pharisees. The word *Pharisee* means "the separate ones." They were lay preachers and scholars who cared about ordinary people, not the religious games and systems of the wealthy and elites. They lived with and hung out with everyday people, not the super wealthy and the super religious with all the power.[5] Their life was about monitoring and living out all the legal requirements of God's laws, plus 613 additional laws written to make sure you didn't even get close to breaking God's original laws.[6]

Second, Nicodemus is part of the Jewish ruling council called the Sanhedrin. This council was made up of the high priest, the priest class, and religious scholars. They were the greatest minds in law, Jewish faith, and history and had jurisdiction over every Jew on earth. It was like Israel's Parliament, the Supreme Court, and Vatican all rolled into one.

Third, he is called the teacher of Israel. Nicodemus was regarded as one of the best religious teachers in Israel. He was a serious thinker. This guy has the real questions; he would have had the PhD plus. He was the incarnation of smarts and religion, a real lover of truth worked out in life, and he loved people![7]

The educated, religious, committed, looked up to him. Most observers would point to his life, his giving, his teaching, his service to everyday people, and say, "That guy, he knows God, he reflects God, he understands God. He is a model for us! I am sure God must be so impressed with him. I sure am. If anyone knows God, it must be him." Yet this man is about to come face to face with the God he has spent a lifetime representing. He is about to come face to face with Jesus and find out the truth. Never forget how John starts his gospel: "In the beginning was the Word, and the Word was with God, and the Word was God. He was with God in the beginning" (John 1:1–2).

Their conversation begins like this: "He came to Jesus at night and said, 'Rabbi, we know that you are a teacher who has come from God. For no one could perform the signs you are doing if God were not with him'" (John 3:2). Why at night? Was he afraid? Did he want to guard his reputation? He was a prominent man and could not be seen with such a threat to the institution he represented. Was he personally here as a seeker? Was he here on behalf of other religious leaders to seek, to bring peace, to make sure that an open confrontation would not happen again like it did in the temple already?[8] We don't know, but what we do know is that Jesus wants to be with him, to sit with him, to share space with him.

Notice he calls Jesus "Rabbi," teacher, a term of respect and high esteem. "You have come from God; I know that you are the real deal. I see something in you and your actions. Your miracles point to you being from God!" Okay, notice this again: the signs—the power encounters—started the conversation, but Nicodemus still does not know the true nature of Jesus.

As we have seen multiple times in biblical and modern examples, Jesus will not linger on the miracles long. Jesus cuts Nicodemus off and goes straight to the heart of the matter: "Jesus replied, 'Very truly I tell you, no one can see the kingdom of God unless they are born again'" (John 3:3). Jesus says you cannot be part of the kingdom of God *unless*. You are not in the sphere of God *unless* you are reborn from above. Think about it: Birth is not something we can do ourselves. We cannot conceive ourselves, and we cannot get ready for our own births; our existence and our birth are the decisions of others. So too with salvation. It's a God deal. He starts the process; he brings us to life and to faith. He gives the relationship. It is all a gift, a miracle, from start to finish. It is another stepping in to make us exist!

"So Nicodemus, you think you are part of the kingdom of God because you are a Jew? Because you own, read, and try to obey the Scriptures, because you are religious, because you are good, because your body has the mark of covenant? Hold on, have you been born from above?" Jesus's words sit in the air as they always do with all-in religious people.

Nicodemus's response is telling. Either he really does not get it, or he does but wants to avoid this part of the conversation. So he says, "This is ludicrous, Jesus!" "'How can someone be born when they are old?' Nicodemus asked. 'Surely they cannot enter a second time into their mother's womb to be born!'" (John 3:4).

As one New Testament scholar wrote about Nicodemus (and all of us):

> He is a bundle of doubts, uncertainties, wishes, hopes, fears and habits, good and bad, built up throughout the years. It would be

> wonderful to break the past and make a completely fresh beginning. But how can this possibly be done? Can physical birth be repeated? Since this lesser miracle is quite impossible how can we envisage a much greater miracle, the remaking of a person's essential being? Regeneration is sheer impossibility.[9]

And Jesus responds, "Very truly I tell you, no one can enter the kingdom of God unless they are born of water and the Spirit" (John 3:5). Water and Spirit—what does that mean? There are four prominent views:

1. Water was John's baptism; a water baptism of repentance in preparation, then salvation.
2. Water means Christian baptism, and then you get the Spirit. The problem is that this act had not been given in the Christian sense yet.
3. Water in rabbinical circles is used for sperm, so the idea is that you must be conceived physically and then spiritually.
4. Water refers to a woman's water breaking just before the birth of a baby.[10]

I think the last two are what Jesus meant. Jesus is saying that we are born but we need another birth. That's why the next verse says, "Flesh gives birth to flesh, but the Spirit gives birth to spirit" (John 3:6). In other words, there is no evolution from flesh to Spirit. You cannot use your own power or the power of religion, good works, education, psychology, science, story, pain, or rights to meet God personally. It takes divine intervention.

That night under the stars, Jesus looks at this man he made, this very good, sincere man and says, "You should not be surprised at my saying, 'You must be born again'" (John 3:7). The bomb drops. Don't miss the offence of Jesus. Don't miss the call of Jesus to this good, moral, kind, religious person. No one, *no one*, can initiate a relationship with God, no matter their history, race, or religious acts! All your theological learning, all your spiritual insights, all your doubts, uncertainties, wishes, hopes, fears, and habits will not gain you entrance. They are not all evil, but they will not save you.

Jesus is accessing every bridge—the shared religious language, agreed-upon religious texts, and the human questions shared by everyone. He's saying, "Nic, you know God's will, you have the Ten Commandments, the Torah, and the prophets from Genesis to Malachi—you have learned all of it from childhood. You know who God is, what his will is for the world, for families, and for relationships. You can discern right from wrong, which makes you superior, right? You think you are far beyond the ignorant masses that flock to the idols and demons. Because you as a Jewish man are circumcised, you have God's mark and you are good, right? No, a real person that knows God does not trust in what they do because they cannot do it all the time! God is perfect and demands perfection; you need heaven to change you because your best efforts, Nicodemus, *your best efforts* don't cut it . . . no pun intended."

I have always loved this illustration:

> An Arabian Chicken Little story tells of a young Arab who was traveling along a road on his donkey when he came upon a small, fuzzy object lying in the road. He dismounted to look more closely and found a sparrow lying on its back with its scrawny legs thrust skyward. At first he thought it was dead, but closer investigation proved the bird to be very much alive. The young man asked the sparrow if he was all right. The sparrow replied, "Yes." Then the young man said, "What are you doing lying on your back with your legs pointed toward the sky?" The sparrow responded that he had heard a rumour that the sky was falling, so he was holding his legs up to support it. Then he replied, "You surely don't think you're going to hold it up with those two scrawny legs, do you?" The sparrow, after a very solemn look, retorted, "One does the best he can."[11]

Jesus keeps going, "The wind blows wherever it pleases. You hear its sound, but you cannot tell where it comes from or where it is going. So it is with everyone born of the Spirit" (John 3:8). "With no knowledge of scientific meteorology as we understand it, wind for the ancients had something mysterious and unpredictable about it."[12] As with the wind, so with the Holy Spirit. God moves in and calls, saves, redeems, transforms! The Spirit is unexpected, powerful, all consuming, and never starts with you being good or moral.

The penny drops. "'How can this be?' Nicodemus asked. 'You are Israel's teacher,' said Jesus, 'and do you not understand these things?'" (John 3:9–10). Desperately, Nicodemus is pulling out all his philosophy, his theology, and his religious background, which has taught him that religion—the act of personal righteousness and ethnic history—will gain one a relationship with God. Jesus is saying faith first and then action. Good works come after being born again, not as entrance but as signs of a new life given!

> Very truly I tell you, we speak of what we know, and we testify to what we have seen, but still you people do not accept our testimony. I have spoken to you of earthly things and you do not believe; how then will you believe if I speak of heavenly things? No one has ever gone into heaven except the one who came from heaven—the Son of Man. (John 3:11–13)

Jesus is saying something like this: "Listen, Nic, you and I both know no person in their own power has ever ascended into heaven. That was the sin of Satan, the son of the dawn, but he could not do it. Think on Babel, as we the human race tried and could not do it. Every time you try going up, you always fall down. But I'm different. My authority comes from heaven. I have more authority than you, more than all the books that have been written. I have more authority than the temple. See, humans cannot physically ascend to heaven, but God can come among us and come as a man. Me—that is what I am saying! And just in case you are missing what I am saying, I am the Son of Man, and I existed before I was born and I came from heaven."

Nicodemus was an Old Testament expert. Right when Jesus said "Son of Man," Nicodemus knew what Jesus was claiming. This thirty-something uneducated, unaffirmed, backwater leader was claiming to be from heaven. Even more, he was claiming to be the One they all had been waiting on for generations. Back to Daniel 7 we go once again.

Before Nicodemus could respond, Jesus keeps going and uses the

Old Testament bridge again: "Just as Moses lifted up the snake in the wilderness, so the Son of Man must be lifted up, that everyone who believes may have eternal life in him" (John 3:14–15). Nicodemus would understand this reference and all the implications. Jesus refers back to Numbers 21,

> They traveled from Mount Hor along the route to the Red Sea, to go around Edom. But the people grew impatient on the way; they spoke against God and against Moses, and said, "Why have you brought us up out of Egypt to die in the wilderness? There is no bread! There is no water! And we detest this miserable food!"
>
> Then the LORD sent venomous snakes among them; they bit the people and many Israelites died. The people came to Moses and said, "We sinned when we spoke against the LORD and against you. Pray that the LORD will take the snakes away from us." So Moses prayed for the people.
>
> The LORD said to Moses, "Make a snake and put it up on a pole; anyone who is bitten can look at it and live." So Moses made a bronze snake and put it up on a pole. Then when anyone was bitten by a snake and looked at the bronze snake, they lived. (Numbers 21:4–9)

Just as our Jewish ancestors had to only look up and trust in God's work to be saved, so you must do the same. "Nicodemus, *look up*. Trust and give your life to the One that will be lifted up and you will be healed in all ways. And by the way, Nic, I am going to be lifted up! To be born again, to be born from above, to be known, to be forgiven for sin against God, you need to look to me and stop looking at yourself." Here is the point: Jesus is telling him that "new birth comes through the simple gaze of faith; not by a perfect faith!"[13]

What lessons do we see in how to witness well? What is the pattern we must follow, especially to deeply religious people? Face-to-face conversations are best. Access common beliefs, assumptions, Scriptures, images, and ideas. For example, I have found that talking about what Christian images mean (the pelican and peacock, the gospel animals, the Chi Rho, the dove, the Alpha and Omega, the cross, the victorious lamb, the anchor, the fish) with nominal Christians is an amazing way to speak about the gospel. We did a full sermon series on these images, and so many found it helpful to bring the gospel to cultural Christians or those who are otherwise religious.

No matter where the conversation starts, it must lead to repentance, resurrection, and personal relationship, to the killing of religious activity as salvation, and to the denial of moralism as the answer to purpose, life, and eternal hope. We must show them the absurdity and hollowness of self-trust.

This was clearly demonstrated to me on an airplane flight from New Jersey to Louisville, Kentucky. I was on my way to speak at a church about implementing spiritual gifts and spiritual disciplines well in their conservative context. There are no direct flights from Toronto to Louisville, so I had to go through Jersey. As I was preparing to get on the plane, I was suddenly surrounded by a large number of Muslim men.

Now this is a pretty normal experience for me, living in Toronto, and I'm very comfortable with my friends from different parts of the world, but I was shocked to see so many on a flight to Louisville, Kentucky. I was perplexed, not expecting this as I flew into the south of the United States. But what I didn't know was that Louisville has become a key hub for immigrants. I got on the plane, sat down, started getting ready to watch some Netflix, and the Holy Spirit said, "Jon, do you see that man?" I said, "Yes, I see him." He said, "He's Muslim," and I said, "Yes, that's obvious by his dress." "There is more, he is an imam," He said. "He's going to sit beside you and you need to witness to him."

My heart sank, because I really wanted to watch Netflix and I did not want to have a massive debate with this Muslim man. Obviously, I don't have the gift of evangelism and obviously, I need to read the book I am writing and you are reading right now. Anyway, of course he sat beside me and we began to talk. He asked me, "What do you do for a living?" I told him that I am a pastor and he said, "Oh, I have never met a Christian pastor before." I asked him what he did for a living and he said, "I am a Muslim imam." I almost said out loud, "I know . . . I've been expecting you." But I didn't. Well, you can imagine how the conversation went: Is Jesus prophet or the son of God? Is the Bible corrupted or not? How does one get saved? The conversation went on and on. Then we got to the idea of someone dying for you, replacing your work for his. "That is ludicrous," he said. I responded, "No, it's not ludicrous; it's mercy. This is the only hope we have." I was shocked at his kind of arrogance about his own ability.

I asked him directly, "Do you actually think on judgment day, when you face Allah in all of his holiness, that you will be able to stand, that your good will outweigh your evil?" He replied, "Yes. I know myself. I know what I think, how I've treated myself and others and so do you." I responded, "There is no way that your good will outdo your evil. Your self-trust is a massive gamble." And then I read him John 3:16–18. "I will trust another's work because no matter who I am or what I do, it will never be enough." I went on Amazon and pointed him to books on why the Bible is not corrupt, and then we kindly parted ways to both go and speak at religious gatherings in the city, but for different kingdoms. The hardest people to convince about their need for a Saviour are those who are the most committed to their own saving through their own actions. That is why Jesus started the Sermon on the Mount with the words "Blessed are the poor in spirit"—not the poor, the *poor in Spirit*. Blessed are those who are lowly and humble, those who truly know their condition before God.[14]

Only when a person knows they are in this trouble without and before God do they become poor in spirit. It is the ancient cry, *God be merciful to me, a sinner!* This saying is for when a person admits that they have a deep need for God and then they will enter the kingdom. This saying is not about self-hatred or saying we don't have personal value. It is an honest acknowledgment of the truth that we need God. This is the fullest form of repentance. One scholar said this saying is "a full, honest, factual, conscious, and conscientious recognition before God of our personal moral unworthiness."[15]

Many people that are deeply religious cannot believe the gospel of grace because it either undermines their self-righteousness and self-ability or, I suspect more often than not, seems too good to be true. Deeply engrained in us by the fall is this idea of a scale—that good must outbalance bad. And of course because of Jesus, we know that's not true, and yet communicating that to our deeply religious friends is a difficult task. Let me just give two illustrations, two word pictures, that come from the worlds of money and garbage.

I have heard in France there are generational mortgages. That is, the cost of certain homes or buildings are so expensive you will never pay off the debt. The mortgage is passed down generation to generation. So imagine if you had a $300 million mortgage. The truth is, you couldn't pay it off; your children could not pay it off, and probably your great-great grandchildren could not pay it off either. You are drowning in debt, and there's no way out. Then unexpectedly, someone, out of mercy, walks into the bank and pays off not only the $300 million but also the penalty for breaking the mortgage for you and your family. That is what the gospel is! Rare, yes; shocking, yes; hardly ever seen, yes.

The other one is from the world of garbage. Garbage—really, Jon? Yes. My favourite day of the week is garbage day. It's like the dishwasher. There are always two people in a marriage—the one who stacks the dishwasher with precision, knows how everything fits for that perfect wash, and when it is finished knows where every dish and utensil goes. The other is an insane, out-of-control individual who throws everything in, slams it shut, and hopes it works. (If you're married or you have roommates, you know who you are.) The same is true with garbage. I am the organized control freak. All week long, I organize recycling into plastic, paper, and cardboard. I have four different bins, and I love organizing all of it. And when it's garbage day, I take out our garbage and recycling in an orderly way, and suddenly my house feels lighter and more free. Then I go to work, and these magic fairies come, all my garbage disappears, and I move on with my life.

But imagine that one day, there is a knock at your door. There stands a man and behind him is every single piece of trash you have produced. Every used tampon and piece of toilet paper. Every fast food container; all the boxes, bins, clothing, shampoo bottles—every single piece of garbage you have discarded since you were born. This man says, "This is your problem. You did this; you need to take care of all this garbage and pay for its proper disposal." How overwhelming! And the truth is, we could not even deal with many of the items because they take thousands or tens of thousands of years to decompose.

You must be born again—you must pay off the mortgage, you must deal with your garbage. It is impossible, unless there is a third way, less tiring way, a kinder way, the only Way.

I love the idea that Gerald Bray outlined in his book *God is Love*:

> The point Jesus was trying to make is that moral behaviour, good and necessary as it is, can never get to the heart of the problem, which is fundamentally spiritual. Outward observances have their place and may indeed be necessary if society is to function the way it should, but they are no substitute for a living relationship with God. When morality leads to moralism, it creates a simulacrum of Christianity which resembles the real thing about as much as a wax figure at Madame Tussaud's resembles the human being it represents. From a distance we can easily be fooled, but the closer we get to it the more we see that what appears to be vibrant with life is in fact a mute object incapable of fulfilling the promise it seems to hold out to those who pass by.[16]

I'm reminded of one woman who came to faith in our community. She had a deep Catholic history but had never encountered Jesus in a personal way. When she finally understood the Christian faith and message, I said, "Isn't it so amazing? You now know the person on the crucifix personally!" She said, "Yes!" Then I said, "Now when you say the Apostles' Creed, you mean it; it's really true. You don't just recite it but confess it!" The joy was incredible, but it took work to get there.

In our increasingly diverse surroundings, it is wise to share God's love with those who have the most bridges. But they are not the only ones we need to share with.

Faith is a fairy tale for people afraid of the dark.

—STEPHEN HAWKING

Atheism is a fairy story for people afraid of the light.

—JOHN LENNOX

Christians believe in the Virgin birth of Jesus. Materialists believe in the virgin birth of the cosmos. Choose your miracle.

—GLEN SCRIVENER

My argument against God was that the universe seemed so cruel and unjust. But how had I got this idea of just and unjust? A man does not call a line crooked unless he has some idea of a straight line. What was I comparing this universe with when I called it unjust?

—C. S. LEWIS

CHAPTER 15

Finding Bridges to Christian Critics

There truly is nothing new under the sun. If you read Roman critics of Christianity in the first four hundred years of church (Pliny, Galen, Celsus, Porphyry, and Julian the Apostate), the attacks they levelled at us are basically the same as those today. In his amazing book *The Christians as the Romans Saw Them*, Robert Wilken summarizes the attacks as these:

> What the pagan critics say about Christianity is not insignificant for Christian theology. Many of the themes which have played a role in the history of Christian thought and are still debated today were first adumbrated in the dialogue between Christianity and the classical intellectual tradition. Some of these are: faith and reason, the relation of God to the world, *creatio ex nihilo* (creation out of nothing), the relation of Christianity to Judaism, the status of Jesus and His relation to God, the historical reliability of the Scriptures, Christianity and civil religion, and revelation of God in history.
>
> In some cases—for example, the doctrine of creation out of nothing—it was a pagan critic who first grasped that Christian statements about God required a new view of the process of creation. Several decades before Christian thinkers had given attention

> to the problem, Galen pointed out the philosophical difficulties of the biblical presentation of creation. Christian thinkers were forced to think through their views with greater care. Not long after pagans had raised the issue in debates with Christians, Christian theologians began to assert, for the first time in the history of Christian thought, that creation out of nothing is a fundamental doctrine.[1]

The Roman attacks are still around today, plus many, many more. And so this next section is meant to summarize and provide resources for thinking deeply about the faith, so when you listen to that podcast, see that new Netflix show, or talk to a neighbour, you have given some thought to your faith and have access to strong Christian thinking.

One of the most common criticisms from atheists, Muslims, liberal Christians, or the latest conspiracy podcast is that the Bible is not reliable—the texts are corrupted, they are written later than stated, the list goes on. But if you slow down and listen and read, you will find how amazing and trustworthy the texts are. It was a conversation between a Christian friend and Nabeel Qureshi (who we talked about in the last chapter) that, when he walked through the trustworthiness of Scripture, brought him before Jesus's face. After hours of conversations, he summarized his friend's response with this:

> First, while there are indeed many variations of the Bible obtained from more than 5,000 Greek manuscripts, there is such a large amount of early manuscript evidence and such a concordance between those manuscripts that we can reconstruct the Bible and be certain of about 95% of the original content. Second, no doctrine of the Bible is in jeopardy by any of the variations.
>
> Third, there are so many quotations of and references to the New Testament from the ancient world that we can reconstruct practically all of it from early quotations alone. Fourth, there are multiple fragments of manuscripts that can be dated to within a couple of centuries after Christ's death which we have in our possession even now (the earliest dating to less than 100 years after Christ, AD 125). Fifth, . . . whole copies of the Bible are available

> from around three centuries after Christ's death. Finally, the previously mentioned estimate of 95% accuracy was a conservative one; in actuality it is closer to 98 or 99%.[2]

Another great summary comes from Alister McGrath, a world-renowned theologian and scientist from Oxford. His summary from the Alpha film series begins to show how much strength and evidence there is as one uses the academic discipline of textual criticism.

> Textual criticism examines the number of copies of early texts that we have available to us today, and it looks at the time gap between the original document and the earliest copy that we have. Basically, the more manuscripts we have, and the earlier they are, the less dark there's going to be about the original.
>
> So let's compare the Bible to other texts in ancient history, ones that are widely used in schools and universities. Let's look at the Greek historians Herodotus and Thucydides. They both wrote in the fifth century BC. But the earliest copy of their writings that we have dates from AD 900, and that makes a 1,300 year time lapse, and even then, we only have eight copies of these manuscripts in the first place. Or look at the roman historian Tacitus. There's a thousand-year gap between his book being written and our first manuscript, and we only have twenty copies. Or another classic, Caesar's *Gallic Wars*: 950 years between the book being written and our first manuscript copy, and even then we only have nine or ten copies of these manuscripts. Again, with Livy's famous *History of Rome*: a 900 year gap between the book being written and our first manuscript, and we only have twenty copies of this. But when it comes to the New Testament—well, it's very different.
>
> The New Testament was written between about AD 40 and 100; we have manuscript evidence going back as early as AD 130, with full manuscripts by AD 350. We have more than 5,300 Greek manuscripts, 10,000 Latin translations, and 9,300 others. So you know we can be pretty confident in the accuracy, the authenticity, and the integrity of the New Testament Scriptures that have been passed down to us today. The remarkable thing about the Bible is

> there's such a short chronological distance between the events being described and our first manuscripts. So in many ways, Bible scholars are in a very fortunate position of being able to check these things out and finding that they are much more reliable than, for example, some of the alternatives you're looking at.
>
> As a scholar I am more than happy to say I trust this. I take it very, very seriously. I rely on it.[3]

Beyond the historical reliability of the text, never underestimate the power of just getting people to read the Bible. Never forget the written Word of God is alive, active (Hebrews 4:12), and God-breathed (2 Timothy 3:16). Scripture is not just intellectually engaging and internally coherent; it is the place where God speaks. This is seen in the amazing conversion story of James Orr, now the associate professor of philosophy of religion at the Faculty of Divinity at Cambridge University. The summary of his conversion was outlined in a conversation with Justin Brierley:

> At school, James had studied Greek and Latin. He was almost fluent in reading Greek by the time he arrived at university for a degree in classics. Up to that point, James says he had only read the ancient works of the great playwrights and philosophers that were part of his reading list. But one day, a Christian friend gave James the New Testament in its original language—Koine Greek. James says he vividly remembers the thrill of being able to read the Gospels in their original language. Of course, he had frequently heard English translations of the Bible being read in public before but had never really thought about it as a historical book. . . .
>
> As James started to read the Gospels for himself in Greek, he realized these accounts were written to be understood as real historical records just as much as any of the histories and annals he was familiar with from Thucydides, Herodotus, and Plutarch. James was also impressed by how well preserved these texts were compared to most of the ancient literature he was familiar with. Most significantly, the life of Jesus also suddenly came to life in a new way. Having become intrigued as an undergraduate by the

> discovery of a real, historical Jesus of Nazareth, he went on to test whether the Christ of history may also be the Christ of today. . . .
>
> Yet something had ignited inside James. The Jesus of history who had consumed his intellectual interest now began to come into focus as the same God who was leading him inexorably towards the Christian faith. James eventually became part of a church community, where he found others who had made similar journeys. They seemed to him to be "the real deal." "There was something self-authenticatingly true about this community," he says.[4]

This happens time and time again. In our church, a couple from Iran began formal studies at a local university. One was doing a doctorate, and the other a master's degree in scientific and mathematical fields of study. Someone from our congregation invited them to church, and they said yes. They came to church one normal Sunday and sat in the balcony. As the service began, one of them looked over at the wall where there were large banners with some Scriptures on them, and in that moment they had their eyes opened. It was not the sermon, the environment, or the worship, but the Scripture they had read on the wall.

After extended times of hospitality and conversations about Christianity, both became followers of Jesus. I remember the day we baptized them. We asked everyone not to post anything on social media because of safety, yet we celebrated joyously as a church. It was the woman's testimony in the baptismal tank that reminded me of the power of Scripture. She shared with us that she told her family back home she had become a follower of Jesus. They of course were incensed and angry that they had left Islam. The family was so determined to show them the error of their ways they all got Bibles to read so they could disprove the Christian faith. I will never forget what the woman said in the tank that Sunday morning. She laughed and joyfully proclaimed, "They all have bought Bibles thinking this will be the way to show us that Jesus and Christianity is not true, but what they do not realize is that the Bible is living and active and they are soon going to hear God's voice!" And they did. Much of their family in Iran did come to faith and joined one of the fastest growing churches around the world today.

Now there is so much more to this. I recommend reading *Why Trust the Bible? Answers to Ten Tough Questions* by Amy Orr-Ewing. She considers the issues of text and manuscripts but goes farther, dealing with questions like: Isn't it all a matter of interpretation? Can we know anything about history? Are the original manuscripts reliable? What about the canon? What about other holy books? Isn't the Bible sexist? What about all the wars? Isn't the Bible out of date on sex?[5]

Several other books could help as well, such as *Trustworthy: Thirteen Arguments for the Reliability of the New Testament* by Benjamin Charles Fox Shaw[6] or the massive volume *Jesus and the Eyewitnesses* by Richard Bauckham.[7] The evidence is strong and will stand up.

We need to face the honest questions of those around us, such as: Isn't Christianity harmful—just a Western colonial religion, hateful to sexual diversity, a driver of war and injustice? In many places, humility about where we have sinned will be the best way to cross the bridge, but we must also correct the skewed readings of history and lack of biblical awareness and understanding.

As we are talking about philosophical bridges, there are so many more truths to think about, present, and access. The next one is one of the best examples of finding that altar to an unknown god—storytelling. The power of storytelling is accessing what is real behind human stories. As Russ Ramsey once said, "Story is a Trojan horse for truth. It can sneak past the gates of our defenses and prepare our hearts to hear things we might have resisted if they had come as mere declaration."[8]

This was the heart of J. R. R. Tolkien's idea of true myth, which led to C. S. Lewis's conversion. When we read, what we find in stories, in movies, and in songs points us to something more, something real. Here is the summary of a series of conversations between Tolkien, Dyson, and Lewis about real myth:

> Now what Dyson and Tolkien showed me was this: that if I met the idea of sacrifice in a Pagan story I didn't mind it at all: again, that if I met the idea of a god sacrificing himself to himself. . . . I liked it very much and was mysteriously moved by it: again, that the idea

> of the dying and reviving god (Balder, Adonis, Bacchus) similarly moved me provided I met it anywhere except in the Gospels. The reason was that in Pagan stories I was prepared to feel the myth as profound and suggestive of meanings beyond my grasp even tho' I could not say in cold prose 'what it meant'. Now the story of Christ is simply a true myth: a myth working on us in the same way as the others, but with this tremendous difference that it really happened. . . .
>
> On September 28, 1931—just nine days after Lewis's conversation with Tolkien on Christ being the true myth—Lewis took the final step in embracing the divinity of Christ while riding in his older brother's motorcycle sidecar on the way to the newly opened Whipsnade Park Zoo in Bedfordshire.[9]

This is why Lewis's and Tolkien's writings, and now the globally watched movies based on their work, move us so much to see where truth is. Tim Keller was famous for preaching from this idea within his New York church.

> As Keller told Redeemer in 1997, the good news of Jesus is the story behind all the other stories. "The gospel story is the story of wonder from which all other fairy tales and stories of wonder take their cues." How, exactly, did Tolkien see the gospel as the mold for fantasy stories? It's in the moment when you think all hope has been lost, as when the disciples huddled together, hidden away in a house after Jesus' death on the cross. It's when victory seems to emerge from nowhere in the least likely way, as when the risen Jesus walked through walls into that house and greeted his old friends and followers. It's when someone's greatest weakness becomes the source of greatest strength. It's what Tolkien called *eucatastrophe*, or the "joyful catastrophe, the tragedy that turns out to be a triumph, the sacrifice that turns out to bring joy, the weakness that ends up being strength, the defeat that ends up being victory."
>
> Tolkien's own stories include no shortage of *dyscatastrophe*, the point when all hope seems lost, as in the Battle of the Black Gate when the Host of the West dwindle against the orcs of Mordor,

> who outnumber them more than ten to one. As the heroes battle on, hoping to distract Sauron from Frodo and Sam's quest to destroy the One Ring in the fires of Mount Doom, they look for *euangelium*, good news that they will not die in vain. The *eucatastrophe* commences when Gollum bites off Frodo's finger and unwittingly destroys the Ring, ending Sauron's malevolent hold on Middle-earth. For Tolkien, the incarnation of Jesus is a *eucatastrophe* after generations of men died without hope. And the resurrection is a *eucatastrophe* of the incarnation, which had appeared to fail when they laid Jesus' lifeless body in the freshly cut tomb owned by Joseph of Arimathea.
>
> When you know the Story behind the stories, you see it everywhere, "from the ugly duckling who turns out to be a swan, to Beauty and the Beast, the Beauty who gives up all of her happiness to throw herself in the arms of this Beast and, because of her incredible sacrifice, gets a love and frees this person beyond anything she ever understood."
>
> When you pluck the string of the gospel, it never stops reverberating in your heart.
>
> "There really is a Beauty who kisses the beast," Keller told Redeemer in 1998. "There really is a Hercules who defeats the villain. There really is a hero. There really is Jesus."[10]

The role of storytelling, real myth, and power encounter is a growing influence once again across the West. Only recently the conversion of Martin Shaw, a famed professor of mythology, shows this in real time.

His father and brother were preachers, and his family was deeply rooted in the Christian faith. And though they were in charismatic circles in the 1980s, they did not hold onto the anti-intellectualism found in many in that part of that family. He said, "My dad would often tell me fairy tales or talk about folklore and, without the pressure to believe, my imagination felt more liberated. . . . I was used to great stories from the Bible, but my mum and dad never regarded myth as the enemy."[11]

So this brilliant young man went the way of the prodigal son but never forgot myth, let alone faith. Over thirty-two years he talked candidly about depression, divorce, entering the music industry, and doctoral work in myth, becoming one of its leading scholarly voices. But he says that the reason he stayed away from Jesus for so long was not unbelief but the fact that Jesus is all consuming and cannot be domesticated. Years later he had a personal encounter with Jesus in the middle of a forest.

> Friends were appalled at my conversion, because they felt I had taken on the colonial religion that devastated our culture. That's been agony for me. People have lost interest in what I write. But, when I read the Gospel of Mark, Yeshua doesn't spend a lot of time checking out your insurance policies before He tells you to come with Him. I feel like I'm in the middle of a spiritual audit that I have no control over. And He's going into all sorts of rooms I don't want Him to look at. That requires proper, profound surrender. For a big, egotistical, middle-aged man, it has been astonishingly beautiful and difficult to go down this road.[12]

This brings up another key place of not only defending the good news of Jesus, but the way to lead people up to the second level of the house. History is one of the most important bridges. The Christian faith unashamedly roots itself in real history, and as one really explores history, that evidence becomes much stronger. In 2017, Richard Dawkins was debating John Lennox in the Natural History Museum over the existence of God. You should go listen to it when you have time. It summarizes so much of what we are talking about in this chapter. In the middle of the debate, John Lennox basically said (my paraphrase): "The problem you have, Richard, is you have no understanding of the power of history. Not everything can be reduced to a test tube or scientific experiment." His point was Jesus did exist and the proofs of the resurrection could not just be quickly dismissed.[13]

Did Jesus exist as a human? Yes, the evidence is overwhelming. Famed agnostic professor Bart Ehrman, when interviewed on *Atheist Radio* on December 30th, 2011, stated: "There is no serious historian who doubts the existence of Jesus. There are a lot of people who want to write sensational books claiming that Jesus didn't exist, but I don't know any serious scholar who doubts the existence of Jesus."[14]

And is there evidence that Jesus lived, died, and rose again? Yes. Again, the evidence is compelling. (See the QR code on the inside of the front cover for additional resources.) William Wand, Oxford University church historian, wrote, "All the strictly historical evidence we have is in favour of the empty tomb, and those scholars who reject it must recognize that they do so on some other ground than that of scientific history."[15] In a massive study of all critical scholars in this area from 1975 till 2005, 75 percent of all scholars now hold to the resurrection being historically authentic in some form.[16]

There was a young man in my congregation who was deeply intellectual (actually in many ways I think he might've been a genius). We talked about the Christian faith, and in the end he began to attend church and said he became a Christian. He also struggled with mental illness, specifically bipolar disorder, so when he was high and excited, his faith was amazing, but when he was low and broken, his faith was doubted. We worked hard to help keep him grounded and at the same time grow in his faith. Eventually he left our church and the faith for a period of time. Then he joined another church and was all in again for a significant period of time, but then left again and was unsure. Years later I ran into him during a very low period. He was doing doctoral work in philosophy at the University of Toronto. He started talking to me about why God might not exist and about some mixture of philosophy and almost New Age thinking. As the conversation continued and more and more semi-agnostic arguments came out, I stopped him and simply said, "Did Jesus exist and did he physically rise from the dead or not? If he did, everything else is answered. The question is, have you really done your work to see if that is true no matter how you're feeling, no matter what you're thinking, no matter where you're struggling?"

I am not sure where he ended up, but as I wrote in *Perseverance*:

> Since Jesus rose from the dead, atheism is answered. Since Jesus rose from the dead, agnosticism is resolved. Since Jesus rose from the dead, every religion must reevaluate itself at its core. Since

> Jesus rose from the dead, death is answered and we know what fully lies beyond the grave because someone came back from it. Since Jesus rose from the dead, the human family does not now need to ask who God is and what he is like or if he is involved. Since Jesus rose from the dead, you can meet God. Since Jesus rose from the dead, there is purpose in your life more than money, sex, power, and being moral or religious. And since Jesus rose from the dead, the coffin or cremation fire is not your end.[17]

The truth of the resurrection doesn't mean we shouldn't walk down to the first level of the house and work through the grand philosophical and scientific arguments on why God exists. These are the lowest hanging fruits and easiest bridges for many around us. One of the most famous, and of course controversial, is the ontological argument of St. Anselm (1033–1109)—that is, you can know God is real by the definition of God. Simply put, since God is a "being that which nothing greater can be conceived," we realize that his essence implies his existence.[18]

There are three other major arguments for God's existence. The cosmological argument, at its heart, says everything must have a cause for it to begin. One professor summarizes it like this:

> St. Thomas Aquinas (1225–1274) famously offered "Five Ways" of demonstrating God's existence, each of which can be understood as a kind of cosmological argument. For example, one of the Five Ways argues that any *motion* (change) has to be explained by some *mover* (cause). If that mover itself exhibits motion, there must be a *prior* mover to explain it, and because there cannot be an infinite regress of moved movers, there must be an original *unmoved mover*: an eternal, immutable, and self-existent first cause.[19]

Theologians and philosophers have adjusted this argument over the years. One of the best is by William Lane Craig.[20]

The teleological argument says that, simply put, with the beauty, complexity, and unity of creation, there must be a designer to all this design, like with everything else that is made. When my son was very young, he asked me if God exists, and if so, how do I know. We were sitting in his room, so I asked him to look at everything in his room and point to something. He ended up pointing to his bookshelf. I said, "What is that?" He answered, "It's a bookshelf." I said, "Noah, how did that bookshelf come to exist?" He said that someone made it. So I replied, "That's right. Now look around at your room again, and list as many things as you can." He did, and every time he listed a new item, I asked him where it came from, and he would tell me who made it or where it came from. Then I said, "Do you really think that the universe, earth, birds, giraffes, elephants, stars in the sky, and leaves with all their beauty and complexity just came to be with no creator? If everything you see has a designer, why would not reality itself have the same kind of beginning?"

It was William Paley (1743–1805) who is best known for his argument from analogy, which compares functional arrangements in natural organisms to those in human artifacts such as pocket watches. While design arguments suffered a setback with the rise of the Darwinian theory of evolution, which purports to explain the apparent design of organisms in terms of undirected adaptive processes, the so-called intelligent-design movement has reinvigorated teleological arguments with insights from contemporary cosmology and molecular biology while exposing serious shortcomings in naturalistic Darwinian explanations.[21] You can see these ideas and more expressed in real time in that debate between Dawkins and Lennox. And you can read books like those of Francis Collins, who mapped the human genome and wrote the book *The Language of God*.[22]

It was the teleological argument that led to one of the greatest shocks in the atheistic community. Antony Flew was a pioneer in modern atheism. His famous paper "*Theology and Falsification*" was first presented at a meeting of the Oxford Socratic Club chaired by C. S. Lewis and went on to become the most widely reprinted philosophical publication of the last five decades. Flew earned his fame by arguing that one should presuppose atheism until evidence of a God surfaces. He now believes that such evidence exists, which he outlined in his book *There Is a God*.[23] It was the argument from design that first moved him.

Then there is the religious and moral argument. Why is there a universal shared morality? If humanity shares moral laws, then there must be a moral law-giver. C. S. Lewis, in his books *Mere Christianity* and *The Abolition of Man,* walks through this argument many times. He wrote,

> Give me a bit of your orange, I gave you a bit of mine—come on, you promised: People say things like that every day, educated people as well as uneducated, and children as well as grown ups. Now what interests me about all these remarks is that the man who makes them is not merely saying that the other man's behaviour does not happen to please him. He is appealing to some kind of standard of behaviour which he expects the other man to know about... These, then, are the two points I wanted to make. First, that human beings, all over the earth, have this curious idea that they ought to behave in a certain way, and cannot really get rid of it. Secondly, that they do not in fact behave in that way. They know the Law of Nature, they break it.[24]

Lewis also argues from desire itself. Desire to worship and desire for the eternal, which is a shared human experience written into the very DNA of every human heart.

> The Christian says, Creatures are not born with desires unless satisfaction for those desires exists. A baby feels hunger: well, there is such a thing as food. A duckling wants to swim: well, there is such a thing as water. Men feel sexual desire: well, there is such a thing as sex. If I find in myself a desire which no experience in this world can satisfy, the most probable explanation is that I was made for another world. If none of my earthly pleasures satisfy it, that does not prove that the universe is a fraud. Probably earthly pleasures were never meant to satisfy it, but only to arouse it, to suggest the real thing. If that is so, I must take care, on the one hand, never to despise, or to be unthankful for, these earthly blessings, and on the other, never to mistake them for the something else of which they are only a kind of copy, or echo, or mirage. I must keep alive

> in myself the desire for my true country, which I shall not find till after death; I must never let it get snowed under or turned aside; I must make it the main object of life to press on to that country and to help others to do the same.[25]

Finally, there has been an explosion of philosophical understanding connected to Lewis's argument of desire that many people around the globe have found convincing. It is based on what we talked about in the chapter on beauty and is rooted in Solomon's statement in Ecclesiastes 3:11: God has made everything beautiful in its time. He has also set eternity in the human heart, yet no one can fathom what God has done from beginning to end. John Calvin put it like this, "There is within the human mind, and indeed by natural instinct, an awareness of divinity."[26]

Another scholar describes the movement like this:

> In the 1980s, a number of Protestant philosophers led by Alvin Plantinga, Nicholas Wolterstorff, and William Alston developed a sophisticated defense of Calvin's notion of the *sensus divinitatis*. Dubbed the "reformed epistemologists," they argued that theistic beliefs can be (and normally should be) *properly basic*: rationally justified even without empirical evidences or philosophical proofs. On this view, believing that God exists is comparable to believing that the world of our experience really exists; it's entirely rational, even if we can't philosophically demonstrate it. Indeed, it would be quite dysfunctional to believe otherwise.[27]

If you want a deep dive into all of this, then a great place to start is with a famous lecture given by Alvin Plantinga in 1986 called "*Two Dozen (or so) Theistic Arguments*." This lecture became a sensation in philosophical circles and truly was a modern Mars Hill moment. It was so explosive that many scholars started interacting with Plantinga's ideas, as best summarized in the book *Two Dozen (or so) Arguments for God: The Plantinga Project*.[28] This stands as an outstanding work for arguing in favour of the existence for God. Despite the increasingly scientific and secular age we live in, many people are still searching for a bigger story and want purpose and embodied life again.

And that relatively short description above brings us to a less accessed bridge: being tired. So many will become tired in time. They will see the lack of fulfillment in so much of what they trust in. Jim Carrey, the actor/comedian, brilliantly said, "I wish everyone could get rich and famous and have everything they ever dreamed of, so they will know that it's not the answer."[29]

We have not even talked about hustle and comfort culture in this book. These are newish secular expressions with spiritual feeling.

> By comfort culture, we mean Netflix bingeing, online gaming, hours of *Candy Crush*, scrolling Instagram reels, fantasy sports, self-indulgent Amazon sprees, foodie culture addiction—all comfy couch consolations to fill the meaning gap. Essentially, this is consumerism in late modernity as a form of spiritual transcendence. It's not that these activities are bad in themselves. But they can become a problem when they create a "comfort culture" that idolizes rest to the point of finding meaning in slothfulness. . . . It's the mindset of working merely to make play possible.[30]

And then there is hustle culture:

> If you doubt the prevalence of hustle-and-grind ideology in today's world, consider how many people listen to *The Joe Rogan Experience*. The show has over 13 million subscribers and billions of views. *Billions*. Although Rogan covers an extremely wide range of topics (from martial arts to alternative medicine to alien spacecraft), there's a strong thread that runs through the show about working hard, challenging yourself, never giving up, and grinding until you win. Rogan's massive influence (particularly among young men) speaks to the appeal of this increasingly popular map of meaning.[31]

Give it time; the shine will fade. These driving forces are great if you have money, if you are young, if you have energy. But old age, sickness, burnout, and boredom will come, and then there is again that chance to show not only a more beautiful and better way but the Saviour they deeply long for.

It's like at the Paris 2024 Olympics. I, like millions of others, not only watched the games but followed the social media feeds of all sorts of athletes—from the food they loved and hated in the Olympic Village, to the famous cardboard beds, to their joys and losses in their competitions. But on day two, on multiple feeds, I started seeing something so intriguing. Multiple athletes began commenting about how they loved waking up in the morning to the singing of the Fujian athletes. Other athletes and news outlets would post videos of these athletes and their supporters singing gorgeously outside their quarters every morning. As I heard the songs, I immediately wondered if they were Christian hymns. They had the feeling and the sound of worship. So I researched and found out that most, if not all, of the songs were Christian hymns sung to the glory of God amidst a gathering of all nations.[32] This is what is happening generationally, as people are getting tired of hustle culture, comfort culture, secular ideology, sexual promiscuity, gender confusion, the never ending call in spirituality to find inner peace, and the religious treadmill. Suddenly, the simple, beautiful gospel can make people turn their heads and wonder if there's something better. Simple singing can cause the most intense, most combative, most competitive, most driven, most in shape, most beautiful, most diverse gathering of humans to go silent and wonder.

I want to encourage you to listen, to read, and to be ready in this mixed moment. More and more people are looking for answers, and beneath the hostility, pain, and information gluttony lies a growing openness to God in our culture. And we not only possess plausible answers but *the* answer in the living person of Jesus Christ.

Christianity is not an intellectual system, a collection of dogmas, or moralism. Christianity is instead an encounter, a love story.

—CARDINAL JOSEPH RATZINGER

Someone read from Luther's Preface to the Epistle to Romans. About 8:45 p.m. while he was describing the change which God works in the heart through faith in Christ, I felt my heart strangely warmed. I felt I did trust in Christ, Christ alone for salvation; and an assurance was given me that He had taken away my sins, even mine, and saved me from the law of sin and death.

—JOHN WESLEY

CHAPTER 16

The Undeniable Need for an Encounter

We now arrive at something essential. To witness well today, there are four major ideas we need to embrace, whether we love intellectual arguments or we barely made it through the last few chapters. The question before us is: How do we witness well in this moment, let alone in any time or place? The next four ideas are true for all moments, places, and people.

The first has already been hinted at: Sometimes, after all the arguments are done and given, we just need to let people come to the end of their ropes, the end of their worldviews, and the end of themselves. I love what Alister McGrath says about those who elevate science to a godlike status in *The Reenchantment of Nature*:

> As E. F. Schumacher pointed out with great sadness in his last book, *A Guide for the Perplexed*, the view that the natural sciences determine all things declares many of the most fundamental questions of human longing to be illegitimate and the answers sincerely given to be totally false. "The maps produced by modern materialistic Scientism leave all the questions that really matter unanswered: more than that, they deny the validity of the questions." Yet a love for the natural sciences need not lead to this materialist reductionism,

> nor to the suppression of the human yearning for a transcendent dimension to life."[1]

Second, Christians need to be deeply confident in our message and the person we represent, but we must not be fanatical. I love this quotation from the famous book and movie *Tinker Tailor Soldier Spy*: "That is how I know he can be beaten. Because he is a fanatic. And the fanatic is always concealing a secret doubt."[2] I find those who are the most intense and brash about our faith are secretly concealing doubt, and many of them end up deconstructing or leaving our faith in the long run. Again, we need to show everyone, both inside and outside the church, that we are okay with doubt. Doubt is not a death knell to our faith. It is normal, and it should be expected, needed, and wanted. McGrath in another one of his books, *The Sunnier Side of Doubt,* gives three very important definitions when thinking through faith connected to struggle.

> Unbelief: The decision not to have faith in God. Unbelief is an act of the will, rather than a difficulty of understanding.
>
> Skepticism: The decision to doubt everything deliberately, as a matter of principle.
>
> Doubt: Asking questions or voicing uncertainties from the standpoint of faith. You believe, but you have difficulties with that faith, or you are worried about it in some way. Faith and doubt aren't mutually exclusive, but faith and unbelief are![3]

We must be honest about what we don't know and where we have more work to do. Not only does it show humility to those we are trying to reach, but it does not allow unvoiced skepticism to develop into unbelief. People in the modern West want to see authenticity and humility more than they want to see someone being right. Recapturing this in our own minds, in our own walks, and in our public conversations will be a stronger magnetic point than many of us think.

We need to understand and live the difference between bold and fanatical. It is so interesting that Peter wrote these words as a former fanatical and violent man who over time was deeply changed: "But in your hearts revere Christ as Lord. Always be prepared to give an answer to everyone who asks you to give the reason for the hope that you have. But do this with gentleness and respect" (1 Peter 3:15). No more ear cutting, no more overpromising and underdelivering; instead, freely given gentleness and respect. When you have confidence, you demonstrate a peace in your soul that is the opposite of the angry fundamentalist. Your peaceful rest can become a place with an attractive and magnetic pull.

Third, after everything is given, it does not mean they will believe or cross the line of faith. There still needs to be a supernatural encounter. I remember in high school there was a Jehovah's Witness who tried bringing me to "real" Christianity. He was attracted to my intensity about Christianity and thought he could convince me that his version was the true version. This was in grade 11, so I made him a deal: "I know you need a certain amount of door-knocking hours to get eternal life, right? I will meet with you two lunches a week for the next two years, and I can become your quota." He agreed. So for two years we met. And for two years we debated. I did all the research on Jehovah's Witnesses beliefs and even bought their old books to show him the changes in their beliefs. Back and forth the conversations went, lunch after lunch. Then after two years, he ran out of arguments. I will never forget the moment. I was sitting in the library and said to him, "You know I'm right, and you know what you've grown up believing is not right, not biblical, and not historically defensible." And then he said these words, "Jon, I know you're right, and I know I'm wrong, but I'm still right." I could not believe what he said, but there it was. This was where our two years of conversation ended. The cost was too high for him. His response shows why intellectual work is never enough. We need the Holy Spirit to give faith, to walk people up to Jesus and bring them to life. Truly we must be born from above because the Spirit does blow where he wants.

Think about the two disciples walking on the road to Emmaus. Jesus had to walk into their lives for them to see: "Then their eyes were opened and they recognized him, and he disappeared from their sight" (Luke 24:31). He had to open their eyes, and this was done in and through encounter. Likewise, Jesus is restoring history. He overcame the results of that first eye opening decision (Adam and Eve) and opened their eyes so they could see the only One who can give forgiveness, love, and a path back to God, which is Eden restored.

Think about the famed leaders in the New Testament. Thomas, for example, had been personally called by Jesus. He had been with Jesus very close to the beginning; he had preached, cast out demons, and healed people in Jesus's delegated power. He was willing to die for Jesus and called others to be willing also (John 11:16). Thomas's inquisitive nature and real questions led to one of the most significant salvation and eternity statements given by Jesus: "I am the way and the truth and the life. No one comes to the Father except through me. If you really know me, you will know my Father as well. From now on, you do know him and have seen him" (John 14:6–7).

If you read Thomas's whole story carefully pre-Good Friday, you see that by this point Thomas had been promised eternal life and guaranteed presence with Jesus in the new heaven and new earth. And all of that does not include when he helped feed the five thousand, when he witnessed Legion being cast out, when he heard the Sermon on the Mount, when Lazarus was raised from the dead—he was there with the rest of the disciples. Then Jesus dies, all is lost, and Thomas is absent when Jesus physically appears on Sunday. Ask yourself: What moved Thomas from deconstruction to reconstruction? What moved him to say, "My Lord and my God" (John 20:28)? Nothing less than encounter.

Think about Jesus's brother, James. James and much of Jesus's family did not believe. They were not seekers; they thought Jesus was crazy, a liar, or worse, demon possessed. They were angry and wanted to shut him up and shut him down. They thought he was a danger to himself and to them. Years later, after Jesus's life, miracles, teaching, death, and resurrection, James finally confesses that his brother was who he claimed to be, the Messiah, the Son of God, God in flesh! But what made the difference? Encounter. It took a postresurrection experience to fully convince him. Only when James met his dead brother, Jesus, now fully alive, did he fully believe! As Paul tells it, "Then he appeared to James, then to all the apostles" (1 Corinthians 15:7).

Then there is Paul, formerly known as Saul of Tarsus. Religiously, Saul was like the person that received the Pulitzer Prize for writing, the Oscar for acting, the Victoria Cross for military bravery, the Heisman Trophy for football, or a gold medal at the Olympics. This guy was the real deal! He was not just Jewish, not just educated, but a Roman citizen who grew up in Tarsus, a cosmopolitan centre. He spoke and wrote in multiple languages. He would have had the equivalent to at least one PhD, maybe two. He studied under Gamaliel, who was the greatest teacher of Judaism in his time and is still considered today as one of the great intellects and leaders of Judaism. Oh, and Saul hated Christians! This story becomes very clear as recorded in Acts. When Stephen declared Jesus was the Messiah and had risen from the dead, Saul helped get Stephen killed. He killed and jailed followers of "the Way." But then came the radical one-eighty. Saul became Paul, the greatest thinker of Christianity. Why the change? Intellect, facts, advantage, gullibility, instability, just because the tomb was empty? No, he encountered the risen Jesus. Again, Paul was one of the best Jewish thinkers of his day. He would have believed in the resurrection of everyone at the end of time. It would have been unthinkable and wrong to say only one person would rise from the dead. The only thing that could change his deepest held beliefs was an encounter with the risen Jesus.

> He fell to the ground and heard a voice say to him, "Saul, Saul, why do you persecute me?"
>
> "Who are you, Lord?" Saul asked.
>
> "I am Jesus, whom you are persecuting," he replied. "Now get up and go into the city, and you will be told what you must do." (Acts 9:4–6)

We must never stop praying for and expecting divine encounter. I love how my friend David Bennett recounts his encounter with the Holy Spirit. He is a scholar of theology at Oxford. If you read his work or hear him speak, you will quickly recognize he is an expert on theology and sexual ethics, and as a gay man, he has become a leading voice on the biblical view of sexuality and how that works while rebuking and rightly correcting both the Left and the Right. But where did all this start? Some brilliant argument? No. Encountering Jesus's love through the Holy Spirit at a gay party in a pub in the gay quarter of Sydney. Listen to his story:

> It was a busy Friday night, just after my nineteenth birthday. The bridge across Sydney Harbour was packed with cars. From the back of my cab, I looked out over the water and spotted the iconic white sails of the Opera House. Then I lay my head back, relieved to have a break from the monotony of life.
>
> I was worn out from political conferences and late nights spent editing the university student magazine. Instead of the more raucous options available for my night, I decided to go to a small pub to celebrate a writer friend's birthday. It was late March.
>
> As I got out of the cab, the streets were filled with the buzz of Sydney's nightlife. A rainbow flag flew above a building just doors down. I was only a street over from Oxford Street, Sydney's famous gay quarter, which held fond memories of Mardi Gras parades, nights out, and coffee dates with friends.
>
> I walked up the pub stairs and scanned the room. Not many people I knew had arrived yet, but I did spot a friend of a friend holding a drink and sitting alone.
>
> Madeline was a finalist in one of the largest short film competitions in the world, a huge accomplishment for a young creative. Everyone was talking about her in my screenwriting class, and I wanted to interview her for the student magazine. It would easily make the best feature article.
>
> Unlike a lot of my peers, whose creative projects centred on them, Madeline was using her gifts to raise awareness for those often misunderstood or forgotten—people with disabilities. Having a disabled uncle, I found her work inspiring.
>
> As I approached, her brown eyes warmed in recognition, and we said hello. Her hair was cut short, and she wore red lipstick and a black dress. Right away I launched into the question I wanted to ask.
>
> "How did you become a finalist? You just graduated!"

"That depends," she said. "Do you want the real answer or the interview answer?"

I laughed, unprepared for what would follow. "The real answer, of course!"

"God led me to make the film."

Madeline must have seen the shock on my face. I remembered the conversation with my aunt and uncle over Christmas lunch. *Please don't mention Jesus,* I thought. I couldn't see how Christianity had anything to do with her work. How could a faith that oppressed me and so many others motivate her to do such good?

"So, which God?" I asked, with a hint of sarcasm. "We talking, like, Vishnu here?"

"Jesus," she said. A thousand objections flooded me as I thought of this God who stood in the way of my community's progress in society. And yet . . . Madeline wasn't like the other moralizing, intolerant, anti-intellectual, homophobic, anti-feminist Christians I'd met.

She explained that she too struggled with Christian stereotypes and the small-mindedness found in parts of the Christian community. The key word in John 3:16, she said, was *whoever*: "God so loved the world that he gave his one and only Son, that whoever believes in him shall not perish but have eternal life." I realized Madeline didn't see my homosexuality as a hindrance to knowing God. She clearly wanted my community to find the same love she had discovered.

Madeline paused. I knew she had seen that my reaction to her faith wasn't positive. Only my admiration for her work prevented what otherwise would have been a very rude response.

"Do you think there's a God?" she asked. Not a hint of ulterior motive or trying to convert me. Just an open question.

"Well, I'm basically an atheist, but I believe there's a *Something,* I guess. I'm a spiritual person, and I think you have to be blind to believe there's absolutely nothing behind life," I said, looking down at my drink. "I just don't like organized religion. I'm gay, so I know this Christian God isn't an option for me. I've never understood how if he existed, he'd give me these desires, then condemn me."

Madeline paused. I expected her to quibble or awkwardly change the subject, like many of my Christian friends. But Madeline didn't hesitate. "David, have you ever experienced the love of God?"

"What do you even mean? No." My only impression of him was that of an angry, distant deity.

"God loves everyone right where they are," Madeline said. I wanted to recoil at her words, yet something drew me deeper.

Suddenly her eyes widened. "David, I can feel God's presence so strongly right now." She paused. "He loves you so incredibly much. I'd never usually ask this, but . . . can I pray for you?"

Instantly I had an internal war over how to respond. *Should I say yes or no?*

A voice in my mind whispered, *You're a good agnostic; you have to be open to prayer, because you don't know if there's a God. Any other response is intellectually dishonest and closed-minded.*

Another thought, this one louder, came on its heels: *Get away from this crazy fundamentalist! She's brainwashed like those Christians you read about in the newspaper!*

The gentler voice won. "Yes, you can pray for me," I said finally. "But I don't think anything is going to happen."

As Madeline laid her hands on me and prayed, the bustle of the pub faded away. I entered into a stillness, a peace. Soon I felt a soft tingling on the crown of my head that slowly intensified, as if someone were pouring oil over me. The warm sensation ran down my entire body like a current of water. It was unlike anything I'd ever felt before.

In a moment, in that experience so totally from outside me, so totally unasked for, everything turned upside down in my mind. All my searching in religion, in relationships, in atheism—none of it compared with this love coursing through me like electricity.[4]

And the rest is history but it started with encounter.

Finally, we must end like Thomas, James, Paul, and my friend David did, with the gospel. The clear proclamation of Jesus's life, death, and resurrection for the forgiveness of sins. After the bridges were crossed and the arguments were given on Mars Hill, Paul still points to the simple gospel. Many scoffed, but a few believed. We were told it was going to be like this:

> For the message of the cross is foolishness to those who are perishing, but to us who are being saved it is the power of God. . . . Jews demand signs and Greeks look for wisdom, but we preach Christ crucified: a stumbling block to Jews and foolishness to Gentiles, but to those whom God has called, both Jews and Greeks, Christ the power of God and the wisdom of God. For the foolishness of God is wiser than human wisdom, and the weakness of God is stronger than human strength. (1 Corinthians 1:18, 22–25)

We must always be ready to be fools and never forget that the gospel offends in every direction because it undoes and breaks pride, no matter the expression—religious, secular, and spiritual. I don't know if you have ever been to the Holy Land. I have a few times. The first time we went to Bethlehem. We stepped off the bus for the fourteenth time that day and stood in front of the famous Church of the Nativity. I expected a large front door, but I was confronted with a small door that we had to bow to duck into. No matter who came, priest, pastor, or pope, religious or not, educated or not, small, big, known or not known, to get into where Jesus was born, you had to bow low. Here lies the scandal and gift of Christianity. Like the Doom paintings reminding us that judgment makes us equal, the invitation to salvation is the same for everyone. I love how Max Lucado describes his experience at that same humbling door.

> A small cathedral outside Bethlehem marks the supposed birthplace of Jesus. Behind a high altar in the church is a cave, a little cavern lit by silver lamps. You can enter the main edifice and admire the ancient church. You can also enter the quiet cave where a star embedded in the floor recognizes the birth of the King. There is one stipulation, however. You have to stoop. The door is so low you can't go in standing up. The same is true of the Christ. You can see the world standing tall, but to witness the Savior, you have to get on your knees. So . . . while the theologians were sleeping and

> the elite were dreaming and the successful were snoring, the meek were kneeling. They were kneeling before the One, only the meek will see. They were kneeling in front of Jesus.[5]

Paul said repent and believe, so we must, no matter the consequence or audience, say the same. Remember, we are never alone in the moment we proclaim the gospel, for the giving of the gospel is a literal, not metaphorical, guaranteed place of encounter. As I wrote in my first book, *Convergence*,

> As Paul wrote to the church in Rome, "I am not ashamed of the gospel, because it is the power of God that brings salvation to everyone who believes: first to the Jew, then to the Gentile" (Romans 1:16). The word power is where we get our word dynamite. The gospel has sheer power; it is dynamic, it is life giving, and it is the place where the Holy Spirit brings the whole of God the Father's calling and the whole of Jesus's work—past, present, and future—into a person's life! As John MacArthur said, "The gospel carries the omnipotence of God, whose power alone is sufficient to save people from sin and give them eternal life." This power brings salvation. The Holy Spirit is always around, above, below, behind and in the giving of the gospel. No matter the results, he is always present. So when you share the good news, you are not alone. Jesus is in the room.[6]

Let me share one last story that I heard years ago. It takes place in Oxford during World War II with the famous London-based preacher, Martyn Lloyd-Jones. In 1941, he preached a sermon called "The Gospel and the Natural Man." This led to another invitation and this is how one summarizes the encounter.

> As a result of that he was invited to preach at St Mary's Church on the Sunday evening, and the students were invited back to the vicarage for a question-and-answer session afterwards. He tells how when questions were called for, the first man to speak was an articulate member of the Union debating society. To become a member of the Union debating society at Oxford, you just have to be so far up

there it's not funny—and so intelligent and so articulate. And this young man addressed a question to Lloyd-Jones. "Surely," he said, "Dr. Lloyd-Jones, that despite the logic, arguments, and arrangements of your sermon, there was no apparent reason why your same sermon should not have been preached in exactly the same way to a congregation of agricultural labourers in Oxfordshire." See? "You've come here into the university, to the intelligentsia of the British Isles, and you come in here, and there certainly was logic, and it was a good sermon, but frankly, couldn't it just have been preached just as well to a bunch of people who are turning over the fields around us here in Oxfordshire?"

That was his question, and the chairman called upon MLJ to respond.

There was only one thing to say. Says Lloyd-Jones,

> I freely confessed that until that moment, I had always taken the view that even the undergraduates at the University of Oxford were only ordinary common human clay like everybody else, and that from the standpoint of the gospel, there is no difference between your brilliant undergraduate and your so-called agricultural labourer. That is what the gospel itself says: "There is none righteous, no not one, for all have sinned." Yes sir, I would preach the same sermon to agricultural labourers, because when you're face-to-face with the gospel, there is no difference between one and the other.[7]

After we do all the work and cross all the bridges through love, power, and intellect, we cannot forget that to maintain presence, to witness well in all moments, we must give time for people to see their thirst. We must be confident, but not fanatical; we must always see the prominence of encounter; and we must preach the gospel, even if it makes us look like fools.

PART 4

RESIDE

to live, have your home, or
stay in a place

At the heart of racism is the religious assertion that God made a creative mistake when He brought some people into being.

—FRIEDRICH OTTO HERTZ

You can safely say you've created God in your own image when it turns out that God hates all the same people you do.

—ANNE LAMOTT

Harm to the vulnerable people begins not with violence but with language we use to subtly make them seem less human, unborn babies become fetuses, immigrants become invaders, the elderly become burdens. But God sees vulnerable people for who they are: His image-bearers.

—DANIEL DARLING

God does not love us because Christ died for us; Christ died for us because God loved us.

—JOHN STOTT

Therefore go and make disciples of all nations, baptizing them in the name of the Father and of the Son and of the Holy Spirit, and teaching them to obey everything I have commanded you. And surely I am with you always, to the very end of the age.

—MATTHEW 28:19–20

Let every nation praise your name
Let every tribe upon you call
Let all the universe proclaim
That Jesus Christ is Lord of all.

—TWI WORSHIP CHORUS

CHAPTER 17

Would You Even Want to Go to Those People?

In January of 1907 a revival broke out at a Bible conference in Pyongyang, now the capital of North Korea. Those attending the conference came under deep conviction of sin, especially when a preacher called them to repent of their traditional hatred of the Japanese. Of course, the Korean Christians had accepted the fundamental truths of the gospel of grace, and yet these had not sunk in deeply enough for them to forgive the Japanese. They felt morally superior to a nation they saw as oppressive and cruel. In the light of the gospel, however, the Koreans at the conference saw that they stood before God as equally sinful and condemned with all other human beings, yet rescued by the sheer and costly grace of Christ. This drained away their pride and bitterness. They returned to their homes with a newness to repent of wrongdoing. People went house to house repairing relationships and returning stolen articles. The worship services were filled with a new power. The result was explosive growth of the church. The Methodist church, for example, doubled in membership size in a single year.[1]

We live in a complex world. One part of this is that Christians are now, in many places, a cultural minority. Jesus's identity and mission are clear, the gospel is clear, your identity is secure, beloved, called, alien, and stranger. God's fingerprints are so plentiful we can miss them only by apathy or by intention. Like fish unaware that they swim in water, human beings are unaware of God's presence surrounding them. The bridges abound around us in the worlds of religion, shared spatial experience, art, philosophy, nature, human kindness or hospitality, poetry, and song.

It is one thing to outline what we face, another thing to be clear about truth, and another thing to think through what bridges exist and how we can—through love, power, and intellect—point, prove, and invite others in our culture into life with God. But what we have only hinted at so far is the motivation. Are we willing to walk with others into places of ongoing difficult decision? The real question for us as Christians, and even more so for us as Christian leaders, pastors, or priests, is, *Who cares?* It is one thing to know there is beauty, and it is another to know that bridges are everywhere but to wonder if I don't like the bridges. Do I want to cross them? Do I want to burn them down? We might say with our lips, in our songs, and in our sermons that we love the world, we need to go, and we will go. But I doubt that always rings true. As A. W. Tozer once said, "Christians don't say lies. They just go to church and sing them."[2]

This is why Jonah's story is such a gift. I am not going to go through the whole story, but his journey has a lot to teach us and, if we are willing, has the ability to expose the true posture of our hearts.

You could boil down Jonah's story to four questions: Do they deserve forgiveness? Do they deserve the message? Do they deserve my presence? What would I do if God showed them mercy? These questions are the heart-questions for every generation of Christians, and they are especially potent for us. I don't know how you were introduced to Jonah, but my introduction was in Sunday school through the cutting-edge technology called "flannelgraphs." If you have no clue what I am talking about, let me share my 1970s core Christian memory with you. This is in the time before iPhones, iPads, iPods, and flatscreen televisions. In the ancient time before apps, before Instagram, Snapchat, and TikTok. Before DVDs and CDs there was the flannelgraph. This cutting-edge storytelling system used a board covered with flannel fabric, usually resting on an easel. The Sunday school teacher would stick images to the board using Velcro. Flannelgraphs were used to teach me about Noah's ark, David and Goliath, the tabernacle, and, of course, Jonah.

I remember it clearly: There was Jonah and a whale. We would all cheer and yell, "Throw him over! Throw him over!" The Sunday school teacher would take the Jonah figure and put him into the whale's mouth, and we'd all cheer, which upon reflection, is disturbing on so many levels.

Years later, I was arriving in the nation of Israel. We had flown all night, and the sun was rising. Before we got to Tel Aviv, we were taken to the ancient city of Jaffa. I didn't know where we were. I just knew it was sunny and beautiful; there was the ocean in front of me, and I was battling jet lag. So we sat down, looking like tourists, and behind me was this fountain that wasn't working with an ugly whale in the middle of it. I remember thinking, why is the fountain not working and—as I kept looking at it—why is there an ugly whale there?

I began to notice all these people kept coming and taking photos of a broken fountain. And in my jet lag and not feeling filled with the Holy Spirit moment, I was asking, "Why are these people taking photos of such terrible art? What's going on?" Then the guide stood up and said, "Welcome to Israel! We're so glad you're here." She pointed north. "You can just see Tel Aviv right over there, but we are in the ancient city of Jaffa. If you know your Bible . . ." Here's when I thought, "Oh no, oh no! I'm a pastor. What have I missed already?" She kept speaking, "If you know your Bible, you're in the town of Joppa." The significance of that statement still did not register. As I tried to pull out YouVersion, she said, "You're standing in the very spot where

Jonah ran from God." I thought, "Thank God no one asked me. I'd lose my job." I would say this is a place we should take pilgrimages to because Jonah is an echocardiogram and stress test for our hearts.

Yes, the days are long, but the years are short. Yes, we are naive about the technological optimism of the moment. Yes, Western culture has created waves of rage and shame, which has led to a bitter divide—the rise of tribalism, angry nationalism, fear of change, partisan silos, sectarian lines, fear of the outsider, or what many now call "othering." It's difficult to navigate. And unlike our friends who are not Christians, we are called to live by grace and truth in the middle of all of this. We are called not to lie or promote lies, we are called to love our neighbour yet at the same time call sin, sin. What to do? What can help us get out of the holes we don't even know we are in? Well, it goes back to the flannelgraph and the whale fountain. If there is one little book that discusses race, nationalism, different religions, evangelism, God's mercy, God's love, God's justice, our role in the world, and our role in the city we live in, while at the same time rooting out our biases and hate, it is the little book of Jonah.

Some of you may be saying, "Jon, I know this. I've spoken on this. I've read books on this." Good! Then, read Jonah slowly again, and don't just compare my words with your prior knowledge, where your interpretation might be different. Ask the Holy Spirit to once again pierce your heart.

To the famed story we must go! Maybe we don't know or have forgotten the community and times Jonah lived in. Jonah was a prophet of the northern kingdom of Israel, whose predecessors were Elijah and Elisha. Hosea and Amos would likely have been contemporaries. We read about Jonah in 2 Kings:

> In the fifteenth year of Amaziah son of Joash king of Judah, Jeroboam son of Jehoash king of Israel became king in Samaria, and he reigned forty-one years. He did evil in the eyes of the Lord and did not turn away from any of the sins of Jeroboam son of Nebat, which he had caused Israel to commit. He was the one who restored the boundaries of Israel from Lebo Hamath to the Dead Sea, in accordance with the word of the Lord, the God of Israel,

> spoken through his servant Jonah son of Amittai, the prophet from Gath Hepher. (2 Kings 14:23–25)

Don't forget that the people of God were no longer one nation but two: Israel in the north and Judah in the south. The Northern Kingdom was involved in all sorts of sin and compromise; there was not one faithful king in Israel towards God. When we read the story of Jonah as a prophet from the Northern Kingdom, everyone down south would go, "Of course he ran away. Of course he compromised." Unlike Amos and Hosea, who confronted their ongoing compromise and sin, Jonah was saying that God was going to increase their borders. Why even listen to him?[3] Already this is a much-needed insight—a word in season for the church. God speaks through people we struggle with. Oh, we want God's message, but we don't always like the messengers, so be careful. God uses who he chooses. In these days, we cannot afford not to listen to our brothers and sisters who, like us, are trying not only to be faithful but are also trying to bring the kingdom of God into this complex moment. Yes, there are false Christians,[4] but most Christians you disagree with are not heretics. They are just from our "north."

By the way, if you tend to read and quote amazing Christian leaders from the past, but at the same time say those who hold the same beliefs today are not Christians, give your head a shake and acknowledge the hypocrisy! We are so much kinder to the living dead than to the living. In my circles, people love to quote Augustine, Athanasius, or Chrysostom for example, but then say that most Roman Catholics or Orthodox living today are not saved Christians. It's like loving to quote Puritans like Samuel Rutherford, George Gillespie, Richard Baxter, or the great Baptist preacher Charles Spurgeon from England, while attacking charismatics and ignoring the repeated and ongoing documented spiritual experiences in their lives that are clearly power gifts.[5] You see the problem, right? There are serious issues to work out, but in times of turmoil and confusion, God might speak through "them," so be slow to speak and quick to listen.

Okay, back to Jonah.

Jonah was active between 786 and 747 BC. Twenty-five years later, the Northern Kingdom would be overrun and utterly destroyed by the Assyrians.[6] The story begins like this: "The word of the LORD came to Jonah son of Amittai" (Jonah 1:1). God speaks to him, calls him. This is direct; it is God's will that this man would become his spokesman, his prophet, his ambassador. Again, let's pause and see the power of this. We say all the time, "If only God would speak to me so directly, then everything would be clear, and I would obey!" Really? The pattern much of the time in Scripture is God speaks and the faithful (or not always so faithful) hear and *run*, not hear and obey. By the way, you may want to pray again right now because this whole next section is about our heart posture. You could pray, "I want to obey, help me out of my disobedience."

The name Jonah means "dove."[7] Interestingly, this leads us back to the time after Noah's flood. A dove found an olive branch. Jonah will be God's peace and mercy, which is already revealing a problem. Jonah does not think the Ninevites should have peace and mercy, just like we can feel about others. The name Amittai means "truth, truth telling, truth of God." So his name means dove and truth—God's peace, God's truth![8]

Then God says to God's peace and truth, "Go to the great city of Nineveh and preach against it, because its wickedness has come up before me" (Jonah 1:2). *Go*—a simple yet all-consuming word, a word that changes the course of one's life. *Go* is a command. Go to the great city of Nineveh. Many of us don't understand what God asked. But this command is the worst, the most dangerous, and totally wrong! Nineveh was the capital of the Assyrian empire. This royal city was 550 miles from Jerusalem and 220 miles north of Baghdad. In two periods spanning over 270 years, it would dominate and wreak havoc in the Middle East.[9]

This empire was Israel's chief enemy. The Assyrians were powerful and well-developed, and even at this point, Israel was paying tribute taxes. The Assyrians were like the mob—you need to pay for protection, and if you don't, they would kill you. But to really get the flavour of this, just read this summary:

> Assyrian kings often recorded the results of their military victories, gloating of whole plains littered with corpses and of cities

> burned completely to the ground. The emperor Shalmaneser III is well known for depicting torture, dismembering, and decapitations of enemies in grisly detail on large, strong relief panels. Assyrian history is "as gory and bloodcurdling a history as we know." After capturing their enemies, the Assyrians would typically cut off both legs and one arm, leaving the other arm and hand so they could shake the victim's hand in mockery as he was dying. They forced friends and family members to parade with the decapitated heads of their loved ones on elevated poles. They pulled out prisoners' tongues and stretched their bodies with ropes, so they could be flayed alive and their skins displayed on city walls. They burned adolescents alive. Those who survived the destruction of their cites were fated to endure cruel and violent forms of slavery. The Assyrians have been called a "terrorist state."[10]

And by the way, I did not mention *who* the Assyrians worshipped, the god Ishtar, goddess of war and sexual love. Their chief deity was a blend of divine violence and fornication, demonic at its core.[11] Years later, when the Assyrian empire collapsed, the prophet Nahum wrote: "All who hear the news about you clap their hands at your fall, for who has not felt your endless cruelty?" (Nahum 3:19).

So God says, "Go, Jonah; preach against it." But this call is ultimately for relationship and restoration. God wants them to see their wickedness and sin so they can see their need for salvation and the mercy of God.

Well, Jonah quickly understood the restorative nature of God's call, and he knew God does not change his mind. Jonah's reaction? "This is radical, this is *crazy*, this must not happen, this must stop!" It was not just because they were not Jews, which was bad enough. As another wrote, "How long for example would a Jewish rabbi have lasted in 1941 if he had stood on the streets of Berlin and called on Nazi Germany to repent? At the most practical level, the prospects of success were none, and the chances of death were high."[12] But more than personal danger and not being part of God's people, the Assyrians were evil and did not deserve God's love or forgiveness. And Jonah was probably thinking, "This is so bad for God's reputation."

Has God lost his mind? What about his holiness? What about his wisdom? What about his justice?[13] So with these facts in place, the path was clear to Jonah: "But Jonah ran away from the LORD and headed for Tarshish. He went down to Joppa, where he found a ship bound for that port. After paying the fare, he went aboard and sailed for Tarshish to flee from the LORD" (Jonah 1:3).

Jewish rabbinic interpretations suggest that Jonah was wealthy. So "to flee from God, Jonah must have sold his home, left everything behind and set off at the risk of his life."[14] Oh, do you see it? What we talked about at the beginning—the running away. Here again is the resurfacing of the fortress mentality; salt and light is replaced by retreat, as well as the wrongheaded belief that we must protect God's reputation or our community's reputation. Jonah's story is the prodigal son's story in reverse. This time, Jonah is the older son running from the father.

Tarshish is located among the beautiful beaches of Spain, a place most of us would like to go to right about now. In Jonah's day, it was the opposite side of the known world. He runs away as far as he can. He is the only prophet who is recorded as having run away from God. The hero becomes the antihero. But he knows who God is personally; he is a prophet. He knows the truth in Psalm 139:7: "Where can I go from your Spirit? Where can I flee from your presence?"

Jonah is not just running from God; he is running from the temple. Jonah is running from the guaranteed place of encounter between heaven and earth.[15] Unlike so many other books, Jonah repeatedly references the temple and God's presence. And Jonah decides to run as far away from that place as he can! As I discovered when I was in Joppa years ago, it is the closest port to Jerusalem. So, basically, Jonah is saying, "Get me out of here right now as fast as you can and as far away as you can."

There are tons of Christians looking for their Joppa these days. They read the Bible, they know God, they sing the songs, but in their heart of hearts, they don't want God to speak to them personally.

Off Jonah went on his Mediterranean cruise, but God will not be brushed aside and ignored. As the Bible says, God is the potter, and we are the clay. He is Lord, and we are not! You know what happened next? "Then the LORD sent a great wind on the sea, and such a violent storm arose that the ship threatened to break up" (Jonah 1:4). In other translations it says that God hurled a great wind, threw a storm at the boat.[16]

When the storm hit, the sailors, who did this for a living, knew this was not a normal storm: "All the sailors were afraid and each cried out to his own god. And they threw the cargo into the sea to lighten the ship. But Jonah had gone below deck, where he lay down and fell into a deep sleep" (Jonah 1:5). The crew were from all nations, connected to many gods, so they prayed to all of them, seeing if any would answer. They knew that this storm was supernatural, but which deity was responsible? They prayed . . . and nothing. They threw the cargo into the sea to lighten the ship . . . and nothing. And where is Jonah? Praying? Crying out? Helping throw stuff off? Not just snoozing, not just drifting, he's in a deep sleep.

Exhausted, yes, but this is escapism—temporary relief from sin, from God himself. This is what the famous Scottish pastor Hugh Martin called the sleep of sorrow.[17] For many of us today it could be the "sleep" of Netflix or video games to avoid reality.

In a panicked state, the captain yells at Jonah to pray, because Jonah's god could be behind this storm. We might hit the god jackpot and pick the right one. "The captain went to him and said, 'How can you sleep? Get up and call on your god! Maybe he will take notice of us so that we will not perish'" (Jonah 1:6). This is like divine slot machines. Now the most ironic thing is, Jonah is living among non-Jews, among pagans. He is running right into God's mission once again. And don't miss this: Jonah has the most amazing opportunity to witness, to show these lost people who God is, to show them the power of God and the love of God, but Jonah remains defiantly silent.

The sailors needed a backup plan: "Then the sailors said to each other, 'Come, let us cast lots to find out who is responsible for this calamity.' They cast lots and the lot fell on Jonah" (Jonah 1:7). Both Jews and gentiles used lots to understand reality. Lots were used to know God's will in Joshua, 1 Samuel, and Acts. Even in Proverbs it reads, "The lot is cast into the lap, but its every decision is from the LORD" (Proverbs 16:33).

“So they asked him, ‘Tell us, who is responsible for making all this trouble for us? What kind of work do you do? Where do you come from? What is your country? From what people are you?’” (Jonah 1:8). This whole investigation is happening as massive waves are crashing over the ship. Fear, anger, anxiety, panic—what is your race, who are your people, and of course, what gods are connected to you? In this time your nationality was connected to your gods.

Notice the response; it tells us so much. “He answered, ‘I am a Hebrew and I worship the LORD, the God of heaven, who made the sea and the dry land’” (Jonah 1:9). As one scholar wrote, “Since Jonah identifies himself first ethnically, then religiously, we may infer that this ethnicity is foremost in his self-identity.”[18] This gets at the root of his revulsion at God’s command to love his neighbours, his enemies. Jonah’s identity should be in God first and nation second, but it is not. And yet in the middle of this ungodly order is one of the best summaries of truth, orthodoxy confessed in the middle of rebellion against God’s mission. You can have the correct theology and be in relationship with God and still run from the heart and mission of God. Welcome to the church in the West right now.

Jonah said, “I worship the LORD, the God of heaven, who made the sea and the dry land.” Jonah’s God is the only true God. He is the supreme deity, the ultimate source of all power and authority, the creator of all sea and land.

Stunned, the sailors look at him and say, “You worship the King of kings, the Lord of Lords, God Almighty?” This terrifies them more than the storm: “This terrified them and they asked, ‘What have you done?’ (They knew he was running away from the LORD, because he had already told them so.) The sea was getting rougher and rougher. So they asked him, ‘What should we do to you to make the sea calm down for us?’” (Jonah 1:10–11).

In this moment, does Jonah repent? No, he does not. Maybe he thinks he is too far gone. Or more likely, he is angry and so against God’s command that he would rather die than obey: “Pick me up and throw me into the sea,” he replies, “and it will become calm. I know that it is my fault that this great storm has come upon you” (Jonah 1:12). The only way to deal with this appropriate God-given wrath is to give his life; his sin has now affected everyone. He also realizes that no prayer or ritual can compensate for his disobedience.[19] It's like Jonah is saying, "I will take the bullet. My life for your life. I will take the storm so you don't have to."

The sailors, however, feel even more trapped. They don't want to kill a person and make his god angrier by murdering Jonah, so they try again to do everything in their own power: "Instead, the men did their best to row back to land. But they could not, for the sea grew even wilder than before. Then they cried out to the LORD, 'Please, LORD, do not let us die for taking this man's life. Do not hold us accountable for killing an innocent man, for you, LORD, have done as you pleased'" (Jonah 1:13–14). They have tried everything! Calling on other gods, lightening the ship, asking Jonah to pray, casting lots, asking Jonah for advice, rowing, pleading.

With blackness to the north, south, east, and west, salt in their eyes, waves crashing over the decks, two of the men grab Jonah and steady themselves. Jonah closes his eyes. I wonder if for a second he thinks back to his childhood, teen years, his parents, and then the cold of the raging sea hits him: "Then they took Jonah and threw him overboard, and the raging sea grew calm. At this the men greatly feared the LORD, and they offered a sacrifice to the LORD and made vows to him" (Jonah 1:15–16). Amazingly these non-Jews, these pagans, use God's covenantal name, his relationship name, Yahweh. They become followers of this God above all their other gods. They still may have believed in the other gods, but the God of the Hebrews is the Lord of Lords. He is the Almighty God; he is Creator; he is deliverer.[20]

So the good news spreads westward and eastward, for God's mercy is stronger than Jonah's escapism, rebellion, and sin. And what does God do for Jonah? "Now the LORD provided a huge fish to swallow Jonah, and Jonah was in the belly of the fish three days and three nights" (Jonah 1:17). Remember our goal is to consider our heart posture in all of this. Interestingly, this again brings up where we started together. If you place your core identity in the wrong place, it will deeply affect your view of the world and your obedience to God. This passage once again asks who you are. Where is your identity? Jonah said, "I am a Hebrew who knows God."[21] Building your identity on any foundation other than Jesus is trouble. Your core identity might be Canadian, American, Jamaican, Korean, man, woman, sinful, painful, smart, beautiful, ugly, educated—the list goes on and on. Your core identity should be child of God, friend of God, through Jesus Christ.

But the story of Jonah is not just about misplaced identity, it's also about wrestling with the idea that God might have mercy on "them" like he has on you. It's not just about us struggling with going to *those* people, but God confronting in us the idea that I might think my story is more important than God's love for those I do not like.

This came home to me in a personal way when my family was on vacation in the beautiful and charming country of Turkey, doing all the things that tourists do, excited to see this ancient country, especially because it has so much Christian history. I knew I couldn't see everything on this trip, but we visited a few places that were touchstones connecting me to my spiritual grandparents. I remember visiting Ephesus, seeing the ancient town, the famous library, and some other parts of town that I won't mention here. If you know, you know. As I walked through the ancient city, I thought about the apostle Paul. I thought about Acts 19. I thought about the book of Ephesians. I kept saying, "I am walking where Paul walked!" This is where the Ephesian church met, and one day I will meet them face to face.

Then we arrived at the Great Theatre, located on the slope of Panayir (Pion) Hill opposite Harbour Street. I was excited because this was the place where Paul had his encounter in Acts 19. I asked our Muslim guide, "This is the theatre where there was such trouble for Paul, right?" "Yes, yes," he said, "It's in the New Testament, but I remind you this is a Muslim country." I was struck by the soft hostility.

Well, we made our way to Istanbul (historically, Constantinople), which has now become one of my favourite cities on earth. You can literally, physically, emotionally, and culturally see the mix of East and West. The colour, the smells, the people—all were so amazing. It is a city that, other than the Holy Land, has been at the centre of so much of history, as Richard Temple pointed out, "[Constantinople] was Paris, London, New York, all in one—and more."[22]

We crossed over the Bosphorus Bridge, visited the Topkapi and Dolmabahçe Palaces, and then arrived at the famed Blue Mosque. My wife and I entered after she covered her head. The sight was stunning—beauty and colour everywhere. As all the tourists took photos, we stood quietly beside each other and prayed, asking for Jesus to be welcome and that people would see him as the Son of God. We prayed that he would enter the dreams of the leaders and the people.

Then we arrived at the place I wanted to see the most, Hagia Sophia. At that time in Turkey's history, it was no longer a site of worship but a national museum. That has changed again since our visit, and Hagia Sophia is now a functioning mosque again, to the joy and anger of many in Turkey and around the world. As I walked around with my wife and parents, we began to see the Christian imagery behind the dust, in the shadows and alongside of the much more predominant Islamic writing. We could see where one grand mosaic of Jesus had been. Then another of Mary holding the baby Jesus and, as I looked up at the centre of this grand historic church, I could see where there were still remnants of four Seraphim, their wings covering their bodies like in the book of Revelation.

On the second level, where I could look out across the vast structure, I glanced down and unexpectedly saw, etched into the ancient stone railing, a small cross. Suddenly anger began to well up in me. This place was dedicated to Jesus! New worship songs were written for the holy Trinity in here, a place where generations of Christians gathered, prayed, listened to God's Word, and dedicated their children. A thousand years of Christian worship happened here, and now it's a museum (and later a mosque). "How dare they?" I thought. "This is our place. This is our church. This is our land. How dare they desecrate it?" Where had my prayers in the Blue Mosque gone, only a few hours earlier?

And then it happened: The Holy Spirit whispered, "Really, Jon? This is the church?" I said, "Yes, God, this is your church, your space, and they have stolen it, desecrated it!" But then he reminded me that the church is his people, not buildings, though they are important. "I live in people, Jon," he said. I could feel the rebuke behind those words. I was beginning to hate those I was called to love and pray for. I was starting to harbour deep resentment towards those I was called to invite to know the one the building was first dedicated to. The unsettling truth is that I love mercy when it is for me, but when mercy is being extended beyond, it begins to feel like collaborating with the enemy rather than collaborating with the heart and mission of God. I was as exposed as Jonah had been before me.

Over and over again in Jonah we see that God is holy love. Over and over again we see that God is drawn to mercy, to compassion, towards people like the Assyrians—violent, angry, sexually and relationally sinful, wholly ignorant of God and his ways. So from the water to the fish to the vomiting, we arrive at the end of the moment. Now we understand the history of the Assyrians, and we know the gravity of Jonah's mission. What happened next is honestly one of the most amazing responses to preaching in history. His enemies, those with all the power, who were the most violent and most oppressive of all people, responded to Jonah's message.

And we would think, coming to the end of the story, that Jonah would be like, "Mission accomplished! God, you are amazing, and I am pretty amazing too because I am a missionary, and I wanted this people to be changed." But no, not really. Jonah loves his country more than the world. When Nineveh repented, and God had mercy on them, Jonah's reaction was, "I feel betrayed, I feel used, I feel like a fool; I hate all of this!" Why this response? Why this anger? As we've already seen, Jonah has made the Jewish relationship with God into an idol because God's love and ongoing forgiveness should only be theirs, right? Remember the analogy of going to Nazi Germany and calling for repentance? Let me take it farther—what if it worked? It would be like Hitler and all his key leaders, along with the whole nation, repenting of the invasions and ongoing Holocaust in 1942. It would be like them giving back all the land, admitting to all the murders, showing people the extermination camps, and God forgiving them! They had already committed the atrocities, already killed, maimed, raped, and destroyed, and God lets you off the hook.

"No, no, no, this is not right," Jonah would say after the awakening. Jonah, by chapter 4, has waited and waited for judgment, but nothing took place. No plagues, no fire from heaven, no invading army, nothing. This mercy threatened, undermined, shocked, and broke his view of God's justice. If God forgives people like this, then he must be lowering himself.[23] Jonah feels wounded, perplexed, undone. So after one of the greatest moves of God in history, one of the greatest responses to preaching, "But to Jonah this seemed very wrong, and he became angry" (Jonah 4:1).

Jonah is actually furious. I imagine his mind filled with words that a man of God should not entertain. His face flushed red, his pace frantic and irritated, yet his anger did not move him from the posture of prayer. Let us not forget that God himself is angry with sin and this nation's wickedness. Remember what the king said about God in Jonah 3:9: "Who knows? God may yet relent and with compassion turn from his fierce anger so that we will not perish."

God is rightly angry and Jonah says, "I am rightly angry." But this is only part of the story. Jonah only likes God as holy and God as judge; he does not want God as mercy and God as compassionate. He wants the fullness of God towards him and his people, but not towards all people.[24] Jonah knows the wholeness of God, that is the fullness of God, will spill over even to his enemies. What had scared him the most is that God might treat them like He has treated Israel. "Who is a God like you who pardons sin and forgives the transgression of the remnant of his inheritance? You do not stay angry forever but delight to show mercy" (Micah 7:18).

Now as most of you know, Jonah has it out with God, "He prayed to the LORD, 'Isn't this what I said, LORD, when I was still at home? That is what I tried to forestall by fleeing to Tarshish. I knew that you are a gracious and compassionate God, slow to anger and abounding in love, a God who relents from sending calamity'" (Jonah 4:2).

"Are you serious? My worst fears have come true. I am disgusted that you asked me to talk to these people in the first place. I cannot stomach this! Why do you think I ran to Tarshish? I hate these people, and I was afraid for my life. But more than personal danger and that they are not part of God's people, they are evil and do not deserve your love or forgiveness!" And even deeper, Jonah was probably thinking about how the Assyrians were bad for God's reputation. Has God lost his mind? What about his holiness, his wisdom, his justice? "I need to defend your reputation, God, even if you will not step up and do your job!"

Years ago, I was walking through my local Chapters, which is sort of like a Barnes and Noble or Waterstones—a large bookstore chain. I made my way back to the religious section to see what Christian books they had in stock. On the way, I walked past the self-help section, the New Age section, the witchcraft section, and all the books from other formal faiths. Then, after arriving at the Christian section, I found it filled with books written by people who had not done their homework, who are spreading conspiracy theories and half-baked academic ideas about the historicity of Jesus. Not only that, but all the gnostic gospels were present, with descriptions on their back covers proclaiming that they had been hidden but were now rediscovered and were equal to the canonical gospels. As I watched people pick up these books and saw others picking up Tarot cards in the witchcraft section and self-help books about mindfulness, I was so upset. I felt like I needed to go to every single one of them and say, "Don't listen to that bad scholarship," or "It's just a lie," or "It will not lead to enlightenment, only eternal loss!" But then the Holy Spirit said, "Jon, I've got this. You don't have to defend me every single time." I was reminded that there is a time to speak and a time not to speak, and in the end, even if I did speak every single time, I would still never be able to catch everyone. But God is everywhere. He's got this. In the end, his character and name will not be overcome.

Jonah, however, had not yet come to trust God with his own reputation, let alone with doing his own job. I love Tim Keller's summary of Jonah's thoughts at this moment in the story, "I just knew you might do something like this! These people are evil, and they only changed because they were scared. They merely promised to start changing and you bestow mercy on them for that! It's good you are a God of mercy but this time you have gone too far."[25] Jonah accuses God for being good, but good to the wrong people: "I knew that you are a gracious and compassionate God, slow to anger and abounding in love, a God who relents from sending calamity" (Jonah 4:2). Jonah has done it again, just like he did on the boat. He has spoken one of the greatest creedal statements about God found in the Hebrew Scriptures. This description is usually spoken towards God's chosen people, the Hebrews, but now it is extended to all people, even violent, abusive, systemically unjust idol worshipers. Sit with that for a while. If God is like this to the ancient version of slavers or Nazis, then our view of how much mercy should be extended is threatened, especially if like Jonah you have been on the receiving end of darkness.[26]

This confession of God's nature is given again and again in the Old Testament. Just after God forgave his people for worshipping the golden calf, this is what we read: "God passed in front of Moses, proclaiming, 'The LORD, the LORD, the compassionate and gracious God, slow to anger, abounding in love and faithfulness'" (Exodus 34:6). David repeats this truth in Psalm 103:8–12, and near the end of the Old Testament, Joel says judgment is coming, but there is still time, because God is merciful: "Rend your heart and not your garments. Return to the LORD your God, for he is gracious and compassionate, slow to anger and abounding in love, and he relents from sending calamity" (Joel 2:13).

But now this love and forgiveness is extended beyond God's people—even to their enemies. When we meditate on what these words mean, we might find there is even more power to this. The words *gracious* and *compassionate* are reserved for God in the Bible.[27] *Compassionate* means tender in his affections. *Gracious* means he longs for and favours others. The word *merciful* is related to the womb, pointing to motherly love. *Slow to anger* means that God does not delight in the punishing of the wicked, nor does he act quickly. *Abounding in love* means God is loyal in love, faithful to a covenant; it is pure marriage love, the Hebrew idea of *hesed*.[28]

Jonah thinks none of these attributes should be extended to the Ninevites. They have committed war crimes and mass killings; they oppress God's people, hate God's Word, break all God's laws. They are dangerous. They are rebellious. Where is God's justice? Where is his protection? Jonah is wondering, "How can I trust you with my future, with my people's future? If you forgive them, will they really change?" If God lets them off the hook, when will it end? Where is the deterrent?

"Now, LORD, take away my life, for it is better for me to die than to live" (Jonah 4:3). Jonah responds, like a child yelling in exaggeration, "Over my dead body; just kill me now!" What cannot be forgotten is that Jonah himself has been forgiven so much, even in this story, but he cannot accept that non-Hebrews should receive that same forgiveness. But there is yet another layer to this that we tend to miss. Many rabbis saw Jonah's story in a more condemning and rebuking way. One scholar wrote,

> They argued that the repentance of the heathen was a judgement on the unrepentant Israel. Jonah was therefore reasoning, Since the heathen are nearer to repentance, I might be causing Israel to be condemned. Rather I would die. In other words recognizing that the heathens of Nineveh might repent in response to God's word, Jonah is aware of the failure of his own people to repent . . . As an Israelite he would rather die than see the heathen repent and shame his own people.[29]

This is like looking in a mirror, realizing what you have become, and then taking it out on others.

What does God do in response? Kill Jonah? Turn him into a pillar of salt? No, God comes close to speak gently: "But the LORD replied, 'Is it right for you to be angry?'" (Jonah 4:4). Jonah chooses not to respond; he just walks away: "Jonah had gone out and sat down at a place east of the city. There he made himself a shelter, sat in its shade and waited to see what would happen to the city" (Jonah 4:5).

In Hebrew, this can read that he "left through the east side of the city." He had entered the grand city through the west side, preached and walked for three days through, and then left out the other side. Not ready to hurry home, not ready to leave everything into God's hands, not praying and asking God for mercy, he stands on the other side of the city hoping for his desired outcome. The forty days are not over, so he still is hoping for judgment.[30]

Oh, but there is more. Jonah made himself a shelter. The word *shelter* is the same word used for the shelters made by the Jews as they wandered the desert for forty years. Later God declared a festival called the Feast of Booths, or the Festival of Tabernacles, to remember this wandering and celebrate God's provision during those years. And why does this matter here? The shelter Jonah makes is the same as the ones built to remind God's people of God's mercy towards them when they rebelled against him. But more, this festival told God's people that God's mercy was for everyone.[31] "Then the survivors from all the nations that have attacked Jerusalem will go up year after year to worship the King, the Lord Almighty, and to celebrate the Festival of Tabernacles" (Zechariah 14:16).

So Jonah is sitting in the historic symbol of mercy, reminding the reader of God's heart for all people. But as he sits in that physical reminder of mercy, he still wants nothing to do with mercy. It is like us sitting in a church building or reading our Bibles and not wanting to give mercy to those we fear or hate.

Well, God does not walk away from Jonah even though Jonah walked away from God. The shelter was rough, so "the LORD God provided a leafy plant and made it grow up over Jonah to give shade for his head to ease his discomfort, and Jonah was very happy about the plant" (Jonah 4:6). The God of the sea, who provided a big fish, is also the God of the earth and plants, and God caused a plant to spring up in a miraculous way. The leafy plant was most likely a castor-bean plant, which grows rapidly in hot climates, is eight to twelve feet tall, has huge leaves, and is easily killed if the stalk is injured. It's a plant found in India, Israel, Africa, and the Middle East.[32]

The plant is better than his shelter, so Jonah is happy. His mood changes. This was selfish joy because of his own comfort. He now had shade from the hot sun. Yet God is about to show him that his joy over personal comfort is nothing compared to the joy and love he should have over the salvation of a whole city. What does God do? "But at dawn the next day God provided a worm, which chewed the vine so that it withered" (Jonah 4:7). A simple worm, a grub, kills Jonah's joy.

But God is not done. Earlier, God had sent a huge storm, a massive wind, a fish, and then a worm. Now he sends more wind. "When the sun rose, God provided a scorching east wind, and the sun blazed on Jonah's head so that he grew faint. He wanted to die, and said, 'It would be better for me to die than to live'" (Jonah 4:8).

Hot, angry, lonely, tired, sunburned, exasperated by the loss of the plant, full of anger that God has not destroyed the city, again Jonah wants to die. Jonah's love shrivels just like the plant's leaves. "Just kill me now!"

> But God said to Jonah, "Is it right for you to be angry about the plant?"
>
> "It is," he said. "And I'm so angry I wish I were dead."
>
> But the Lord said, "You have been concerned about this plant, though you did not tend it or make it grow. It sprang up overnight and died overnight." (Jonah 4:9–10)

God reminds Jonah, "You did not tend it or make it grow" (Jonah 4:10). God did. I love what another author wrote about this passage:

> Let's analyze this anger of yours, Jonah.... It represents your concern over your beloved plant—but what did it really mean to you? Your attachment to it couldn't be very deep, for it was here one day and gone the next. Your concern was dictated by self-interest, not by genuine love. You never had the devotion of a gardener. If you feel bad as you do what would you expect the gardener to feel like who tended the plant and watched it grow only to see it die? This is how I feel about Nineveh, only much more so. All those people, all those animals—I made them; I have cherished them all these years. Nineveh has cost Me no end of effort, and it means the world to Me. Your pain is nothing compared to Mine when I contemplate their destruction.[33]

God points out how Jonah's proud and angry posture had led him to have greater pity for a small shrub than for a whole city of people. Jonah had moved from thinking of these people as those made in the image of God to being almost subhuman. Jonah became what he hated and did not even see it. He was thinking like the Ninevites had thought about Jonah's own people. And then it happens. God points Jonah to look westward to the great walls of the city and says with compassion, "Should I not have concern for the great city of Nineveh, in which there are more than a hundred and twenty thousand people who cannot tell their right hand from their left—and also many animals?" (Jonah 4:11).

Concern is the word for *compassion*; it literally means to grieve over, to have your heart break, to weep over something. This is amazing—God is saying, "Should I not be concerned? Can you not see that I am heartbroken, weeping over this city?"[34]

It's like God is saying, "Jonah, they cannot tell their right hand from their left; they are spiritually blind, left to false gods, to their own strength, thinking that sex, money, and power is the only thing, nothing more. They don't know me, that there is salvation now and forever. I keep having mercy and forgiving you and the Jewish people for sin, why not them also?"

Once again God is undoing Jonah's wrong view. God did not choose the Jews to be his people at the expense of all others. He chose them, walked with them, and gave them his Word and covenant—all for the sake of the world! This is why Israel was called: "I will also make you a light for the Gentiles, that my salvation may reach to the ends of the earth" (Isaiah 49:6).

And of course, the story of Jonah famously ends with us not knowing Jonah's response, only God's questions. For me, that seems right. God is asking us, the Western church, these same questions, and we are still not sure which way we will turn. The book of Jonah is a heart check for you, your ministry, your church, your kingdom movement. If we don't check our hearts, or if we choose another path, there may be little hope for the church in the West, let alone for the billions of souls connected in this moment.

To check your hearts, ask yourself the following three questions. First, *have you forgotten you were once Nineveh?* When we forget what we have been saved from, we become like Jonah. When we forget that we all were blind and all deserving of hell and separation from God, then anger, resentment, confusion, and bitterness will replace faith, love, and hope. When we forget his mercy extended to us, we will become hard. When our comfort becomes the gravitational centre of our thinking and acting: the comfort of what we already know, the comfort of what was, the comfort of how we used to do church, the comfort of the Christian holy huddle, where everyone looks the same, talks the same, and walks the same. As one author said it, "There is a Jonah that lurks in the heart of every Christian, smug prejudice, empty traditionalism, exclusive solidarity."[35]

Second, let's be honest about who we struggle with. I am sure you have caught this: I love history, and I love personal history. We live in a moment where we can access so much of our genealogy online. I found the boat manifest with my grandfather's name when he immigrated to Canada from the UK. His wife, my maternal grandmother, was a direct distant relative of the famed composer Bach. My other grandfather did tons of family research showing French, Irish, and Scottish roots. He also uncovered scandal and assault, which resulted in my family's very beginnings, dark as they were. It's funny how when you travel to a place your ancestors came from, see a picture, or find an ancient governmental document, you feel connected, whole, home.

We love to watch others find their history and see their emotion, their heartache, their feeling of belonging. Many of us love watching shows like, *Who Do You Think You Are, Roots Less Traveled, Relative Race, Long Lost Family, The Generations Project, Ancestors,* and *Genealogy Roadshow.*

Right now, in this decolonization period, more people are looking to recover what was killed, buried, lost, and stolen. There is a deep ache for home, and the journey is needed. Even within missional Christian communities, the mess and damage of the past is hard to wade through. I don't think there will ever be full unity before the new heaven and the earth. Although this journey is important, let's not believe that our histories—known or lost—are the promised land.

What I have found fascinating when talking to others is the idea that finding one's cultural roots will uncover a more whole, purer culture. But you won't find that. You might find a culture that provides deep personal meaning or a sense of home or belonging, but then as a Christian, you will quickly see how that culture also was an oppressor and was sinful, just in different directions. When I sit with my African friends and hear them speak about the deep pain related to slavery, this comes up again and again. For example, before the transatlantic slave trade, there were four hundred years of tribal slavery in many areas. One does not excuse the other, nor should it be weaponized to justify injustice and sin. My point is this: Depravity is a human condition. One's search for ancestry does not negate that our core identity is in Christ.

Which brings up the real question: *Who do we mistrust, who do we struggle with, who do we hate?* Government leaders, teachers, white people, Black people, "those" immigrants, Muslims, gays, men, women, trans, straight, Democrats and Republicans, progressives, Jews, Palestinians, Chinese, Taiwanese, Korean, or Japanese. The Liberals are crazy; no, it's the Conservatives; no, I am Indian and let me tell you what the Pakistanis have done! Just fill in the blank. There are over 3,000 formal tribes in the African context today, and the divisions are deep, real, and dangerous. The list goes on and on: your neighbour, boss, former friends, family members, and even yourself—don't count out self-hate! "I don't deserve God's love; you don't know what I have done, what I think."

Each person or group mentioned or not mentioned are all fallen in the same way (original sin and total depravity) and are marked by many different sins. The truth is not grey; it is absolute. Did you notice that God called Jonah to go and preach against the sin of Nineveh? There's plenty of sin to go around! God sent Jonah to preach so they would be saved, so that they would know God. God sent Jonah to love his neighbour.

So who do you think does not deserve God's love? Understand this: *No one* is going to get away with sin. But God tends to call us to those we want nothing to do with so they will be saved, and so we will see our own great need—because we are *just as in need* of his mercy as those we hate!

One of the best exercises at this point of the book would be to write out every group or person you struggle with. Look at the list, sit with it, pray over it, and ask the Holy Spirit to work, for this is the key to turning the tide.

Here's the third and final question: When was the last time you wept over the lostness of your neighbours, friends, and family—your great city? God had compassion and grieved over that evil city. Later,

Jesus did the same over the great city of Jerusalem. "As he approached Jerusalem and saw the city, he wept over it. . . . 'They will not leave one stone on another, because you did not recognize the time of God's coming to you'" (Luke 19:41, 44).

If you read the Gospels, the pattern is shocking: Jesus cries twenty times for every time he laughs. This is not saying Jesus was out of control or that he was depressed or having mood swings. His emotional state shows the true nature of God and the true nature of the world. If you have never wept over or been deeply moved over the lostness of people, you have not fully entered into and known the heart of God. Ask God to move you to weep as the God you love weeps. This sorrow can only come as a gift from God. Some of you that have a certain expression of the spiritual gift of intercession have had this happen. But for the vast majority of us, this will need to be a God-given gift. If you are willing, start praying today that God shows you the world as he sees it and keep asking until it happens. When you see how lost you were, and when you know the heart of God, then your eyes will open up.

The darker the night, the brighter the stars. The deeper the grief, the closer is God.

—FYODOR DOSTOEVSKY

When I saw you from afar, I thought you were a monster. When you got closer, I thought you were just an animal. When you got even closer, I saw that you were a human, but when we were face to face I realized that you were my brother.

—AFRICAN PROVERB

All evil began with some attempt at superiority.

—G. K. CHESTERTON

CHAPTER 18

Would I Even Want to Live Beside Those People?

It is one thing to see beauty; it is another not to cross bridges; and it is yet another to preach judgment at them and see those we don't feel comfortable with or who we do not like get saved. But then we can just cross the bridge back over to our "safe" side, right? We always have our God-given "out." No, to win in this repaganizing and pluralistic world for God, we need to stay.

This is not some short-term mission trip. We need permanent presence. Wonder—just wonder—if God asks you not just to preach and shake the dust off our shoes but to settle and *live in* Nineveh? It is one thing to be willing to go, but it is another thing altogether to stay, to live with all "those" people! You, your kids, and your friends will be exposed day in and day out to their way of life, their worldview, their attempts to subtly or brutally conform you to the ways of the world. Could you live there for the rest of your life knowing that you will never get back to the promised land, to the place where it is so much godlier, safer, just . . . *better*. Again, this is our cultural moment right now whether we like it or not. And it is here, for a brief moment, that Daniel becomes our teacher.

How do we weep and witness at the same time? This is the real question of this whole book. What does it mean to thrive in exile, to live well in a de-Christian, post- or pre-Christian, postmodern, pluralistic, multicultural world? How do we thrive when the Christian faith is less and less affirmed, less and less at the centre and more on the margins? When I ask myself these questions, Daniel comes to the forefront of my mind.

The most helpful part for us comes before the lion's den and before the fiery furnace. God's people were about to be exiled from their land for seventy years, and the temple built by Solomon would eventually be destroyed. As we know, this all took place because God's people would not obey God's Word and live within their covenant. The prophets Isaiah and Jeremiah had warned them about their sin. The prophets tried to tell the people to turn back to God or they would be judged. Unfortunately, the people didn't listen.

> Therefore the LORD Almighty says this: "Because you have not listened to my words, I will summon all the peoples of the north and my servant Nebuchadnezzar king of Babylon," declares the LORD, "and I will bring them against this land and its inhabitants and against all the surrounding nations. . . . This whole country will become a desolate wasteland, and these nations will serve the king of Babylon seventy years. (Jeremiah 25:8–9, 11)

But we are not at wholesale destruction yet. This happens later under Jehoiakim's brother. The story of Daniel falls between disaster and full out destruction—in the middle of a really bad time, something interesting for us to reflect on living in this transitional moment.

Later we can hear their pain and deep longings living in exile as the people of God sang in Psalm 137:1–4:

> By the rivers of Babylon we sat and wept
>   when we remembered Zion.
> There on the poplars
>   we hung our harps,
> for there our captors asked us for songs,
>   our tormentors demanded songs of joy;
>   they said, "Sing us one of the songs of Zion!"

> How can we sing the songs of the LORD
> while in a foreign land?

But that's later. Daniel begins like this: "In the third year of the reign of Jehoiakim king of Judah, Nebuchadnezzar king of Babylon came to Jerusalem and besieged it" (Daniel 1:1). Babylon, the world's superpower of its time and known for its cruelty in conquest, is also the birthplace and epicentre of worship to Marduk. We see its starting point as a nation is all the way back in Genesis 11, when their ancestors built the tower of Babel. Now the roots of Babel have morphed into a global superpower.[1]

As we read the story of Daniel, we need to feel the military might, the political dominance, and the religious darkness. But don't get stuck in the looming large storm. God is not unaware, nor has he given up control. Listen again: "And the Lord delivered Jehoiakim king of Judah into his hand" (Daniel 1:2). God's name here is not Yahweh, God's marriage or covenantal name. The Hebrew name used is Adonai, which means God is Lord, is master, is superior.[2] By the use of this name, we know God is in control. When evil seems to have the last say, it does not; God always has the last say! Yet the upcoming journey is painful even as God oversees it. Not just the king has been taken, but also "some of the articles from the temple of God. These he carried off to the temple of his god in Babylonia and put in the treasure house of his god" (Daniel 1:2). Those items represented sacrifice, prayer, forgiveness, grace, and relational connection. They would have been brought to the largest of the fifty-plus temples in Babylon, a tower just like Babel, and there God's items would have been laid beneath and submitted under the demonic idol Marduk.[3] But unlike holy history when God's very presence overcame the idols and the powers behind them (see 1 Samuel 5), this time nothing happens.

Just like in our day, the declaration in their day is *"Our god is stronger than your god."* Can you imagine the pain, the powerlessness, the thought of God's people—maybe our God is not the all-powerful, only God? Don't forget that in the ancient Near East kings were the representatives of their gods!

But this is where the story helps us in our day. For God's people, things move to darker places:

> Then the king ordered Ashpenaz, the chief of his court officials, to bring into the king's service some of the Israelites from the royal family and the nobility—young men without any physical defect, handsome, showing aptitude for every kind of learning, well informed, quick to understand, and qualified to serve in the king's palace. He was to teach them the language and literature of the Babylonians. The king assigned them a daily amount of food and wine from the king's table. They were to be trained for three years, and after that they were to enter the king's service. (Daniel 1:3–5)

Many think these young men were around twenty, but others think they might have been much younger, more like thirteen to sixteen years old. But the description of these young men is key. They are all good looking, intelligent, already educated, and from the right type of homes.

As a modern reader, we can miss what is really going on. This is about assimilation. This is about propaganda. The goal is clear: eradicate Jewish belief, faith, and custom. And how? Well, get the best and brightest of the Jewish community fully assimilated into Babylonian society. This is intentional seduction. This conversion would be complete if they stayed and joined the system or, even better, if they went home and started making their homes like Babylon. They would be religiously, economically, spiritually, politically, sexually, linguistically, and relationally transformed, thus becoming evangelists for the Babylonian way of life. This was a three year, twenty-four hours a day, all-in process,[4] and it was similar to what our schools and social-media feeds are attempting to do to our children and to us today.

Years ago, my children came home from public school, all of them under grade five, and told me that pride month had started, which is normal here. But what we did not know was the whole school was gathered outside and made to stand as the gay pride flag was raised above the school. Then they heard a series of speeches on why this is good and right and faithful to agree with as Canadians. As another example, my country has rightly tried to repair and reconcile for our terrible history with the Indigenous communities whose land this was before any other. The painful struggle to work through this is needed and must happen. But the line between understanding and participation becomes blurred sometimes. More than once my children have been asked to participate in specifically religious indigenous ceremonies in their public schools. They've had to say no respectfully while still trying to learn in order to make a difference in our shared history. The line is hard to see sometimes. Trust me, from podcasts to reels to TikTok influencers, so many people want to disciple our children in their ways.

The question in Daniel—like it is in our day—is this: Would these young men, God's people, give in to the easier path, or would they remain holy and different? Does God still own these young men body and soul, or does the court of Nebuchadnezzar own them? So they have been captured and brought in, and they will be taught, trained, given the best of the best that Babylon has to offer, and the indoctrination will not be complete until it touches the core of personal identity.

In ancient cultures like Daniel's, a person's core identity was intrinsically bound up in their name: "Among those who were chosen were some from Judah: Daniel, Hananiah, Mishael and Azariah. The chief official gave them new names: to Daniel, the name Belteshazzar; to Hananiah, Shadrach; to Mishael, Meshach; and to Azariah, Abednego" (Daniel 1:6–7). As I have shared before, I grew up going to Sunday school. I had heard these names so many times. These famed young adults had been on the flannelgraph like Jonah. But only recently did I come to know what their old and new names meant:

Daniel means "Israel's God is my judge."
Hananiah means "Israel's God has been gracious."
Mishael means "Who can compare to my God, no one!"
Azariah means "Israel's God is my help."
Belteshazzar means "May a god protect his life or Lady goddess, protect the king."
Shadrach means "I am fearful of Marduk."

Meshach means "I am despised, humiliated."
Abednego means "a slave of Nabu."[5]

Their new Babylonian names are directly connected to pagan gods. The new names are given to eradicate Jewish cultural identity, to undermine Jewish faith, and to humiliate these young leaders. The names remove the name of the true and living God that each one of them bears. The new names make other gods and pagan kings the centre of their lives. Every time their new names would be uttered by themselves or by others, they will be reminded of their losses and that they are defeated slaves. Their Babylonian indoctrination begins at the core of their personalities.

And yet, was life so bad? They got off better than most. They were young, good looking, and smart. They had access to power and its benefits, and if they moved away from the Jewish faith of their parents, if they compromised, who knows? Since God had not shown up to help, and the king's word is law, maybe compromise is a good, logical, helpful, freeing thing.

However, "Daniel resolved not to defile himself with the royal food and wine, and he asked the chief official for permission not to defile himself this way" (Daniel 1:8). Why did Daniel and his friends choose not to eat the king's food? Some say the food was dedicated to idols. Yes, that is part of what is going on here, but that is not the full answer. Others point out that they are good, orthodox, religiously observant Jews and would not eat food that was considered religiously unclean. Yes, but what about the wine? Wine was not unclean according to Jewish law. More is going on here than meets the eye. Their refusal helped them avoid the allure of the whole moment.[6]

Already in eight small verses, we begin to see what each one of us must cling to and live out to thrive in exile. What do we already see? Daniel trusted in the sovereignty of God. Daniel made God's written Word central to his life. He knew God had the final say and chose to obey God over the king. But what we cannot read into this story is constant protest. This was not constant revolt; it was not countercultural living at every single moment. We have to pair Daniel's no with God's yes.

What did the prophet Jeremiah speak to the exiled community? Did he say, "Listen to the call of God—protest only, countercultural only, on the margins only, monastery and hiding only?" No, God says I have placed you in Babylon, so *thrive* in exile. Flourish where I have planted you. How much clearer could God's word have been?

> This is what the LORD Almighty, the God of Israel, says to all those I carried into exile from Jerusalem to Babylon: "Build houses and settle down; plant gardens and eat what they produce. Marry and have sons and daughters; find wives for your sons and give your daughters in marriage, so that they too may have sons and daughters. Increase in number there; do not decrease. Also, seek the peace and prosperity of the city to which I have carried you into exile. Pray to the LORD for it, because if it prospers, you too will prosper. (Jeremiah 29:4–7)

We are called to increase in number in exile. Love the city we are in. Participate in the life of the city. Have families, work, be people of peace, love your enemies. Be in the city but not fully of the city, and pursue a normal way of life, knowing deliverance will come.

Pray for the city that invaded you. Pray for the city that destroyed the temple of God. Pray for those who are trying to make you worship idols and for those who have changed your names. Pray for those who killed your friends and neighbours. Pray for the city full of wickedness. Pray for the city that kills and overcomes. But don't just pray "God, go kill them. Give them what they deserve." No, ask God to grant the city peace, God's blessing on every dimension of life—physical, emotional, mental, and spiritual—healing and wholeness for Babylon! God is saying, "Daniel, don't divorce. Dive in!"

Here in Toronto we have over 6.4 million people. We live in the most multicultural city on earth. There are 150 plus heart languages spoken every day. It is sexually diverse in every direction, and every religion on earth is here—Muslims, Hindus, Baha'i, Sikhs, Witches, Buddhists, Jews, and the list goes on and on. We have spiritualism, agnosticism, and atheism. Our city is creative, artistic, and the engine of the economy for our country, with banking, fashion, and trade. It is fast paced, intensive, vibrant, global.

How do followers of Jesus live in a city like this, in a country like ours? Don't panic. Do not grow suspicious or angry, and don't get so excited when people start moving back towards the idea of God or his values without meeting him personally. Atheism is not our greatest enemy; theism is (that is, believing in God without knowing him). We see true Christianity retreat and cultural Christian-ish renewal at the same time. No matter, we are all called to be like Daniel: He protested when needed and lived, loved, and served as he could with a clear conscience before God.

We see the fruits of Daniel's choices developing in the next part of chapter 1: "Now God had caused the official to show favor and compassion to Daniel" (Daniel 1:9). God is fully in control. From the arc of human history, to redemption in time, to one little situation among so many, God is working. God caused favour from Daniel's boss—you know, the boss who worshipped demons and worked for the king that had destroyed his nation and killed off family and friends before enslaving him and his other friends. "But the official told Daniel, 'I am afraid of my lord the king, who has assigned your food and drink. Why should he see you looking worse than the other young men your age? The king would then have my head because of you'" (Daniel 1:10). In other words, "I will die if you do not obey me; the king's word is law. I respect you guys and really want to help you, but my life is on the line and so is yours."

Daniel, living with such God-given wisdom, knew this was no picketing moment. This was not some "I am going to show these pagans why they are so very wrong, don't you know my rights, I am writing my MP, my congressmen, just watch what I post on social" moment:

> Daniel then said to the guard whom the chief official had appointed over Daniel, Hananiah, Mishael and Azariah, "Please test your servants for ten days: Give us nothing but vegetables to eat and water to drink. Then compare our appearance with that of the

> young men who eat the royal food, and treat your servants in accordance with what you see." So he agreed to this and tested them for ten days. (Daniel 1:11–14)

Notice the Jewish names are used again, not the Babylonian names. Yes, in the middle of the first great test, we hear the names "Israel's God is my judge," "God is still gracious," "Who can compare to my God, no one," and "Israel's God is my help." Daniel is saying something like this: "Let us be the demonstration of our God to you. Let us be the gospel to you, great and powerful chief official. Here is the test: In only ten days, we will look better, feel better, and be stronger than all the others. It will be because of Yahweh, not Marduk."[7]

By the way, this is not a call to be vegetarian or vegan. The point of the test and fast is to let God do the impossible with less resources in an allotted time that is seemingly impossible. And notice how polite Daniel was. Not angry, or "This is my right," or "You stupid pagan, don't you know who I am?" Gentleness and respect. Years ago, I heard a pastor talking about how to protest with gentleness. He pointed out the different ways one could respond to the question, "Hey, do you want a smoke?" You could say, "No, thank you. I don't smoke." Or you could say, "Me, smoke? Are you stupid? That will give me cancer! I don't want your death sticks in my face. I would not give cigarettes to anyone. Do you hate me? Do you want my doctor's number?" Do you see the difference? It is not the protest but the attitude and the method that matter so much.

And what happened? "At the end of the ten days they looked healthier and better nourished than any of the young men who ate the royal food. So the guard took away their choice food and the wine they were to drink and gave them vegetables instead" (Daniel 1:15–16). Now the protest back in verse 8 can be more fully understood. They are not just obeying God's word because of idols and unclean food. More is happening. Who gets praise for the coming successes of these young men? Is it the king, his table, his food, his education, his gods? Or is it God? Daniel makes the countercultural decision and steps out in such a profound public way that either he totally fails or God steps in and does the impossible.

God moved and kept moving: "To these four young men God gave knowledge and understanding of all kinds of literature and learning. And Daniel could understand visions and dreams of all kinds" (Daniel 1:17). For a third time in the passage it says, "God gave." Three times God moves—from the largest to the smallest of details, God is aware, involved, and keeps his story going. Here God moves in the natural and supernatural. God blesses these teenagers with wisdom and visions. God empowers them with natural ability, learned ability, and spiritual gifts—all leading to God's glory and, ultimately, to one of the greatest divine interventions in human history.

Thriving in exile is possible: "At the end of the time set by the king to bring them into his service, the chief official presented them to Nebuchadnezzar. The king talked with them, and he found none equal to Daniel, Hananiah, Mishael and Azariah; so they entered the king's service" (Daniel 1:18–19). Yes, we *can* be out of sync with culture and yet live in it. We can bring wisdom in an age of folly. The question for us is: Is this a time for protest, or is it a time for transformation? The answer is yes. Daniel shows us what real presence looks like.

Did you just read that and move on? Don't. God knows you by name, right? He decided that you should live here and now, right? In this time and place, right? Have you asked God to give you the peace to settle in Babylon? Remember, since the Holy Spirit lives in you, even your presence brings light into darkness.

As you slowly lose your debate with God about settling down and staying, remember these two things. First, the sovereignty of God is stronger than any king, any massive change, or any decline. The way we live in freedom, the way we are not washed away by fear, the way we choose not to compromise, the way we thrive in exile living is that we know, confess, and believe that this is God's world. God is creator, even as things are changing around us. Do not fear, because God is in charge, and he will make all things right. Sovereignty is the underpinning to faithfulness.

The people's sin brought this exile about, so Daniel could have said, "God, this is not fair; I have the right to be bitter. God did this, so I am out." Daniel instead had a profound sense of God's hand in the situation. Do you think God is in heaven looking down saying, "Oh, no!

All these churches are closing in Canada and in the West. What am I going to do?" No, God is still on the throne, and he will accomplish his purposes. Do you trust him to stay in Babylon?

Second, this case study once again brings up the role of God's Word in our presence and witness. God's Word was central for Daniel thriving in exile. Nine chapters later, we see the centrality of God's Word: "I, Daniel, understood from the Scriptures, according to the word of the LORD given to Jeremiah the prophet, that the desolation of Jerusalem would last seventy years" (Daniel 9:2). The reason Daniel would not defile himself at the king's table was based on God's law and God's revealed purposes. For Daniel and for us, the Scriptures are the ultimate authority for faith, life, and practice. Our culture likes to undermine absolute truth. We are told to live our own truth and that everything is flexible and up to debate. We are told that life, gender, sexuality, justice, politics, money, business, relationships, and religion are just opinions, personal choices, and are not grounded in anything absolute. No, God is our Lord, and God has spoken the truth. How do we thrive in exile? We continue to choose to be formed by and live under God's good and kind Word. We in Canada, for example, must make the decision now about God's Word before full collapse of the church. King David put it best when he wrote in the Psalms, "My heart is set on keeping your decrees to the very end. . . . I consider all your precepts right, I hate every wrong path" (Psalm 119:112, 128). Generations later, Paul wrote it this way, "Watch your life and doctrine closely. Persevere in them, because if you do, you will save both yourself and your hearers" (1 Timothy 4:16).

In the story in Daniel, notice that there was not a hint of a double life among these young, strong, smart, good looking young adults. They had it all but chose to honour God. The way of Babylon that Daniel faced, which is mirrored by what we are being told and offered today, is that you can be a follower of God and live a double life and believe all will be okay. You can eat at the tables of the false king and the true king. Babylon living is compromised living; it is mixing truth and error. Will we be like Daniel and choose to risk everything for God, or will we compromise?

Hundreds of years later, Paul wrote to a group of Christians living in an ancient city that was different yet similar to Babylon. We can hear echoes of Daniel. Paul wrote to those who already followed Jesus:

> Or do you not know that wrongdoers will not inherit the kingdom of God? Do not be deceived: Neither the sexually immoral nor idolaters nor adulterers nor men who have sex with men nor thieves nor the greedy nor drunkards nor slanderers nor swindlers will inherit the kingdom of God. And that is what some of you were. But you were washed, you were sanctified, you were justified in the name of the Lord Jesus Christ and by the Spirit of our God. (1 Corinthians 6:9–11)

And lastly, to thrive in exile God must have the final say over our names. Who gets to name you? No matter what family says, work says, the government says, friends say, or enemies say, God is the one who knows us and names us. Babylon looks for the most beautiful, the smartest, the families with advantage to model and form. Sound familiar?

But what does Jesus say? "I am the good shepherd; I know my sheep and my sheep know me" (John 10:14). He has the final say over us! We are his sheep. You are—because of Jesus Christ—forgiven, without blemish, reconciled to God, free from accusation, not owned by Satan, and seated with Jesus above evil. You are saints; you have been given grace and peace with God. You are chosen, called, foreknown, adopted sons and daughters of Adonai. You are redeemed, sealed by the Holy Spirit, and guaranteed physical resurrection. Made in the image of God, you have been baptized into Jesus's death and baptized into Jesus's resurrection. You are the actual temple of the Holy Spirit, have been bought with a high price, and have been guaranteed eternal life. You are his possession, justified, crucified in Christ, no longer a slave to sin but a slave to Jesus, loved by Jesus. You have acceptance and security in the love of God. This is the content of your name. This is who you truly are.

Many would end the book here, but it would be the wrong place to end. One question remains: Is there ever a time to say, "Enough is enough"? Is there a time we get to stand and fight and say no? When do we stand and say, "I will not bow down to the king's image no matter what"? Moses disobeyed Pharaoh, Jesus disobeyed the Pharisees and Sadducees, Peter and John the Sanhedrin, and Paul the Emperor of Rome. And the answer is yes. There is a time, but we must be clear when it *is* time and when it is *not* time.

Wherever politics tries to be redemptive, it is promising too much. Where it wishes to do the work of God, it becomes not divine, but demonic.

—POPE BENEDICT XVI

A Man with God is always in the majority.

—JOHN KNOX

But Peter and John replied, "Which is right in God's eyes: to listen to you, or to him? You be the judges! As for us, we cannot help speaking about what we have seen and heard."

—ACTS 4:19–20

"Ya Rabbi Yassou" ("O Lord Jesus").

—THE LAST WORDS OF TWENTY-ONE YOUNG CHRISTIAN MEN WHO WERE BRUTALLY SLAUGHTERED ON A LIBYAN BEACH BY ISLAMIC STATE MEMBERS

CHAPTER 19

When It Is Good and Right to Say No

Some of you will remember November 15, 1982. The Cold War was still raging. On that day, something massive took place at the funeral of Leonid Brezhnev, the leader of the Soviet Union. Many of you reading this were not alive and don't remember the long shadow of that Cold War. I was seven when this took place. It was the height of the Cold War, and the Soviet leader had just died. But it was his wife that did something shocking, dangerous, and unexpected. One wrote,

> She was the First Lady of the Soviet Union for 18 years. Her husband, a loyal and lifelong communist, used the KGB to quell any opposition to his repressive regime. For Brezhnev and his wife in this environment, the Church did not exist. They never spoke of religion and certainly never practiced it. Faith was seen as a weakness in Soviet culture, to be controlled and limited by the government. No one with any government aspirations could be known as a person of faith. Brezhnev imprisoned priests and believers, closing seminaries and churches whenever they got in his way. When her husband died, something extraordinary took place. As Vice President, George Bush represented the U.S. at the Brezhnev's funeral, Bush was deeply moved by a silent protest carried out by Brezhnev's widow. She stood motionless by the

coffin until seconds before it was closed. Then—just as the soldiers touched the lid—Brezhnev's wife performed an act of great courage and hope, a gesture that must surely rank as one of the most profound acts of civil disobedience ever committed: she reached down and made the sign of the cross on her husband's chest. There, in the citadel of secular, atheistic power, the wife of the man who had run it all hoped that her husband was wrong. She hoped that there was another life, and that that life was best represented by Jesus who died on the cross, and that the same Jesus might yet have mercy on her husband.[1]

As I mentioned in the previous chapter, religiously inspired civil disobedience is found throughout all the Bible. In the story of Exodus, the midwives were commanded to kill every Jewish boy, but they did not and lied about it to Pharaoh. Daniel and his friends broke the law by not worshipping the king and not bowing down to idols. When do we do the sign of the cross in public, no matter the consequences? When do we have God's blessing and backing to break the law?

For me, these questions are paramount, and Paul shows us if, when, and how, but let's begin with Esther to set the scene. This book is such a gift for us. You may wonder why this book that is over 2,400 years old is helpful to you today. It is helpful in the strangest ways because this historical book is unlike any other in the Bible:

1. God is not mentioned once in this whole book.
2. There are zero Messianic promises in Esther—Jesus and future hope are not found here.
3. No person in the book explicitly prays, reads the Scriptures, or gives to the poor.
4. God's Word or law is mentioned only once, and it is hated when mentioned. But the laws of the land, the secular laws, are mentioned fourteen times. God's law feels weak and small, but the state law and culture feel overwhelmingly strong and in charge.
5. There is no reference to the promised land, to the temple, or to God's promises to his people.

6. This book takes place during a potential genocide.
7. A woman is the centre of the story, which happens only one other time in Ruth.[2]

That short summary of Esther is what many of us often feel. As I have shared throughout this book, we are starting to look around and ask: Where is God? Where are his promises and his help? We feel like strangers in our own countries, no matter our gender or ethnic background, simply because we are Christians.

To understand the potency of this story, we need to take a moment to do a bit more historical research. The story of Esther takes place nearly five hundred years before Christ and about fifty years after Ezra led the Jews back to Jerusalem from captivity. Yet many of the Jewish people still lived in the land of Persia. Esther and Mordecai, along with many other Jews, had chosen not to make the trek back to Judah. They seemed content to stay in Susa, the capital city of Persia, where the story is set.[3] Those who stayed had ongoing, peaceful coexistence, but the fragile peace is suddenly broken.

So in our day as peace is also seemingly broken, what do we do about growing government oversight? What do we do about corporations like banks, schools, medical, and clinical oversight organizations that keep saying we must support, teach, and agree to things that go against the Christian faith that has been held for 2,000 years? When is it okay to say no to the government, to your boss, or to an organization because of your worldview rooted in faith? Well, it is not as often as some of you want but more often than is comfortable for others. Esther is such an amazing book for us because this is one of the times where godly people break the law for the greater good.

For our conversation, the best place to start is midway through the book:

> When Esther's words were reported to Mordecai, he sent back this answer: "Do not think that because you are in the king's house you alone of all the Jews will escape. . . . For if you remain silent at this time, relief and deliverance for the Jews will arise from another place, but you and your father's family will perish. And who knows

> but that you have come to your royal position for such a time as this?" (Esther 4:12–14)

God had placed Esther in a palace in this pagan government for his purposes. I think we need to pause and say this out loud, "I, my family, my church, and the kingdom initiative I oversee have all been placed in this moment by God." Sometimes simply remembering that can bring needed clarity and courage. The courage for Mordecai was rooted not only in providence but in God's promises. Mordecai knew God had promised that the Jews will never be fully destroyed, just like we know the church will not be overcome. But more importantly, Mordecai demonstrates that one person can change everything. One person can make such a difference for good or evil. When one person is placed by God into a situation, even one person can change the world, but they have to be willing to partner with God to do daring things.

Esther's response is powerful. She says to Mordecai: "Go, gather together all the Jews who are in Susa, and fast for me. Do not eat or drink for three days, night or day. I and my attendants will fast as you do. When this is done, I will go to the king, even though it is against the law. And if I perish, I perish" (Esther 4:16). This pattern of three days and three nights runs throughout Scripture. On the third day Abraham was going to sacrifice Isaac, and God sent an angel to stop him. Jacob was running from Laban, who was going to hurt Jacob, but on the third day God stopped him. Jonah was three days in the belly of the fish. Hosea had a promise of restoration on the third day. All of this is pointing to the coming of the most important of three days: Good Friday through Easter Sunday, three days that will change the world forever! Even here in a moment of loss and death, we find hope. Not optimism, but real, God-given, historically rooted hope.

Now back to the story. So much is at stake, and yet God can handle anyone. Have you ever thought about that? God is not taken aback; God is not afraid; God is not intimidated by anyone, including those with all the power. Those with all the military might, those with the best laid plans—they are no match. Fast forward to Esther 5: "On the third day Esther put on her royal robes and stood in the inner court of the palace, in front of the king's hall. The king was sitting on his royal throne in the hall, facing the entrance" (Esther 5:1). This can be read in the original language as "she wore the kingdom." She prepped. She came dressed for success. She knew that this was a great risk. So she dresses to kill. She knew that the king would see her before she even entered the forbidden court.

We need to remind ourselves this act was illegal. The king was sitting in his amazing 350-square-foot audience hall. Historians point out that there are pictures of the king sitting on his throne. In his hand was a large golden scepter. But beside the throne was a soldier with a large axe. This soldier was not to guard the king. If the king did not call for you, then you die. If you got into the throne room, and he did not extend his scepter towards you, then you die.[4] You'd get your head cut off by that big axe. Do you feel how serious this is?

After three days of fasting, Esther goes and breaks the law. Would she live or die? The queen comes in all her royal breathtaking beauty: "When he saw Queen Esther standing in the court, he was pleased with her and held out to her the gold sceptre that was in his hand. So Esther approached and touched the tip of the sceptre" (Esther 5:2). Can you imagine her relief? She was not killed; she was in the door, and the axe was not lifted.

But there is so much more danger on the other side of the door; the real dangerous moment is just beginning: "Then the king asked, 'What is it, Queen Esther? What is your request? Even up to half the kingdom, it will be given you'" (Esther 5:3). From this moment forward, she is referred to as Queen Esther. We might think that Esther is going to get Haman, because of the evil he had done to the queen. But that's not what happened. Do not read into her motivation. This is not revenge. It is about trust and timing.

She knows the king loves a good banquet, so she has prepared one: "'If it pleases the king,' replied Esther, 'let the king, together with Haman, come today to a banquet I have prepared for him'" (Esther 5:4). Esther is dressed like she is walking on a Paris runway, and she is looking for the right place for the real conversation to come. Notice that she shifts the place of power. Esther moves it from the king's banquets in the king's royal hall to her place in the palace. But more—she is the opposite of Vashti, the other queen in the story. She is more subtle, less confrontational, and preparing the real setup for Haman.[5] Listen to what happens next:

> "Bring Haman at once," the king said, "so that we may do what Esther asks."
>
> So the king and Haman went to the banquet Esther had prepared. As they were drinking wine, the king again asked Esther, "Now what is your petition? It will be given you. And what is your request? Even up to half the kingdom, it will be granted."
>
> Esther replied, "My petition and my request is this: If the king regards me with favour and if it pleases the king to grant my petition and fulfill my request, let the king and Haman come tomorrow to the banquet I will prepare for them. Then I will answer the king's question." (Esther 5:5–8)

This is not fear or weakness or second guessing; this is strategic, this is tactical. Both the king and Haman follow the will of a woman, the opposite of the command in chapter 1. But more than strategic thinking, underneath this is holy waiting—this is about God's timing. But things are far from okay. After this banquet the Jews are still going to be killed. If you read the rest of the chapter, Haman conspires with his wife and closest family and friends to kill Mordecai by impaling him, but in the end Haman is the one who dies and the Jews are saved.

What we really need to focus on for this book, however, is Queen Esther's religiously inspired civil disobedience. Mordecai also broke the law when he refused to bow down to Haman even after the king had made it law. The Bible has many other moments where God's people say, "No, we will not obey the government, my boss, or my family." Let's return to that image I used near the beginning of the book—forest fires.

One day, while I was a kindergartener, I was over at my cousins' home. We had always dreamed of being firefighters. We looked up to firefighters, and we wanted to be them so badly. So I got a crazy idea. Across from my cousin's house was a small wooded area with brush in front of it. I thought it would be a good idea to start a fire, and then we could put the forest fire out and become firefighters. So the game began. We had plastic fireman hats that we put on. Then we lined up all our little sand buckets in a row. I remember them distinctly—blue, red, and yellow. There was a hose attached to the house. We filled the small buckets, and then somehow we found matches. I don't recall where we found them, but it was probably in the kitchen.

We ran across the street, remembering to look both ways for cars, and arrived at the brush in front of the trees. We tried lighting our matches, but it did not work, so I had another idea—to get a magnifying glass and use the sun to start the fire! With the magnifying glass that I had used many times to look at stamps and burn ants with, we returned to the brush. We sat patiently, focusing the sunlight on a small pile of leaves, pine needles, and brush. For a while there was nothing, then a wisp of smoke, and then a small fire!

When the fire started, we were so excited. This was incredible! We were starting a fire that would lead to a forest fire that we got to put out! Immediately we shouted with glee and started running back and forth and back and forth and back and forth, grabbing our little buckets of water and throwing them on the fire.

Some smaller parts of the fire went out as we threw our buckets of water. "We are firemen!" we kept saying. But the fire kept spreading, growing until there were flames spreading in the brush and around the trees. The smoke was growing and billowing. For us, this was incredible. We were living our best lives and doing it so young. Well, a neighbour suddenly looked out her window and saw kindergarteners fighting a very large fire. I suppose she was a bit disturbed. I have this recollection of running across and throwing the next bucket of water as this woman screamed and ran towards us. We didn't understand the problem. She was yelling about how we shouldn't be doing this and that we need to call the fire department, but we thought we got this! "We started it! Do you want to be a firefighter with us?" The shock on that woman's face is etched in my memory. You can imagine that it didn't go well. From that moment she physically scooped us up to carry us away, and she ran with us under her arms into her home and dialed on her rotary phone. Then things got even better in our minds—real firefighters came. This was even more epic and more amazing! Up came the truck and out came the hoses. The fire was quite large by this point. I was a little guy, so in my mind the firemen were gigantic. The firemen started putting out the fire. What were we doing? We were cheering on the other side. It was incredible. After the fire was out, however, things deeply changed. We had a conversation with those firemen and our parents about not lighting fires that I have never forgotten—and I'm forty-nine years old!

Why in the world am I talking about fires and my childhood juvenile delinquency when we are trying to find out when God-inspired Christian civil disobedience is needed? The answer comes back to forest fires. Sometimes forest fires are needed to clear out brush and bring new life to a dying forest. Local authorities will start them to save forests from much larger and more destructive fires. But other times, forest fires bring nothing but destruction and death. When and how you start a forest fire matters. In the same way, when and how Christians are moved to civil disobedience in God's name has the potential either to bring new life or to cause massive destruction. In this age of rage, when Christians feel culturally transplanted, when we are living between fear (what if) and faith (even if), when the siren voices of hatred and mistrust and the echo chambers of social media call us to always react, we must be slow to use the nuclear option. If you don't have all the facts when you intentionally start a forest fire to prevent bigger problems, your actions may be harmful and dangerous. The *reason* you start the fire makes all the difference.

So when does God give us his permission to disobey the law? When are you Daniel or Esther, and when do you think you are Esther but are not and are instead sinning? Both Paul and Peter tell us how to do this well and right in God's eyes. Paul gives us the rules for how to be Esther in our day in Romans 13.

The emperor Claudius had expelled all the Jews from Rome because of the dispute between them about Jesus, as recorded in Acts. After a time, they were allowed to return, but it was tense. After the death of Claudius, Paul wrote his letter to the Romans afterwards, during Nero's reign, which we will talk about in a minute.[6] The church was in a tough spot. Anti-Jewish and anti-Christian sentiment was growing. Paul knew he needed to address how Christians interacted with government because some of them were Zealots by background. If the church was filled with an anti-Roman mentality, that could invite another set of big problems.

Yet there was another wrong attitude that Paul also needed to address. That is, some started thinking, "I'm a Christian, and Jesus is coming back and is going to make everything right, so why even get involved in civic affairs at all? It's a waste of time. Just run away and let God deal with it all." But Paul is about to charge Christians to live in "horizontal grace." Since God has given us grace, mercy, and kindness, we must do this with other Christians as well as with those who run the land. Responsible citizenship is at the heart of Christian worship. Paul commands the Christian in Romans 13: "Let everyone be subject to the governing authorities, for there is no authority except that which God has established. The authorities that exist have been established by God" (Romans 13:1).

Okay, if you are a Christian, if you have named Jesus as Saviour and Lord, then you must be subject to—that is, stand under—the government. This is a military term meaning "a voluntary deference to the wishes of another." Put yourself under the government or authority willingly.[7] Now again, before you start going to all the exceptions, consider the last time you put yourself under a leader you don't like or don't agree with. Is that your starting posture as a Christian?

God's Word says right here in black and white that God has established the government. They may be good or bad, but God always uses them to accomplish his purposes. As one wrote, "After God created the world, he filled it, organized it, and gave purpose to each created thing. When governments establish laws and prosecute justice they honour His created order, even when they don't do it perfectly. Anarchy, however, is bad for everyone."[8]

Obey the law, remain productive, pay taxes, stop at red lights, don't steal, don't invade another's privacy, don't rob banks. All of these are good things, but the common good is not enough. For Christians, this is about worship, and notice the power of the statement.[9] Resisting the government is fighting against God's plan and authority. Many of you don't like the government, and you post on the internet against the government 24/7. Stop and ask, when was the last time you said, "God allowed this government right now, so it is his will"? This one verse confronts several of the hate-filled conspiracy theories that are supported by so many Christians across so many countries.

Now, of course, this has been totally misused. Paul is not teaching blind devotion to the government either. Submission does not equal total obedience. Many of the churches under Hitler used Romans 13 to teach that one could not and should not stand up. We will get to the question of when it is okay to disobey soon, but too many of you are jumping there too quickly. Stop for now. Pause. Let it sink in that your worship is connected to your thoughts and actions towards those who have authority over us. This is as important to God as you singing on Sunday morning or denying yourself. Do you place this on the same level as other acts of worship? Just keep listening to God's Word. "Consequently, whoever rebels against the authority is rebelling against what God has instituted, and those who do so will bring judgment on themselves" (Romans 13:2).

There are two reasons we should obey. First, it allows us to worship, to please God, to honour him. Second, it allows us to serve God freely. If we keep disobeying the law, then fines, a bad reputation, and prison sentences will kill our testimony and remove our time to serve God. Richard Halverson, former chaplain of the United States Senate, wrote:

> To be sure, men will abuse and misuse the institution of the State. People because of sin have abused and misused every other institution in history including the Church of Jesus Christ, but this does not mean that the institution is bad or that it should be forsaken. It simply means that men are sinners and rebels in God's world, and this is the way they behave with good institutions. As a matter of fact, it is because of this very sin that there must be human government to maintain order in history until the final and ultimate rule of Jesus Christ is established. Human government is better than anarchy, and the Christian must recognize the "divine right" of the State.[10]

As a general rule, obey and it will go well with you: "For rulers hold no terror for those who do right, but for those who do wrong. Do you want to be free from fear of the one in authority? Then do what is right and you will be commended" (Romans 13:3). If you break the law, you will always be looking over your back. But if you obey, you will have less to fear. Again, I know this is only a general rule. I have never had to have the talk with my kids about being wrongfully stopped by the police like my friends who are people of colour. But as with Proverbs, this is not promise but wisdom. This is the general rule.

Paul just keeps going, and he gets more in our face:

> For the one in authority is God's servant for your good. But if you do wrong, be afraid, for rulers do not bear the sword for no reason. They are God's servants, agents of wrath to bring punishment on the wrongdoer. Therefore, it is necessary to submit to the authorities, not only because of possible punishment but also as a matter of conscience. This is also why you pay taxes, for the authorities are God's servants, who give their full time to governing. (Romans 13:4–6)

The sword was the symbol for Roman judicial power. God has given the authority of law and consequence to governments. Notice they are called God's servants. The same word is used for "deacons" in the New Testament and priests serving in the temple in the Old Testament.[11] When is the last time you said that (fill in the blank with whichever leaders you disagree with most) are God's servants? Really? Yes, really.

So we don't simply obey the government because we don't want to get in trouble, lose time, reputation, and money. We obey as a matter of conscience. That is, obedience is God's will, and we love God and want to follow him as Saviour and Lord. And so we follow the law as worship.

Two thousand years ago, Jewish Christians struggled with this because it was to a pagan government. The issue was not greed but holiness and worship. Jews thought that by paying taxes they were giving God's money to Caesar and Rome. Like many today, I don't want my money going to support abortion or buy army tanks. But Jesus says in Matthew 22:21, "So give back to Caesar what is Caesar's, and to God what is God's." So simple.

Paul also teaches us to pay our taxes. Doing so is for the common good and is worship. But then he goes further than most of us want: "Give to everyone what you owe them: If you owe taxes, pay taxes; if revenue, then revenue; if respect, then respect; if honour, then honour" (Romans 13:7). We are called to fulfill the requirements of good citizenship. Doing so may create opportunities to share the good news with greater freedom. Respect and honour are key when we deal with anyone in authority over us. As one preached, "As Christians we may deplore the politics of a particular person in office. We may be repelled by his or her scandalous conduct. But that does not disallow us from respecting the office they hold."[12]

Do you honour who God has placed over you? Really? That means you can never say, "So and so is not my prime minister, not my president, not my boss, not my . . ." What did Peter say about this? "Submit yourselves for the Lord's sake to every human authority: whether to the emperor, as the supreme authority, or to governors, who are sent by him to punish those who do wrong and to commend those who do right. . . . Show proper respect to everyone, love the family of believers, fear God, honour the emperor" (1 Peter 2:13–14, 17). Peter says holiness and godly living are found in one very difficult, shocking, jarring word—submit. What does *submit* mean? The definition means "be subject to, subordinate to, order yourself under according to the order in that relationship."[13]

Peter says submit to every authority, including the emperor Nero. In AD 64, the famous Roman fire broke out, and the population and government officials blamed Nero. But as one scholar explained,

> Nero, always a man desperate to be popular, therefore looked for scapegoats on whom the fire could be blamed. He found it in an obscure new religious sect, the Christians. And so many Christians were arrested and thrown to the wild beasts in the circus, or they were crucified. Many of them were also burned to death at night, serving as "lighting" in Nero's gardens, while Nero mingled among

> the watching crowds. It is this brutal persecution which immortalized Nero as the *first Antichrist* in the eyes of the Christian church.[14]

Submit to Nero? Honour Nero? Really? If those Christians were called to honour Nero, then we are called to honour whoever leads us, right? Do you need to pause here and really think about the implications of this?

Let's not forget what these passages are *not* saying. Paul, Peter, Mordecai, and Esther are not naïve about government abuse and power. They had all been abused by the government more than once. Some of them are very aware that behind many of the powers and rulers are spiritual forces that are hostile to God. So can we ever disagree with leaders? Can we choose not to obey?

The answer is yes, on rare occasions, when we have no choice but to obey God over the government. Don't forget that Paul never shares which form of government is best, even democracy. I have travelled the world. I have sat with people who have lived under communism, fascism, dictatorships, ongoing injustice, real abuse, and lack of power. I know what we have in the West. I am not sure if Winston Churchill did say this but it rings true: "Indeed it has been said that democracy is the worst form of Government except for all those other forms that have been tried from time to time."[15] Much of the heart of democracy is rooted in Judeo-Christian perspective and values, but again this is not guaranteed. Paul does not tell us what to do in the middle of a revolution, but it would seem, as I have read many commentaries, there are three times when we can and must disobey.[16]

1. *When those in power tell us to violate a direct command of God revealed in the Bible.* We saw this in Acts 4 and 5 when the church was told they could not talk about and preach in Jesus's name. What was Peter's response? "We must obey God rather than men!" The command of God always takes precedence.[17] If anyone tells us we cannot say that Jesus is the Son of God or the only way to heaven, if we are told we

cannot talk about heaven and hell, if we are told we cannot call people to repentance or speak about life, sexuality, or gender from a biblically informed worldview, then we must not obey.

2. *If we are told to commit an immoral or unethical act—to lie, kill, or affirm things God has said no to.* No Christian doctor or nurse should have to take a life in the womb or the life of an aging patient, for example. You might lose your job or be demoted, but you must obey God rather than people. If your boss tells you to change some notes or lie on some reports, you should say no in Jesus's name. The list grows quickly and becomes more difficult as we touch on education and the sexual revolution.[18]
3. *If something goes against a Christian conscience informed by Scripture and the Spirit of God.* Now Christians do not agree about everything. Some believe it is always wrong to be involved in war or take up arms, and others think there must be action to deal with ramped up evil and defending the weak. The famed Dietrich Bonhoeffer was part of the plot to kill Hitler. Many Christians in the 1960s talked about never working on nuclear weapons. Others are divided on what one should do for a job or what one should protest related to the environment. Both root their views in Scripture. But remember we must really consult God's Word, community, and think critically—not just three social media posts and two websites. As we have already seen in Paul's life in Philippi, the gospel comes before rights every single time. This should be our Christian reflex and decision.[19]

So where does this leave us?

1. *Honour your leaders.* What does God's Word tell us? "Show proper respect to everyone, love the family of believers, fear God, honour the emperor" (1 Peter 2:17). Respect every person you ever meet. All people—those of different religions, different politics, different views, different moralities, and

different sexualities—treat them with dignity! Treat others like you want to be treated. This does not mean we have to agree with them or justify what they believe or what they do or how they act. Human dignity is directly connected to being in the image of God, not money, status, power, race, sexual orientation, political belief, and so on. Remove God, remove human dignity. This had never been heard of before the Christian revolution, not like this. Do you need to repent about honouring the government or other authorities?

2. *Pray for our leaders.* "I urge, then, first of all, that petitions, prayers, intercession and thanksgiving be made for all people—for kings and all those in authority, that we may live peaceful and quiet lives in all godliness and holiness" (1 Timothy 2:1–2). I know many who pray for leaders but with prayers that are not filled with any compassion. They pray for their removal or God's wrath upon them. Much of the time, the prayers don't follow God's own charter and actions—mercy first and then judgment. When we pray, we should pray for wisdom, justice, and their conversions. We should pray for their blessing, for their families. We should pray for them like we pray for our own families. Only after we pray like that should we pray for divine chastisement or judgment.
3. *Don't break the current law just because that law might be used in a wrong way.* The Bible does not let us preemptively break the law. Does this mean you can never voice your opinion? Of course not. Does it mean we should vote very carefully and try to keep laws that help everyone flourish? Yes. Should we be involved by helping to form and direct laws that build freedom and respect? Of course. Can Christians be involved in open protest? Yes. But much of the time we act too quickly before the real fight begins. Remember, tone matters, context matters, truth matters, and the gospel matters more than all of it.

I love this summary,

> It is essential for the full expression of religious freedom that believers be welcome, in law and in social custom, to bring their religiously based moral convictions into the ongoing public debate over how we ought to order our common life. Religiously informed moral argument does not establish religion or impose sectarian values on a pluralistic society. Such charges are undemocratic, for they deny to fellow citizens and religious communities the right to bring the sources of their deepest convictions into public life. For their part, believers often have the resources to make their arguments in the public square in ways that every citizen, irrespective of religious belief or the lack thereof, can engage. Thus we seek neither a naked nor a sacred public square, but a civil public square open to the full range of convictions.[20]

I know things can change quickly, and I also know that even in one country, experiences are not the same depending on where you live. That is why incarnation is so unbelievably important. I realize that freedom can be removed and suffering might come quicker than we think. It's what happened during that Disney vacation I started the book with. We were on vacation for just under two weeks. People were taking care of our house. But when we returned, the hedges in front of our house had all died. Those who had taken care of our house had watered them, but it didn't make a difference. For most of the time they were taking care of our home, the hedges appeared just fine, but beneath the green something terrible was happening. The hedge was infected by something called spider mites. At first it looked like a small spiderweb in our evergreen hedges. But they are not actually spiders. In less than seven days they ate and destroyed our hedges. Likewise, religious freedom and freedom of conscience can be lost so quickly. We absolutely can protest and point out our fading freedoms, but never at the expense of the gospel.

So we must try to influence while we can, but in the end we still might lose. And in that moment, we will have to suffer. In my book *Convergence,*[21] I talk about why suffering for the kingdom is a guaranteed place of encounter, and in *Perseverance*[22] I talk about why suffering must be taught and embraced as a normal part of the Christian life and public witness. So can we break the law? Yes, you can break the law—but only when the Bible says yes.

This is starting to happen in Australia, England, and in Canada bit by bit. Christians might lose jobs or be publicly lied about. There might be a time when we must be Esther. And we must be ready, as parents, teachers, lawyers, doctors, politicians, plumbers, and bankers to say no if needed. There will be a need to stand and suffer. Church father John Chrysostom said the famed words below. Some think it was when he was brought before the Roman Empress of his time who threatened him with banishment for life if he remained unchanged in his Christian preaching and exhortations to those in power. Others think this was his advice to others who had to stand. But no matter, the dialogue is recorded like this:

> Chrysostom replied, "You cannot banish me for this world is my father's house."
>
> "But I will kill you," the empress said.
>
> "No, you cannot, for my life is hid with Christ in God."
>
> "I will take away your wealth," said Eudoxia.
>
> "No, you cannot do that either for my treasure is in heaven and my heart is there."
>
> "But I will drive you away from people and you will have no friend left," Eudoxia responded.
>
> "No, you cannot," said John, "for I have a friend in heaven from whom you cannot separate me. I defy you. For there is nothing that you can do to hurt me."[23]

But let's not break the law before the time is called for. The questions for us in this transitional moment, especially if you are a Christian leader or a Christian with influence, are:

What might you need to change in your thinking?
Where did you or do you react too quickly?
What do you need to repent of? What posts, thoughts, actions,

public declarations, or sermons broke God's word according to Romans 13?

When was the last time you prayed for those in power, and was your prayer filled with holy love?

What do you need to keep working out in your context?

What do you need to say no to, even if it costs you your job or reputation?

PART 5

REVIVAL

to duplicate life

The sovereign act of God, in which he restores his own backsliding people to repentance, faith and obedience.

—STEPHEN OLFORD

The return of the Church from her backslidings, and the conversion of sinners.

—CHARLES FINNEY

An extraordinary movement of the Holy Spirit producing extraordinary results.

—RICHARD OWEN ROBERTS

A community saturated with God.

—DUNCAN CAMPBELL

Conservatives would rather work to reform church theology and practice. Intellectuals doubt supernatural intervention. Rationalists dismiss emotional enthusiasm. All convene committees and organize campaigns but few will plead for revival.

—MARTYN LLOYD-JONES

Reformation is a return to the sound doctrine of the Bible. Revival is the practice of that sound doctrine under the power of the Holy Spirit.

—FRANCIS SCHAEFFER

CHAPTER 20

Where Does Revival Fit In?

I know that many of you reading this might still be asking a different question: Where does revival fit into all of this?

Couldn't revival be the answer for us in this moment? Is it not true that "if my people, who are called by my name, will humble themselves . . ."? Is it not true that God wants to be wanted? Is it not true that God will come to the places he is wanted? I often hear that "we are not post-Christian but pre-revival." As I talk to my own teenagers and travel the world, there is something happening in Gen Z and Gen Alpha that really feels different. It feels real, humble, and hungry, and there are signs of God breaking in. But are we seeing this everywhere, and will it last?

Yes, God does come where he is wanted, and yes, revival will break out. I will say, revival is breaking out, but that does not mean that God's arrival always looks like revival. Hopefully you underlined that.

I have seen and taught for years that expectations can inspire or kill faith, both communities and ministries. Ministry can be seen in two simple ways, with two lenses—common faithfulness and specific assignment.

The most famous and fundamental description of common faithfulness, that is, what every single church must look like no matter their denomination, cultural expression, or size, is found in Acts 2:42–47. Teaching, community, communion, prayer, the presence of God, giving, loving the poor, large and small gatherings, baptism, and evangelism—every church is called to this. And we are all called to fulfill the last words of Jesus: "Therefore go and make disciples of all nations, baptizing them in the name of the Father and of the Son and of the Holy Spirit, and teaching them to obey everything I have commanded you. And surely I am with you always, to the very end of the age" (Matthew 28:19–20). That is common faithfulness. This whole book has been outlining the ways Jesus calls us to faithfulness today, and most of what has been discussed is transcultural: It can and should be used five hundred years from now. But there is another category I call "specific assignment."

Beyond common faithfulness, sometimes out of holy listening, comes God-given vision. I have come to believe that Jesus uniquely speaks to congregations and movements just as he did in the book of Revelation to the church in Sardis, Philadelphia, Smyrna, Ephesus, and more. The Scriptures are full of leaders being issued God-given assignments. The same mission is assigned to all churches, but specific calling is usually given to leaders: "Moses, I have called you to do this"; "Paul, do that"; "Philip, go there"; "When we were fasting and praying, the Spirit said go!" In these moments, God speaking should become the inception point for the dynamic vision of each church. But hearing God speak implies being open and learning to listen through spiritual disciplines; this presumes empowering people within their gift mix to discern what is actually from God versus what is just human, the devil, or the tacos you had last night.

Mission (Acts 2, Matthew 28) is common faithfulness and never changes in any environment. Vision, however, is God-given for a season and will be replaced by new ones.[1] The idea of revival is found in the uncommon, not guaranteed, sovereignly started. Revival is given to start new movements and to move people and communities forward over very long periods of time. Sometimes God gives revival not just to people or communities but to generations.

We should be encouraged because God does break through, and he has done so many times over the last one hundred and fifty years, in the middle of all the events that have created the world we are trying to reach and live in today. Mark Shaw, in his book *Global Awakening*, outlines how revivals between 1900 and 2000 triggered a Christian revolution that has made Christianity the fastest growing and most diverse movement on earth.[2] He focuses on six major moments in our global family.[3]

Now this does not include the many other moves of God, such as the Welsh Revival (1904–1905) or the Hebrides revival in Scotland (1949–1953), the impact of which still ripple around the world today. I shared in my first book, *Convergence*, how our church had a three-year documented move of God that deeply changed us. And as I speak and travel, I have seen moments of revival taking place in Asbury, New York, London, Oxford, Los Angeles, France, and on US college campuses. God is pouring out his Spirit in so many communities and in many different denominational tribes. Across the world, Gen Z and Gen Alpha are displaying a God-given hunger that we have not seen in over a hundred years. The tide could be turning, and truthfully, as this book comes out or is read years from now, there might be or have been a global move of God. But if this move happens in a few years or does not pan out the way we thought, it does not remove the need for this chapter.

As I shared at the beginning of the book, if there are Christians left at all, then revival is possible. But in this repaganizing, pluralistic moment, so many are praying for, hoping for, and counting on revival to be the difference maker in the West. To that I say, "Yes, Lord!" But . . . I cannot put all my eggs in one basket, even if I love and desire it so much. Oh, don't misread that; I'm not hedging my bets. This is not gross pragmatism or lack of faith. The Scriptures do not let me guarantee what I want to be guaranteed.

There's a group of Christians that say revival can and should happen anywhere. Basically, expect it. The phrase I keep hearing is, "God goes where he's wanted." That mind-set builds the expectation that if we really want God, and we're desperate for his presence, then he's going to show up in revival. Many other people wonder if this will ever happen or should happen. Other Christians don't even think about revival, and others still are somewhere in between.

Now there are guaranteed places of encounter that happen in common faithfulness, which is where we should be building guaranteed expectation. These guaranteed places of encounter are the giving of the gospel, Scripture, spiritual disciplines, spiritual gifts, worship, communion, baptism, and in the suffering for Jesus. Salvation is not earned by our acts or habits, though they are all guaranteed places of ongoing encounter. When understood, they build right expectation for the church community. But just because you meet God in an ongoing way does not mean fire, angels, or profound life-changing moments. It means he is there every time in a unique way. This is like going to the gym or doing an activity over a long period of time. The habit leads to lasting change, and when people come to these spiritual places and activities knowing that God is there, their faith grows deeper.

Why does this matter? All these spiritual environments and actions translate across cultures; they are globally Christian. They can be and must be the centre of any ministry, no matter the size or makeup. These practices can be used in different styles of church or ministries. Numbers are not a barrier, money is not the centre, and Jesus is always present. Let us meet him, build our ministries around him, and lead people to him. You should build your discipleship model around these ongoing places of encounter.[4]

So what about revival? After leading through one and being in the middle of other marked moves of God, what I suggest below is how to think theologically and practically through revival and how to ask God if he will move. The first question I asked so long ago was this: Are there distinctions between renewal, revival, and awakening? Yes. Here's a simplified answer we use in our context: *Renewal* is when God touches the heart of a single individual. *Revival* is when God touches a community of faith at large. And *awakening* is when the wider society is impacted through mass conversion and life change.

One of the Bible passages that best describes God's unique work in this area is the event we call the transfiguration of Jesus. This account is recorded in three of the Gospels (Matthew 17:1–13; Mark 9:2–13; Luke 9:28–36). Let's follow Matthew's account and see what Jesus was trying to show us and tell us through the lens of revival. What happened just before this event is crucial: Peter's confession of

Jesus at Caesarea Philippi. "You are the Messiah, the Son of the living God" (Matthew 16:16). Jesus asked Peter and the other disciples a question that everyone must answer. The answer given leads to eternal life or death; it's the answer that changes one's life trajectory.

Since Peter's confession, that truth has rocked the ages, brought hope to billions, and been a stumbling block to many more. But at the transfiguration, the Father and the Son chose to pull back the veil a little more to show three of the disciples that the one they know, the one they have served with, eaten with, and seen heal, and the one Peter claimed is the Christ is actually the one they have heard and read about from Genesis to Malachi. The one they hang out with is none other than the God of Adam, Noah, Abraham, Isaac, Jacob, David, Isaiah, and Jeremiah.

"It's time," heaven says. So the Son of God, Jesus of Nazareth, in obedience to the Father, sets the stage for a revival of sorts. At first, it is only for a small group, Jesus's inner circle within the twelve: "After six days Jesus took with him Peter, James and John the brother of James, and led them up a high mountain by themselves" (Matthew 17:1).

The phrase "after six days" should send up an Old Testament flare for us. In six days God created all of reality, beauty, colour, and life, and then said it was good. In six days God spoke and existence came to be. Yet another new creation was about to happen through Jesus's perfect life, death, and resurrection, a new creation that would not only bring us back into a relationship with God but also signal the beginning of the end, which will culminate in the restoration of Eden, the new heavens and the new earth.

There is still more to understand about the significance of the six days. What is about to unfold is connected to Moses's personal encounter with God at the giving of the Ten Commandments. Notice the timeframe in Exodus 24 as well as words like *fire*, *cloud*, and *glory*, which show up in Matthew too:

> "The Lord said to Moses, 'Come up to me on the mountain and stay here, and I will give you the tablets of stone, with the law and commands I have written for their instruction.' . . .

> When Moses went up on the mountain, the cloud covered it, and the glory of the LORD settled on Mount Sinai. For six days the cloud covered the mountain, and on the seventh day the LORD called to Moses from within the cloud. To the Israelites the glory of the LORD looked like a consuming fire on top of the mountain. (Exodus 24:12, 15–17)

Notice back in Matthew 17:1 that it says Jesus led them up. He started the process. They didn't know where they were going, and they didn't know what was going to happen, but they had agreed to follow him, wherever he led.

So here are Peter, James, John, and Jesus up on this mountain. Luke notes they went to pray and to connect with the Father until, like all of us sometimes, they fell asleep. It says in Luke 9:32 that Peter and his companions "were very sleepy." As their eyes were closing and dreams were coming into their minds, as yawning turned into a losing battle with slumber, everything suddenly changed. The heavens ripped open, and the mountaintop was consumed with unnatural light, fire, and brilliance. Terror and fear came in milliseconds as the three wondered if this was dream or reality. They were so scared they lost their ability to move. Sleep was gone, and all five of their senses were overwhelmed. They were transfixed, frozen, and full of wonder.

Matthew simply said of Jesus, "There he was transfigured before them." *Transfigured*—what does that mean? It means that Jesus was changed in appearance. The original word in Greek is where we get our word *metamorphosis* from. He was transformed such that in the moments that followed he was seen as fully human and fully God. These three men got a glimpse of Jesus as he will be seen in heaven! Jesus the Christ, the Son of God, was manifest and revealed, so Peter, James, and John saw him in his heavenly splendour. As R. T. France wrote, "This transformation is not so much a physical alteration as an added dimension of glory, it is the same Jesus, but now with an awesome brightness 'like the sun' and 'like light.'"[5] Peter's confession "you are the Christ" is now fully realized!

Matthew continued by describing this beyond-yet-present experience as best he could, given the stunned testimony of his three witnesses: "His face shone like the sun, and his clothes became as white as the light" (Matthew 17:2). Mark, probably listening to Peter struggle to verbalize the unspeakable, recorded it this way: "His clothes became dazzling white, whiter than anyone in the world could bleach them" (Mark 9:3).

For a moment the veil was lifted, and they saw fully. Jesus and his clothing gleamed and glittered, shining brighter than any modern light we have ever seen or invented. This light was coming from *within* him and descending from above him. As Peter, James, and John looked on, and their vision adjusted to heavenly light, they suddenly saw two others, the most famed persons in Jewish faith and history. They are called the fathers of faith, great men that these three had heard about since they were little boys. *"Just then there appeared before them Moses and Elijah, talking with Jesus"* (Matthew 17:3). Both the figures now talking with Jesus had lives that ended in supernatural ways, and both were great leaders who spoke with God at Mount Sinai. Moses was the great lawgiver, the one who led Israel out of Egypt. Elijah was the greatest miracle-working prophet who came to represent all the prophets. They were present to witness and to testify that the one with whom they were conversing was the fulfillment of the Old Testament.

The entire unfolding of God's plan in history, allegory, poetry, and prophecy was to prepare the world for the coming of Jesus. The Law and the Prophets show us our sin and our need for an external Saviour; they give us hope. At this moment, time was shattered; heaven and earth kissed, and Jesus, God in flesh, was about to start the process that would lead to greater miracles and a greater second exodus.

Remember that Peter, James, and John were orthodox Jews. They must have been thinking, "Moses and Elijah! Are you kidding me? I have heard about and revered you my whole life, and now here you are. And this is the long-awaited Messiah! I am seeing more in this moment than any Jew has ever seen before. It cannot get better than this. The kingdom has come, heaven on earth, and all Jewish hopes and fears are now dealt with."

How did Peter respond? He said to Jesus, "Lord, it is good for us to be here. If you wish, I will put up three shelters—one for you, one for Moses and one for Elijah" (Matthew 17:4). Notice again that although Peter usually called Jesus Rabbi, Teacher, or Master, Peter now went much, much further and called him Lord, the name of God from the Old Testament.

In confusion and amazement, Peter basically said, "Let's stay here! This is great. Our prayers are answered! We want it all now, so let's plant a flag and declare this the kingdom of heaven right here and now!" Peter wanted the momentary experience of the long-anticipated reality to be fulfilled. "We want to live here, to commune with you. We don't want to go back to the mundane, the boring, the seven-day work week, to sickness and family fights, to the Romans, politics, war, and dealing with diseases and demons. You keep talking about dying and death, but you don't need to do that. Let's go buy some tents from Mountain Equipment Company and make camp!" Do you really think you and I would think something different?

The suggested placement of the shelters also shows us something. One famed preacher said, "Peter, bewildered by the heavenly vision and not knowing what to say, proposed to build three shelters, one for Christ, one for Moses and one for Elijah. He seemed, in fact, to place the lawgiver and the prophet side by side with his divine Master, as if all three were equal. At once, we are told, the proposal was rebuked in a marked manner."[6]

As Peter was working on a strategic plan to camp forever with Jesus and his heavenly posse, another act of heaven interrupted Peter's thoughts, desires, and human agenda: "*While he was still speaking, a bright cloud covered them, and a voice from the cloud said...*" (Matthew 17:5).

"A bright cloud covered them." The image of the cloud is central to everything we're talking about in this book. The cloud is a form of the Shekinah glory (which means "dwelling of God"), referred to often in the Old Testament. A supernatural cloud is always connected to the brilliance, glory, fire, and overwhelming presence of God. That presence was experienced at the giving of the Ten Commandments but also throughout the wilderness wanderings when a pillar of cloud led Israel by day and a pillar of fire by night. It was experienced at both

the dedication of the tabernacle (Exodus 40:34) and of the temple (1 Kings 8:10–11). The same cloud came down and consumed the sacrifice and altar on Mount Carmel when Elijah invited God to display his power. The cloud was seen at the call of Isaiah (Isaiah 6:1–4) and Ezekiel (Ezekiel 1:4) and was the glory that shone around the shepherds when the angels sang and announced the birth of Jesus (Luke 2:9). That same cloud appeared at the transfiguration of Jesus and at the birth of the church in Acts 2:2–3 when the Spirit came as tongues of fire. It was also seen at the death of Stephen and at the conversion of Saul on the road to Damascus. And out of that cloud, on the mountaintop, from the fire, the voice of the Father speaks, "This is my Son, whom I love; with him I am well pleased. Listen to him!" (Matthew 17:5).

The Holy Spirit, now in the form of a cloud, was given to affirm Jesus's identity, so his life, death, resurrection, and ascension would be valid. Here we see God in Trinitarian fullness, as at Jesus's baptism: the Father's voice, the Son of God in flesh, and the Spirit in the form of a cloud. We see the reality of the God who is one, found in three persons for ever and ever amen! And what does God say? "Listen to him" (Matthew 17:5).

The disciples' response is far too rare among people who claim to seriously follow Jesus today: "When the disciples heard this, they fell facedown to the ground, terrified" (Matthew 17:6). How often are we "facedown" in God's presence?

The disciples were "terrified." In that shocking and sudden exposure to ultimate reality, they knew that only God is God, and they, most definitely, were not. In those terrifying moments, there is not only a spiritual response but also a physical one. At that moment they knew their own sinful, imperfect condition before the holy God, yet they also knew that they were invited and allowed, guests with no other right to be there. During unusual moves like this, our omnipresent God becomes palpably present; he who is transcendent comes near. In those terrifying moments, there is not only a spiritual response but also a physical one.

When God moves in such ways—and he still does—it is for his glory, for our freedom, and to empower us to move forward in our ministry for others. Isaiah experienced God's presence as God prepared him for the challenges of being God's prophet: "'Woe to me!' I cried. 'I am ruined! For I am a man of unclean lips, and I live among a people of unclean lips, and my eyes have seen the King, the LORD Almighty'" (Isaiah 6:5).

This has always been the pattern in revivals. I love how J. I. Packer outlined this process years ago in a small book called *God in our Midst*:

1. *Awareness of God's presence:* "The first and fundamental feature in revival is the sense that God has drawn awesomely near in his holiness, mercy and might."
2. *Responsiveness to God's Word:* "The message of Scripture which previously was making only a superficial impact, if that, now searches its hearers and readers to the depth of their being."
3. *Sensitiveness to sin:* "Consciences become tender and a profound humbling takes place."
4. *Liveliness in community:* "Love and generosity, unity and joy, assurance and boldness, a spirit of praise and prayer, and a passion to reach out to win others, are recurring marks of renewed communities."
5. *Fruitfulness in testimony:* "Christians proclaim by word and deed the power of the new life, souls are won, and a community conscience becomes informed and Christian values emerge." [7]

Peter, James, and John have now seen more than any other Jewish person in history. They experience Moses, Elijah, the Messiah, the Shekinah glory of God, and the Father's voice. Of course they want to stay. Of course they think this can never get better. Even in their undoing, they know it's what is best.

Encountering God in all aspects of relationship is always full of terror and euphoria, fear and adoration. The transfiguration story concludes, "But Jesus came and touched them. 'Get up,' he said. 'Don't be afraid.' When they looked up, they saw no one except

Jesus" (Matthew 17:7–8). As soon as it happened, it was over. Moses and Elijah had vanished and the cloud was gone, and they returned to reality. What a letdown! All the emotion, adrenaline, terror, and euphoria was here and gone in an instant. And what does Jesus say? He says something like, "Let's go. Time to go down the mountain, back to real life, to the Romans and politics, the diseases and demons and struggles of faith, back to the everyday. And yes, back to ministry, now in a deeper, more empowered way." Like Jacob you will walk with a limp for the rest of your life, but your name will be changed, and nations will be born from this moment.

So this is how we learn to see what God might do. This is how we learn how to ask. This is the rule no matter East or West, no matter where we lead or in what time; here is what I believe the Scriptures say. First, we, personally and corporately, must be willing to be led up the mountain by Jesus; that is our only part. We don't know what he will do when we reach the top. That is why we must continually seek his presence and practice common faithfulness in the low country while we pray for revival. Second, if God in his sovereignty wants this, then he is the one who leads us up. We worship Yahweh, not Baal. We cannot draw him down.

The preparation for revival is always marked when God gives a promise that we must start praying back to him. This is the signal that he is about to lead us up the mountain. When I led a church through a revival and in the other revivals and movements I have connections to, God made a promise to a leader, a prayer group, or a community. God always gives the yes before the yes. Think about Jacob wrestling with God (Genesis 32). The wrestle for the blessing was key, but God had already given him the promise in Genesis 28. We are just agreeing with his decision to move in a unique way. The yes is not always there, the yes is not given to every church, leader, or generation. That is why we must ask if there is a yes, knowing he might say no.

Then, in his time, if there is the yes, we pray his promise back to him, and he sends the Holy Spirit and reveals himself fully. He moves from omnipresence to palpable presence. We will be terrified, we will confess sin, we will know our need, and we will see our pain exposed.

Let me be clear: When God moves from omnipresence to palpable presence—that is, manifests presence—God's nature is not changing. Nor are we more aware because of anything we do. This is all grace. God makes the environment change; he makes it a thin place. In those very special moments, we encounter under his will and direction more of the fullness of God. Jesus was the same person we were with hours before, but now we have access to a fuller experience of his immutable reality.

Much of the time, if we will let the witness of history speak, there will be accompanying physical manifestations like falling over, shaking, weeping, and trembling at the presence of God. Every time God moved in great power in the Scriptures there were physical reactions by the people or the leader. Study church history—accounts from Jonathan Edwards, John Wesley, and the Welsh revivals are full of the unusual work of God: from holy laughter to weeping and falling over. Do these always happen? No. Do they make you more holy or spiritual? No. But when God moves very close, strange things do happen, because it is impossible to be close to God and not overwhelmed. The results will prove if God's move was real or if that move was accepted and internalized. Let me take this a little farther.

Think about John the disciple. John was Jesus's closest friend; he walked with Jesus and saw all he did. John was at the transfiguration. He was at the cross and held his newly adopted mother as Jesus bled out. He was there for Jesus's resurrection and ascension to heaven. Yet much later, John had another remarkable encounter. At ninety years old, John received the book of Revelation from Jesus as he was worshipping on a Sunday in exile: "I turned around to see the voice that was speaking to me. . . . When I saw him, I fell at his feet as though dead. Then he placed his right hand on me and said: 'Do not be afraid. I am the First and the Last. I am the Living One; I was dead, and now look, I am alive forever and ever! And I hold the keys of death and Hades.'" (Revelation 1:12–18)

Picture a ninety-year-old senior citizen falling before Jesus. There is a physical reaction to the proximity of the divine. Weird is not always wrong. And yet people during revivals will make mistakes around the weird even though God is present. John himself goes wrong. In fact, he does something wrong not once but twice after he fell over with Jesus. Here is one example: "I fell down to worship at the feet of the angel who had been showing them to me. But he said to me, 'Don't do that! I am a fellow servant with you and with your fellow prophets and with all who keep the words of this scroll. Worship God!'" (Revelation 22:8–9).

You will know it is the glorified Jesus and that the Spirit of Christ is among you in a new and close way when you feel that you must die because of your sin, yet you are loved and assured of forgiveness at the same time. Holy love and terror held together is an overwhelming experience. The Holy Spirit comes in full power: The cloud, the fire, and the dove come to give the church, for a time, an extraordinary movement, producing extraordinary results in personal lives, in families, in the church, and then in the community.

During this time, we will be pointed to Jesus only. He will be all we can see, and he will be the only one we care about. His will, his agenda, and his glory will become central. We will be able to read the following verses and know they are true: "We live by faith, not by sight. We are confident, I say, and would prefer to be away from the body and at home with the Lord. So we make it our goal to please him, whether we are at home in the body or away from it" (2 Corinthians 5:7–9).

Let me summarize: Common faithfulness, spiritual gifts, and spiritual disciplines are the ongoing, guaranteed reality of God's persistent work in and through his church. Revivals are sovereignly started, occasional, unguaranteed, intense moments God gives his people. And awakenings always include mass conversions of people to Jesus.

A common mistake is to pair the outworking or unusual manifestations of the Spirit during revival with the gifts that are always present in the daily Christian life. When people try to replicate the physical activity of revival after it is done, it's rotten manna, a dead ritual just like any other liturgy can become when done without a believing heart. Revival settings are not about gifts or disciplines. Spiritual disciplines are for all to exercise at any season of life. Spiritual gifts are sovereignly assigned and are normative, day in and day out. But revival is not normal and not guaranteed, and neither are the results.

Much of the time during revival, there is a greater power and presence of God, which means the disciplines are used more and the power behind the gifts is stronger. But revival is started and ended only by God. Otherwise, we all would want to build tents like Peter, and historically some have tried but were not allowed because God does not dwell in temples or monuments built by human hands. These seasons are given to send us out and to sustain us over a lifetime. Don't pair one experience with the other. Some revivals last days, others last months, still others last years.

Here's what I want to give you as fellow Christians trying to do presence well. If you are Christian leaders, pastors, key volunteers, elders, theologians, or influencers, pay close attention. Should we pray for, ask for, and expectantly wait for God to move in revival? Should we say to the Lord, "We want revival"? Should we say, "God, I need renewal"? Absolutely.

If God says no or not yet, that does not affect the gifts he has given or the disciplines he has modelled for a normal Christian life. This fact should help leaders set expectations about manifestations and outworking. But if God says yes, then we should claim it. We should agree with heaven. We persistently pray, "Lord, you must come because you said you would." We pray back the promise until he comes.

On the one hand, many churches that *did* have a real work of God in the past keep trying to replicate it. We must accept it when that time is done, and we must go back to gifts and holy habits and the last part of Acts 2—good old common faithfulness. God can do something new in his own timing.

On the other hand, too many of us have never asked to see if Jesus wants revival, to see if God would give us a promise to pray back to him, because of fear and ungodly control. So many of us like singing songs about revival, but we secretly don't want one because we know everything will change. A lot of us don't want to see revival because we're afraid of our sin being exposed or of control and fear being confronted. There are so many leaders for whom the reason in your heart of hearts that you really don't want revival is because you are afraid, you are fear-driven, and you are controlling. If God really showed up in great power like he did in the transfiguration or in revelation, what would you do with the weird stuff that takes place? Maybe you can't handle that, so you don't want God to move in power. Is your fear worth it?

My point is that there is one set of experiences and overarching expectations for a revival and another for everyday ministry. For a time, they can fuse together, if God so chooses, but not necessarily. Pastors and leaders should understand this and never confuse these factors so that their expectations for revival are neither too low nor too high. We must keep our expectations anchored to Jesus, who never disappoints.

So what should you do after reading this chapter? Don't look at stats, don't look at your city, don't look at your family. Instead, just go to the Father, by the Holy Spirit, through Jesus, and ask, what is your will? Yes or no? This might feel very exposing and risky, for both answers can confront fear, control, desire, and expectation. No matter what answer you get, when you get your answer, pray, plan, and prepare accordingly.

During the move of God in our church, we prayed two prayers that launched us forward just before and during God's unusual move. Both prayers are written below, and you may want to use them as a guide:

Prayer 1

God, do anything you want in my life, for your glory and my freedom, so others will see Jesus clearly. Amen.

Prayer 2

Father, we ask that the tide of God's favour would continue to flood into our community. Increase our spiritual hunger and draw people in our region to yourself. We ask for many people to turn to you, Lord Jesus. Give us a heart for the lost in our neighborhoods, cities, and beyond. Pray Zechariah 8:20–22: "This is what the Lord Almighty says: 'Many peoples and the inhabitants of many cities will yet come, and the inhabitants of one city will go to another and say, "Let us go at once to entreat the Lord and seek the Lord Almighty. I myself am going." And many peoples and powerful nations will come to Jerusalem to seek the Lord Almighty and to entreat him.'"

Avoid banquets with outsiders and the unschooled. Yet, if you do end up attending such an occasion, be alert, lest you lapse into the behaviour of the unschooled. For be assured of this: the one who keeps company with the impure becomes impure even if he should happen to be pure.

—EPICTETUS

The Son of Man came eating and drinking, and they say, "Here is a glutton and a drunkard, a friend of tax collectors and sinners." But wisdom is proved right by her deeds.

—MATTHEW 11:19

CHAPTER 21

Collaborating with the Enemy

At the beginning of the COVID-19 crisis, I was walking through my local grocery store in southern Ontario with no clue that we would be living in lockdown longer than most people in the world. The crisis truly came home for me in the fruits and veggies section. A day or two earlier, I had been with church leaders in a confidential meeting in downtown Toronto, talking about strategic partnerships and mergers. It was Wednesday, the day before the world started closing down. We were wondering how long it was going to last, and they were asking if we had any plans to go digital. I told them that we had started building a studio three days earlier and preparing as best we could. That same day, I was looking around in that grocery store and started seeing a few people wearing masks. I remember thinking, all of this is *real*, and then I remember coming to the vegetable section. I looked at the plastic bag, and I looked at the vegetables, and I thought, how in the world am I going to do this? If someone has coughed or breathed on the vegetables—or on the bags—then I can get whatever this thing is, right? In that moment, I suddenly realized that my world was not the same. I did not feel safe. I didn't know how much of another person's presence would make me sick or even kill me. Their presence—my association with them in the same room—could deeply affect me or my family's health, even our very lives.

Now don't read the above politically. This was before we knew what we know now—good, bad, exaggerated, tested, and proven. My point is that a great number of religious Jews felt this way when being around "sinners" and non-Jews. Presence, let alone relationship, they taught, could spiritually contaminate you. This was the common view held 2,000 years ago. And today, as things have gotten darker, many Christians who claim they have been saved by grace don't fully believe this but instead hold to views held by our religious great-great-grandparents.

So one last time, let's go through this: It is one thing to see beauty; it is another to cross bridges instead of burning them. It's another thing to preach and see those we don't feel comfortable with get saved. It's a whole *other* thing to give the gospel and just cross the bridges, heading back over to our side after we are done. It is even *another* thing to obey God and not just preach but settle and live in Nineveh, Babylon, in some hostile modern city. But now we must take that very last step. It is one thing being willing to go, and another when you are called to stay and to live, but God calls us to more. He says don't just live and work alongside these people but go and eat with those people. He tells us to *be in relationship* with them.

So if there is one person that is the icon for our moment, it must be Levi, a man hated by his family, a man hated by his own people, a person in power, whose whole lifestyle was based on compromise, political injustice, bribes, and ripping off the poor. His story is the story of a collaborator, an institutional thief, a tax collector.

Jesus had a wide variety of personal encounters. Nicodemus came asking, the adulterous woman was forced to come, Saul was confronted, the rich young ruler came begging and went away sad, but now this last man, Levi, is curious but not really seeking Jesus. But let us again see God's power meet and change yet another person.

Let us admit there is a vast difference between *among* versus *with*. And let us also admit that Jesus was always eating *with* people. Over those meals, he broke down barriers and shattered expectations. He shows what it is like to love your neighbour. And in those moments he reveals who he is and what he is calling people into. So this is where a book about presence must end: over food.

There is no better way to check out the Christian faith than with food and Jesus. If you took the time to read about every meal Jesus had with others in the Gospels, you would see quickly that Jesus calls us to be with *others*, to be with those who are *not like us*, to see the power of hospitality, and furthermore why it is a problem to connect exclusively with those we are comfortable with. Jesus loved to associate with a broad cross section of people over food: normal people, flagrant sinners, tax collectors, prostitutes, farmers, fishermen, housewives, artists, the intellectual and religious elite. Again, Jesus shows us why we reach out broadly to those around us.

To Levi's story we go: "As he walked along, he saw Levi son of Alphaeus sitting at the tax collector's booth. 'Follow me,' Jesus told him, and Levi got up and followed him" (Mark 2:14). Jesus calls a *tax collector* to be a follower and leader. Tax collectors were middlemen between the Jewish people and the occupying Roman government. Tax collectors have a bad rap in our day (we tend to not like our money being taken away), but this was bigger. This is about institutional injustice. Jewish collectors had made a deal with the devil; they had sold their soul for money. They were working for the Romans, an occupational force who had removed ethnic rights, who had killed thousands, and to the Jewish mind, who represented everything antithetical to the one true living God. Many historical references to tax collectors point out that they were involved in mass exploitation through lying, cheating, bribes, and stealing; they overtaxed their own people and in the process became very wealthy.[1]

If you have read the story of Zacchaeus in Luke 19, you should note that though the story is similar, the main difference is that Zacchaeus is the chief tax collector. He is the district manager, a ruler who had real power and privilege. You had to bid for this position, and Zacchaeus got it. He was rich—I mean really, *really* rich. And he had gained his fortune not from landed or generational wealth but from entrepreneurial activity of the worst kind. He would take a cut of commission from all the other tax collectors off the backs of his own people.[2]

Oh, there is more! If you, as a Jew, decided to do this job, you became an outcast from society. You were disqualified as a judge or witness in legal cases because you were that untrustworthy. You were excommunicated from the synagogue, banned from worship, and a disgrace to your family (immediate and extended). To get rich this way, you had to leave everything and burn every bridge.[3]

See the scandal for what it is. Levi was working for a military occupational army. This is like a French or Polish citizen working for the Nazis during World War II and getting rich doing it. Tax collectors were collaborators. Yet this hated man got up and followed Jesus after Jesus invited him to. *What?*

Later that day, Jesus ends up having dinner with him and others as we see recorded by Mark: "While Jesus was having dinner at Levi's house, many tax collectors and sinners were eating with him and his disciples, for there were many who followed him" (Mark 2:15). Can you imagine Levi's joy? This amazing person, this leader, this healer, this respected religious guy wants to hang out with me? But not just me, but all these so-called disqualified sinners!

We need to understand what *sinner* means so we don't misread or mispreach this—and so we can see ourselves in the story. There are two expressions of sinner in a Jewish worldview:

1. Those who lived in sin (i.e., moral breakdown, those who break the Ten Commandments). All of us are sinners in this sense.[4]
2. Those who did not meet the religious standards of the time. That is, they broke the Old Testament purity laws and broke the oral law, which were rules that were not in God's revealed Word but were good ideas to stop you from sinning. The goal was to have you trip over these extra oral laws and never cross the threshold of sin according to God's Word. By the time of Jesus, the two kinds of laws had been fused together as one, and Jesus calls these "human traditions" (Mark 7:8).[5]

N. T. Wright observes, "He ate with 'sinners' and kept company with people normally on or beyond the borders of respectable society; which of course in his day and culture meant not merely social respectability, but religious upbringing, proper covenant behaviour, loyal to the tradition and to the aspirations of Israel."[6]

So many Jewish people—including Levi—fit both bills. So what did the pastors, elders, deacons, the small-group-going, every-week-tithing, Bible-caring people say? "When the teachers of the law who were Pharisees saw him eating with the sinners and tax collectors, they asked his disciples: 'Why does he eat with tax collectors and sinners?'" (Mark 2:16). The obvious response was anger and frustration: *What are you doing, Jesus*? We love your miracles, your deliverances, your teaching, but we don't love your personal associations. Do you know what you're doing? Levi is a thief with Roman backing. He is a thug and a traitor to God, his family, and every Jew. And by the way, Jesus, you say you are holy, but eating with him—let alone staying at his house—is tantamount to saying his lifestyle and sin are okay. Are you okay with sin, Jesus?

Again, the religious leaders of the day were upset because they taught purity was connected to association. If you ate, spent time with, lived with people that were not following God's standards or other religious standards, you were saying it was okay, and thus you would be tainted. If you ate with a sinner, you yourself became a sinner.[7] Like a virus, like COVID-19 or a cold, you would catch it just by being around people.

But Jesus never excused anyone's sin by associating with them. This is key. Many Christians have started to act and believe that association equals justification of worldviews and sin. It does not. Over these encounters and meals, Jesus still called sin, *sin*.

In the encounter between the religious leaders and adulterous woman, Jesus makes it clear that the religious leaders were hypocrites, and he calls the woman to go and sin no more. Jesus did not care about ceremonial cleanliness. He calls out all parties. How can you be salt and light if you don't have relationships with those who are lost?

"On hearing this, Jesus said to them, 'It is not the healthy who need a doctor, but the sick. I have not come to call the righteous, but sinners'" (Mark 2:17). Now hold on—is Jesus saying that he only came for sinners and not for good or religious people? No, there's a hint of sarcasm here. Jesus knows that Levi and his friends and the religious leaders *all* need salvation, so he confronts two expressions of flagrant sin: moralism and hedonism. To use the prodigal son story, Jesus always calls both the older brother and the younger brother to repentance. The key is that both the tax collector and the scribe are the same; both need Jesus to change them, as we have seen throughout this book.

What happened to this sinner, this collaborator, this traitor, this cheat and so-called God hater? Years later, Levi, who we today call Matthew, helped change the world. He wrote the gospel of Matthew to convince the Jewish community that Jesus was the fulfillment of the Jewish faith. Just sit with the backwards logic of that. That fact also lends credibility to the truthfulness of this whole story. We know that Levi (Matthew) preached in Egypt and Ethiopia, started and strengthened the church, and then laid down his life for Jesus. Tradition tells us he was speared to death for his faith.

So why end our thinking here? Simple. Again and again we are tempted to give in to the darkness by separating ourselves from the world. We all have struggles, and we should not place ourselves in areas we cannot handle. But many times separation is an easy excuse to ignore relationships. It is easier not to have the hard conversations, and truly the shadow of Jonah shows up in thinking we are better than them and they don't deserve mercy.

I would invite you to really stop and think through all of what has been written. I know you will not agree with everything. That's okay and expected. But are you willing to be like Jesus in this repaganizing and pluralistic moment whether or not revival comes? Will you risk disappointment or discomfort for the sake of getting to know those who need Christ? Are you willing to spend time, have relationship with, and talk to those in your community?

The gospel is a pivoting gospel; it moves in multiple directions to so many different people, and so must we. People might say no to relationships. They might mock you, persecute you, or try to seduce you back to one of the many forms of worldliness. Pivoting is hard. Reaching out to many, knowing that most will not say yes might be difficult, but God has placed us in this moment. I leave you with the words of Paul:

> To the Jews I became like a Jew, to win the Jews. To those under the law I became like one under the law (though I myself am not under the law), so as to win those under the law. To those not having the law I became like one not having the law (though I am not free from God's law but am under Christ's law), so as to win those not having the law. To the weak I became weak, to win the weak. I have become all things to all people so that by all possible means I might save some. (1 Corinthians 9:20–22)

Christianity has died many times and risen again; for it had a God who knew the way out of the grave.

—G. K. CHESTERTON

Do not say, "Why were the old days better than these?" For it is not wise to ask such questions.

—ECCLESIASTES 7:10

We had no rest, but we were harassed at every turn—conflicts on the outside, fears within.

—2 CORINTHIANS 7:5

The church has outlived great empires, philosophical systems, totalitarian systems. The things that seem to occupy the whole horizon of public thinking now will be simply phantoms, half remembered from the past, twenty years from now. But the church will still be there.

—LESSLIE NEWBIGIN

Stand at the crossroads and look; ask for the ancient paths, ask where the good way is, and walk in it, and you will find rest for your souls.

—JEREMIAH 6:16

CHAPTER 22

Notes to an Unknown Future

Since I speak and write for a living, I have an ever-growing library. At the time of writing, I'm forty-nine years old. I've lived through the digitized revolution, but I prefer paper over screens. If you came into my office, you would see almost two thousand books, but I don't think you would ever guess which one is my most valuable and cherished. Between the textbooks, commentaries, and some very old and rare family Bibles, there is a small, red-covered book bound together with red string. It has frail, hole-punched, photocopied pages. The book is not beautiful, eye-catching, or artistically stunning, nor can I actually read what's inside of it. Each page is written in Hungarian. Its contents are songs. This hymn book was given to me by an underground Baptist leader who lived through the Cold War. During the thirty years of communism and suppression of the church, he ran a camp for orphans and quietly led many of them to Christ. I had the privilege of visiting this camp after communism fell, and while we were there, he handed me this little red book. This hymn book is so precious because it is the language of resistance. It is the language of hope in dark times, and its very existence proves that the gates of hell do not prevail against the church. We need to be reminded of this fact so that we can rest during the worst storms like Jesus did. Very few humans love change, yet we are living in a time of seemingly never-ending change. The temptation for you—for us—can be to give in to distraction, despair, or burnout. Many of us are becoming spiritual "booktroverts," or people that prefer fictional worlds and characters over real life. Or as a friend of mine said, we will be tempted to check out, tap out, or flame out. But God has placed us here now, for such a time as this.

We need a pivoting gospel, a multidirectional gospel that can speak into our digital, multigenerational, multicultural, pluralistic, global, local, modern, postmodern, religious, spiritual, secular, repaganizing, prerevival moment. Christians need to have the ability to speak and invite the deeply religious Nicodemus, the collaborator Levi, the dark-minded Mary Magdalene, the deconstructing prodigal child, the jaded skeptic Thomas, the unbelieving brother James, the blood enemy Paul, the intellectual Epicureans and Stoics, and Zeus worshippers of our time to meet their Creator through the work and person of Jesus from Nazareth.

With that in mind, let me give eight reflections on how we might thrive and win the West for Christ once again.

The Church Is Doing Fine; It Just Looks Different

When we feel alone, much of the time we cannot see truth. And the truth is that there is a movement on earth that touches more people than the Chinese Communist Party and is more multicultural and multilingual than the European Union and the International Monetary Fund, you fill in the blank with other global movements. It is the Christian church. The church is more connected and exerts more influence than anyone else.[1] For example, the last 126-plus years have shown us what God is up to. When the great Edinburgh Missionary Conference was held in 1910, over 80 percent of the world's affiliated Christian population lived in Europe and North America. Now it is less than forty percent. When you read the stats, they're not great. For example, Christians in Europe are among the world's least active Christians in terms of church attendance, Bible reading, and Christian education.[2]

And yet God is doing something so amazing. He has moved the centres of anointing and influence from the north to the south. Thinking on God's heart for Africa, one scholar wrote: "The way to restore a vision for God's purpose for Africa is to return to the call of Abraham. Just as Abram turned his back on the old nation of Ur to become a new nation, the implication is that God is doing a similar thing in our day with the shift from global North to global South."[3] We should all shout amen! In 1900, Africa was home to 8.7 million Christians. Today there are 542 million, with estimates that by 2050 this will rise to 1.2 billion. While Africa makes up 14.9 percent of the global population, it holds 21.9 percent of the world's Christians.[4]

And it's not just in Africa; God is answering the prayers and honouring the work of a thousand years. Here are just a few examples. In 1960, there were thirty known Christians in Nepal; today, there are more than 1.4 million.[5] Next door in China, the stats are incredible. In and around 1949—less than one hundred years ago—there were about one million Christians. Today, Chinese Christians are estimated to number 100 million or more. "If the growth continues at the rate of 7 percent, Christians could be 32.5 percent of the Chinese population by 2040 and 66.7 percent by 2050."[6] We may feel lonely as Christians in the West, but we're not at all. We're more like Elijah, who said, "I am the only one left," and God responded, "No, I have over seven hundred prophets."

The global statistics on evangelicals, Pentecostals, charismatics, and neo-charismatics alone are amazing: Brazil (79.9 million), followed then by the United States (75.2 million), China (54.3 million), India (33.5 million), South Africa (21.2 million), the Philippines (20.0 million), Congo-Zaire (17.7 million), Mexico (13.0 million), South Korea (9.1 million), and the list goes on and on.[7] Many think that the fastest growing church in the world is in Iran, saying it is nearing or just surpassed a million.[8] These numbers do not even include Catholics, Coptics, or Orthodox, which all hold to the agreed-upon Ecumenical creeds (the Apostles' Creed, Nicene Creed, and Athanasian Creed).

But these stats are not just for our encouragement. This is one of the ways the West will be won again. The revivals of the last hundred years, the tidal waves of immigration, and the many refugee crises are God's way of reseeding these ancient lands with the gospel. Global revivals are producing reversed missions.[9] Take Brazil as an example. More than 10,000 Brazilian Christian workers are missionaries in Britain, France, Germany, and Italy. There are more than 35,000 who are missionaries to the United States.[10]

I witness the global Christian church every single day. Our current senior executive pastor is Brazilian. The Lord told him and his wife to become missionaries to Canada. Now here they are, working alongside us and helping lead our church. Our church is home to over fifty-five ethnic groups, all worshipping the Trinity in the most multicultural city on earth. Another one of our site pastors is half Greek and half Canadian. She is married to a Ghanian pastor. For a period of time, he oversaw our young adult ministry and then our global initiatives. Now she works on our staff, and he is doing his doctorate on the role of the Holy Spirit, leadership, and the revitalization of the Free Methodist Church in Canada. Our staff includes people who are Korean, Chinese, Filipino, Jamaican, Nigerian, Brazilian, Sri Lankan, Eritrean, and many more.

Everywhere I travel in the West, historic, orthodox, Bible-believing, evangelical, charismatic, Anglican, Presbyterian, or Baptist churches are filled with people from around the world who hold to the true gospel. Two other stories come to mind that illustrate this ongoing God-move so profoundly. John Newton, who wrote the song "Amazing Grace," lost his mom at seven, and his dad was borderline abusive. The abused boy became an abuser, and the man who was a slave himself became a slaver. Newton's personal journey was full of drinking, partying, and premarital sex. Rebellious and lost, he meets Jesus.[11] "Amazing grace (how sweet the sound) that saved a wretch like me!"

Newton did not shy away from the human condition, for he had seen it. Not just "I am broken," not just "I am traumatized," not just "I learned bad behaviour." No, he said we are all wretched sinners in need of salvation. Our world does not want to hear it—and neither do many in churches—but we need to say it because it is true. Generations later, a friend of mine who is a Nigerian Pentecostal was called by the Holy Spirit to become an Anglican priest and now oversees John Newton's church. It is filled with young adults from multiple ethnic communities worshipping the triune God. It's not just irony; it's divine pleasure and providence that John Newton's church is led by Africans pointing London back to the giver of amazing grace. This is what God is up to all around the world, and we should celebrate God's ongoing moves!

Here's another example: My great-grandmother was in charge of prayer ministry at one of the greatest missionary-sending churches of Canada, actually in all of North America—the People's Church. When the founder, Oswell J. Smith, died, Billy Graham spoke at the funeral. This church has invested millions of dollars into global evangelism and has sent more missionaries than nearly every church in Canada. My great-grandmother, along with others, interceded for the nations, prayed over missionaries, asked the Lord for workers for the harvest, and wrestled for the world. God has been answering her prayers since 1928.

When a major refugee crisis broke out in Toronto, the city of Toronto used the plan written by this church to welcome refugees and help them assimilate. But even more amazing, those refugees who became Christians from hundreds of different backgrounds because of the missionaries sent out by the People's Church have now come to Toronto looking for the church that led their ancestors to Christ. Now they are growing, leading, and building the People's Church in Toronto to witness today.

I know there are honest disagreements and deeply difficult decisions to be made related to safety, terrorism, antidemocratic worldviews, jobs, money, and health coverage regarding immigration, refugees, and hosting countries. It is too simplistic to say Jesus wants open borders or nation over refugees. The questions surrounding legal and illegal immigration are immense. And I believe God has established nations (Acts 17:26) so national identity and sovereignty are not necessarily sinful or evil. So I feel torn between compassion and allowing immigration for those who do not believe in modern liberal democracies. Nonetheless, Christians need to take heaven's view. God is using ongoing crises to bring life back into the dying church of the West, and he is bringing the nations to us so that we can show them the hospitality, the truth, and the power of Jesus.

There are as many Ruths as there are Sauls of Tarsus among us. We must ask ourselves: Has God brought even our enemies (those who oppose our faith or hate our nations) so they might hear the gospel? This fits no political box, but it sure feels like Providence. As I have said, if Toronto was touched overnight by the Holy Spirit, then within twenty-four hours the whole world would be touched. The whole world could be impacted in twenty-four hours. Never has the church had such an opportunity in its last two thousand years.

The Role of Family in Evangelism

Though I don't think we need a full monastic hunker-down moment, we do need to think small. Christian families are key in passing on the faith. If faith is going to root itself once again in the West, family evangelism is going to be key. The church is so important, but prayer, Bible reading, and discipleship at home is nonnegotiable. What Moses said just before Joshua entered the promised land should be our rallying cry:

> Hear, O Israel: The LORD our God, the LORD is one. Love the LORD your God with all your heart and with all your soul and with all your strength. These commandments that I give you today are to be on your hearts. Impress them on your children. Talk about them when you sit at home and when you walk along the road, when you lie down and when you get up. (Deuteronomy 6:4–7)

There is only one God. We must love him more than anything or anyone else. And since this is true, pass the faith on to your children and to those in the next generation. Faith should be talked about and embedded in the mundanities of everyday life, not reserved for worship gatherings.

As we share our faith with those coming up, remember to show your kids, nephews, nieces, and grandkids your brokenness and doubt, and when you don't know something, admit it. Help them see the difference between politics and the nonnegotiables of faith. If you speak about these things in the same tone, how will they see which one will last in the new heaven and the new earth? Again, Timothy's conversion can be an example for us. I summarize it like this in *Perseverance*:

> Then we finally arrive at one of the most important verses about encounter, conversion, perseverance, and generational faith in the whole of the Bible. It's one we often miss because it's so boring, normal, family based, and unspectacular that we don't grasp the power of it. "I am reminded of your sincere faith, which first lived in your grandmother Lois and in your mother Eunice and, I am persuaded, now lives in you also" (2 Tim. 1:5). Okay, so let's talk about Timothy's family! We have one other passage, in the book of Acts, that gives us just a small insight into this family, Paul came to Derbe and then to Lystra, where a disciple named Timothy lived, whose mother was Jewish and a believer but whose father was a Greek. The believers at Lystra and Iconium spoke well of him. Paul wanted to take him along on the journey, so he circumcised him because of the Jews who lived in that area, for they all knew that his father was a Greek. (Acts 16:1–3)
>
> Timothy's mother was Jewish and so was his grandmother. Within that worldview 2,000 years ago, Timothy would be considered Jewish. But his dad was Greek. Why does this matter? Well, that means his mother had become a nominal Jew—an apostate Jew, outside of God's love and family because she had married an outsider. She married a man who did not worship the true living God. But more, their whole family would be considered unclean because as a Greek, he would eat, wear, and touch unclean things. They would not be considered faithful, synagogue-going Jews.
>
> Also, Timothy was not circumcised, despite being considered ethnically Jewish by everyone else. Circumcision was a physical sign of the Jewish faith, and this was God's idea. As one explains it, "No doubt this surgery was symbolic of the sinfulness of man that was passed from generation to generation. The very procreative organ needed to be cleansed of a covering. So, man at the very centre of his nature is sinful and needs cleansing of the heart. This graphic symbol of the need for removing sin became the sign of being a Jew."

But by Paul's day, the rabbis were teaching that this was what kept you from hell. So, as I read and reflect, Timothy's mom and grandmother were ethnically Jewish and religiously sort of Jewish; Timothy was raised Jewish, sort of, and his dad was a pagan. To everyone else, Timothy would be considered Jewish but to the Jewish community, he was not saved and was either going to hell or was at least in trouble. And yet in the middle of this, Timothy's mom and grandmother came to faith in Jesus Christ and shared their faith with Timothy. So Paul says, "I am persuaded, now lives in you also" (2 Tim. 1:5).

Timothy's faith is sincere; Paul says this faith that was on the inside of your mom and grandma, this indwelling faith, now also lives in you. Do you see this—the Christian faith is not inherited; it must still be accepted by every generation. As Billy Graham said, "God has no grandchildren." And yet the role of faith passed on in the home is central to Timothy's story. So much evangelism must be done within families."[12]

The Need for *Bothandism*

Like all those faithful followers of Jesus that have gone before us, we walk a tightrope. We are called to say no to licentiousness and at the same time say no to legalism. And we are called to live, fight for, and find the middle space between theological liberalism and unbiblical fundamentalism. This is difficult on the best days, but it is the right place to be.

Years ago, one of my favourite shows, *The West Wing*, was a behind-the-scenes story about living and leading in the White House. Now it was a liberal fantasy for sure. At points, I was frustrated by how they framed certain conservative values, especially in the early seasons. But the dialogue was incredible, the stories compelling, and famous hallway walking scenes showed people talking and walking and arguing. One episode in season five called "The Supremes" is about choosing Supreme Court justices. At the end of the episode, President Jed Bartlett chooses a conservative and a liberal justice at the same time, making sure the court was balanced. This of course is not what happens in the United States, but in its day, it struck a chord with many people as a hopeful way to keep that country together. The episode was fun, amazing, and intriguing, but there was a short conversation between the president and one candidate who was not chosen, Judge Shelton. He was not conservative or liberal but a clear-minded, insightful, and gutsy moderate. This is how the dialogue went:

Jed: Affirmative action is going to be back in the next few years. Let's start there.
Shelton: What do I know about it?
Jed: What do you think about it?
Shelton: I don't know. Not the answer you were looking for?
Jed: Not really.
Shelton: Unnerving, isn't it?
Jed: Is there another topic you'd be more comfortable with?
Shelton: Nothing comes to mind.
Jed: Perhaps you should make something up.
Shelton: I'm not trying to be cagey, but I don't position myself on issues, and I don't know what I think about a case until I hear it. There are moderates who are called that because they are not activists. And there are moderates who are called that because sometimes they wind up on the Left and sometimes on the Right.
Jed: You think I want somebody who will vote with Ashland?
Shelton: I think you are looking for somebody who will vote with him now and replace him later.
Jed: And that's not you?
Shelton: Wish it were. He's a giant. But my allegiance to the eccentricities of a case will reliably outweigh my allegiance to any position you might wish I held.[13]

The line that stood out to me years ago was, "Sometimes they wind up on the Left, and sometimes on the Right." This judge was loyal to the law over political positions. Yes! His mind-set is so needed, especially if we are going to let the Bible form us and have the ultimate say.

Someone asked me my thoughts on preaching the other day on a podcast and this is how I responded: Here are a few ideas that have been foundational over the last twenty-five years. To be a good preacher, first, I must live under Scripture, not over it. I must be formed by God's Word. I don't naturally agree with a lot in Scripture, but I know it's right, no matter what I feel or struggle with. Second, when reading or preaching, if the text goes hard left, I go hard left. If it goes hard right, I go hard right. If it goes to the middle, then I must walk in the middle. I have observed that if you are not regularly bothering both those on the political right and the political left, you are not preaching well. Personally, if I am not regularly both encouraged and disturbed when reading and preaching Scripture, then I am not listening well. Sometimes you should sound out of touch to popular culture, and at other times you should be deeply disturbing to church culture. If you say the Bible is the ultimate source of faith, life, and practice, then you have no choice but to feel a bit of *bothandism*.

This posture allows us to reach out well and be formed well inside, making sure no theological reflex or national agenda has more authority than the Scriptures. Many people have left our church over the years for various reasons, but one of the most frequent responses in our exit interview has been about us being inconsistent to a political, theological, or ethnocentric expectation. The Bible and its Author set the boundaries, and rarely does our comfort—or the preconceived boxes we desire—do well with that!

Tell the Whole Truth

I don't know if it's me, but—at least in my country—I always smile or smirk when I watch a pharmaceutical ad. There are always people dancing or baking or running or hiking, showing us the best of the world as they're talking about some needed medicine. In every one of these ads, especially during the images of the amazing life we all want to live, they list all the things that might go wrong if you take this drug. This drug will help you with cholesterol, or with your heart, or with weight loss, but if you take it, you might become suicidal, get migraines, or even die, and then they list twenty other possible issues. I always smile because the happiest images of life appear when they talk about the worst things. But like these ads, we too are called to tell the whole story! We saw this with Peter in Acts 2 and with Jonah in Nineveh. We must talk about both judgment and mercy, eternal loss and eternal life. We are all fallen, all owned by sin, all blind, all dead, and all under judgment. Just listen to the Scriptures:

> You see, at just the right time, when we were still powerless, Christ died for the ungodly. (Romans 5:6)
>
> The god of this age has blinded the minds of unbelievers, so that they cannot see the light of the gospel that displays the glory of Christ, who is the image of God. (2 Corinthians 4:4)
>
> As for you, you were dead in your transgressions and sins. . . . All of us also lived among them at one time, gratifying the cravings of our flesh and following its desires and thoughts. Like the rest, we were by nature deserving of wrath. (Ephesians 2:1, 3)

The Bible is explicitly clear about the bad news before the good news.[14] The Bible says we are under the just wrath of God; we are spiritually dead, blind, powerless, and enslaved to evil. We cannot *not* sin, and we are destined for an eternity without God that we call hell. Yes, there is so much good in the world. Yes, there is common grace all around us. Yes, we are not utterly depraved, but it is still really bad. The worst and the best, the most unreligious and the most religious, the weak and powerful—this is our condition. We are not just sick or in trouble; we are not born mostly good but a little off. We are under God's wrath because of sin, and the holy God must bring honest judgment. It was James Finley who powerfully wrote, "There is something in me that puts fig leaves of concealment, kills my brother, builds towers of confusion, and brings cosmic chaos upon the earth. There is something in me that loves darkness rather than light, that rejects God and therefore rejects my own deepest reality as a human person made in the image and likeness of God."[15]

Rebellion, wrath, dead, blind, slave, positionally possessed by evil, complete loss—these are not just words but our lived-out experience. But then, into that darkness of night, into that unchangeable situation, the God who walked in the coolness of the day with Adam and Eve steps back in. He returns to save, to buy us back, to deliver, to recover, to provide escape, to rescue. And he does not send anyone else but himself; he sends his Son, Jesus. This is when it gets so good! Only when we see the truth of our condition does the work of Jesus become powerful. It's not just good news; it is the best news! Seeing the bad news alongside the good news, we get the whole story.

The gospel does not tell us we are innocent, but it tells us we are loved. And in asking us to receive and consent to that love, it asks us to identify with and make our own love. Let us not forget that this is news, not advice. This is not something you do but something already done for you. It happened:

> For God so loved the world that he gave his one and only Son, that whoever believes in him shall not perish but have eternal life. For God did not send his Son into the world to condemn the world, but to save the world through him. Whoever believes in him is not condemned, but whoever does not believe stands condemned already because they have not believed in the name of God's one and only Son. (John 3:16–18)

Don't shy away from the whole truth.[16]

The gospel is still the power of God unto salvation; after the bad there is the best—forgiveness of sin, reconciliation, eternal life, human flourishing! As one scholar said, "In any situation of forgiveness, four elements are actually in play. Three are obvious; the offender, the offended, and their relationship. But a fourth must be borne in mind, else the cross makes no objective sense as sacrifice.... Jesus repairs it. Jesus pays it. Jesus bears it. Jesus absorbs it. Jesus, somehow, and whatever 'it' is, makes things right by his sacrifice of himself."[17]

Be Prepared to Be a Fool

I have been told, first from the Left and now from the Right, "You are on the wrong side of history." Well as Christians, we are going to be on the wrong side of history much of the time, for history is influenced by sinful, worldly systems and demonic influences. We must remind ourselves that true history is owned by God, so ultimately we will be on the right side of history because our Father owns history. I think we need to start using the medieval phrase "the year of our Lord" so we are reminded whose year it actually is! It is not better to be on the wrong side of history than on the wrong side of the Author of history. Fear God, not people!

But as we wait for Jesus's return, which will make his Father's kingdom be fully expressed across time and space, we must settle in and be prepared to be called all sorts of things, including fools. When rebuking the arrogance of the Corinthian church, Paul said in 1 Corinthians 4:10, "We are fools for Christ, but you are so wise in Christ! We are weak, but you are strong! You are honoured, we are dishonoured!"

"Fools," "weak," and "dishonoured." Yup. This is our lot in life. We are often tempted to replace meekness with power. I have heard that when Alexander the Great lay dying at age thirty-three, he was asked to whom he would leave his kingdom. "To the strongest," he said, which led to two hundred years of war. Our King was on a cross—beaten, naked, and humiliated—and said, "Forgive them, Father." So why are we shocked that we need to be fools? Paul summarizes it best: "We preach Christ crucified: a stumbling block to Jews and foolishness to Gentiles" (1 Corinthians 1:23). This has not changed! But don't be disheartened because the gospel is still the same and the power has not changed. Just become okay with being a fool.

> For the message of the cross is foolishness to those who are perishing, but to us who are being saved it is the power of God. (1 Corinthians 1:18)

We Need Each Other

In these transitional and turbulent times, we need each other as fellow Christians. Now I do believe that many people that call themselves Christian are not Christian. Many don't have a personal relationship with Jesus; others are false teachers and false Christians. I also know that even confessional, orthodox, biblically centred Christians cannot agree on much. I still have many deep concerns related to my Catholic and Orthodox friends, and I remain unconvinced by many of their demands and beliefs (the need for apostolic succession, ultimate Papal authority, the veneration of Mary, the role of tradition, the intercession of the living dead [the saints], the role of works connected to eternal life, etc.).[18] And yet I still believe that there is an unchanging core of unity between us. The late J. I. Packer beautifully outlined this years ago. He wrote that the great tradition of Christian faith and life that we all hold includes the following:

> Recognizing the canonical Scriptures as the repository and channel of Christ-centred divine revelation. Acknowledging the triune God as sovereign in creation, providence and grace.
>
> Focusing faith, in the sense both of belief and of trust, on Jesus Christ as God incarnate; as our crucified and living Saviour, Lord, master, friend, life and hope; and as the one mediator of—and thus the only way to—a filial relationship with God, His Father.
>
> Seeing Christians as a family of forgiven sinners, now supernaturally regenerated in Christ and empowered for godliness by the Holy Spirit.
>
> Seeing the church as a single supernatural society, and the two dominical sacraments as necessities of obedience: gestures of worship and means of communion with God in Christ.
>
> Practicing prayer, obedience, purity, love and service, and sanctifying all relationships in the home, the church and the wider world, as the Christian's proper individual lifestyle.
>
> Reckoning with the personal reality of evil and maintaining purposeful hostility to sin and the devil.

> Expecting death and final judgment to lead into the endless joy of heaven, where the glorified saints will live with Christ and each other forever. The great tradition has from time to time embraced different ways of explicating these things, but the things themselves are the nonnegotiable of Christianity according to Christ.[19]

If you can say yes and amen to what Packer said, then we are likely brothers and sisters in Christ. And if we are going to spend eternity together, we should try not only to get used to each other but to work with each other, especially in this time we are facing. In his unique and controversial book *The End of Protestantism: Pursuing Unity in a Fragmented Church*, Peter J. Leithart outlines what he hopes this will look like. He calls it Reformational Catholicism.

> Each congregation will view itself as a congregation of a single, global communion of congregations. Each congregation will pray for the others that it knows, and will pray continuously for even deeper and broader unity among Christians. This may sound utopian. It may seem that this church will exist only at the last day. But it is not utopian. It is essentially what the church was for the first several centuries, what the Western church was before the Reformation. It is what happened in South India in the mid-twentieth century, as formerly Methodist and Reformed and Anglican churches died to their old names and rose to become the united Church of South India. Can we say more?
>
> The reformed, united church of the future will be a biblical church. It will not ignore the riches of Christian history. Pastors and theologians of the future church will draw on the whole tradition of biblical commentary and theology, all the tradition's wealth of pastoral wisdom and liturgical beauty, as they go about their work. Former Lutherans will discover fresh insights in the writings of former Mennonites and Calvinists; former Baptists will study encyclicals from Rome with appreciation; former Methodists will deepen their insight into the liturgy by studying Eastern Christian writers. Everyone will accept the whole of the tradition, East and West and beyond, past and present, as a treasure entrusted by the

> Spirit to the church. Origen and Augustine and Aquinas and Luther and Barth will be remembered and honoured. A millennium from now, everyone will be studying the Latin American and African "church fathers" of the twenty-first century. Confessions and creeds will remain in play. Churches will unite around the early creeds and will continue to use the treasures of the great confessions of the Reformation, of Trent and the Catholic Catechism, and of the hundreds of creeds and confessions that the global South will produce between now and then. . . . Confessions, however, will cease to serve as wedges to pry one set of Christians from another. Confessions will be used for edification rather than as a set of shibboleths for excluding those who mispronounce.[20]

Now even when I read the above desire and dream, I have a lot of questions and difficulties. I am still ultimately an evangelical protestant,[21] even though Trent says I am not family.

But relationally on the ground and through reading, podcasts, and conversations, denominations are reconnecting and conversing everywhere I go. From the bastion of complementarian Calvinism at Southern Seminary to the Wesleyans at Asbury and the evangelical charismatic Anglicans in London, from the spiritual formation movement to the classic evangelical preaching movement, libraries, podcasts, and bookstores are filled with the great traditions talking to each other once again. The whole family forms and challenges us, showing us where real unity might be.

The famous Southern Baptist W. A. Criswell, leader of the largest Baptist church in the world in his time and former president of the Southern Baptist Convention, came to the same conclusion: "I have no common denominator with a Protestant liberal at all, the man that doesn't believe the Bible, the Word of God. . . . I would be more comfortable praying with a Catholic priest who believes in the virgin birth, the blood atonement, and the deity of Christ than with a liberal Protestant who doesn't."[22]

This idea, of course, is deeply opposed by many faithful others. But I find that quietly—even in those tribes—there is a growing underground river ultimately calling us to remain, to boldly confess, to give holy presence, and witness well alongside each other in this repaganizing and pluralistic, apathetic, hostile, possible-revival moment. Whether we know it or not, together we are praying for—and in small ways seeing—renewal, which might become revival, that we pray might become an awakening. As I read church history, I am unaware of an awakening fully taking place in a fully multicultural environment like our world today. I hope and pray that somewhere, somehow such a move of God takes place so that many would be saved in an eye-opening, head-turning, makes-no-sense way!

We Need Love, Power, and Intellect to Break Through

Many will come to faith by being loved into the kingdom. Others will be taught or thought into the kingdom. Yet my on-the-ground experience and growing conviction is that the vast majority will come to faith through power, through encounter with Jesus. All these doors must lead to the real Jesus of Scripture, and there must be repentance of sin, faith in Christ for salvation, and the hope of physical resurrection. But if you don't have all these paths to faith in your church, some doors to evangelism will be closed that need not be. Even though all these gifts work, some doors will not attract certain people or groups. This is why all the gifts must be understood and used. Whether it's a Muslim having a dream about Jesus, a university student listening to a Christian Oxford professor on the historical validity of the resurrection, a sick person being loved, cared for, and prayed over by a Christian nurse, a sermon by the preacher that broke the power of darkness, the point is that in a pluralistic, multicultural, socio-economically diverse world, we need all God's doors open to see the kingdom of God in its fullness on this side of the new heaven and new earth. Love, word, and power are the keys to walking across all the bridges.

We desperately need in our time what is true for all times. We are called to be a hospitable, intellectually engaging movement of encounterism. Let me say it again, for this summarizes almost all my work and worldview: hospitable, intellectual, encounterism. This is how Jesus worked; this is how Peter and Paul worked. This is why the spiritual gifts are grouped as they are. This is what the many incarnations of the early church looked like. They were loving, merciful, and hospitable alongside miracles, dreams, deliverances, and healing, while at the same time outlining and defining the rational, intellectual, and historical validity of the faith. I think spiritual gifts are key to this,[23] but in more general terms this is how the gospel pivots and addresses many needs, many audiences from many different backgrounds. We need all three legs of our three-legged stool, or we all fall down.

We Are Not Alone

You are not alone, and knowing where your true home lies is one of the most foundational ideas for living not only a fulfilled Christian life but persevering amidst so many ideas, voices, and cultural change.

I end this book with one last personal story. Every culture has its own food, candy, drinks, and so on. One of Canada's most famous snacks is ketchup chips (others of you call these "crisps"). Don't dismiss them; they're amazing. If you have heard me speak a few times, you'll know I'm a Christmasholic. Christmas music and decorations go up on November 1. I put baby Jesus out on Halloween. We set up six Christmas trees. We also have stockings. The debate between my wife and me is that I think stocking gifts need to be wrapped and she doesn't. Every year I get a bag of ketchup chips in my stocking. You may think, "Wow, Jon, that's really random and weird," but it holds deep meaning for me. Ketchup chips at Christmas make me feel at home. I'm a third-culture kid. I grew up in Ecuador in the 1980s, preinternet. When I was growing up in a different culture, there were moments where I deeply missed home, and for some reason, in my little grade three mind, I equated ketchup chips with Canada. When we moved from Ecuador back to Canada, my mom started putting ketchup chips in my stocking to remind me I was home. I'm forty-nine now, and we still do it. Many of you reading this might be immigrants or the children of immigrants, so you have lived the tension of coming to a new country and trying to make it feel like home. And yet sometimes you miss your original home. Or maybe you have moved to a different part of your own country. That missing thing can be a person, a smell, a place, or, more often than not, a food. You know this is true, because when you meet up with others that have similar backgrounds, the whole conversation tends to be about what you miss. For me, it's ketchup chips.

Let my Christmastime ketchup chips remind you: Don't forget where home is and who is there. Jesus profoundly said in John 14:

> Do not let your hearts be troubled. You believe in God; believe also in me. My Father's house has many rooms; if that were not so, would I have told you that I am going there to prepare a place for you? And if I go and prepare a place for you, I will come back and take you to be with me that you also may be where I am. You know the way to the place where I am going. (John 14:1–4)

As we wait, we have his Spirit, and that is how he chooses to be with us to the end of the age.

At this moment, Jesus is making all things right, and one day you and I will see him face to face. When Jesus's best friend John saw him at age ninety, he fell over because he was *that* amazing. Over 1,200 years later, Thomas Aquinas met the One he had written about, spoken about, preached about, invited others to meet. While Aquinas was saying Mass at Naples in 1273, he had a mystical experience. He refused to work—or could not return to working—on the *Summa Theologica*. Famously, he told a friend that everything he had written now seemed to him "like straw in comparison to what he had seen." The third part of the *Summa*, the part about Jesus, his body here on earth, and the sacraments he gave his church, Aquinas left unfinished. He died only a few months later, shortly after striking his head on a tree branch on his way to a church council.[24] Jesus is that beautiful, that terrifying, that comforting, that transcendent, that intimate. He is not just preparing our home, but he is our home, and we are never alone. As we wait for him, we must commit to holy presence and to witness. We must be love, we must demonstrate and proclaim the life, death, and resurrection of Jesus in this modern or postmodern, sort of Christian, sort of post/pre-Christian, secular, spiritual, religious, repaganizing, pluralistic, divided age. No matter the seasons that will come, a greater retreat from Christianity or a fourth great awakening, we must walk in God's ways.

As we do this, dear Christian, never forget you are not alone! Right now from an isolated village in Peru to the boundless energy of New York City, from the slums of Calcutta and Nairobi, to basements in Riyadh and high rises in Hong Kong, from Toronto to Tokyo, Manchester to Moscow, from the jungles in Thailand and Brazil to the steppes in Tibet, you will find brothers and sisters. Right now, you are connected to them because we are all possessed by the same Spirit; we share one Saviour, who gives us all access to our Father.

Today, from free to liturgical, from cathedral to house church, from the megachurch to neighbourhood church, we are all connected. We are even connected to those who have already died and are in the presence of Jesus. Even death cannot stop our connection, for we are a people united globally and dimensionally by the Holy Spirit of Christ. Keep going, for the great cloud of witnesses is not mere metaphor but reality itself! And what do they say to us in our God-given moment and assignment?

> Therefore, since we are surrounded by such a great cloud of witnesses, let us throw off everything that hinders and the sin that so easily entangles. And let us run with perseverance the race marked out for us, fixing our eyes on Jesus, the pioneer and perfecter of faith. For the joy set before him he endured the cross, scorning its shame, and sat down at the right hand of the throne of God. (Hebrews 12:1–2)

Notes

Introduction

1. *Mr. Universe* (Netflix, 2012).
2. Scotty Smith, "A Prayer for Becoming a More Attentive, Engaged Listener," The Gospel Coalition, June 1, 2013, https://www.thegospelcoalition.org/blogs/scotty-smith/a-prayer-for-becoming-a-more-attentive-engaged-listener/.

Chapter 1: This World Is Not My Home . . . Or Is It?

1. Kevin DeYoung, *"An American Evangelist," First Things,* May 2023, https://www.firstthings.com/article/2023/05/an-american-evangelist.
2. DeYoung, "An American Evangelist."
3. DeYoung, "An American Evangelist."
4. Andrew F. Walls and Brian Stanley, *The Missionary Movement from the West: A Biography from Birth to Old Age,* Studies in the History of Christian Missions (Grand Rapids: Eerdmans, 2023), 51.
5. Athanasius, *Life of St. Anthony of Egypt,* in Nicene and Post-Nicene Fathers, second series, vol. 4, trans. Philip Schaff and Henry Wace (Buffalo, NY: Christian Literature, 1892).
6. Claire Gilbert, *I, Julian: The Fictional Autobiography of Julian of Norwich* (London: Hodder & Stoughton, 2024).
7. Dallas Willard, *The Divine Conspiracy: Rediscovering Our Hidden Life in God* (San Francisco: HarperSanFrancisco, 1998), 121–23.
8. N. T. Wright, *Matthew for Everyone, Chapters 1–15* (Louisville: Westminster John Knox, 2023), 31.
9. R. Kent Hughes, *The Sermon on the Mount: The Message of the Kingdom* (Wheaton, IL: Crossway, 2013), 79.
10. Michael J. Wilkins, *Matthew: From Biblical Text—to Contemporary Life,* NIV Application Commentary (Grand Rapids: Zondervan, 2004), 121–23.
11. D. A. Carson, *Jesus' Sermon on the Mount: And His Confrontation with the World; An Exposition of Matthew 5–10* (Grand Rapids: Baker, 1999), 30.

12. Hughes, *The Sermon on the Mount*, 81.
13. Hughes, *The Sermon on the Mount*, 82–83.
14. Wilkins, *Matthew*, 213.
15. Marianne Sawicki, *Crossing Galilee: Architectures of Contact in the Occupied Land of Jesus* (Harrisburg, PA: Trinity Press International, 2000), 165.

Chapter 2: The Decline of Christendom in the West

1. Andrew F. Walls and Brian Stanley, *The Missionary Movement from the West: A Biography from Birth to Old Age*, Studies in the History of Christian Missions (Grand Rapids: Eerdmans, 2023), 23–24.
2. Jon Thompson, *Deliverance: A Journey Toward the Unexpected* (Ajax, ON: Sanctus Church, 2018), iii.
3. George R. Hunsberger and Craig Van Gelder, eds., *The Church Between Gospel and Culture: The Emerging Mission in North America* (Grand Rapids: Eerdmans, 1996), 43.
4. J. I. Packer, *Finishing Our Course with Joy: Guidance from God for Engaging with Our Aging* (Wheaton, IL: Crossway, 2014), 23–24.
5. Andrew F. Walls and Brian Stanley, *The Missionary Movement from the West: A Biography from Birth to Old Age*, Studies in the History of Christian Missions (Grand Rapids: Eerdmans, 2023), 8.
6. "Prime Minister Justin Trudeau Marches at Montreal's Pride Parade," *The Canadian Press*, August 19, 2018, https://globalnews.ca/news/4396252/prime-minister-justin-trudeau-set-to-walk-in-montreals-pride-parade/.
7. "Harvard Professor, Diana Eck, on the Difference between Pluralism and Relativism," The Veritas Forum (channel), hosted by YouTube, posted January 7, 2016, https://www.youtube.com/watch?v=hUmDG0KlkUs.
8. Tim Keller (@timkellernyc) "Roman Empire: You Christians are too exclusive," X, April 6, 2023, 6:23 a.m. https://x.com/timkellernyc/status/1643922244060553223.
9. John T. McGreevy, *Catholicism: A Global History from the French Revolution to Pope Francis* (New York: Norton, 2022), 43.
10. Oliver Samson, "Drag Queens Admit Paris Olympic Games Performance as Parody of 'The Last Supper,'" Radio Veritas Asia, August 2, 2024, https://www.rvasia.org/asian-news/drag-queens-admit-paris-olympic-games-performance-parody-last-supper.
11. Rod Dreher, *Live Not by Lies: A Manual for Christian Dissidents* (New York: Sentinel, 2020), xi.
12. Dreher, *Live Not by Lies*, 31.
13. Hannah Arendt, *The Origins of Totalitarianism* (New York: Mariner Classics, 2024) 761.

14. Dreher, *Live Not by Lies*, 33–34.
15. Dreher, *Live Not by Lies*, 35–41.
16. Dreher, *Live Not by Lies*, 7–8.
17. Caroline De Sury, "Record 12,000 People Were Baptized in France on Easter," *America Magazine: The Jesuit Review*, April 4, 2024, https://www.americamagazine.org/faith/2024/04/04/france-easter-adult-baptism-record-247629; Caroline De Sury, "France to See a Record 17,800 Catechumens Baptized at Easter, with Requests Still 'Pouring In,'" *Catholic Review*, April 14, 2025, https://catholicreview.org/france-to-see-a-record-17800-catechumens-baptized-at-easter-with-requests-still-pouring-in/.
18. C. S. Lewis, *The Pilgrim's Regress*, ed. David C. Downing, Wade annotated edition (Grand Rapids: Eerdmans, 2014), 156.
19. "*Richard Dawkins: I'm a Cultural Christian*," LBC (channel), posted on YouTube, April 1, 2024, https://www.youtube.com/watch?v=COHgEFUFWyg.

Chapter 3: The Incarnation as Our Model

1. Charles R. Swindoll, *Insights on John*, Swindoll's New Testament Insights (Grand Rapids: Zondervan, 2010), 17.
2. Leon Morris, *The Gospel According to John*, rev. ed., The New International Commentary on the New Testament (Grand Rapids: Eerdmans, 2008), 67.
3. R. Kent Hughes, *John: That You May Believe*, Preaching the Word (Wheaton, IL: Crossway, 1999), 16.
4. Swindoll, *Insights on John*, 24.
5. Hughes, *John*, 17.
6. Dean S. Gilliland, "The Incarnation as Matrix for Appropriate Theologies," in *Appropriate Christianity*, ed. Charles H. Kraft and Dean S. Gilliland (Pasadena, CA: William Carey, 2005), 494–95.
7. Andrew F. Walls, *The Missionary Movement in Christian History: Studies in the Transmission of Faith* (Maryknoll, NY: Orbis, 1996), 27.
8. Dean S. Gilliland, *The Word Among Us: Contextualizing Theology for Mission Today* (Eugene, OR: Wipf and Stock, 2002), 123–26.
9. Timothy George and Thomas G. Guarino, eds., *Evangelicals and Catholics Together at Twenty: Vital Statements on Contested Topics* (Grand Rapids: Brazos, 2015), xxi.
10. Stephen B. Bevans, *Models of Contextual Theology*, rev. ed., Faith and Cultures Series (Maryknoll, NY: Orbis, 2002), 44.
11. Gilliland, "The Incarnation as Matrix for Appropriate Theologies," 493.
12. Darrell L. Whiteman, "The Function of Appropriate Contextualization in Mission," in Kraft and Gilliland *Appropriate Christianity*, 53.
13. Luke Stamps, "Biblical Reasoning," *Gregorian Eclecticism* (blog),

February 18, 2015, https://secundumscripturas.com/2015/02/18/gregorian-eclecticism/.
14. Andrew F. Walls, *The Missionary Movement in Christian History: Studies in the Transmission of Faith* (Maryknoll, NY: Orbis, 1996), 47, 97.
15. James S. Cutsinger, ed., *Reclaiming the Great Tradition: Evangelicals, Catholics and Orthodox in Dialogue* (Downers Grove, IL: InterVarsity Press, 1997), 186.
16. C. S. Lewis, *Mere Christianity* (Rockville, MD: Wildside, 2019), 9.
17. Bevans, *Models of Contextual Theology*, 118–21.
18. Bevans, *Models of Contextual Theology*, 122.
19. Stanley Hauerwas, *A Community of Character: Toward a Constructive Christian Social Ethic* (Notre Dame, IN: University of Notre Dame Press, 1981), 32.
20. Jon Thompson, *Convergence: The Transforming Power of Living Like Jesus Through Spiritual Gifts, Disciplines, and Unusual Experiences* (Grand Rapids: Zondervan Reflective, 2026), 14.
21. Molly Worthen, interview with Collin Hansen, "What Happened to Historian Molly Worthen?," *Gospelbound* (podcast), May 9, 2023, https://www.thegospelcoalition.org/podcasts/gospelbound/happened-molly-worthen/. The transcript has been revised for readability.
22. John Wortley, ed., *The Book of the Elders: Sayings of the Desert Fathers; the Systematic Collection*, Cistercian Studies Series 240 (Collegeville, MN: Liturgical, 2012), 308.
23. "Church of England Resources," *A Church of England Prayer for Christian Unity* (blog), September 17, 2010, https://www.churchofengland.org/sites/default/files/2017-11/praying-for-unity-english-arc.pdf.

Chapter 4: Learning from the Past

1. Christopher A. Hall, *Reading Scripture with the Church Fathers* (Downers Grove, IL: InterVarsity Press, 1998), 14.
2. Jon Thompson, *Deliverance: A Journey Toward the Unexpected* (Ajax, Ontario: Sanctus Church, 2018), 9.
3. I appreciate Gavin Ortlund's simple summary, "The core Protestant intuition leading to sola Scriptura: God is ontologically unique; therefore, his speech is ontologically unique. As the Scripture is unique in nature, so it is comparably unique in authority." Gavin Ortlund (@gavinortlund), X, "The core Protestant intuition leading to sola Scriptura" August 19th, 2025, 6.33 pm., https://x.com/gavinortlund/status/1957933894981845382
4. Jon Thompson, *Convergence: The Transforming Power of Living Like Jesus Through Spiritual Gifts, Disciplines, and Unusual Experiences* (Grand Rapids: Zondervan Reflective, 2026), 12–13.

5. Christopher A. Hall, *Reading Scripture with the Church Fathers* (Downers Grove, IL: InterVarsity Press, 1998), 21.
6. Hall, *Reading Scripture with the Church Fathers*, 23–24.
7. Millard J. Erickson, *Christian Theology* (Grand Rapids: Baker, 1992), 16–17.
8. D. A. Carson, *The Gagging of God: Christianity Confronts Pluralism* (Grand Rapids: Zondervan, 1996), 18.
9. Carson, *The Gagging of God*, 23.
10. George R. Hunsberger and Craig Van Gelder, eds., *The Church Between Gospel and Culture: The Emerging Mission in North America* (Grand Rapids: Eerdmans, 1996), 6–7.
11. Luke Timothy Johnson, *The Mind in Another Place: My Life as a Scholar* (Grand Rapids: Eerdmans, 2022), 12.
12. Johannes Hartl, "Leadership Conference 2024 (Alpha)" (Royal Albert Hall, London, May 5, 2024), https://www.leadershipconference.org.uk/watch.

Chapter 5: Living in Retreat and Revival All at Once

1. Rod Dreher, *The Benedict Option: A Strategy for Christians in a Post-Christian Nation* (New York: Sentinel, 2018).
2. John T. McGreevy, *Catholicism: A Global History from the French Revolution to Pope Francis* (New York: Norton, 2022), 418.
3. One problem with Christian nationalism is that it guarantees what is in the "not yet" and places it in the "now." Yes, Jesus is king and has been given all nations (Psalm 2). Yes, Jesus sits at the right hand of God and has all authority (Acts 7:55–56; Romans 8:34; Ephesians 1:20; Colossians 3). And yet his full reign will not be experienced in full measure until his second coming (1 Corinthians 15:26–28; Revelation 20–21). As I wrote in *Perseverance*: "Stop here for a moment and reflect (even if you don't really want to)—as Christians we were never promised religious liberty in the Bible. Many of us have had that religious liberty, and it has been good, but that doesn't mean we get to keep it. And let me bring this closer to home for some of you: Biblically-engaged churches must reject and renounce what we see happening in many churches that have given in to a different idol, one that feels nice but is not of God—the idea of Christian nationalism. This is not an American story alone. Here is what one American author wrote that helps us define and understand the temptation before us no matter where you might live or serve:

   > Christianity is a religion. It's a set of beliefs about ultimate things: most importantly, about the life, death, and resurrection of Jesus Christ. It's drawn from the Bible, from the Nicene Creed, and the Apostles' Creed. Christian nationalism is a political ideology about American identity.... It idealizes and advocates a fusion of Christianity with American civic life. That's a great way of understanding it. Christian nationalism believes that the

> American nation is defined by Christianity and that the government should take steps to keep it that way to sustain and maintain our Christian heritage. It's not merely an observation about American history. It is a prescription for what America *should* do in the future. We should sustain and continue our identity as a Christian nation. That's Christian nationalism. (Morgan Lee, "Christian Nationalism Is Worse Than You Think," *Christianity Today*, January 2021, https://www.christianitytoday.com/podcasts/quick-to-listen/christian-nationalism-capitol-riots-trump-podcast/.)

There is no such thing! Christians are people who accept Jesus Christ as Savior and Lord. We belong to the kingdom of God, and of course we are called to be amazing citizens, to vote, sometimes protest, and influence the law, but when you declare a nation as Christian, you water down the gospel and remove the call for real conversion and real life change. This is something the disciples had to learn; they wanted a political religious kingdom (as did the Pharisees), but what did Jesus teach? "Jesus replied, 'The coming of the kingdom of God is not something that can be observed, nor will people say, "Here it is," or "There it is," because the kingdom of God is within you'" (Luke 17:20)." Jonathan Thompson, *Perseverance: Fifteen Reflections on Christian Ministry at the Halfway Point—An Invitation to Make It to the Finish Line Well—Oh God, Help* (2023), 10–11.

4. Stanley Hauerwas, "Peacemaking Is Political: An Interview with Stanley Hauerwas by Charles E. Moore," *Plough*, March 16, 2021, https://www.plough.com/en/topics/justice/nonviolence/peacemaking-is-political.
5. Arthur F. Glasser and Charles Edward van Engen, *Announcing the Kingdom: The Story of God's Mission in the Bible* (Grand Rapids: Baker Academic, 2003), 2013.
6. "Verdure," in *Merriam-Webster*, n.d., https://www.merriam-webster.com/dictionary/verdure.
7. Philosophy of Life(@PhilOfLife_), "'There's a Japanese legend that says," X, December 29, 2023, 12:49 p.m., https://x.com/PhilOfLife_/status/1740792043113431238.
8. Mary Ann Glendon, *In the Courts of Three Popes: An American Lawyer and Diplomat in the Last Absolute Monarchy of the West* (New York: Image, 2024), 17–18.

Chapter 6: Who Is Jesus?

1. "1896 Frederic Remington Portrait | Extraordinary Finds," *Antiques Roadshow, PBS*, 2020, posted on YouTube, https://www.youtube.com/watch?v=c3L4V9qsAvk.
2. Michael J. Wilkins, *Matthew: From Biblical Text to Contemporary Life*, The NIV Application Commentary (Grand Rapids: Zondervan, 2004), 557.

3. Marie-Claire De Villiers, "Artza, the Holy Land Delivered," *7 Interesting Facts About Caesarea Philippi in Israel* (blog), July 9, 2024, https://www.artzabox.com/a/blog/number-interesting-facts-about-caesarea-philippi-in-israel.
4. Wilkins, *Matthew*, 557.
5. Daniel J. Harrington, *The Gospel of Matthew*, Sacra Pagina Series 1 (Collegeville, MN: Liturgical, 1991), 247.
6. Wilkins, *Matthew*, 562–64.
7. R. T. France, *The Gospel According to Matthew: An Introduction and Commentary*, Tyndale New Testament Commentaries (Grand Rapids: Eerdmans, 1985), 255.
8. Wilkins, *Matthew*, 565; France, *The Gospel of Matthew*, 624.
9. Wilkins, *Matthew*, 567–68.
10. France, *The Gospel According to Matthew*, 99–100.
11. France, *The Gospel of Matthew*, 134–35.
12. Wilkins, *Matthew*, 160–61.
13. Henri J. M. Nouwen, *In the Name of Jesus: Reflections on Christian Leadership* (New York: Crossroad, 2002), 73–79.
14. John Macmurray, *Persons in Relation* (Amherst, NY: Humanity, 1999), 121.
15. C. S. Lewis, *Mere Christianity* (Rockville, MD: Wildside, 2019), 55–56.
16. John T. McGreevy, *Catholicism: A Global History from the French Revolution to Pope Francis* (New York: Norton, 2022), 182–83.
17. McGreevy, *Catholicism*, 181.
18. Arthur F. Glasser and Charles Edward van Engen, *Announcing the Kingdom: The Story of God's Mission in the Bible* (Grand Rapids, Mich: Baker Academic, 2003), 37.
19. Peter J. Leithart, *The End of Protestantism: Pursuing Unity in a Fragmented Church* (Grand Rapids: Brazos, 2016), 14–15.

Chapter 7: What Is the Gospel?

1. Richard John Neuhaus, *Death on a Friday Afternoon: Meditations on the Last Words of Jesus from the Cross* (New York: Basic, 2000), 203.
2. John Dunnett, "Making Sense of Living in Love & Faith after General Synod Vote," Church of England Evangelical Council (CEEC), hosted by YouTube, November 29, 2023, https://www.youtube.com/watch?v=GBhT9ixxg2U.
3. William J. Larkin, *Acts*, IVP New Testament Commentary Series 5 (Downers Grove, IL: InterVarsity Press, 1995), 53; F. F. Bruce, *The Book of the Acts*, rev. ed., New International Commentary on the New Testament (Grand Rapids: Eerdmans, 2009), 60.
4. Larkin, *Acts*, 53–54.
5. Dean Pinter, *Acts*, Story of God Bible Commentary (Grand Rapids: Zondervan Academic, 2019), 67.

6. Ajith Fernando, *Acts*, NIV Application Commentary (Grand Rapids: Zondervan, 1998), 102.
7. Fernando, *Acts*, 102–3.
8. John Piper, *Fifty Reasons Why Jesus Came to Die* (Wheaton, IL: Crossway, 2006), 20.
9. Darrell L. Bock, *Acts*, Baker Exegetical Commentary on the New Testament (Grand Rapids: Baker Academic, 2007), 122.
10. Fernando, *Acts*, 103.
11. Bruce, *The Book of the Acts*, 63–64.
12. Timothy Keller, *The Reason for God: Belief in an Age of Skepticism* (New York: Dutton, 2008), 101.
13. Larkin, *Acts*, 57–58; Fernando, *Acts*, 105.
14. D. W. Gooding, *True to the Faith: The Acts of the Apostles; Defining and Defending the Gospel* (Coleraine: Myrtlefield, 2013), 67.
15. Larkin, *Acts*, 58.
16. Grace Hamman, *Jesus Through Medieval Eyes: Beholding Christ with the Artists, Mystics, and Theologians of the Middle Ages* (Grand Rapids: Zondervan, 2023), 108.
17. Michael Green, *Thirty Years That Changed the World: The Book of Acts for Today* (Grand Rapids: Eerdmans, 2004), 88.
18. Douglas J. Moo, *Romans*, NIV Application Commentary (Grand Rapids: Zondervan, 2000), 73.
19. Hamman, *Jesus Through Medieval Eyes*, 25–27.
20. Pinter, *Acts*, 66.
21. T. D. Alexander, *From Paradise to the Promised Land: An Introduction to the Pentateuch*, 2nd ed. (Grand Rapids: Baker Academic, 2002), 24; Tremper Longman, *Genesis*, Story of God Bible Commentary (Grand Rapids: Zondervan, 2016), 150.
22. Victor P. Hamilton, *The Book of Genesis: Chapters 1–17*, New International Commentary on the Old Testament (Grand Rapids: Eerdmans, 2006), 356.
23. Arthur F. Glasser and Charles Edward van Engen, *Announcing the Kingdom: The Story of God's Mission in the Bible* (Grand Rapids: Baker Academic, 2003), 52.
24. Pinter, *Acts*, 63; Bruce K. Waltke and Cathi J. Fredricks, *Genesis: A Commentary* (Grand Rapids: Zondervan, 2001), 184.
25. D. A. Carson, *A Call to Spiritual Reformation: Priorities from Paul and His Prayers* (Grand Rapids: Baker, 1992), 109.
26. George Thornton, *The Radical Book for Kids: Exploring the Roots and Shoots of Faith* (Greensboro, NC: New Growth, 2016), 4.

Chapter 8: What Is Our Identity?

1. *Collins Dictionary*, s.v. rebellion, https://www.collinsdictionary.com/dictionary/english/rebellion.
2. John Mark Comer, *Practicing the Way: Be with Jesus, Become like Him, Do as He Did* (New York: Random House, 2025), xvi.
3. John Tyson (@jontyson) "Here are the 3 main stories about sexuality in our world today," Instagram photo, August 29, 2023.
4. Rowan Williams, *Resurrection: Interpreting the Easter Gospel*, rev. ed. (Cleveland: Pilgrim, 2004), 89.
5. Donald W. McCullough, *The Trivialization of God: The Dangerous Illusion of a Manageable Deity* (Colorado Springs: NavPress, 1995), 38.
6. David G. Benner, *The Gift of Being Yourself: The Sacred Call to Self-Discovery* (Downers Grove, IL: InterVarsity Press, 2004), 47–48.
7. Neil T. Anderson, *Living Free in Christ* (Ventura, CA: Regal, 1993), 11.
8. F. F. Bruce, *The Letter of Paul to the Romans: An Introduction and Commentary*, 2nd ed., Tyndale New Testament Commentaries 6 (Grand Rapids: Eerdmans, 1997), 166.
9. Douglas J. Moo, *Romans*, NIV Application Commentary (Grand Rapids: Zondervan, 2000), 263.
10. R. Kent Hughes, *Romans: Righteousness from Heaven*, Preaching the Word (Wheaton, IL: Crossway, 1991), 154.
11. Moo, *Romans*, 247.
12. J. M. Houston, ed., *Sources of the Christian Self: A Cultural History of Christian Identity* (Grand Rapids: Eerdmans, 2018), xvi.
13. James M. Scott, "N. T. Wright's Hypothesis of an 'Ongoing Exile': Issues and Answers," ed. James M. Scott, in *Exile: A Conversation with N. T. Wright* (Downers Grove, IL: IVP Academic, 2017), 8.
14. N. T. Wright, "Yet the Sun Will Rise Again: Reflections on the Exile and Restoration in Second Temple Judaism, Jesus, Paul and the Church Today," in Scott, *Exile*, 29.
15. Scott, "N. T. Wright's Hypothesis of an 'Ongoing Exile,'" 8.
16. James K. A. Smith, *On the Road with Saint Augustine: A Real-World Spirituality for Restless Hearts* (Grand Rapids: Brazos, 2019), 46–47.
17. Darrell L. Bock, *Luke: The NIV Application Commentary from Biblical Text—to Contemporary Life*, NIV Application Commentary Series (Grand Rapids: Zondervan, 1996), 232.
18. Stanley Hauerwas, *Matthew*, ed. R. R. Reno (Grand Rapids: Brazos, 2015), 129.
19. Curt Thompson, "Feeling Shame & Accepting Compliments," The Veritas

Forum, hosted by YouTube, Uploaded on March 29, 2021, https://www.youtube.com/watch?v=UgwnJ0SQs_c.
20. "Hyde Park Corner," *The Crown* (Netflix, November 4, 2016), https://www.imdb.com/title/tt5095274/characters/nm0040586.
21. "Act of God," *The Crown,* Netflix, released November 4, 2016. See https://www.imdb.com/title/tt5170842/characters/nm0040586.
22. See Jonathan Thompson, *Perseverance: Fifteen Reflections on Christian Ministry at the Halfway Point--An Invitation to Make It to the Finish Line Well--Oh God, Help* (2023), chapter 3.

Chapter 9: Seeing Beauty with New Eyes

1. Russ Ramsey, *Rembrandt Is in the Wind: Learning to Love Art through the Eyes of Faith* (Grand Rapids, Michigan: Zondervan, 2022), 16.
2. Aidan Nichols, *Discovering Aquinas: An Introduction to His Life, Work, and Influence* (Grand Rapids: Eerdmans, 2003), 24, 37.
3. Gordon D. Fee, *Paul's Letter to the Philippians,* New International Commentary on the New Testament (Grand Rapids: Eerdmans, 1995), 36–37.
4. Gordon D. Fee, *Paul's Letter to the Philippians,* New International Commentary on the New Testament (Grand Rapids: Eerdmans, 1995), 408.
5. As cited in Edward M. Bounds, *E. M. Bounds on Prayer* (Peabody, MA: Hendrickson, 2006), 205.
6. Fee, *Paul's Letter to the Philippians,* 409.
7. Fee, *Paul's Letter to the Philippians,* 417.
8. Fee, *Paul's Letter to the Philippians,* 417.
9. Fee, *Paul's Letter to the Philippians,* 17–18.
10. Fee, *Paul's Letter to the Philippians,* 418.
11. Frank Thielman, *Philippians,* NIV Application Commentary Series (Grand Rapids: Zondervan, 1995), 220–21.
12. Quoted in Ramsey, *Rembrandt Is in the Wind,* 2.

Chapter 10: Seeing Bridges That Already Exist

1. Thomas Aquinas, *Scripture Series* (Albany, NY: Magi, 1966), 95.
2. Norman L. Geisler, *Thomas Aquinas: An Evangelical Appraisal* (Grand Rapids: Baker, 1991), 58.
3. Millard J. Erickson, *Christian Theology* (Grand Rapids: Baker, 1992), 500.
4. Erickson, *Christian Theology,* 500.
5. Erickson, *Christian Theology,* 500–501.
6. J. I. Packer, *Concise Theology: A Guide to Historic Christian Beliefs* (Wheaton, IL: Tyndale, 1993), 71–73.

7. Aidan Nichols, *Discovering Aquinas: An Introduction to His Life, Work, and Influence* (Grand Rapids: Eerdmans, 2003), 21, 37–38.
8. Richard J. Mouw, *He Shines in All That's Fair: Culture and Common Grace* (Grand Rapids: Eerdmans, 2001), 40.
9. John Calvin, *Institutes of the Christian Religion*, ed. John Thomas McNeill, vol. 1, Library of Christian Classics (Louisville: Westminster John Knox, 1960), 273.
10. Ramsey, *Rembrandt Is in the Wind*, 39.
11. Claus Westermann, *The Psalms: Structure, Content & Message* (Minneapolis: Augsburg, 1980), 10–28; Gerald Henry Wilson, *Psalms*, vol. 1, NIV Application Commentary (Grand Rapids: Zondervan, 2002), 65–74.
12. Donald A Leggett, *"The Psalms,"* seminary course, Tyndale Seminary, North York, Toronto, fall 1999.
13. Claus Westermann, *The Psalms: Structure, Content and Message* (Minneapolis: Augsburg, 1980), 94.
14. Wilson, *Psalms*, 1:374–75.
15. As quoted in Collin Hansen, *Timothy Keller: His Spiritual and Intellectual Formation* (Grand Rapids: Zondervan, 2023), 234.
16. Bruce K. Waltke and Cathi J. Fredricks, *Genesis: A Commentary* (Grand Rapids: Zondervan, 2001), 62–63.
17. Wilson, *Psalms*, 1:364–65.
18. Wilson, *Psalms*, 1:369.
19. J. H Bavinck, *An Introduction to the Science of Missions* (Philadelphia: P&R, 1960); Dan Scott, "Unpublished Lecture Notes on Contemporary Religion," North York, Toronto, Fall 1997.
20. Michael Green, *Thirty Years That Changed the World: The Book of Acts for Today* (Grand Rapids: Eerdmans, 2004), 110.
21. I go into this in depth in my book *Convergence: The Transforming Power of Living Like Jesus Through Spiritual Gifts, Disciplines, and Unusual Experiences* (Grand Rapids: Zondervan Reflective, 2026), 103.
22. Jon Thompson, *Convergence: The Transforming Power of Living Like Jesus Through Spiritual Gifts, Disciplines, and Unusual Experiences* (Grand Rapids: Zondervan Reflective, 2026), 231.

Chapter 11: Power Within Our Presence

1. I go into this in detail in *Convergence* and *Deliverance.*
2. F. F. Bruce, *The Book of the Acts*, rev. ed., New International Commentary on the New Testament (Grand Rapids: Eerdmans, 2009), 246.
3. Darrell L. Bock, *Acts*, Baker Exegetical Commentary on the New Testament (Grand Rapids: Baker Academic, 2007), 442.

4. William J. Larkin, *Acts*, IVP New Testament Commentary Series (Downers Grove, IL: InterVarsity Press, 1995), 193.
5. Jon Thompson, *Deliverance: A Journey Toward the Unexpected* (Ajax, ON: Sanctus Church, 2018), 78.
6. Bruce, *The Book of the Acts*, 297; Bock, *Acts*, 444.
7. Bock, *Acts*, 444.
8. Larkin, *Acts*, 194.
9. Dean Pinter, *Acts*, Story of God Bible Commentary (Grand Rapids: Zondervan, 2019), 326–27; Michael Green, *Thirty Years That Changed the World: The Book of Acts for Today* (Grand Rapids: Eerdmans, 2004), 108–9.
10. Bock, *Acts*, 476.
11. Pinter, *Acts*, 327.
12. Kisilu Kombo, "Witchcraft: A Living Vice in Africa," *African Journal of Evangelical Theology* 22, no. 1 (2003): 73–85.
13. J. I. Packer, *A Quest for Godliness: The Puritan Vision of the Christian Life* (Wheaton, IL: Crossway, 1994), 219–30.
14. The four challenges are as follows: (1) Are not all power acts such as exorcism tied and limited to the apostles? No. Read Tim Challies, *"Continuationism and Cessationism: An Interview with Dr. Wayne Grudem,"* December 13, 2005, https://www.challies.com/interviews/continuationism-and-cessationism-an-interview-with-dr-wayne-grudem/; Sam Storms, "TGC U.S. Ed.," *Why I Am a Continuationist*, January 22, 2014, https://www.thegospelcoalition.org/article/continuationist/; and Wayne Grudem, *Systematic Theology: An Introduction to Biblical Doctrine* (Grand Rapids: Zondervan, 1994), 55–103, 1031–42. (2) Doesn't Paul in 1 Corinthians 13 say gifts will cease? No. Read D. A. Carson, *Showing the Spirit: A Theological Exposition of 1 Corinthians* 12–14 (Grand Rapids: Baker, 1987); Wayne Grudem, *Systematic Theology: An Introduction to Biblical Doctrine* (Grand Rapids: Zondervan, 1994), 1034–35; Gordon D. Fee, *The First Epistle to the Corinthians*, New International Commentary on the New Testament (Grand Rapids: Eerdmans, 2010), 646–74. (3) Does Jude 9 imply that Christians should not cast out demons? No. Read C. Peter Wagner, *The Kingdom and the Power: A Biblical Look at How to Bring the Gospel to the World with Power*, ed. Gary S. Greig and Kevin N. Springer (Ventura, CA: Regal, 1993), 75–76. (4) Is it not a historical fact that the miraculous gifts ceased within the early history of the church? No. Read Craig S. Keener, *Miracles Today: The Supernatural Work of God in the Modern World* (Grand Rapids: Baker Academic, 2021); Jon Thompson, *Deliverance: A Journey Toward the Unexpected* (Sanctus Church, 2018), chs. 8–9; Wayne Grudem, *The Gift of Prophecy in the New Testament and Today* (Wheaton, IL: Crossway, 2000), 346–59.

Chapter 12: Make Christianity Weak Again

1. Andrew F. Walls and Brian Stanley, *The Missionary Movement from the West: A Biography from Birth to Old Age*, Studies in the History of Christian Missions (Grand Rapids: Eerdmans, 2023), 13–14, 17.
2. Darrell L. Bock, *Acts*, Baker Exegetical Commentary on the New Testament (Grand Rapids: Baker Academic, 2007), 533.
3. Ajith Fernando, *Acts*, NIV Application Commentary (Grand Rapids: Zondervan, 1998), 444.
4. See Jon Thompson, *Deliverance: A Journey Toward the Unexpected* (Sanctus Church, 2018).
5. Jon Thompson, *Deliverance: A Journey Toward the Unexpected* (Ajax, Ontario: Sanctus Church, 2018), 80.
6. William J. Larkin, *Acts*, IVP New Testament Commentary Series (Downers Grove, IL: InterVarsity Press, 1995), 193–96.
7. Bock, *Acts*, 537–538.
8. Dean Pinter, *Acts*, Story of God Bible Commentary (Grand Rapids: Zondervan, 2019), 386.
9. Pinter, *Acts*, 386.
10. Ajith Fernando, *Acts*, The NIV Application Commentary (Grand Rapids, Mich: Zondervan, 1998), 455.
11. Larkin, *Acts*, 240.
12. Stephen B. Bevans, *Models of Contextual Theology*, rev. ed., Faith and Cultures Series (Maryknoll, NY: Orbis, 2002), 40.
13. Walls and Stanley, *The Missionary Movement from the West*, 9.
14. Miroslav Volf, *Exclusion and Embrace: A Theological Exploration of Identity, Otherness, and Reconciliation* (Nashville: Abingdon, 2008), 124.
15. Robert V. Young, *Shakespeare and the Idea of Western Civilization* (Washington, DC: Catholic University of America Press, 2022), 87.
16. Lesslie Newbigin, *Foolishness to the Greeks: The Gospel and Western Culture* (Grand Rapids: Eerdmans, 1986), 125.
17. Henry Gariepy, *Christianity in Action: The International History of the Salvation Army* (Grand Rapids: Eerdmans, 2009), xv.
18. Gariepy, *Christianity in Action*, 167.
19. William Wilberforce, *A Practical View of Christianity* (Carol Stream, IL: Tyndale, 2006).
20. Dean S. Gilliland, *The Word Among Us: Contextualizing Theology for Mission Today* (Eugene, OR: Wipf and Stock, 2002), 199.
21. See John Ortberg, *Overcoming Your Shadow Mission* (Grand Rapids: Zondervan, 2008).

22. Steve Jones, "Throw a Toonie into a Salvation Army Kettle This Christmas," *President's Blog*, The Fellowship, December 9, 2024, https://www.fellowship.ca/blog/916/Throw-a-Toonie-into-a-Salvation-Army-Kettle-this--Christmas; John Ortberg, *Overcoming Your Shadow Mission* (Grand Rapids: Zondervan, 2008).
23. Jonathan Thompson, *Perseverance: Fifteen Reflections on Christian Ministry at the Halfway Point--An Invitation to Make It to the Finish Line Well--Oh God, Help*, 2023, ix.
24. Colby Itkowitz, "Her Son Shot Their Daughters 10 Years Ago. Then, These Amish Families Embraced Her as a Friend.," *The Washington Post*, October 1, 2016, https://www.washingtonpost.com/news/inspired-life/wp/2016/10/01/10-years-ago-her-son-killed-amish-children-their-families-immediately-accepted-her-into-their-lives/.
25. *Ted Lasso*, season 1, episode 9, "All Apologies," written by Phoebe Walsh, directed by MJ Delaney, aired September 25, 2020, on Apple TV.
26. Franciscans of Canada, "The Mission Office of the Franciscans of the Holy Spirit Province of Canada," *A Franciscan Blessing* (blog), February 28, 2018, https://www.franciscanfriars.ca/blog/holy-spirit-province/a-franciscan-blessing/.

Chapter 13: Answering the Right Questions

1. Ajith Fernando, *Acts*, NIV Application Commentary (Grand Rapids: Zondervan, 1998), 473.
2. William J. Larkin, *Acts*, IVP New Testament Commentary Series (Downers Grove, IL: InterVarsity Press, 1995), 251.
3. Fernando, *Acts*, 473.
4. Darrell L. Bock, *Acts*, Baker Exegetical Commentary on the New Testament (Grand Rapids: Baker Academic, 2007), 560.
5. Fernando, *Acts*, 474.
6. F. F. Bruce, *The Book of the Acts*, rev. ed., New International Commentary on the New Testament (Grand Rapids: Eerdmans, 2009), 329; John R. W. Stott, *The Message of Acts*, 2nd ed. (Downers Grove, IL: Inter-Varsity, 1991), 281.
7. Dean Pinter, *Acts*, Story of God Bible Commentary (Grand Rapids: Zondervan, 2019), 406.
8. Fernando, *Acts*, 474; Pinter, *Acts*, 406.
9. Ben Witherington, *The Acts of the Apostles: A Socio-Rhetorical Commentary* (Grand Rapids: Eerdmans, 1998), 514.
10. Pinter, *Acts*, 406.
11. Larkin, *Acts*, 253.
12. Larkin, *Acts*, 561–62.
13. Pinter, *Acts*, 25.

14. N. T. Wright, *The Resurrection of the Son of God, Christian Origins and the Question of God 3* (Minneapolis: Fortress, 2008), 35, 81, 83–86.
15. Bock, *Acts*, 563.
16. Larkin, *Acts*, 253–54.
17. Fernando, *Acts*, 475.
18. Don Richardson, *Eternity in Their Hearts*, rev. ed. (Ventura, CA: Regal, 1984), 16–17; Larkin, *Acts*, 255–56.
19. Michael Green, *Thirty Years That Changed the World: The Book of Acts for Today* (Grand Rapids: Eerdmans, 2004), 108.
20. Bruce, *The Book of the Acts*, 339.
21. Green, *Thirty Years That Changed the World*, 108.
22. C. S. Lewis, *Christian Reflections* (Grand Rapids: Eerdmans, 2014), 167–69.
23. Larkin, *Acts*, 257.
24. Green, *Thirty Years That Changed the World*, 111.
25. Green, *Thirty Years That Changed the World*, 111.
26. Andrew F. Walls and Brian Stanley, *The Missionary Movement from the West: A Biography from Birth to Old Age*, Studies in the History of Christian Missions (Grand Rapids: Eerdmans, 2023), 135–36.

Chapter 14: Finding Bridges to Religious People

1. Nabeel Qureshi, *Seeking Allah, Finding Jesus: A Devout Muslim Encounters Christianity*, 3rd ed. (Grand Rapids: Zondervan Reflective, 2018).
2. J. Dudley Woodberry, Russell G. Shubin, and G. Marks, "Why Muslims Follow Jesus? The Results of a Recent Survey of Converts from Islam," *Christianity Today*, October 2007, www.christianitytoday.com/ct/2007/october/42.80.html.
3. Chloe-Arizona Fodor, "Nearly Half of the World's Migrants Are Christian," *Christianity Today*, August 21, 2024, https://www.christianitytoday.com/2024/08/christian-migrant-immigration-religion-world-pew-research/.
4. *Thailand Report, Christian Witness to Nominal Christians Among Protestant Christians*, Lausanne Occasional Papers 23 (Wheaton, IL: Lausanne Committee for World Evangelization, 1980), 5.
5. R. Kent Hughes, *John: That You May Believe*, Preaching the Word (Wheaton, IL: Crossway, 1999), 74–75.
6. Charles R. Swindoll, *Insights on John*, Swindoll's New Testament Insights (Grand Rapids: Zondervan, 2010), 69.
7. Swindoll, *Insights on John*, 69.
8. Charles R. Swindoll and Charles R. Swindoll, *Insights on John*, Swindoll's New Testament Insights (Grand Rapids, Mich: Zondervan, 2010), 67–68.
9. Leon Morris, *The Gospel According to John*, rev. ed., New International Commentary on the New Testament (Grand Rapids: Eerdmans, 2008), 190.

10. Morris, *The Gospel According to John*, 191–93.
11. Hughes, *John*, 82.
12. Morris, *The Gospel According to John*, 195.
13. Hughes, *John*, 83.
14. John R. W. Stott, *The Message of the Sermon on the Mount (Matthew 5–7): Christian Counter-Culture*, The Bible Speaks Today (Downers Grove, IL: InterVarsity Press, 1985), 38–41.
15. D. A. Carson, *Jesus' Sermon on the Mount: And His Confrontation with the World: An Exposition of Matthew 5–10* (Grand Rapids: Baker, 1999), 18.
16. Gerald Bray, *God Is Love: A Biblical and Systematic Theology* (Wheaton, IL: Crossway, 2012), 425–26.

Chapter 15: Finding Bridges to Christian Critics

1. Robert Wilken, *The Christians as the Romans Saw Them* (New Haven, CT: Yale University Press, 1984), xvi.
2. Nabeel Qureshi, "Crossing Over: An Intellectual and Spiritual Journey from Islam to Christianity," *Answering Islam*, https://www.answering-islam.org/Authors/Qureshi/testimony.htm.
3. *"Alpha Short #2 // Alister McGrath,"* The Lighthouse UK, uploaded on April 29, 2021, hosted on YouTube, Alpha Film Series, https://www.youtube.com/watch?v=Qz5WYhZQJ4s.
4. Justin Brierley, "The Conversion of a Classicist: Why Reading a Greek New Testament Led James Orr to Christ," *Think Faith*, April 13, 2024, https://justinbrierley.beehiiv.com/p/conversion-classicist-reading-greek-new-testament-led-james-orr-christ. Text is an excerpt from episode 17 of *The Surprising Rebirth of Belief in God* podcast.
5. Amy Orr-Ewing, *Why Trust the Bible? Answers to Ten Tough Questions*, rev. ed. (Nottingham, UK: Inter-Varsity Press, 2020).
6. Benjamin Shaw, *Trustworthy: Thirteen Arguments for the Reliability of the New Testament* (Downers Grove, IL: IVP Academic, 2024).
7. Richard Bauckham, *Jesus and the Eyewitnesses: The Gospels as Eyewitness Testimony*, 2nd ed. (Grand Rapids: Eerdmans, 2017)
8. Russ Ramsey, *Rembrandt Is in the Wind: Learning to Love Art through the Eyes of Faith* (Grand Rapids: Zondervan, 2022), 14.
9. Justin Taylor, "TGC Us Ed.," *85 Years Ago Today: J. R. R. Tolkien Convinces C. S. Lewis That Christ Is the True Myth* (blog), September 20, 2016, https://www.thegospelcoalition.org/blogs/evangelical-history/85-years-ago-today-j-r-r-tolkien-convinces-c-s-lewis-that-christ-is-the-true-myth/.
10. Collin Hansen, *Timothy Keller: His Spiritual and Intellectual Formation* (Grand Rapids: Zondervan, 2023), 57–58.
11. Justin Brierley, "There's Nothing Reassuring About Jesus. That's Why

I Stayed Away from Him for so Long," *Premier Christianity*, June 24, 2024, https://www.premierchristianity.com/testimonies/theres-nothing-reassuring-about-jesus-thats-why-i-stayed-away-from-him-for-so-long/17830.article.
12. Brierley, "There's Nothing Reassuring About Jesus."
13. "Richard Dawkins vs John Lennox | Has Science Buried God? Debate" Larry Alex Tauton (YouTube channel), posted June 1, 2017, hosted by YouTube, video recording of a debate that took place in Oxford, England, https://www.youtube.com/watch?v=OVEuQg_Mglw.
14. "Atheist Refuted by Agnostic Historian (Bart Ehrman) on the Existence of Jesus," MrShazoolo (YouTube channel), posted December 30, 2011, hosted by YouTube, https://www.youtube.com/watch?v=u9CC7qNZkOE.
15. William Wand, *Christianity: A Historical Religion?* (Valley Forge, PA: Judson, 1972), 93–94.
16. Gary Habermas, "Resurrection Research from 1975 to the Present: What Are Critical Scholars Saying?," *Journal for the Study of the Historical Jesus* 31 (2005): 135–53.
17. Jonathan Thompson, *Perseverance: Fifteen Reflections on Christian Ministry at the Halfway Point--An Invitation to Make It to the Finish Line Well--Oh God, Help* (2023), 155.
18. Cynthia Rostankowski, "Can We Prove God Exists? The Ontological Argument," in *Classic Philosophical Questions*, ed. James A. Gould and Robert J. Mulvaney, 11th ed. (Upper Saddle Rive, NJ: Pearson Prentice Hall, 2004). See https://www.sjsu.edu/people/cynthia.rostankowski/courses/HUM119BS14/s0/Anselm-The-Ontological-Argument.pdf.
19. James Anderson, "*The Existence of God*," The Gospel Coalition, https://www.thegospelcoalition.org/essay/the-existence-of-god/.
20. William L. Craig, "*The Kalam Cosmological Argument*," *Reasonable Faith*, https://www.reasonablefaith.org/writings/popular-writings/existence-nature-of-god/the-kalam-cosmological-argument.
21. James Anderson, "*The Existence of God*," The Gospel Coalition, https://www.thegospelcoalition.org/essay/the-existence-of-god/.
22. Francis S. Collins, *The Language of God: A Scientist Presents Evidence for Belief* (New York: Free, 2007).
23. Antony Flew and Roy Abraham Varghese, *There Is a God: How the World's Most Notorious Atheist Changed His Mind* (New York: HarperOne, 2008). The little appendix written by N. T. Wright at the end of *There Is a God* is one of the best summaries of Jesus, resurrection, and history.
24. C. S. Lewis, *Mere Christianity* (Rockville, MD: Wildside, 2019), 16, 19, 35–36.
25. Lewis, *Mere Christianity*, 136–137.
26. John Calvin, *Institutes of the Christian Religion*, ed. John Thomas

McNeill, vol. 1, The Library of Christian Classics (Louisville, KY: London: Westminster John Knox, 1960), 3.1.

27. Anderson, "The Existence of God."
28. Jerry L. Walls and Trent Dougherty, eds., *Two Dozen (or so) Arguments for God: The Plantinga Project* (New York: Oxford University Press, 2018).
29. *YouTube*, "A Broken Genius–The Real Jim Carrey," T&H–Inspiration & Motivation, posted on August 26, 2024, hosted by YouTube, https://www.youtube.com/watch?v=vNm6t_eQYbA.
30. Cory Brock and Andrew Kelley, "TGC U.S. Ed.," https://www.thegospelcoalition.org/article/comfort-culture-hustle-ideology/, *How Comfort Culture and Hustle Ideology Fill the Meaning Gap* (blog), December 14, 2022, ttps://www.thegospelcoalition.org/article/comfort-culture-hustle-ideology/.
31. Cory Brock and Andrew Kelley, "*How Comfort Culture and Hustle Ideology Fill the Meaning Gap*," The Gospel Coalition, December 14, 2022, https://www.thegospelcoalition.org/article/comfort-culture-hustle-ideology/a.
32. Kelsey Kramer McGinnis, "*Yes, Fiji Olympians Are Singing Hymns*," *Christianity Today*, August 6, 2024, https://www.christianitytoday.com/2024/08/fiji-hymns-singing-team-rugby-hymn-viral-olympics/.

Chapter 16: The Undeniable Need for an Encounter

1. Alister E. McGrath, *The Reenchantment of Nature: The Denial of Religion and the Ecological Crisis* (New York: Doubleday, 2002), 168.
2. *Tinker Tailor Soldier Spy*, dir. Tomas Alfredson, StudioCanal, 2011. See https://www.imdb.com/title/tt1340800/quotes/.
3. Alister E. McGrath, *The Sunnier Side of Doubt* (Grand Rapids: Academic, 1990), 12.
4. David Bennett, *A War of Loves: The Unexpected Story of a Gay Activist Discovering Jesus* (Grand Rapids: Zondervan, 2018), 77–80.
5. Max Lucado, *The Applause of Heaven* (Nashville: Thomas Nelson, 1999), 71.
6. Jon Thompson, *Convergence: The Transforming Power of Living Like Jesus Through Spiritual Gifts, Disciplines, and Unusual Experiences* (Grand Rapids: Zondervan Reflective, 2026), 261.
7. Alistair Begg, "*Martyn Lloyd-Jones, the Preacher*," *Truth for Life*, May 14, 2001, https://www.truthforlife.org/resources/sermon/martyn-lloyd-jones/.

Chapter 17: Would You Even Want to Go to Those People?

1. Timothy Keller, *The Prodigal Prophet: Jonah and the Mystery of God's Mercy* (New York: Viking, 2018), 86.
2. A. W. Tozer (@TozerAW), "Christians don't tell lies they just go to church and

sing them." X, February 2nd, 2018, 2.49 pm., https://x.com/TozerAW/status/959514047325458432

3. Phillip Cary, *Jonah* (London: SCM, 2008),32–33.
4. Jonathan Thompson, *Perseverance: Fifteen Reflections on Christian Ministry at the Halfway Point--An Invitation to Make It to the Finish Line Well--Oh God, Help*, 2023, chapters 10–13.
5. Sam Storms, "*When a Cessationist Prophesies, or, What Are We to Make of Charles Spurgeon?*," *Enjoying God*, https://www.samstorms.org/enjoying-god-blog/post/when-a-cessationist-prophesies—or—what-are-we-to-make-of-charles-spurgeon; Wayne A. Grudem, *The Gift of Prophecy in the New Testament and Today*, rev. ed (Wheaton, IL: Crossway, 2000), 353–56.
6. James K. Bruckner, *Jonah, Nahum, Habakkuk, Zephaniah*, NIV Application Commentary (Grand Rapids: Zondervan Academic, 2010), 40–41.
7. Cary, *Jonah*, 30.
8. Cary, *Jonah*, 30.
9. Bruckner, *Jonah, Nahum, Habakkuk, Zephaniah*, 41.
10. Timothy Keller, *The Prodigal Prophet: Jonah and the Mystery of God's Mercy* (New York: Penguin, 2018), 10–11.
11. Thomas Edward McComiskey, *The Minor Prophets* (Grand Rapids: Baker Academic, 2009), 621.
12. Timothy Keller, *The Prodigal Prophet: Jonah and the Mystery of God's Mercy* (New York: Viking, 2018), 14.
13. Keller, *The Prodigal Prophet*, 15.
14. McComiskey, *The Minor Prophets*, 511.
15. Bruckner, *Jonah, Nahum, Habakkuk, Zephaniah*, 42, 75.
16. Bruckner, *Jonah, Nahum, Habakkuk, Zephaniah*, 42.
17. Keller, *The Prodigal Prophet*, 33.
18. As quoted in Keller, *The Prodigal Prophet*, 50.
19. Rosemary A. Nixon, *The Message of Jonah: Presence in the Storm*, The Bible Speaks Today (Downers Grove, IL: InterVarsity Press, 2003), 113–115.
20. Keller, *The Prodigal Prophet*, 66–67.
21. Keller, *The Prodigal Prophet*, 30–31.
22. Richard Temple, icons lecture, Temenos Academy, 2021.
23. Phillip Cary, *Jonah* (London: SCM Press, 2008), 128–129.
24. Keller, *The Prodigal Prophet*, 96.
25. Keller, *The Prodigal Prophet*, 100.
26. Keller, *The Prodigal Prophet*, 100–101.
27. Nixon, *The Message of Jonah*, 186.
28. Nixon, *The Message of Jonah*, 186–88.
29. Nixon, *The Message of Jonah*, 184.

30. Nixon, *The Message of Jonah,* 194.
31. Bruckner, *Jonah, Nahum, Habakkuk, Zephaniah,* 113.
32. McComiskey, *The Minor Prophets,* 586.
33. Jill Briscoe, *Jonah and the Worm* (Nashville: Thomas Nelson, 1983), 12.
34. Keller, *The Prodigal Prophet,* 118.
35. Leslie C. Allen, *The Books of Joel, Obadiah, Jonah, and Micah,* New International Commentary on the Old Testament (Grand Rapids: Eerdmans, 2008), 246.

Chapter 18: Would I Even Want to Live Beside Those People?

1. Wendy Widder, *Daniel,* Story of God Bible Commentary (Grand Rapids: Zondervan, 2016), 22–24.
2. Leon James Wood, *A Commentary on Daniel* (Grand Rapids: Zondervan Pub. House, 1978), 30.
3. John Lennox, *Against the Flow: The Inspiration of Daniel in an Age of Relativism* (Oxford: Monarch, 2015), 30–31.
4. Tremper Longman, *Daniel,* NIV Application Commentary (Grand Rapids: Zondervan, 1999), 47–49.
5. Longman, *Daniel,* 50–51; Lennox, *Against the Flow,* 46.
6. Ajith Fernando, *Spiritual Living in a Secular World: Applying the Book of Daniel Today* (Grand Rapids: Zondervan, 1993), 16–17.
7. See Longman, *Daniel,* 53.

Chapter 19: When It Is Good and Right to Say No

1. Gary Thomas, "Wise Christians Clip Obituaries," *Christianity Today,* October 3, 1994.
2. Marion Ann Taylor, *Ruth, Esther,* Story of God Bible Commentary (Grand Rapids: Zondervan Academic, 2020), 85–96; Karen H. Jobes, *Esther,* NIV Application Commentary (Grand Rapids: Zondervan, 1999), 41–45.
3. Jobes, *Esther,* 26–27.
4. Jobes, *Esther,* 444.
5. Taylor, *Ruth, Esther,* 158.
6. Charles R. Swindoll, *Insights on Romans,* Swindoll's New Testament Insights (Grand Rapids: Zondervan, 2010), 15–16.
7. Douglas J. Moo, *Romans,* NIV Application Commentary (Grand Rapids: Zondervan, 2000), 422, 429.
8. Swindoll, *Insights on Romans,* 304.
9. Swindoll, *Insights on Romans,* 273.
10. As quoted in R. Kent Hughes, *Luke: That You May Know the Truth,* Preaching the Word (Wheaton, IL: Crossway, 2015), 701.
11. R. Kent Hughes, *Romans: Righteousness from Heaven,* Preaching the Word (Wheaton, IL: Crossway, 1991), 243.

12. Hughes, *Romans*, 244.
13. Donald Senior and Daniel J. Harrington, *1 Peter*, Sacra Pagina Series 15 (Collegeville, MN: Liturgical, 2003), 68–69.
14. Franco Cavazzi, "Emperor Nero," The Roman Empire, Roman-Empire.net, https://roman-empire.net/people/nero; Barry Strauss, *Ten Caesars: Roman Emperors from Augustus to Constantine* (New York: Simon & Schuster, 2019), 96–101.
15. "The Worst Form of Government," International Churchill Society, https://winstonchurchill.org/resources/quotes/the-worst-form-of-government/.
16. Moo, *Romans*, 426–30.
17. Hughes, *Romans*, 240.
18. Hughes, *Romans*, 241.
19. Hughes, *Romans*, 241.
20. Timothy George and Thomas G. Guarino, eds., *Evangelicals and Catholics Together at Twenty: Vital Statements on Contested Topics* (Grand Rapids: Brazos, 2015), 142.
21. Jon Thompson, *Convergence: The Transforming Power of Living Like Jesus Through Spiritual Gifts, Disciplines, and Unusual Experiences* (Grand Rapids: Zondervan Reflective, 2026), 277–78.
22. Jonathan Thompson, *Perseverance: Fifteen Reflections on Christian Ministry at the Halfway Point--An Invitation to Make It to the Finish Line Well--Oh God, Help*, 2023, 179–92.
23. "*Chrysostom's Invincibility Before the Byzantine Empress*," Pioneer Library, November 12, 2017, https://olddeadguys.com/2017/11/12/chrysostoms-reply-to-eudoxia/.

Chapter 20: Where Does Revival Fit In?

1. Jon Thompson, *Convergence: The Transforming Power of Living Like Jesus Through Spiritual Gifts, Disciplines, and Unusual Experiences* (Grand Rapids: Zondervan Reflective, 2026), 58.
2. Mark Shaw, *Global Awakening: How 20th-Century Revivals Triggered a Christian Revolution* (Downers Grove, Ill: IVP Academic, 2010).
3. Kil Sun Ju and the Korean revival of 1907, Joseph Babalola and the Aladura revival of 1930, V. S. Azariah and the Dornakal revival in India, William Nagenda and the East African revival in Uganda, Billy Graham and the revival of American evangelicals, Paulo Borges Jr. and the revival in Brazil, African Pentecostalism and reverse mission, and the Chinese house-church movement.
4. Jon Thompson, *Convergence: The Transforming Power of Living Like Jesus Through Spiritual Gifts, Disciplines, and Unusual Experiences* (Grand Rapids: Zondervan Reflective, 2026), 233–43. A lot of the following section comes from this previous book.

5. R. T. France, *The Gospel of Matthew*, New International Commentary on the New Testament (Grand Rapids: Eerdmans, 2007), 647.
6. J. C. Ryle, *Matthew*, Crossway Classic Commentaries (Wheaton, IL: Crossway, 1993), 150.
7. J. I. Packer, *God in Our Midst: Seeking and Receiving Ongoing Revival* (Milton Keynes: Word, 1987); Ray Ortlund, "*J. I. Packer: A Personal Appreciation from Ray Ortlund*," The Gospel Coalition, July 17, 2020, https://www.thegospelcoalition.org/article/j-i-packer-a-personal-appreciation-from-ray-ortlund.

Chapter 21: Collaborating with the Enemy

1. Daniel L. Akin, *Exalting Jesus in Mark*, ed. David Platt and Tony Merida (Nashville: Holman, 2014), 48.
2. Darrell L. Bock, *Luke*, vol. 2, Baker Exegetical Commentary on the New Testament (Grand Rapids: Baker, 1994), 1516.
3. Akin, *Exalting Jesus in Mark*, 48.
4. John R. Donahue and Daniel J. Harrington, *The Gospel of Mark*, Sacra Pagina Series 2 (Collegeville, MN: Liturgical, 2002), 102.
5. William L. Lane, *The Gospel According to Mark*, New International Commentary on the New Testament 2 (Grand Rapids: Eerdmans, 2010), 101–2.
6. N. T. Wright, *Jesus and the Victory of God*, Christian Origins and the Question of God 2 (Minneapolis: Fortress, 1996), 149.
7. Akin, *Exalting Jesus in Mark*, 46.

Chapter 22: Notes to an Unknown Future

1. John T. McGreevy, *Catholicism: A Global History from the French Revolution to Pope Francis* (New York: Norton, 2022), ix.
2. Mark A. Noll, *The New Shape of World Christianity: How American Experience Reflects Global Faith* (Downers Grove, IL: InterVarsity Press, 2013), 89.
3. Mark Shaw, *Global Awakening: How 20th-Century Revivals Triggered a Christian Revolution* (Downers Grove, IL: IVP Academic, 2010), 169.
4. Brian C. Stiller, *From Jerusalem to Timbuktu: A World Tour of the Spread of Christianity* (Downers Grove, IL: InterVarsity Press, 2018), 12.
5. Stiller, *From Jerusalem to Timbuktu*, 15.
6. Stiller, *From Jerusalem to Timbuktu*, 14.
7. Noll, *The New Shape of World Christianity*, 90.
8. Jayson Casper, "Researchers Find Christians in Iran Approaching 1 Million," *Christianity Today*, September 3, 2020, https://www.christianitytoday.com/2020/09/iran-christian-conversions-gamaan-religion-survey/.
9. Shaw, *Global Awakening*, 174.

10. Noll, *The New Shape of World Christianity*, 10.
11. Jonathan Aitken, *John Newton: From Disgrace to Amazing Grace* (Wheaton, IL: Crossway, 2007).
12. Jonathan Thompson, *Perseverance: Fifteen Reflections on Christian Ministry at the Halfway Point--An Invitation to Make It to the Finish Line Well--Oh God, Help* (2023), 169–70.
13. "The Supremes," dir. Jessica Yu, *The West Wing*, created by Aaron Sorkin, March 24, 2004, http://www.westwingtranscripts.com/wwscripts/5-17.txt.
14. Larry Dixon, *The Other Side of the Good News* (Wheaton, IL: Victor, 1992), 20–24.
15. James Finley, *Merton's Palace of Nowhere*, 25th anniv. ed. (Notre Dame, IN: Ave Maria, 2003), 77.
16. Jonathan Thompson, *Perseverance: Fifteen Reflections on Christian Ministry at the Halfway Point--An Invitation to Make It to the Finish Line Well--Oh God, Help* (2023), 122–23.
17. John G. Stackhouse Jr., "Generic Evangelicalism," in *Four Views on the Spectrum of Evangelicalism*, ed. Kevin T. Bauder, Andrew David Naselli, and Collin Hansen, Counterpoints (Grand Rapids: Zondervan, 2011), 134–35.
18. Norman L. Geisler and Ralph E. MacKenzie, *Roman Catholics and Evangelicals: Agreements and Differences* (Grand Rapids: Baker, 1995); Timothy George and Thomas G. Guarino, eds., *Evangelicals and Catholics Together at Twenty: Vital Statements on Contested Topics* (Grand Rapids: Brazos, 2015); Bradley Nassif and James J. Stamoolis, eds., *Three Views on Eastern Orthodoxy and Evangelicalism*, Counterpoints (Grand Rapids: Zondervan, 2004).
19. James S. Cutsinger, ed., *Reclaiming the Great Tradition: Evangelicals, Catholics & Orthodox in Dialogue* (Downers Grove, IL: InterVarsity Press, 1997), 156.
20. Peter J. Leithart, *The End of Protestantism: Pursuing Unity in a Fragmented Church* (Grand Rapids: Brazos, 2016), 26–28.
21. I remain a Protestant. I think the Reformation was a needed correction and still is needed much of the time today. Overall, my heart still holds to the Scriptures being supreme, that grace is sovereign, and Jesus is enough. Though I tend to lean towards a more Anglican view on many theological ideas, I still see a more congregational expression of church in Scripture and love to see what the Lord of the church is calling/doing in each community and movement (Revelation 2–3). I believe the Holy Spirit ultimately is the glue that unites all true Christians and Christian communities together (Romans 8).
22. O. S. Hawkins, *Criswell: His Life and Times* (Brentwood, TN: B&H, 2024), 152.
23. See my books *Convergence* and *Deliverance*.

24. Grace Hamman, *Jesus through Medieval Eyes: Beholding Christ with the Artists, Mystics, and Theologians of the Middle Ages* (Grand Rapids: Zondervan, 2023), 108.

Scripture Index

Convergence

The Transforming Power of Living Like Jesus Through Spiritual Gifts, Disciplines, and Unusual Experiences

Jon Thompson

Jon Thompson asks, "If Jesus chose to limit his divine attributes and power, how did he do all of this?" Here Thompson finds the convergence of three things that should ultimately shape our own lives:

1. **Jesus used spiritual disciplines (or practices)** to walk with the Father and to develop and learn as we do.
2. **Jesus used spiritual gifts** (not his inherent power) to carry out his ministry while on earth.
3. **Jesus used the promptings he received** from the Father and the Spirit to lead his disciples into moments of revival.

In *Convergence: Spiritual Gifts, Practices, and Unusual Works of the Spirit*, you will come to realize that Jesus as God in flesh isn't just our Savior and our Lord. He's also our model for understanding what the normal Christian life should look like.

This comprehensive resource aims at understanding the intersection of spiritual gifts (love, word, and power), spiritual disciplines (or practices), and unusual works of the Spirit (revival) in the life of the local church.

Available in stores and online!

ZONDERVAN®
.com